COSMIC LITURGY

HANS URS VON BALTHASAR

Cosmic Liturgy

The Universe According to
Maximus the Confessor

Translated by
Brian E. Daley, S.J.

A COMMUNIO BOOK
IGNATIUS PRESS   SAN FRANCISCO

Title of the German original:
Kosmische Liturgie: Das Weltbild Maximus' des Bekenners
Third edition
© 1988 Johannes Verlag, Einsiedeln

Cover art by Christopher J. Pelicano
Cover design by Roxanne Mei Lum

Dedicated to Louis Bouyer

~

There is amongst us a set of critics who seem to hold that every possible thought and image is traditional; who have no notion that there are such things as fountains in the world, small as well as great; and who would therefore charitably derive every rill they behold flowing from a perforation made in some other man's tank.

— S. T. Coleridge

CONTENTS

TRANSLATOR'S FOREWORD

To publish a translation of a long and difficult book, now almost sixty years old, which deals with an even more difficult, still relatively obscure Greek theologian of the seventh century, may seem to call for some justification. Yet to readers even slightly familiar with the thought of either Maximus the Confessor or Hans Urs von Balthasar, such justification will surely be unnecessary: von Balthasar's *Cosmic Liturgy: The Universe according to Maximus the Confessor* deserves to be considered a classic, both because of its own literary character, as a work combining historical interpretation with constructive argument in a way seldom encountered today, and because of its crucial importance in the development of modern scholarship's estimate of Maximus as well as in the growth of von Balthasar's own theology.

Although the great theologians of the early Church exercised a strong influence on von Balthasar's thought throughout his life, his direct scholarly engagement with them was mainly confined to his early career. Von Balthasar's doctoral thesis, largely completed before his entrance into the Society of Jesus in 1929, was a wide-ranging study of the eschatology of eighteenth- and nineteenth-century German romantic literature and philosophy, later published in three volumes as *Die Apokalypse der deutschen Seele* (1937–1939). In 1934, however, von Balthasar was sent to the Jesuit faculty at Lyons/Fourvière, to study theology in preparation for ordination as a priest. There, especially through the influence of Henri de Lubac, he came into contact with the revival of patristic studies then under way, a movement that was to have a powerfully shaping effect on Catholic theology, spirituality, and worship in the decades after World War II and that was to be one of the decisive forces preparing the way for the Second Vatican Council. For de Lubac and his younger contemporaries, the study of the Fathers offered a new approach to the mystery of Christian salvation, as it is contained in the word of Scripture and the living tradition of the Church: a way largely free of the rigid intellectual confines of the scholasticism of twentieth-century theological manuals, more self-consciously rooted in biblical proclamation and liturgical practice and more optimistic about the possibilities of a direct, experiential union of the human subject with the infinite God. For some of von Balthasar's French and German contemporaries, especially some of his young Jesuit confrères, such as Jean Daniélou, Claude Mondésert, Alois Grillmeier, and Heinrich Bacht, the Catholic rediscovery of patristic literature in the late 1930s led to scholarly careers that would set new boundaries for textual and historical scholarship on the early Church; but even for those whose later work would be more in systematic or dogmatic theology, such as Karl Rahner, Otto Semmelroth, and von Balthasar himself, serious study of the Fathers was a decisive force in freeing their thought, early in their careers, for fresh ways of conceiving and formulating the heart of the Catholic tradition.

Almost immediately after finishing his theological studies at Fourvière, von Balthasar began publishing a series of books and articles on the Church Fathers that included critical textual studies and German translations, as well as essays in philosophical and theological interpretation. The focus of his interest was not so much the classical controversies and stages in the early development of Christian dogma, but rather patristic literature of a more explicitly spiritual or mystical character, especially the Platonizing tradition of Origen and his intellectual heirs. The first work he published in this field was a two-part article in French, in 1936 and 1937, while he was still a student at Fourvière, on the notion of mystery in Origen;[1] this appeared twenty years later, with some reediting, as *Parole et mystère chez Origène* (Paris, 1957). In 1938, *Origenes: Geist und Feuer*[2] appeared: an extensive anthology of passages from Origen, which von Balthasar had not only translated but had arranged thematically in a way intended to evoke the systematic substructure of Origen's thought. The following year, von Balthasar turned his attention to Origen's most controversial disciple, the late-fourth-century ascetical writer and speculative theologian Evagrius Ponticus, in two articles—one an important discussion of basic questions of the authenticity and scope of the ascetical works in the Evagrian corpus,[3] the other a briefer treatment of Evagrius' spiritual

---

[1] "Le Mysterion d'Origène", *Recherches de science religieuse* 26 (1936): 514–62; 27 (1937): 38–64.

[2] *Origenes. Geist und Feuer: Ein Aufbau aus seinen Schriften* (Salzburg, 1938; rev. ed., 1952). English translation by Robert J. Daly: *Origen: Spirit and Fire* (Washington, D.C., 1984).

[3] "Die Hiera des Evagrius", *Zeitschrift für katholische Theologie* 63 (1939): 86–106, 181–206.

theology.[4] In 1939, also, von Balthasar published an article in French on the religious philosophy of Gregory of Nyssa,[5] which would become the third and final section of his book on Gregory's philosophy, *Présence et pensée*, published three years later.[6] In that same year, too, his German translation of excerpts from Gregory of Nyssa's commentary on the Song of Songs appeared, with the title *Der versiegelte Quell*.[7] Finally, 1939 saw the publication of an important early article by von Balthasar, "Patristik, Scholastik und Wir" (The Fathers, the Scholastics, and ourselves), in which he attempted to characterize what he saw as both the promise and the danger of early Christian Platonism and to contrast it with the underlying premises of scholastic and modern views of the reality and value of the created order.[8] During the following year, as the firstfruits of his study of the work of Maximus Confessor, von Balthasar published a pathfinding article on the authorship of the earliest commentary on the works of Pseudo-Dionysius the Areopagite: here he showed, by painstaking analysis of the surviving text, that most of this important commentary, attributed variously in the manuscripts to Maximus and to the sixth-century scholar John of Scythopolis, is in fact the work of the earlier writer and that Maximus' role was mainly that of editor and enhancer.[9]

The present book first appeared in 1941, with the title, *Kosmische Liturgie: Höhe und Krise des griechischen Weltbildes bei Maximus Confessor* (Cosmic liturgy: Apex and crisis of the Greek conception of the universe in Maximus Confessor).[10] Von Balthasar's own translation of Maximus' two hundred *Chapters on Knowledge*[11] appeared separately the same year: a translation that presented this perplexing work as both

---

[4] "Metaphysik und Mystik des Evagrius Ponticus", *Zeitschrift für Aszese und Mystik* 14 (1939): 31–47.

[5] "La Philosophie religieuse de saint Grégoire de Nysse", *Recherches de science religieuse* 29 (1939): 513–49.

[6] *Présence et pensée: Essai sur la philosophie religieuse de Grégoire de Nysse* (Paris, 1942). English translation by Marc Sebanc: *Presence and Thought* (San Francisco, 1995).

[7] *Gregor von Nyssa. Der versiegelte Quell: Auslegung des Hohen Liedes* (Salzburg, 1939).

[8] This long and little-known article, which originally appeared in *Theologie der Zeit* (Vienna) 3 (1939): 65–104, has recently appeared in a fine English translation by Edward T. Oakes, S.J.: *Communio* 24 (1997): 347–96.

[9] "Das Scholienwerk des Johannes von Scythopolis", *Scholastik* 15 (1940): 16–38.

[10] Freiburg, 1941. After World War II, the work appeared in a French translation: *Liturgie cosmique: Maxime le Confesseur* (Paris, 1947).

[11] *Die Gnostische Centurien des Maximus Confessor* (Freiburg, 1941).

continuation and critique of the Origenist tradition of speculative theology, by rearranging the order of Maximus' texts and including parallels drawn from Origen and Evagrius. By far von Balthasar's most ambitious work on patristic theology, *Kosmische Liturgie* also signalled the end of this early period of von Balthasar's activity as an interpreter of ancient theology. Two shorter collections of translated patristic texts were to appear in the following two years: an anthology of passages from Augustine in 1942[12] and another drawn from Irenaeus in 1943,[13] each with a brief introduction. The second part of his later systematic work *Herrlichkeit* (*The Glory of the Lord*) would include chapters on Irenaeus, Augustine, and Pseudo-Dionysius, along with many later thinkers, in the context of that work's much larger theological agenda.[14] But nothing in von Balthasar's *oeuvre* would again compare with the depth, thoroughness, and originality of analysis and interpretation given to an early Christian theologian in *Kosmische Liturgie*. In 1961, von Balthasar published a second edition of the work, substantially revised in response to criticisms of the original version and drawing on the results of postwar scholarship for a number of historical issues; in particular, this second edition modified the theory, expressed in the original text, that Maximus had undergone a "crisis"—in the sense both of challenge and of discernment—in his espousal of Origenist theology and had noticeably moved away from the thinking of Origen in his mature works. This change of emphasis on von Balthasar's part, due in large part to the arguments of Dom Polycarp Sherwood and Endre von Ivánka in their studies of Maximus published in the 1950s but also to a nuancing of his own views of Origen and the Platonic element in early Christian theology, can even be seen in the altered title of the (1961) second edition: it was now simply *Kosmische Liturgie: Das Weltbild Maximus' des Bekenners* (*Cosmic Liturgy: The Universe according to Maximus the Confessor*). It is this second edition that I have translated here. [A third printing was done in 1988.]

At the beginning of the twenty-first century, it seems fair to ask what gives this early work of von Balthasar's its claim to lasting value. One

---

[12] *Aurelius Augustinus: Das Antlitz der Kirche* (Einsiedeln, 1942).

[13] *Irenäus. Geduld des Reifens: Die christliche Antwort auf den Mythus des 2. Jahrhunderts* (Basel, 1943).

[14] *Herrlichkeit: eine theologische Ästhetik*, vol. 2: *Fächer der Stile*, pt. 1: *Klerikale Stile* (Einsiedeln, 1962; 2d ed., 1969); English translation: *The Glory of the Lord: A Theological Aesthetics*, vol. 2: *Studies in Theological Style*, pt. 1: *Clerical Styles* (San Francisco, 1984).

aspect of its importance, first of all, is the historical impact that it has had on patristic studies in the second half of the twentieth century. As von Balthasar himself remarks in the foreword to the second edition, Western scholarship before this book had almost universally tended to see Maximus' importance simply in terms of his decisive contribution to the seventh-century debate on the presence of one or two natural wills in Christ; historians classed his other writings on the mystery of Christ and on the interpretation of the biblical and patristic tradition, as well as his many ascetical works, as simply the products of a late compiler, a conscientious but unimaginative drone. After the publication, in 1941, of the first edition of *Kosmische Liturgie*, and clearly under its influence, patristic scholars began to look at the Confessor more seriously; they had been piqued, at least, to curiosity by von Balthasar's impassioned insistence that Maximus was not so much a compiler as a synthesizer of earlier tradition and that he had brought together many varied strands of Christian thought, ancient culture, and even Oriental religious yearning with brilliant and fruitful originality. A glance at the new bibliography we have included with this translation of the work reveals the massive expansion of interest in Maximus since the late 1940s, and the recognition, along with von Balthasar, that he is an author with important and illuminating things to say on many different aspects of the Christian mystery. This interest still goes on, despite the obvious difficulty, even opacity, of Maximus' thought, and despite the fact that many of his most important works are still without modern translations. Von Balthasar's book stands as the fountainhead and continuing inspiration of modern Maximus scholarship.

Secondly, although *Kosmische Liturgie* is a study of the broad lines and implications of Maximus' theology, it also offers an important perspective on the early formation of von Balthasar's own thought. Many features of von Balthasar's mature theological style are already perceptible here, in his presentation of Maximus: his insistence that the heart of all Christian understanding of the world, history, and God is the person and life of Christ, encountered in its fullness in the Paschal Mystery; his frequent allusion to the "dramatic" and "tragic" character of the history of creation before God; his stress on analogy as fundamental to a correct understanding of created being, and his vision of paradox, of the "coincidence of opposites", as a central pattern of both Christian soteriology and Christian ontology. Even von Balthasar's cultural breadth, his tendency—so striking in his mature works—to draw on classical and modern European literature, on music and the theater, for parallels and elucidating categories in theological explanation, is already present here. In this book, von Balthasar has begun, for the first time on a large scale, to develop the rhetorical instruments and intellectual strategies that will become the trademark of his way of writing theology.

A third reason for the lasting importance of *Kosmische Liturgie*, in my opinion, is the fact that it represents an unusual and risky, but fascinatingly suggestive, way of dealing with the thought of other ages and cultures. Von Balthasar writes here, not as a historian, but as a theologian who turns to his historical forebears for instruction. Clearly, he has read the works of Maximus, exhaustively and sympathetically, in all the baroque density of their language and in all the formidable complication of their argument; clearly, too, he is constantly concerned to fit Maximus into the longer stream of Greek patristic thought and the continuing theological tradition of the Church—to see and point out connections, to plot the outlines of his intellectual context. Yet von Balthasar's interest is, just as clearly, *not* to be a detached observer of Maximus in his own milieu, patiently trying to reconstruct the man and his thought from the bewildering mass of evidence we possess; it is to be a critic of what he sees as Maximus' excesses, but even more to be an advocate, an impassioned promoter of the synthetic view of God and creation that he perceives in this seventh-century scholastic and monk, precisely because he sees there many elements of the theological synthesis he hopes to offer to his own world. In so many details of Maximus' thought—his Christocentrism, his fascination with dialectics, his focus on the distinctive ontology of created being, perhaps even his stylistic intensity and linguistic complication—von Balthasar seems to have found signs of a kindred spirit.

The dangers inherent in this kind of historical-theological study are obvious. Even scholars willing to acknowledge the magnitude and interpretive brilliance of this book, especially in reviews of its second edition in 1961, suggested weaknesses in von Balthasar's approach: the questions he asks of Maximus are modern questions, set by the peculiar situation of French and German Catholic theology in the mid-twentieth century; and the picture of Maximus he draws is, in the end, an incorporation of substantial and authentic elements of Maximus' thought into the proportions and shadings of von Balthasar's own theological enterprise.[15] In 1941 and even in 1961, von Balthasar's concern was to find in the Catholic dogmatic tradition—in patristic thought, but also in the Thomist tradition, as seen through the lenses of Joseph Maréchal and Erich Przywara—an intelligent and convincing answer to the seductive call of German idealism to let the concrete reality of creation dissolve into being nothing more than the phenomena experienced by the thinking human subject. Even in his reading of Maximus, von Balthasar's questions are the questions of Hegel, and his answers those of a christologically focused version of the *philosophia* and *theologia perennis*: the real distinction between essence and existence, the analogies of being and of faith, the resolution of the inherent tension between finite and infinite being in the personal unity of Christ, as expressed in the formula of the Council of Chalcedon.

In his valuable and insightful book on von Balthasar's use of patristic theology, Werner Löser characterized the intellectual axis of *Kosmische Liturgie* in the following way:

> Von Balthasar developed his view of the importance of the Confessor within the horizon of patristic thought but also in the broadest possible context of the history of thought. He considers this possible, because he begins with the assumption that there is, *in the final analysis*, one single question for human thought at every time and in every place: whether, and under what conditions, the world can be affirmed in all its finitude. As is evident here, the value that von Balthasar attaches to the work of a thinker is *ultimately* determined by his answer to this question.[16]

Put another way, the underlying issue for von Balthasar in his attempt to interpret the thought of Maximus the Confessor is the way Maximus and the tradition before him understand the relationship of the finite, created being of the world and all its inhabitants, including man, to the infinite, transcendent being of God and to the universal categories of knowledge and truth that are rooted in God's own intelligence. For

---

[15] See Polycarp Sherwood, O.S.B., "Survey of Recent Work on Saint Maximus the Confessor", *Traditio* 20 (1964): 428–37, esp. 433f.

[16] *Im Geiste des Origenes: Hans Urs von Balthasar als Interpret der Theologie der Kirchenväter*, Frankfurter Theologische Studien, 23 (Frankfurt, 1976), 211 (translation mine; italics in the original). For Löser's whole discussion of *Kosmische Liturgie*, see ibid., 181–215. Von Balthasar's critique of what he sees as the tendency in many of the Fathers to overlook the value and autonomy of the created order in its relationship to God is developed at some length in the article mentioned above (n. 8), "The Fathers, the Scholastics, and Ourselves".

von Balthasar, the ever-present danger is a gnosis, an idealism, that refuses to take seriously and to value reverently the finite, ontologically dependent concrete reality of individual material things—a danger he sees in the Origenist tradition of early Christianity as well as in Neoplatonism and in German idealism. The right approach, in his view, can be found in the cosmic sacramentalism of Pseudo-Dionysius, in the scholastic Christology of such sixth-century authors as Leontius of Byzantium, and—most fully developed—in the synthetic system of Maximus Confessor. At its heart, this approach is an affirmation of a paradoxical unity of ontological opposites, rooted in the Chalcedonian understanding of the Person of Christ—"one individual or person subsisting in two natures, without confusion or change, without division or separation". It is only this personal presence of the infinite God in our world as a human individual, and our own potential personal unity with God through and in him, as we walk his way, that can keep us from regarding the world as simply the extension of our own minds, the playground of our own ideologies, or the mirror of our own limitations and vices.

It is, as I have said, clearly a risky business to approach the works of a thinker from another age and culture with such a clear-cut intellectual and theological agenda. *Kosmische Liturgie*, in my opinion, succeeds as historical interpretation more than von Balthasar's other works on the Church Fathers simply because Maximus does, in fact, lend himself to this kind of reading much more readily than do Origen or Gregory of Nyssa. Maximus was interested in questions of ontology, and in the metaphysics of the Person of Christ, far more than either of those earlier writers; his theological method, strongly influenced (through Leontius of Byzantium and his contemporaries) by the sixth-century scholasticism of the Neoplatonic commentators on Aristotle, shows more obvious links to both Thomism and German idealism than does that of the earlier, more exegetically and pastorally oriented representatives of the Origenist tradition.

Understandably, von Balthasar's interpretation of Maximus and his roots can be regarded as dated in a number of ways. His understanding of Origen's own thought—always a complex area—needs to be revised in the light of the work of more recent interpreters, such as Henri Crouzel; his identification of sixth-century Origenism with the Monophysite wing of the christological controversies after Chalcedon also needs to be revised. Von Balthasar's reading of the Antiochene "school" of christological interpretation in the fourth and fifth centuries—based largely on the pro-Antiochene revisionism of a number of Catholic patristic scholars in the 1950s—needs to be rethought, as well: today it seems clearer that the real concern of the Antiochenes in their Christology was not to defend the full humanity of Christ so much as to prevent the transcendence of God from being compromised by too close an involvement in human history. Correspondingly, many scholars today might want to give a more positive appreciation of Cyril of Alexandria's theological breadth and sophistication than von Balthasar suggests. Von Balthasar's understanding of the tortuous christological debates of the sixth century, and of what is today sometimes called "Neo-Chalcedonianism", also needs to be revised in a number of details. And his interpretation of Maximus himself seems, curiously, to neglect the influence of the Cappadocian Fathers, especially Gregory Nazianzen and Gregory of Nyssa, on the shape of Maximus' thought. On the other hand, von Balthasar's insistence on the orthodoxy and the fundamentally Christian inspiration of Pseudo-Dionysius would find growing echoes today, particularly in the work of Alexander Golitzin, after several decades in which the predominant interpretation was to link Dionysius resolutely with anti-Chalcedonian Christology and Neoplatonist philosophy.

In the end, the real value of this book seems to be that it presents us with a powerful, attractive, religiously compelling portrait of the thought of a major Christian theologian who might, but for this book, have remained only an obscure name in the handbooks of patrology. It is surely not the only portrait possible, and it certainly reflects aspects of the painter's own intellectual physiognomy to a degree that even a postmodern critic may find disturbing. Nonetheless, it is a plausible portrait, based on an intelligent and careful reading of Maximus' own writings, and one that is superbly calculated to draw the reader into the central issues of Christian thought and Christian witness in our own age. Here the history of theology has become itself a way of theological reflection.

It seems appropriate to say a few words here about the principles I have followed in making this translation. Basically, I have attempted to be as faithful as possible to both the content and the style of the German text, as it appears in its second edition of 1961. Some of von Balthasar's long, sinuous sentences have had to be divided and reshaped in the interest of intelligibility: English obviously does not lend itself

to lengthy periodic sentences as easily as do more highly inflected lan-
guages like German, Greek, or Latin. But I have tried to present the
rhetorical effect of von Balthasar's prose, as well as its ideas, as far as
that could be done, if only because he is a theologian who is more
seriously concerned with the aesthetics of his own prose than are most
of his colleagues. When I have felt it necessary to add a few words or
a phrase of clarification to von Balthasar's text, I have placed those in
square brackets—though I have kept such additions to a minimum; ordinary, rounded parentheses correspond to von Balthasar's own punc-
tuation. In translating the numerous quotations from Maximus that
appear in the book—some of them quite lengthy—I have decided to
base my English first of all on von Balthasar's German translation, in
order to preserve better the connections he is trying to establish between the passages quoted and his own argument. But I have checked
all the quotations against the Greek original and have corrected them
where necessary to assure a fair representation of Maximus' sense—
even though they are probably farther removed from the Greek, in
some cases, than a direct translation would have been.

The second edition of *Kosmische Liturgie* also included German translations of several of Maximus' works—the *Mystagogia*, the *Four Hundred
Chapters on Love*, and a revised version of his comparative translation
of the *Two Hundred Chapters on Knowledge*—as well as a revision of
his 1940 article on the authorship of the scholia on Pseudo-Dionysius
attributed to John of Scythopolis. I have included here a translation
only of this revised article, as an appendix to the book. The *Mystagogia*, the *Chapters on Love*, and the *Chapters on Knowledge* are available
elsewhere in good modern English translations,[17] and even though von
Balthasar's translation of the last of these works includes a discussion
of comparative material from the Origenist tradition, it seemed best to
allow those who want to pursue this subject more closely to consult
his German text. I have also modernized von Balthasar's references, in
the footnotes, to the Greek text of Maximus' works, making use of the
new editions of those works in the *Corpus Christianorum, Series Graeca*

---

[17] Maximus Confessor, *The Ascetic Life: The Four Centuries on Charity*, trans. Polycarp Sher-
wood, O.S.B., Ancient Christian Writers, 21 (Westminster, Md.: Newman Press, 1955);
Maximus Confessor: Selected Writings, trans. George C. Berthold, Classics of Western Spiri-
tuality (New York: Paulist Press, 1985). See also the translation of the *Mystagogia* by Julian
Stead, O.S.B., entitled *The Church, the Liturgy, and the Soul of Man* (Still River, Mass.: St.
Bede's Pub., 1982).

where possible; I have corrected and completed his references to secondary works (which can often be rather casual) in the footnotes, and have added references to newer literature, in square brackets, where that seemed important and helpful. I have completely revised his bibliography of published works on Maximus and have attempted to include in it all major twentieth-century literature on Maximus. Finally, I have added a new and much more extensive index.

In conclusion, I must add my brief but heartfelt thanks to others who have made the labor of translating this work easier. The first of these is my friend and long-time colleague on the editorial board of *Communio* Professor David L. Schindler, himself one of the leading experts in North America on von Balthasar's thought; it was he who invited me to prepare this translation, more years ago than I care to remember, and who has encouraged me gently through the years to bring it to completion, without ever making encouragement feel like pressure. Second, I am grateful to my confrère Fr. Edward T. Oakes, S.J., for helpful critique and suggestions as this project drew to a close. Finally, I am very grateful to two graduate students at the University of Notre Dame, Dr. Christopher J. Ruddy and the Rev. Paul R. Kolbet, both of whom read the translation through completely in manuscript, caught many of my errors, and made many enormously valuable suggestions of ways to improve its readability. In addition, Paul Kolbet was an indispensable help in checking and correcting the Greek references and in bringing the final revisions of the manuscript to technical realization with unstinting intelligence and care. Through the help of all of these friends, it has been possible to turn this translation project into a corrected and updated version of one of our century's major works of historical theology. It is my hope that it will make the rich theological thought of both Maximus Confessor and Hans Urs von Balthasar more readily available to a new generation of readers, for the good of the Church and the Christian faith.

Brian E. Daley, S.J.
University of Notre Dame
August 12, 1998
(Vigil of St. Maximus the Confessor)

FOREWORD TO THE
SECOND EDITION (1961)

When Herder first published this study, amid the confusion of wartime twenty years ago (1941)—simultaneously with two other related investigations of mine: *Die Gnostischen Centurien des Maximus Confessor* (Herder, 1941) and "Das Scholienwerk des Johannes von Scythopolis", *Scholastik* 16 (1940): 16–38, on the scholia to Pseudo-Dionysius the Areopagite—it was a move into virtually uncharted territory. Aside from the contributions of Grumel, Devreesse, Peitz, and Montmasson on particular aspects of the biography of Maximus or of literary authenticity, the only recent study was the brief but valuable work of M. Viller, which showed the connection between Maximus and Evagrius.[1] As a result, my sketch of the Confessor's world view had the stage to itself. The purpose of the book, above all, was to set a perspective that would put the details in place, to point out the constellation his works present to us in the theological heavens and the lines that connect star with star. The two accompanying studies I have mentioned, on two decisively important works [attributed to Maximus], were meant only to serve this wider expository purpose: most of the scholia on Pseudo-Dionysius could be excluded as inauthentic, whereas the *Centuries on Knowledge*, which make such an odd impression on the reader, had to be recognized as genuine. Further, the book made a first attempt at a chronological ordering of Maximus' writings, something that was also indispensable if one were to get a view of their underlying structure.

Since that first loosening of the soil, a great deal of work has been done. In the same year, Josef Loosen's fine book appeared, *Logos und Pneuma im begnadeten Menschen bei Maximus Confessor*,[2] followed—even more significantly—by the careful, accurate studies of Polycarp Sherwood, O.S.B.[3] These latter works led to clear results on a number of

---

[1] "Aux Sources de la spiritualité de s. Maxime: Les Oeuvres d'Evagre le Pontique", *Revue d'ascèse et de mystique* 11 (1930): 156–84, 239–68.

[2] Josef Loosen, S.J., *Logos und Pneuma im begnadeten Menschen bei Maximus Confessor* (Münster, 1941).

[3] Polycarp Sherwood, O.S.B., *An Annotated Date-List of the Works of Maximus the Confessor* (Rome, 1952); *The Earlier Ambigua of St. Maximus the Confessor and His Refutation of Origen* (Rome, 1955); *St. Maximus the Confessor. The Ascetic Life: The Four Centuries on Charity*, Ancient Christian Writers, 21 (Washington, D.C.: Newman Press, 1955).

points: the Confessor's most obscure works, his *Ambigua*, were now
brought closer to the light; one of his main concerns, the polemic
against Origenism, was appropriately underlined; the chronology of
his life and works was examined and developed with the greatest care;
and the question of the scholia on Pseudo-Dionysius was pursued further. In addition, the confused history of the theological background
to Maximus' Christology was clarified, in many respects, by the research of Marcel Richard,[4] Charles Moeller,[5] Berthold Altaner,[6] and
others; the spiritual side of his work was explained by Irénée Hausherr,
S.J.,[7] Irénée-Henri Dalmais, O.P.,[8] and J. Pegon, S.J. (in his edition of
the *Centuries on Charity*);[9] and many other contributions were made,
which one can find listed in Hans-Georg Beck, *Kirche und theologische
in Literatur Byzantinischen Reich*, Byzantinisches Handbuch, 2:1 [1959],
437–42.

Nonetheless, none of these works—with the exception, perhaps of
Sherwood's *Earlier Ambigua*—had the ambition of piercing to the heart
of the Maximian synthesis, probably because in most minds the old
judgment of Viller and Hausherr continued to hold sway: that such a
unity in Maximus' thought really did not exist—that he remained a
compiler, or at best a reservoir of disparate traditions. That attitude is
precisely what encourages me to attempt this new edition of a book
that argues for the unity of his achievement and to try to establish the
point more clearly. What is presented here is not a historically neu-

---

[4] [See, for example, "L'Introduction du mot 'Hypostase' dans la théologie de l'incarnation",
Mélanges de science religieuse 2 (1945): 5–32, 243–70.]

[5] ["Le V. Concile oecuménique et la magistère ordinaire au VIᵉ siècle", *Revue des sciences
philosophiques et théologiques* 35 (1952): 413–23.]

[6] [Von Balthasar may be referring to Altaner's article, "Der griechische Theologie Leontius
und Leontius der skythische Mönch", *Theologische Quartalschrift* 127 (1947): 147–65 (= *Kleine
Patristische Schriften*, Texte und Untersuchungen, 83 [Berlin, 1967], 375–91).]

[7] ["Les Grands Courants de la spiritualité orientale", *Orientalia christiana periodica* 1 (1935):
126–28; "Ignorance infinie", ibid., 2 (1935): 351–62; *Philautie: De la tendresse pour soi à la
charité selon S. Maxime le Confesseur* (Rome, 1952).]

[8] ["S. Maxime le Confesseur, Docteur de la Charité", *Vie spirituelle* 2 (1948): 296–303
(with a translation of Epistle 2); "La Théorie des 'logoi' des créatures chez S. Maxime le
Confesseur", *Revue des sciences philosophiques et théologiques* 36 (1952): 244–49; "L'Oeuvre
spirituelle de S. Maxime le Confesseur", *Vie spirituelle*, supp. 21 (1952): 216–26; "Un Traité
de théologie contemplative: Le Commentaire du Pater de S. Maxime le Confesseur", *Revue
d'ascétique et de mystique* 29 (1953): 123–59; "La Doctrine ascétique de S. Maxime le Confesseur", *Irénikon* 26 (1953): 17–39.]

[9] [*Maxime le Confesseur: Centuries sur la charité*, Sources chrétiennes, 9 (Paris: Éditions du
Cerf, 1945).]

tral overview of the life and works of this man, but rather an attempt to grasp intuitively, and to make visible, the shape of his ideas. If I have seen that shape correctly, then Maximus surely takes on an unexpected relevance for today's intellectual scene. He is *the* philosophical and theological thinker who stands between East and West. In his self-effacing serenity, and also in the fearless courage of his truly free spirit, he reveals how, and from which directions, these two come together. And "East" means not simply Byzantium, nor "West" simply Rome; "East" really means Asia, and "West" the whole Western world.

In the first edition, I spoke of a "crisis" in the life and work of the Confessor; this drew criticism, especially from Sherwood, and I now omit the expression in order to put the reality I mean in a more positive light. I attempted to illustrate this so-called crisis by a particularly dramatic example from among his writings, the *Centuries on Knowledge*, and tried, by way of suggestion, to connect it with his stay in Alexandria. The tension of ideas I was referring to, however, is, to a greater or lesser degree, present in all his works and in all the stages of his life and belongs, one could say, to the man's very horoscope, to his internal, intellectual "con-stellation". In a similar sense, the no-man's land that seems to stretch between Jews and Gentiles bears the name of Paul and is filled by his presence. Such places, however, are not inhabited by harmless compilers and librarians: the place itself takes charge of the man and shapes him, and what happens there happens in the full light of his consciousness. We will make this intuition our starting point in the pages that follow.

This time, too, we do not intend to present a study that will please scholars in the classical mold by clarifying every tiny detail. What has already been explained by others will either be gratefully noted here or silently presupposed; and there is still much that is unexplained and awaits investigation on its own. No work has yet been done, for instance, on Maximus' relation to Pseudo-Dionysius (as Viller has investigated his relation to Evagrius, and Sherwood and I his relation to Origen); also none on his relation to the Cappadocian Fathers or to the Neo-Chalcedonian Christology of the sixth century. This latter task can be undertaken fruitfully only now that the distorting rubble of Loofs' hypotheses on the work of Leontius [of Byzantium] has, with great labor, been swept away by the work of Junglas. There is also nothing satisfactory written on Maximus and Sophronius, nothing helpful about his relationship to the Byzantine liturgy of the period, nothing on his biblical commentaries, which are buried in the catenae,

nor anything on the relationship—until now assumed, but not proven
—between Maximus, who lived so long in Carthage, and Augustine.

Sherwood, above all, has made substantial accomplishments. His general chronology[10] confirmed my own proposals,[11] I may say, on every
point, though going far beyond them in offering new information, and
has allowed me to forego any further detailed investigation into the
chronology of Maximus' life and work. For that reason, what I published earlier on this subject does not need to be printed once again. I
do not feel particularly under attack, for the most part, by Sherwood's
criticisms of the earlier version of this book, since his most important theses—for instance, Maximus' critique of Origen—agree both
materially and verbally with me: something that is not always made
clear in Sherwood's text. Other points, such as his emphasis on the
imago Trinitatis in Maximus, I consider to be mistaken, even if he has
offered enlightening commentaries on a few individual passages.[12] His
brief presentation of Maximus in Ancient Christian Writers, volume
21, distorts the figure of the Confessor to some extent, despite its eru-
dition, because it paints him simply as a spiritual writer and omits the
philosophical element, which is absolutely fundamental. His complicated attempts to prove that Maximus showed at times that he considered baptism and the Eucharist to be means of grace, even though he
speaks of them so little, seem points hardly worth belaboring for a saint
of the Church; on the other hand, Maximus' allegorical interpretation
of the Eucharist ought not to be dismissed so lightly. Nevertheless,
Sherwood has demonstrated so much that is new and interesting that
his research must remain a starting point for every future scholar. This
new edition makes no claim to take the place of any of his works.

Alongside the desire I have already mentioned of further clarifying
Maximus' overall significance, and apart from many small corrections
and additions, this present edition gives greater emphasis than the first
to a few critical points. First, the meaning of the trinitarian dogma [in
Maximus' work] has been made clearer, both in light of Sherwood's
work and in criticism of it. Secondly, in discussing his Christology, I
have drawn some of the lines connecting Maximus with Chalcedonians
and Neo-Chalcedonians more clearly, but I have also laid more empha-

---

[10] *An Annotated Date-List of the Works of Maximus Confessor.*

[11] See *Gnostische Centurien*, in *Kosmische Liturgie*, 2d ed. [1961], 149–56.

[12] See *Ascetic Life*, 32f.

sis on the speculative synthesis by which he brings ancient Christology to a conclusion. Since the Confessor's terminology is more variable than his basic intuitions, I am suspicious of an overly philological approach to this subject; it seems more helpful to try to observe what simple ideas are meant to be imagined and expressed by the many complicated, often time-worn scholastic or controversial concepts Maximus uses. Thirdly, I have further emphasized the meaning and implications of the *Mystagogia*, within the framework of the earlier ecclesiological tradition.

The study of John of Scythopolis' Scholia on Pseudo-Dionysius [printed here as an appendix] has been included mainly because a number of misprints, particularly in line-numbering, needed to be corrected in its original, somewhat fuller form. This work itself, however, has remained in the same state it had reached in 1940; a full revision would have called for very extensive study—material for a doctoral thesis! The caution raised by Sherwood on aspects of my method is justified but remains only negative criticism. All I can do is point some successor in a direction that will lead him farther along. There is at least this value in my old essay: it has restored to philosophy and theology the man who may well be the most profound thinker of the sixth century. As far as I can see, no one but Charles Moeller has yet seriously recognized this and drawn from it the appropriate conclusions. So it is high time to work out an orderly presentation of the deep and original understanding of the world that lies embedded in these Scholia. In the process, one must also attempt to solve the unanswered question of whether the collection of Scholia really contains nothing at all by Maximus, as Sherwood thinks, or whether one should still ascribe some part of it to him, as tradition has done.

Finally, there are people I must thank: Berthold Altaner, for giving so affirmative a welcome, in the *Theologische Revue* of 1942, to the first version of this study; my revered friend and teacher Henri de Lubac, who first interested me in doing this work, who saw it come into being in a first French draft, and then had the German text [of 1941] retranslated into French, to be part of his *Theologie* series; and finally, the intelligent and devoted French translators of that edition, who did their job superbly.

We search, with our lanterns, for models to imitate, but we do not like to look for them in the distant past. Here is one who seems extraordinarily contemporary: a spiritual world-traveler, who continued to work quietly while the waves of the Persian armies and the still more threatening waves of Islam drove him ever farther from home and while ecclesiastical and political integralism captured him, put him on trial, attempted to seduce him, condemned him, and banished him, until—at the southern end of what was one day to be Holy Russia—he died a martyr.

Pentecost, 1961
Hans Urs von Balthasar

I

INTRODUCTION

1. The Free Mind

a. Opening Up the Tradition

When Staudenmaier, as a young man, recognized that the theological task before him was to uproot the pantheism of Hegel and looked around for a model who would be not only enlightening but sufficiently grounded in history to be reliable, he came upon the figure of Scotus Erigena.[1] It was a happy choice: there the relationship of God and the world, the emergence of all things from God and their return to him, were seen, despite the pantheistic dress of Neoplatonism, with an essentially Christian eye. Even so, because of the interaction of form and content, a shadow still lies across this great figure, who, at the start of the Middle Ages, built from the heritage of Augustine, Gregory of Nyssa, Pseudo-Dionysius the Areopagite, and Maximus the most imposing intellectual edifice to rise before Aquinas. Erigena's achievement never became a theological classic.

Maximus, on the other hand, living two hundred years before his Scottish translator, became—in an equally dangerous and bleak period of history—not only the most daring systematician of his time, but also an incontestable pillar of the Church; this is due to his influence as monk, as spiritual advisor and writer, and as saint, as well as to his martyr's death, along with that of Pope Martin I, in defense of the dogma of Chalcedon. In all its dimensions, the inner form of his work is synthesis: not only because of what it deliberately intended and achieved, but because of its location at a place and historical moment between Byzantium, Africa, and Rome, between the patristic era and the Byzantine and Carolingian Middle Ages, even—in the final christological struggle, in which Maximus truly played the decisive role—between Eastern and Western theology and spirituality themselves.

---

[1] [Franz Anton Staudenmaier, *Johannes Scotus Erigena und die Wissenschaft seiner Zeit. Mit allgemeinen Entwicklungen der Hauptwahrheiten auf dem Gebiete der Philosophie und Religion, und Grundzügen zu einer Geschichte der speculativen Theologie* (Frankfurt am Main, 1834).]

In order to stamp such a paradigmatic form on intellectual history, Maximus' own ability to form and be formed had to be mutually and internally conditioned by destiny. At the deepest level, each of these abilities promotes the other, and each comes to its fullness only when a person has seen his own star rising beyond all the cultural and political configurations and weaknesses of his time and follows it with a freedom that overcomes the world. By taking possession of his own mission, he becomes its possession; the things around him, and the course of history, conform themselves to him. Maximus did nothing to give power to his own achievement: considered externally, his main works are without form, and the collection of his writings incredibly haphazard; as a humble monk, he seems almost deliberately to have avoided or concealed any claim to authority in the intellectual realm—there is never the slightest gesture of pretension. Even his biographical traces are lost for long periods: his fifteen years in Africa are beyond reconstruction. But how suddenly his authority blazes forth in his disputation with Pyrrhus! What supreme precision this contemplative spirit reveals, who seemed to be sunk in "pure prayer"! He never meddles, but he is always available; he seems to crystallize automatically around his higher center. In the cramped monastic communities in which he lives, clouds of envy and calumny ride high, as anyone can immediately see who has eyes to read the *Four Centuries on Charity*. He answers with love alone, a love that has essentially withdrawn itself from the sphere of πάθη, of passionate vulnerability, and has buried itself in the freedom of a universal, catholic benevolence that imitates God. We shall see how much this evangelical love, which has renounced all power of its own, is the ultimate synthetic force of his thought and his life. For him, spirituality and genius, freedom and boldness are never separate from each other. Anyone who knows how to interpret his achievement will see, as something obvious, that his boldest spiritual actions are dictated by a catholic love that always brings two things together: it lets objective, actual values stand on their own, and it brings into unity those values that the heart finds indispensable for its own existence. In this sense, Maximus is one of the greatest models we have for what we call "handing on the Christian tradition".

One must try to grasp his historical situation. Origen lived four hundred years earlier, the great Cappadocians, Chrysostom, Jerome, some three hundred, Augustine a little less. The high period of trinitarian and christological thought had found its end in the two councils of

Ephesus (431) and Chalcedon (451). Shortly afterward Theodoret died, and the end of the fifth century showed unmistakable signs of spiritual exhaustion. Around 500 another star rose, curiously removed from all that is historical: the unknown writer who styled himself "Dionysius the Areopagite". Then came the sixth century, whose Christian face is dominated by the frightening name of Justinian. At the end of this era, around 580, Maximus was born, and his lifetime, too, would stand in the shadow of an imperial name: Heraclius, in whose court he served as first secretary.

The Council of Ephesus was, to an alarming degree, a matter of court politics; the decisions of Chalcedon were ceremoniously extorted by imperial commissioners from bishops who resisted them and who only imperfectly understood the implications of the new terminology. From then on, the imperial court would determine the form of the history of dogma to an increasing degree; gripped in the talons of imperial politics and pointed by them in the desired direction, the Church's thoughtful reflection on revelation could only take a few tiny, timid steps forward. We do not need to rehearse the full tragedy of this religious and political integralism here again; it is significant enough that even the papacy was deeply dishonored and that none of the popes of the period —despite all the sympathy we may feel for Vigilius—reached a genuinely tragic greatness. The mildew of integralism, which was the real point of the period's politically correct dogmatic formulas, meant the death of three things in the Church: a living biblical theology, which was extinguished around the time of Chalcedon; the fruitful exchange between theology and monastic spirituality, which distinguished the whole classical patristic period, whereas after the decisive politicization of theology monasticism withdrew into a realm beyond time; and finally—worst of all—the free republic of the mind, through the branding of some of its greatest citizens as heretics and through the upsetting and ultimately the destruction, by all the stratagems of political power, of the kind of intellectual balance that through dialogue, and dialogue alone, enables all thought—even theological thought—to come to its full development. Chalcedon—not without strong political pressure, as we have said—achieved this dialogical balance one final time; that is why it remained, for the period that followed, a guiding star. Yet even before Chalcedon, Cyril, along with the Alexandrian Christology and outlook, had been victorious over Nestorius and Antiochene thought; already there, spiritual and political power had entered into an alliance

rife with consequences. It was not without effect that the shadowy
name of the imperious and violent patriarch was to shape intellectual
history, from Chalcedon to Maximus, almost as an absolute monarch.
The justice done to Antiochene thought at Chalcedon came too late:
in Cyril's name, the Alexandrian front hardened into Monophysitism,
and not even centuries of crafty imperial politicking succeeded in rout-
ing it from the field. In fact, the ecclesial and theological center fell
in with this political program: today one calls the approach that began
shortly after Chalcedon and held the field practically until Maximus
"Neo-Chalcedonianism", since it attempted to reconcile Chalcedon,
not with the selections from Cyril's work recognized by the Council,
but with the whole of Cyril's thought (which had now been weighed
down by the exaggerations of the Apollinarian forgeries).[2] Clearly, we
are indebted to this movement for much that is valuable; without it, the
Confessor's synthesis would never have been possible. Nevertheless,
we must recognize that it was an expression of a deeply rooted im-
balance. On the bishop's throne of Antioch now sat the Monophysite
Severus; the spirit of Antioch was held incommunicado. Nestorianism
had withdrawn to the eastern borders of the empire and beyond into
Persia and existed in the theological mainstream only as a caricature,
a shadowy puppet-figure one could attack and accuse at will, without
fear of reprisal. The "Three Chapters" controversy, the imposition of
the imperial theology at the Fifth Council (553)—which decreed the
final condemnation of the Antiochenes on the basis of forged texts[3]—
the contradiction between two papal decrees, the more balanced *Con-
stitutum* (May 14, 553) and the forced compromise *Iudicatum* (554): all
make the whole process [of the Council of 553] appear in a highly
questionable light. It shows clearly, as Moeller has demonstrated, that
even the concept "ecumenical council" must be seen as analogical, that
[the decree of] Constantinople II must ultimately be understood only

---

[2] M. Richard, "Le Néochalcédonisme", *Mélanges de science religieuse* 3 (1946): 156–61;
C. Moeller, "Le Chalcédonisme et le néo-chalcédonisme en Orient de 451 à la fin du VIᵉ
siècle", in A. Grillmeier and H. Bacht, *Das Konzil von Chalkedon: Geschichte und Gegenwart*
(Würzburg: Echter, 1951), 1:637–720. [See also S. Helmer, *Der Neuchalkedonismus Geschichte,
Berechtigung und Bedeutung eines dogmengeschichtlichen Begriffes* (diss., Bonn, 1962); A. Grillmeier,
"Der Neu-Chalkedonismus. Um die Berechtigung eines Kapitels in der Dogmengeschichte",
in *Mit Ihm und in Ihm* (Freiburg, 1975), 371–85.]

[3] M. Richard, "L'Introduction du mot 'Hypostase' dans la théologie de l'incarnation",
Mélanges de science religieuse 2 (1945): 21–29.

as an explicatory annex to Chalcedon—as Gregory the Great understood it—and that the second papal document must be judged in the
sense of the first.[4] But what is the point of such modern revisionist
judgments? At the time, all opposition was broken, destroyed by being
made to look ridiculous.

The man who had steered the emperor into this political chess game,
Theodore Askidas, was an Origenist, however, and his own personal
chess game was successful in turning the emperor's attention away from
a destructive crusade against Origen. Only if one keeps the entire phenomenon of Origen in mind—the fervent "man of the Church" who
died a martyr, the great lover of both the letter and the spirit of Holy
Scripture, the daring theologian who tried to take everything good
and positive that Greece and gnosis had conceived and to put it at the
service of Christ's truth—only then can one understand how Origen
can and must always be a source of new and fruitful inspiration for the
Church's reflection. The monks, however, since the time of Evagrius
Ponticus (d. 399), had reduced his work to a two-dimensional ascetical
and mystical schema; in doing so, they had made certain speculative
tendencies, which in the context of his entire work remained within
their proper proportions, into dominant concerns. At the beginning of
the sixth century, fanatical, esoteric propaganda was launched again in
the monasteries of Palestine in behalf of this spiritualistic caricature of
Origen, propaganda that makes the emperor's no less energetic coun-
terattack understandable. Justinian's anathemas against the Alexandrian
master (543), supposedly approved by Pope Vigilius, are really aimed
against the caricature of his thought that the Origenism of the time
offered,[5] to which Origen himself had certainly given some support.
The catastrophe was not so much the condemnation itself as the fact

---

[4] C. Moeller, "Le 5ᵉ concile oecuménique et le magistère ordinaire au 6ᵉ siècle", *Revue des sciences philosophiques et théologiques* 35 (1951): 413–23; see there also a similar conclusion by E. Amann.

[5] "Although the edict and condemnatory judgment of the bishops, in the year 543, laid the anathema first of all on the errors committed by Origen himself and on his person, the new campaign [of 552] was directed against the teachings of the contemporary Origenists in Palestine": F. Diekamp, *Die origenistischen Streitigkeiten im 6. Jahrhundert und das fünfte all-gemeine Concil* (Münster, 1899), 130. One presupposition of Justinian's anathema on Origen himself was the legend, which the emperor took for unvarnished truth, that Origen had not remained faithful in persecution, but that he had denied Christ and worshipped idols (ibid., 74). The emperor decreed that no one, in the future, should receive priestly ordination who had not condemned Origen along with all other certified heretics.

that once again Christian theology had allowed a straw man to be
set up by political integralism, thereby darkening its view of its own
history with the same dire results that would soon follow the Three
Chapters controversy. The wild legends that grew up around Origen
in the Middle Ages, which Henri de Lubac has recounted, bear witness
to the frightening power of politics, even in the intellectual realm; it
was, after all—as in the case of Theodore of Mopsuestia—an attempt
to rub out not simply his teaching but his whole personality, in the
hope that the defamation of his character would finally assure that the
verdict against his teaching would take effect.

As a result, the spring that had nourished not only Didymus and
Evagrius—who were condemned along with Origen—but also Basil
and the two Gregories was now invisible, inaccessible; and when the
springs of the mind lie buried or poisoned, one can no longer live
freely and openly in a world of undistorted thought. At the same time,
however, seemingly from the distant origins of Christianity, the star
of Pseudo-Dionysius began to rise, and freer and more wakeful spirits
immediately began to gather around him. Doubts about his historical
authenticity grew silent remarkably early; it is possible that John of
Scythopolis, his first inspired commentator, campaigned so enthusiastically for him because he saw in him a spiritual force finally powerful
enough to become the center of a new intellectual universe in the dev-
astated inner world of the Church. Nevertheless, the Areopagite was
shown to the public first of all by Monophysite hands, and in the Dialogue of 532 [between Monophysites and Chalcedonians] his works
were rejected by Hypatius of Ephesus, the leader of the orthodox side,
as a forgery. A certain questionable odor seems to have clung to him
throughout the sixth century; he remained, in a sense, an esoteric author read in circles of σχολαστικοί and γραμματικοί, the educated hu-
manists of the time.

Only against this background is it possible to measure the real weight
of Maximus' intellectual accomplishment. To achieve it called for the
highest degree of Christian intellectual freedom. Doubtless, Maximus
had read a great deal,[6] but he rested his intellectual edifice on only a
few well-chosen pillars, which allowed him to reclaim the true form
of a living tradition, untroubled by the lurid figures of villains and
scarecrows. Dionysius must not be left out, and Maximus is the one

---

[6] See I. Hausherr, *Philautie* [Rome, 1952], 43: "Maxime . . . a tout lu."

who assured his permanent citizenship in the world of official, ecclesial theology; this achievement alone proves him to be one of the founders of the Middle Ages, even in the Latin West. But Dionysius was not enough—he is too narrow a pillar to carry the Church's tradition; Origen had to return, as well. There were two, possibly three avenues of approach. The first was named "Cappadocia": Gregory Nazianzen, the personification of orthodoxy yet a man steeped in Origen's thought, was a sturdy bridge; he could serve as an example of what it might mean to return to Origen in this, the seventh century. Accordingly, the title of the Confessor's main work is "An Explanation of Obscure Passages in Dionysius and Gregory" [*Ambigua*]: by systematically interpreting passages in Gregory that sounded classically Origenist, he was able— as no one before or since—to undertake a constructive criticism of Origen himself. This criticism was sharp, pressing forward "to the division of joints and marrow" [Heb 4:12], but it remained objective and just, and so it acquired for Maximus the right to claim the inheritance of the one who had been examined and judged so severely.

This heritage was an overwhelmingly rich one. The harvest is brought home throughout Maximus' writings, most abundantly in the *Two Hundred Chapters on God and on the Mystery of the Incarnation of God's Son*, which we will simply call, from now on, the *Centuries on Knowledge*. Here Maximus dared to take the second avenue of approach, incorporating texts from Origen directly into his own work. These are not simply texts gathered together from a superficial reading of the Alexandrian, but undoubtedly passages that embody his central intentions. Nonetheless, they are texts that must have seemed to their collector—whether by means of their arrangement [in his anthology] or through the light shed on them by their context, whether by means of [his own] careful selection or by free reformulation—to be, not simply acceptable, but even indispensable to a theology of the spiritual life. So we have here an example, unique in the cultural history of the early Church, of a genuine intellectual dialogue being conducted with an earlier author, despite his condemnation (which had clearly been colored by political motives). This dialogue, conducted, not as a snobbish liberal pose, but out of responsibility to the Church, ended by revealing the opportunity, even the duty, to take hold once again of material that had been lost to the mind through suppression by the state and to make the central results of that dialogue one's own.

Still a third avenue of approach was possible, even indicated. Origen's influence on monasticism was exercised through the form into which his disciple Evagrius Ponticus had reshaped him.[7] This radicalized form of Origenism, infectious in its very simplicity, whose powers of cultural penetration one can see in [fifth-century] authors like Palladius and Cassian, was obviously not just past history by the Confessor's day. Evagrius, who had created the only consistently systematic ideology of the monastic life, remained a major power still; anyone who intended, not to hand on the unexplained aspects of the larger Christian [spiritual] tradition blindly, but to take them apart critically, in the hope of clarifying them and of making his own whatever could be responsibly assimilated [from this tradition] in the light of the gospel, had to engage in dialogue with him. Maximus had wrestled with Evagrius, in the *Centuries on Love* and in many other places, with the same dogged determination he had directed toward Origen in the *Ambigua* and the *Centuries on Knowledge*. Superficially, on the purely linguistic level, one can find countless terminological and even ideological parallels between them. Viller was so struck by them that he branded Maximus simply a plagiarist of the older mystical theologian;[8] yet, as we have discovered since, this judgment was unfair. If one looks more deeply, through the similarities of terminology, to the contents themselves, one is amazed —even in a work that is admittedly put together from echoes and quotations, like the *Centuries on Love*—at the differences and at the quiet but deliberate corrections.

Pseudo-Dionysius and Gregory Nazianzen could be alluded to openly, Origen and Evagrius only anonymously. But names were not important to Maximus, provided the great springs could begin flowing again, provided they could be made accessible again, after his personal effort at critical purification, to the free realm of the mind—accessible without causing qualms of conscience, without being hampered even by the "politics" of the heart. Yet one main branch of the Church's tradition was still missing: Antioch. This branch was beyond direct recovery, either by open allusion or nameless citation; such an attempt would immediately have betrayed itself in its old-fashioned terminology, for one could no longer reach back beyond Chalcedon. But it was part

---

[7] "Evagrius is the organizer of the Eastern spiritual doctrine inspired by Origen": I. Hausherr, "Les Grands Courants de la spiritualité orientale", *Orientalia Christiana Periodica* I (1935): 125.

[8] M. Viller, "Aux sources de la spiritualité de s. Maxime: Les Oeuvres d'Évagre le Pontique", *Revue d'ascétique et de mystique* 11 (1930): 156–84, 239–68.

of the Confessor's destiny to restore this missing member, too, in another way: his role in the history of dogma was to a large extent that of stressing the full humanity of Christ, even his human "personality" (although not his human "person")—the element that had been the Antiochenes' main concern. The man Jesus' own active doing and willing—not a passive human nature dependent on the activity of a personal divine Logos, as the Monothelites imagined—was more than simply something to be defended on the conceptual level; it had to be made plausible within the context of a comprehensive understanding of the world.

In Maximus, the real intent of Antioch found victory—anonymously, but truly. On the bedrock of a philosophy of created being that was valid in its own right, the three Alexandrian Platonic theologies of Origen, Evagrius, and Dionysius met and mingled. Gregory [Nazianzen], whose intellectual contours were often the weakest and whose attitude was more often eclectically aesthetic, provided the ecclesial vehicle. And in the background, like a ghost yet near enough to touch, rose the ancient ancestor of the Alexandrians: Philo, present [in Maximus' work] in demonstrable verbal allusions, yet there simply to complete the golden chain of the intellectual tradition and to flesh out a hidden spiritual geometry, perceptible only to the knowing eye. Maximus never shows any of the antiquarian preoccupation that will later appear in Photius. On the contrary, he holds everywhere to the practice of making hard choices: all that is secondary must disappear, only the main supporting pillars should be visible. In this respect, he is both seer and preserver in a time of cultural dissolution, just as, a hundred years earlier, Boethius had been—in his own way also a martyr of the intellectual life.

b. Between Emperor and Pope

The acts of a free mind are not simply produced by nature but occur in the context of historical decisions. After one has taken responsibility for them inwardly, before God, one must sooner or later also take responsibility for them outwardly, before the forces of opposition whom these very acts have overcome on the level of consciousness. Maximus succeeded in tearing the whole organism of the Greek Christian tradition away from the destructive claws of political integralism. It was impossible that the political powers should not hold against him, in their own way, what he had done to them by such a theft. The final trials that brought both him and Pope Martin I to their end were political trials; precisely as such, they set a final seal on the mind's untamable independence before earthly power. Of course, it is true that the [Eastern Church's] great christological decision against monenergism had already been made on the political level; that way of conceiving Christ had, after all, been originally thought up in order to promote political unity, and the whole history of the empire was intimately bound up with these issues. The most unfortunate aspect of the dispute was that the dialogue that decided its intellectual outcome, Maximus' disputation with the deposed and exiled Patriarch Pyrrhus in 645, took place in Carthage—in Africa, a place that had long been a bastion of opposition against the Byzantine court and that had taken on that role more than ever in those years under the influence of the Exarch Gregory, who was himself scheming to become emperor. The disputation took place with Gregory in the chair. In addition, Pope Theodore I (642–649), the first pope after a hundred years of imperial humiliations to dare raise his head against Byzantium, not only received Pyrrhus back into communion when he renounced Monothelitism but "had a throne set up for him next to the altar and honored him as bishop of the imperial city". Theodore only dared to do these things because he had already declared himself for the African usurper, against Emperor Constans II.[9] Gregory's reign was a brief one; he was killed, in 647, in a battle with Arab invaders. On this subject, it is worth noting that even though Maximus was obliged to live in the exarch's region, no document gives even a hint of any kind of political collusion. Thus one cannot put too much weight on Gregory's presiding role in the disputation. Later, during the trial Maximus had to endure in Byzantium after his arrest in Rome a witness alleged that nine years earlier a certain Abba Thomas had arrived from Rome, and had told him: "Pope Theodore sent me to the Patrician Gregory to tell him not to be afraid, because the servant of God, Abba Maximus,[10] saw

---

[9] Erich Caspar, *Geschichte des Papsttums*, vol. 2 (Tübingen, 1933), 549f.

[10] On the erroneous use of the title "Abba" in the acts of the trial, see Vénance Grumel, "Notes d'histoire et de chronologie sur la vie de saint Maxime le Confesseur", *Echos d'Orient* 30 (1927): 32. In Caspar and in Grillmeier and Bacht (*Chalkedon*, 2:834ff.) one still reads "Abbot Maximus". [Von Balthasar seems to take the Greek title *abbas* as meaning the head of a monastic community, parallel to the Western office of "abbot". At this period, however, it

in a dream choirs of angels in heaven, toward the east and toward the west, and the ones in the west began to sing, 'Gregory Augustus, you shall conquer.' "[11] If there is anything true at all in this story (and it could, after all, have risen from a deeper level within the dreamer's soul than the politicians imagined), its implications told at most against the pope, not Maximus. Maximus denied that he had ever had the dream but then argued that even if the story of the dream had been true, dreams are not subject to human freedom; and that even if he had told the pope about it, the consequences the pope drew from it would be his responsibility, not that of the supposed dreamer.

When Theodore's successor, Martin I, condemned Monothelitism, with Maximus' help, at the Roman synod of 649, and was, as a result, arrested and dragged off to Byzantium, the whole spectacle repeated itself. Emperor Constans II had previously sent the Exarch Olympius to Italy in order to take charge, if possible, of the Roman militia and then to arrest the pope and have the *Typos* [a decree banning further discussion of the wills of Christ] published in all the churches. Olympius did take over the Italian armies, but only in order to advance his own cause for three years in a violent rebellion against the emperor; he himself was killed in 652, in a battle with the Arabs in Sicily. Nevertheless, it was under his protection that the Lateran Council [of 649] was able to meet, and the pope, who was later forced to undergo a political trial, naturally could not deny having had contact with Olympius. "How could I have had the power to resist such a man," he protested, "who relied on the mailed fist of the whole Italian army? Was I the one who made him exarch?" The confused stories that cluster around these relationships can be interpreted meaningfully only if one supposes that Olympius "involved the Roman militia with him in a successful coup and dragged the pope into it as well. How far Martin I really was only the hapless victim, drawn along by physical power, as he himself later alleged, is impossible to discern with certitude."[12] One wonders, in fact, whether the pope could have acted in any other way.

---

was probably still nothing more than a title of honor for a venerable monk, with no specific jurisdiction implied.]

[11] *Acta*; PG 90, 112C.

[12] Caspar, *Geschichte des Papsttums*, 2:568. Cf. 573: "An unfortunate stain of earth clings to his reputation as a martyr, which no efforts at apologetics . . . can succeed in wiping away."

On the other hand, it was never possible to implicate Maximus, who in the meantime had also been arrested and put on trial, in any kind of political deal. The imperial *sacellarius*, a fiscal official, presided over the trial—a fact that shows it was intended from the beginning to deal with political, not dogmatic, issues. He accused Maximus of having handed Egypt, Alexandria, the Pentapolis, and Africa over to the Saracens, out of hate toward the emperor: a witness had stated that twenty-two years earlier, when Emperor Heraclius had ordered Peter, the prefect of Numidia, to resist the Saracens, Maximus had advised the prefect not to do it, since God would never support the government of a prince who favored Monothelitism.[13] Maximus rejected this suggestion, too, as pure slander. A cause of greater concern for him was the revelation that Eugenius I, the successor of the martyred Pope Martin I, was showing an inclination to make a deal, through his representative at court, with Pyrrhus, who was again functioning as patriarch of Constantinople and who had long since recanted on the concessions he had made, out of weakness, at Rome. This proposed deal that would, in effect, bargain away the whole dogmatic achievement of the Lateran synod by proposing now to speak both of two natural wills and of one hypostatic will in Christ, depending on whether one was considering him in his two natures or in his single person. Maximus was threatened with excommunication by the pope himself, if he should prove unwilling to follow this new official policy.[14] Peace now seemed to be within the Church's grasp, but it was a peace that hung on the back of the imprisoned Confessor, who seemed to be the price the Roman curia had to pay. In this, his "darkest night of the soul", Maximus remained resolute. He denied that such an opportunistic course of action was possible, even in the face of almost perfect factual evidence that it had already been taken;[15] meanwhile, the gullible Roman legates had returned home, where both clergy and people gave the pope enough moral support[16] to back away from the proposed reunion.

The Byzantines proposed another solution: Bishop Theodosius [of Caesaraea in Bithynia, one of the emperor's representatives at Maximus'

---

[13] *Acta*; PG 90, 89C. Cf. Hefele, *Conciliengeschichte*, vol. 3 (1877), 240.

[14] See the letter of Maximus to Anastasius: *Acta*; PG 90, 132C.

[15] " 'And what will you do, if the Romans approve this step?' He answered, 'The Holy Spirit, through the mouth of the apostles, condemns even angels, if they proclaim something that contradicts the gospel' " (*Acta*; PG 90, 121BC).

[16] Not without the help of the Confessor, as we shall see.

trial in 653] would subscribe to the formula of two wills and two operations in Christ, and Maximus would proclaim his own readiness
to communicate with him and the see of Constantinople. But Maximus refused, on the grounds that he alone, as a monk, did not have
the authority to take such a step; Church law demanded rather that
the emperor, along with the patriarch and his whole synod, should
resume contact with the Holy See, and then he himself would be glad
to accompany the patriarch on a journey to Rome. The whole pro-
posal, however, soon turned out to be a political fiction. During those
months, the fate of Christology depended on the unflinching resolve
of one man; without him, the desire for reunion, both in Rome and
in Byzantium, would presumably have brought about a dogmatic compromise, which would surely have led to the collapse of everything that
had been achieved [at the Lateran synod]. The fact that a victory over
politics "was won in the last moment, that in the end not opportunism
but the serious conviction of faith held good, that 'two wills' was not
merely a verbal formula—all this was the work of Maximus alone, who
is rightfully known in Church history by the title 'Confessor', as the
last great theologian and martyr of the christological controversies." [17]
    The trouble the Byzantines took to change the mind of this maver-
ick monk, the flattering promises made even by the emperor himself,
all show how aware they were of his role as bastion of orthodoxy.
But what was almost unintelligible to a Greek heart was that Maximus, an Easterner, had succeeded for the first time in abandoning the
"caesaropapist" fusion of priestly and imperial power, simply through
the internal consistency of his own intellectual progress, and had come
to make his spiritual home in papal Rome. Even during his stay in
Rome, a man named Gregory, who had brought the imperial *Typos*
to the West, visited him in his cell and asked, in the course of their
conversation, if he thought the emperor was also a priest.

> "I say no," Maximus replied, "for he does not stand at the altar and
> intone the 'Holy, Holy' after the consecration of the bread, nor does he
> baptize or administer the sacrament of anointing or perform the rite of
> laying on hands; he does not make men bishops, priests, or deacons, nor
> does he consecrate churches, nor does he wear the priestly insignia, the
> pallium, and the Gospel-book, as he wears the imperial crown and purple
> robe. You ask, however, 'Why does the Scripture call Melchizedek both

---

[17] Caspar, *Geschichte des Papsttums*, 2:575–76.

priest and king?' I answer: Melchizedek was the unique type (τύπος) of the one divine King. If you quote the phrase, '. . . Another king and priest, according to the order of Melchizedek' (Heb 7:11), then quote the rest: 'Without father, without mother, without family, he has neither a beginning to his days nor an end to his life' (Heb 7:3). And mark the evil that can come from [a misuse of] this passage! For this 'other', we find, is the incarnate God, working our redemption 'according to the order of Melchizedek' and not according to that of Aaron."[18]

This interpretation of the priestly kingship of Melchizedek, which finds its entire fulfillment in the appearance of Christ, after whom there can only be worldly rulers and spiritual priests, probably takes its inspiration from Pope Gelasius I (492–496), although for a long time afterward even the popes continued to address the emperors by the double title.[19]

With this distinction of powers in mind, Maximus constantly cuts apart the seemingly indissoluble unity of political and ecclesial interests and of the symbiotic exercise of office. To the argument that the Lateran synod had no legal standing because the pope who summoned it had been deposed, he answers:

Not deposed, but driven out! Show me the documentation of a synodal, canonical process that clearly attests his legal deposition! And even if he had been canonically deposed, that would still not prejudice our judgment of these synodal decisions, which were made in right faith and according to the holy canons, for all that had already been written by Pope Theodore, of happy memory, agrees with them.

A year later, the difficulty was raised that the Roman synod had no standing because it had met without imperial command. In response, Maximus produced a long list of Arian and other heretical synods that had been summoned by emperors, none of which was recognized as valid by the Church. Other synods—such as the one that deposed Paul of Samosata—were received as binding, even though they had met without imperial permission.[20] With logical consistency, he denied that by rejecting the imperial *Typos* he had set himself in opposition to the emperor's person; he had simply rejected a document composed by the patriarch, which did not even come from the emperor

---

[18] Ibid., 576–77; *Acta*; PG 90, 117AB.
[19] Caspar, *Geschichte des Papsttums*, 2:67 and n. 7.
[20] *Acta*; PG 90, 117Af., 145C–148A.

himself.[21] And when he was accused of arrogance for being the only one to oppose common opinion, he replied: "The three young men condemned no one, when they refused to adore the statue everyone else worshipped, . . . nor did Daniel condemn anyone when he was thrown in the lions' den—he simply preferred to die, rather than to offend God."[22]

Behind all of this stood a single great decision: for Rome, the refuge of free, evangelical faith; against Byzantium, the bulwark of politico-religious integralism. So the *sacellarius* asks him directly, at one point [in his trial], " 'Why do you love the Romans and hate the Greeks?' The servant of God replied, 'We are commanded to hate no one. I love the Romans because I am of the same faith as they are; I love the Greeks because I speak the same language.' "[23] Rome, for him, was objectively the home of right faith: Christ founded both the Catholic faith and the Church on Peter, he proclaims to his judges, "and I wish to adhere to that confession of faith on which the unity of all the Churches is based."[24]

With its Eastern intellectual power, Hellas [in the 640s] came to the support of a papacy that had gone into cultural decline because of the barbarian invasions. Gregory the Great, although he had been papal legate in Byzantium, spoke no Greek. Honorius I [625–638] gave way before the scheming Byzantines and their subtle, obscure distinctions and had to be defended by his successors in some difficult rear-guard actions. An Eastern pope, Theodore I [642–649]—a native of Jerusalem —smoothed over his predecessor's mistake and brought about a turn toward new independence. Although he remained modestly in the background, Maximus was the soul of the Lateran synod of 649; at least two of its canons, 10 and 11, come from his pen, and the Greek monks, who had five monasteries in Rome, were zealous representatives and translators of his position.[25] And even if this Greek victory found, for

---

[21] *Acta*; PG 90, 128B.

[22] *Acta*; PG 90, 121A.

[23] *Acta*; PG 90, 128C.

[24] *Acta*; PG 90, 93D.

[25] See E. Caspar, "Die Lateransynode von 649", *Zeitschrift für Kirchengeschichte* 51 (1932): 75–137; Johannes Pierres, *Sanctus Maximus Confessor princeps apologetarum synodi lateranensis anni 649* (diss., Gregorian University, Rome 1940); cf. B. Altaner, *Theologische Revue* 41 (1942): 50–51. [On the role of Maximus in the composition of the *acta* of the Lateran synod, see Richard Riedinger, "Die Lateransynode von 649 und Maximos der Bekenner", in F.

a while, little affirmative echo in Rome and was practically ignored in Byzantium,[26] the martyrdom of the pope, Maximus, and Maximus' companions in the long run gave the synod prestige, without which the almost effortless victory [of dyothelite Christology] at the Third Council of Constantinople would never have been achieved. Of course, the political Leviathan had, in the intervening years, completely collapsed, and the Arab invasion had derailed any political hopes for union with the Monophysites. But what do such minor disturbances matter, in comparison with the fact that at Constantinople in 681 the Confessor's Christology, which sprouted organically from the Christology of Chalcedon, was there declared, in simple terms, to be identical with the faith of the Catholic Church (DS 553–59)?

2. East and West

a. Religion and Revelation

The two preceding sections have shown the tension in the life and work of Maximus Confessor: a recapturing of the undistorted, integral tradition of the Christian East, alongside an ever-clearer inclination to bring all these recovered treasures to Rome, that Rome might profit from them. And Rome meant for him, as we have just tried to show, not some accidental oasis of political freedom, but the refuge of orthodoxy guaranteed by the gospel itself. More concretely, it was the defender of the balanced faith of Chalcedon against the rank growth of an exaggerated Cyrillian reinterpretation of Chalcedonian teaching.

The tension between East and West is an inseparable dimension of the Confessor's thought. He was rightly called the man who led both East and West into uproar;[27] even the dream he allegedly had in Rome was a dream about dialogue between East and West, in which the West won the day. The decisive question, however, for all the events that

---

Heinzer and C. Schönborn, eds., *Maximus Confessor: Actes du Symposium sur Maxime le Confesseur, Fribourg, 2–5 Septembre 1980*, Paradosis, 27 (Fribourg, 1982), 111–21; Pietro Conte, *Il sinodo Lateranense dell' ottobre 649* (Vatican City, 1989), 105–48.]

[26] Basing his argument on Rome's power of the keys, Maximus himself immediately began to count the Lateran synod as the sixth ecumenical council (PG 91, 137D–140A). As far as doctrinal content is concerned, he was right: the synod of 649 was really the first phase of the discussion completed at the council of 680–81 [Constantinople III].

[27] *Acta*; PG 90, 101B.

were to follow Maximus, was what "East" and "West" here really mean—on what level these concepts are to be understood. It is certainly not simply a question of the immediately geographical and political sphere, the struggle between the Rome of the East and the Rome of the West. It is also—as we have shown already—not simply a question of two styles of thought, of the Greek and the Roman-African patristic traditions: these are not the decisive issues. In spite of Leo's *Tome*, Chalcedon was not merely a "Roman" affair but was just as authentically Greek; even if Maximus thinks in anti-Monothelite terms, his thought is at least as much Greek in style as it is Roman.

The opposition [of East and West] lies at a deeper level. That glorious, dangerous intellectual tradition that Maximus unearthed, despite all the labels of heresy, and to which he tried to lend new brilliance and new validity, is, one can say, the element in Christian thought that had its living roots in Asia; it represents the maternal soil of the human religious instinct: what one—speaking somewhat inexactly— might set in contrast to biblical revelation as "natural religion". Let us briefly characterize this kind of religion. As the elemental groping of man toward God, it is, first of all, a way of renouncing the world— for this transitory, spatio-temporal, destiny-determined world is surely not God! It is a way of stripping off form, in order to find the infinite Absolute in a state of formlessness. The world, compared with God, is unreality, a falling away from the eternal unity. Expressed in terms of this picture of things, an incarnation of God can only mean a concession, the gracious descent of God into multiplicity, into the realm of matter, in order to lead what is multiple back into unity. In the end, it is not so much a synthesis of the One and the Many as a gesture of the One toward the Many, beckoning it home into the One. The religious yearning for a return to God glazes over all the objections and reservations one might raise on the basis of an ontology of created being; these can surely be noted for what they are worth, but they do not occupy the final, decisive position.

In contrast to such thinking stand the powerful forces of the Bible, Greece, and Rome. In the Old and New Testaments, God and the creature stand in an irreducible relationship of confrontation: not emanation and decline, but only the good, free, creative will of God is responsible for the creature's being, an act which, in the end, is justified by the relationship of confrontation within God of three Persons in unity. So the overarching unity of God and the world in Christ is

no attack on the integrity of creation but an act lifting creation beyond itself to fulfillment, an act in which even the Asian longing for
divinization is brought to rest. Greece reflects on this mystery of God
and world in Aristotelian and Stoic terms, taking seriously the nature
(φύσις) of the individual being, in its lasting structure of meaning, and
finding there a revelation of the divine Reason (*logos*, λόγος) that abides
within the world. Rome, with its genius for order, always turns confusion into clarity by making distinctions, dividing in order to conquer.
And then, in the midst of these three contending powers comes the
unprecedented synthesis of Chalcedon: God and man are now one,
"undivided and unconfused" (ἀδιαιρέτως καὶ ἀσυγχύτως). It is biblical
Christology, conceived in the terminology of Greek philosophy under
the inspiration of a Roman pope.

But what then becomes of the East? This was the question Maximus
asked himself, and he recognized that Christianity could not survive
without the religious passion of Asia. But how much of this impulse,
this human way of thinking, can be assimilated into Christianity? How
can it be done without endangering the core of Christianity itself? How
strong, how high must the christological thought structure be built?
How far must Christ be brought toward the center even of theodicy
and the theology of creation in order to make the Christian duality of
God and world bearable for Asian thought?

These are all subtle, endlessly vexing questions, which we find today more difficult to answer than ever. Christian evangelism among
the great Asiatic religions still struggles to make sense of them. Such
questions were posed by Maximus more clearly than they are by many
modern Christians, who dream excitedly of vague syntheses between
European and Asian spirituality. For Maximus saw clearly that the East-
West tension we are dealing with is not simple but threefold, although
its three polarities can never be separated from each other. First of all,
there is the polarity between Eastern and Western styles of thought.
Aristotle has no Eastern counterpart; he represents an irreversible step
forward in human culture, from *mythos* [narrative thought] to *logos* [an-
alytical thought], and the question after him is only what elements of
mythos can be translated into *logos*. Next, there is the polarity between
the impersonal religious thought of the East and the personal categories
of biblical revelation. Here the contrast is between a religion of nature
and a religion of self-communication and of grace, even though traces
of these latter categories can also be discovered in Eastern religions.

And this step, too, is irreversible; from a biblical point of view, at least, there can be no question of equivalency. Finally, there is the East-West polarity in the Church of Christ. Here again, a simple balancing act— on the model of Justinian's policy of treating Rome merely as the "patriarchate of the West"—will not work, since it stands in opposition to Jesus' commission to Peter, which assigned primacy to the Church of Rome. Maximus, then, brings the fullness of Asian religious thought under the triple primacy of the philosophical *logos*, the biblical Christ, and the central authority of Rome.

As far as content goes, there are also three bodies of material to be incorporated into his system. The first is the thought of *Origen*, itself an attempt to sketch out the full biblical message against the golden background of Asia. Here Eastern thought remains so much part of his background that it is almost invisible due to the Christian colors of the picture and shines out strongly only in later Origenism, which plays down the biblical element in Christianity. In Origen's thought, subordinationism is rooted in the metaphysical bias of the system, for which there can be only one supreme God; the creation of the material world is assumed to be a falling of spirits away from their original, collective unity with God, and their restoration (ἀποκατάστασις) must logically imply the final elimination of material being—a conclusion that Origen, as a Christian, never drew.

The second body of material is the thought of *Evagrius*, who added to this Asian background of the picture something Origen had omitted: a consistent ascetical and mystical doctrine. By silencing sensible images and conceptual thought, by eliminating all "form" from the realm of spirit, he seeks to reach the formless inner light of the mind, where the light of God becomes transparent to the act of contemplation.

The third body of material is that of *Alexandrian Christology*: first conceived according to a *logos-sarx* (Word-flesh) pattern, as in the works of Apollinarius, Athanasius, and Cyril, then corrected to speak of "ensouled flesh" (σάρξ ἔμψυχος), yet always riveted on the notion of "one nature" (μία φύσις), until its forward movement comes to a halt— through Dioscorus, Timotheus Aelurus, and Peter Mongus—in the works of Severus and can no longer be shaken by either political cunning or dogmatic compromise. What kind of mysterious fate is it that even today divides Oriental Christianity from the other Churches? One can argue all one likes for the material orthodoxy of the "Monophysites", speak all one will of a "merely verbal Monophysitism"; one can split hairs to prove that the non-Chalcedonians mean by their "one composite nature" (μία φύσις σύνθετος) or "one composite individual" (μία ὑπόστασις σύνθετος) exactly the same, in practical terms, as the bishops meant at Chalcedon;[28] yet the riddle grows only more tantalizing. Was it mere stubbornness? Was Severus really not concerned about something real, some value too precious to abandon? Certainly he was! Behind all the Alexandrian tradition, beyond all the orthodox insistence on preserving the unity of Christ's being, what was at stake—whether admitted or denied, conscious or unconscious—was the Asian dialectic between reality and appearance, divinity and divine self-revelation: [the dominant force was] a kind of thought that used the pure categories of revelation without concerning itself with created reality. For when one begins by presupposing the completeness of Christ's human nature, and so takes seriously the primordial opposition between God and the creature, then one seems—to an Alexandrian christological thinker like Severus—no longer capable of preserving Christ's unity, whether one seeks it in his nature or in his person. Monothelitism was simply the last flowering of this brand of thought: the unity of an active, divine personal center in Christ here ruled out any other existence for his human nature than that of a passive and obedient instrument. So here, too, the full reality of the creature is abandoned for the sake of its union with what is above nature (ἕνωσις) and for the purpose of revealing the divine.

In Maximus' own conclusive struggle with Severus, and with the party of Cyrus, Sergius, and Pyrrhus, he clearly chose the Western tradition. Yet he chose it in such a way that he could bring into Chalcedonian Christology the whole Asian mystique of divinization—on the higher level of the biblical mystery, of the personal synthesis of an incarnate God, rather than on the lower level of natural dissolution and fusion. In taking this path, he essentially also made a decision on the fates of Evagrius and Origen. Origen, as we have already seen, had to undergo a radical disenchantment, by which he would lose enough of his background myth that only what was compatible with the Bible remained: the formal rhythm of the world's emergence and return, from God into God again, and a doctrine of creaturely being that supposes no more than the concrete stages of a nature created, elevated,

---

[28] See Joseph Lebon, "La Christologie du monophysisme syrien", in Grillmeier and Bacht, *Chalkedon*, 1:425–580.

fallen, restored, and deified. Evagrius, of the three, comes off best of all—because his spirituality seemed capable of being transformed from something marginally Christian into something inherently so, with the least amount of friction and noise. One needed only to add to his seemingly Gnostic "passionlessness" (ἀπάθεια) the charity (ἀγάπη) of the Sermon on the Mount and to remove the pantheistic flavor from his conception of "knowledge of the Trinity" by combining it with the Cappadocian and Areopagite ideas of God. Nothing more was necessary.

In this work of translation, *Pseudo-Dionysius* was, like Aristotle, of inestimable value. If Aristotle provided the notion of "first substance" (πρώτη οὐσία)—the irreducible, ultimate substance of a thing, with its inner field of meaning and power defined in terms of potency (δύναμις) and act (ἐνέργεια)—Dionysius pointed to the indissoluble autonomy of the finite world, as a whole and in its individual members, in relation to the infinite reality of God. Nothing could be more Western, nothing points more clearly back, beyond Proclus and Plotinus, to decisively Greek, anti-Asiatic sources. Pseudo-Dionysius remains, with Chalcedon and Augustine, the foundation stone of the Western spirit, which can only breathe in an atmosphere of space and freedom. The salvation, the preservation, the confirmation of finitude by God himself: these are the Areopagite's basic intellectual models. On the other hand, it makes little difference that he thought and wrote, quite possibly, in an atmosphere that was externally Monophysite, that there is an echo of Monophysitism in one or two of his formulations—even though they can be interpreted in an orthodox sense; as a thinker, Pseudo-Dionysius is unconditionally and unexceptionably a Chalcedonian.[29] The terms "unconfused" (ἀσύγχυτος: fourteen times)

---

[29] [Debate on the theological and philosophical "location" of Pseudo-Dionysius and his writings continues, echoing both von Balthasar's judgment here and that of his opponents. The most significant recent studies on Pseudo-Dionysius as a Christian thinker include: Michele Schiavone, *Neoplatonismo e cristianesimo nello Pseudo-Dionigi* (Milan, 1963); Bernhard Brons, *Gott und die Seienden: Untersuchungen zum Verhältnis von neuplatonischer Metaphysik und christlicher Tradition bei Dionysius Areopagita* (Göttingen, 1976); Kurt Ruh, *Die mystische Gotteslehre des Dionysius Areopagita* (Munich, 1987); Andrew Louth, *Denys, the Areopagite* (Wilton, Conn., 1989); Paul Rorem, *Pseudo-Dionysius: A Commentary on the Texts and an Introduction to Their Influence* (New York, 1993); Alexander Golitzin, *Et Introibo ad Altare Dei: The Mystagogy of Dionysius Areopagita* (Thessalonike, 1994); Ysabel de Andia, ed., *Denys l'Areopagite et sa posterité en orient et en occident: Actes du colloque international, Paris, 21–24 septembre, 1994* (Paris, 1997).]

and "inseparable" (ἀδιαίρετος) are not incidental in his vocabulary but
are consciously emphasized,[30] just as are "unmixed condition" (ἀσυμ-
μιξία), "unblended" (ἀσύμφυρτος), "distinction" (διαφορά), "particularity" (ἰδιότης: twenty-seven times), "preserve" (σώζειν: ten times),
to say nothing of his words for order and rank. One can, of course,
make the point that Chalcedonian terminology also made its way into
the accepted and official language of the Monophysites, who had no
qualms about accepting the word "unconfused" (ἀσυγχύτως).[31] But this
is either due to unawareness (just as many Lutheran liturgies remain
close to the Roman Mass) or is an external adoption of words, without
any thoughtful realization of their content. The case is very different
with Pseudo-Dionysius: he is a crystal-clear thinker,[32] and he adopts
Chalcedonian-Aristotelian elements into his metaphysical scheme.

b. Scholasticism and Mysticism

Pseudo-Dionysius, then, was already available as a point of contact.
Aristotle was also there, to an increasing degree, his thought typically
mingled with elements of Stoicism and Neoplatonism in a way that
was not unfruitful and that corresponded to the taste of the time. Even
so, these philosophical building blocks had not yet been formed into
a synthesis; they were used as individual elements for scholastic instruction and for christological polemics, and for that very reason they
were largely not understood, nor did they communicate the slightest degree of spiritual power. The division between scholasticism and

---

[30] See A. van den Daele, *Indices Pseudo-Dionysiani* (Louvain, 1941), 9, 34. Cf. René Roques,
L'Univers dionysien (Paris, 1954), 58: "Unity without confusion is the rule for divine action
on the hierarchical intelligences."

[31] See Hieronymus Engberding, "Monophysitische Liturgien", in Grillmeier and Bacht,
Chalkedon 2:697f., quoting the liturgy of St. Gregory (l. 715): "Without transformation or
change, you united human nature with yourself in your hypostasis, in an ineffable and inconceivable way, without alteration or confusion." And later: "In the one Son and the one
Christ, both natures are preserved completely, along with their particular properties. There
is *one* nature, one person, one individual, one will . . ." (l. 730). The author concludes that
no diminution of the human nature of Christ is clearly perceptible in any of these liturgies.

[32] He is the direct opposite of the enthusiastic illuminate that Ernst Honigmann wants to
make him, in order to identify him with Peter the Iberian: see *Pierre l'Ibérien et les écrits du
Ps-Denys* (Brussels: Académie Royale de Belgique, 1952). In addition, the clear Chalcedonian
accent cannot find any explanation in Honigmann's thesis. Even less can Dionysius, the great
aesthete of late antique Christian thought, for whom everything is alive with beauty, be identified with the strict, austere Severus of Antioch, as Stiglmayr suggested. Such hypotheses
are ruled out by a simple, phenomenological examination of the facts.

mysticism, between the theology of the schoolroom and the spirituality of the monastery, was, in the sixth century, complete. The former, held hostage by politics, kept inventing new distinctions that lacked any genuine basis in the experience of being; the latter had withdrawn from the dogmatic and political theater into a world beyond time. The situation, in this respect, was not unlike the late Middle Ages: dangerous conditions for the sudden deterioration of Church unity.

Maximus must have had an eye on the need for unity between these currents of religious thought from the very beginning. The Areopagite, in his abstract precision and in his flights of enthusiasm, offered the first promising means of approach. A framework for an understanding of the universe had been erected here, which could hold its ground and needed no further modification. But Pseudo-Dionysius did not deal with christological issues eagerly, and when he did—as in the letters—it was only from the loftiest peak of reflection; he never descended into the thick of the theological battle. The task, then, was to carry the spirit of the Areopagite into the heart of [scholastic theology's] academic distinctions; to put it another way, it was to strike mystical and spiritual sparks out of the rough scholastic flint. That could only work to the degree that one tried to grasp Aristotle from within, so that one might gain an insight into the mystery of the God-man with the help of his view of reality.

Maximus must have had a good philosophical training, but we know nothing about it.[33] It must have given him the ability to read the characteristic works of sixth-century scholastic Christology with critical perception. To name the most important authors of that school, we should mention John the Grammarian,[34] Severus' opponent, and John of Scythopolis,[35] both of whom began to develop the Neo-Chalcedonian approach [to Christology] before 520; Leontius of Byzantium, who

---

[33] For a bibliography on Byzantine academic philosophy in the sixth century, see Moeller, "Chalcédonisme", 1:640, especially V. Valdenberg, "La Philosophie byzantine au IVe siècle", *Byzantion* 4 (1927): 237–68; F. Überweg, *Grundriß der Geschichte der Philosophie*, ed. B. Geyer, vol. 2 (Berlin, 1898), 123–26. The *Acta* make much of the philosophical interests of the young Maximus (PG 90, 69f.) but give us no details. [For further information on academic philosophy and theology in the sixth century, see B. E. Daley, "Boethius' Theological Tracts and Early Byzantine Scholasticism", *Mediaeval Studies* 46 (1984): 158–91.]

[34] [Ed. Marcel Richard, CCG 1 (1977). For an analysis of John's theology, see Alois Grillmeier, *Jesus der Christus im Glauben der Kirche*, vol. 2, pt. 2 (Freiburg, 1989), 54–82; English trans. *Christ in Christian Tradition*, vol. 2, pt. 2 (London, 1995), 52–79.]

[35] [See appendix below for an extensive discussion of John of Scythopolis' work and further bibliography.]

flourished about 540;[36] Leontius of Jerusalem, writing before 552;[37] Theodore of Raïthu, whose *Proparaskeuē*[38] appeared around the middle of the century; that mature work known as the *De sectis*,[39] which appeared after 580; from about 600, the so-called *Panoplia* of Pamphilus;[40] and finally, dating from about 650, the anthology called the *Doctrina Patrum*,[41] which may be by Anastasius of Sinai and which includes excerpts from Maximus. The polemical dogmatic *opuscula* of the Confessor belong in this series of writings, too, although they move in a completely different direction—making distinctions only to let the mystery as a whole shine out more brightly, laboring constantly forward in the service of a spirituality. If the spiritual and mystical suggestiveness, the intellectual fruit, of a distinction is not immediately perceptible, in Maximus' work it soon becomes so.

This would not be possible if his philosophical analysis were not grounded in meditation on *Holy Scripture*. Maximus has been called unscriptural, but Scripture is the background and the presupposition for all that he does, to a wholly different degree than in the one-sided scholastic theology or spiritual works of the sixth century. The Confessor's first major work is his set of answers to the questions of his friend Thalassius on passages in the Holy Scriptures.[42] Maximus offers these answers from the fullness both of the exegetical and spiritual tradition and of his own personal meditation. It should not be surprising that he is not an exegete in the style of the fifth-century Antiochenes; in any case, he knows his way around in the Alexandrian and Cappadocian style of spiritual exposition. Besides the *Quaestiones ad Thalassium*, Maximus wrote other exegetical works: a commentary on the Song of Songs and another on Ecclesiastes, both of which were apparently combined with commentaries by Gregory of Nyssa and Nilus of Ancyra into a *Catena of the Three Fathers*, which later was edited and

---

[36] [PG 86, 1268–1396, 1901–76. For a thorough discussion of Leontius' Christology, see Grillmeier, *Jesus der Christus* vol. 2, pt. 2, 194–241; *Christ* vol. 2, pt. 2, 181–229.]

[37] [PG 86, 1400–1901; see Grillmeier, *Jesus der Christus* vol. 2, pt. 2, 291–333; *Christ* vol. 2, pt. 2, 271–316.]

[38] Ed. Franz Diekamp, *Analecta Patristica*, Orientalia christiana analecta, 117 (Rome, 1938).

[39] [PG 86, 1193–1268; see Grillmeier, *Jesus der Christus* vol. 2, pt. 2, 514–23; *Christ* vol. 2, pt. 2, 493–502.]

[40] [Ed. J. H. Declerck, CCG 19 (1989).]

[41] Ed. F. Diekamp (Münster, 1907).

[42] [Ed. C. Laga and C. Steel, CCG 7 (1980); CCG 22 (1990); PG 90, 244–785.]

enlarged by Michael Psellos and others.[43] We also possess a fragment of a commentary on the Apocalypse attributed to Maximus.[44] That he knew not only how to soar in the heights of allegory but also—like Origen—how to descend into the glens of historical detail is proved by his *Computus ecclesiasticus*,[45] from which a "succinct chronology of the life of Christ" was later drawn.[46] Other exegetical works of Maximus are the *Exposition of the Lord's Prayer*, the *Exposition of Psalm 59*, the *Quaestiones et Dubia* (answering other questions, mainly on passages in Scripture),[47] and the short work addressed *To Theopemptus*.[48]

A passage from the report of his trial illustrates well Maximus' attitude to the Scriptures. Bishop Theodosius [the imperial representative] suggests to him, on the subject of the two wills in Christ, that it would be better to stick to the "simple words" of Scripture (ἁπλᾶς φωνὰς δέξασθαι), without entering into elaborate speculations. Maximus answers:

> In saying this, you are introducing new rules for exegesis, foreign to the Church's tradition. If one may not delve into the sayings of Scripture and the Fathers with a speculative mind, the whole Bible falls apart, Old and New Testament alike. We hear, for instance, what David says: "Blessed are they who study his testimonies, who seek him with their whole heart" (Ps 119:2); this means that no one can seek and find God without penetrating study. Again he says, "Give me understanding, that I may study your law, and then may keep it with my whole heart" (Ps 119:34); for speculative study leads to a knowledge of the law, and knowledge arouses love and longing and brings it about that those who are worthy can keep the law in their hearts by observing its holy commands. Again he says, "Wonderful are your testimonies; therefore my soul studies them" (Ps 119:129). Do not the Proverbs demand that we mull over their parables and riddles and dark sayings? Does not the Lord, who speaks in parables, insist that the disciples should understand them,

---

[43] See Michael Faulhaber, *Hohelied-, Proverbien- und Prediger-Catenen* (Vienna, 1902); H. G. Beck, *Kirche und theologische Literatur im Byzantinischen Reiche*, Byzantinisches Handbuch vol. 2, pt. 1 (Munich: C. H. Beck, 1959): 471, 539f., 653. The final version, from the twelfth century, appears in PG 122, 537–686; parts of it are in PG 87, 1755–80.

[44] *Catalogus codicum astrologorum*, 7:100f. (3); cf. Franz Messerschmidt, "Himmelsbuch und Sternenschrift", *Römische Quartalschrift* 39 (1931): 68–69.

[45] PG 19, 1217–80.

[46] Ed. E. Bratke (Bonn, 1892).

[47] Ed. J. H. Declerck, CCG 10 (1982); PG 90, 785–856.

[48] PG 90, 1393–1400.

by explaining their meaning himself? Does he not himself command, "Search in the Scriptures!" (Jn 5:39)? And what does Peter, the chief of apostles, mean when he teaches us that "The prophets have searched and reflected about salvation" (1 Pet 1:10)? What does the divine Apostle Paul mean, when he says, "If the gospel is veiled, it is veiled to those who are being destroyed, whose spiritual eyes the God of this world has blinded, so that the light of the knowledge of Christ might not enter them" (2 Cor 4:3)? It seems you want us to become like the Jews, who have filled their minds with the "simple words" of the Bible—in other words, with the letter of Scripture alone—as if it were so much rubbish, and so have fallen away from the truth; they carry a covering over their hearts, so as not to see that "the Lord is Spirit" (2 Cor 3:17), hidden within the letter, and that he says, "The letter kills, it is the Spirit that gives life!" (2 Cor 3:6). You may be sure, reverend sir, that I will never accept some concept from Scripture if I have not really understood its meaning. I will not openly behave like a Jew.[49]

This passage says more than enough. It entitles us to assume that the theological act of meditating on Scripture, which for Maximus had again become one with the act of spiritual or mystical contemplation, served as the vehicle and medium of all his thought. Hans-Georg Beck has rightly observed that dogmatic theology and the spiritual ascent to God, according to Maximus, offer each other "no opposition. And what is correct in his view, dogmatically and spiritually, is nothing else than the fruit of a deepened understanding of the Bible."[50] If we still possessed his commentaries on the Song of Songs and Ecclesiastes—the same books Gregory of Nyssa had chosen to interpret—we would doubtless find there a confirmation of how much the ultimate encounter of God and the creature in Christ—that meeting point of our knowledge of God in himself (θεολογία) and our experience of God in history (οἰκονομία)—was for Maximus, not a problem of knowledge, of gnosis, so much as one of Christian love and longing, of eros; for that reason, mystical instruction, at its best, provides a wonderful theological witness. In the genuine tradition of Origen (and going beyond Pseudo-Dionysius in this respect), Maximus speaks of the "holy tent of love", hidden in the depths of God, where the "awe-inspiring mystery of union is celebrated beyond the limits of mind and word, a mystery in which God becomes one flesh and one spirit with

---

[49] Acta; PG 90, 149A–D.
[50] Handbuch, 437.

the Church, which represents the soul—and the Church with him. O Christ, I stand amazed by your goodness."[51] In the same sense, he interprets the meeting of lips in the liturgical kiss as pointing to the "growth together" in love of the Logos, who is the mouth of God, and the soul that responds to his word.[52]

Maximus' whole philosophical undertaking [with regard to Christology and soteriology], which we have described, stands in service of this highest synthesis, which is purely biblical; its function is to prevent the creature, understood in its essential identity, from being overwhelmed and dazzled in this loving encounter with God, openly or implicitly, to such a degree that it is reduced merely to the level of an "appearance". By preserving the metaphysical rights of humanity —in the human nature of Christ and in the ordinary human person— Maximus provides the support for man's right to grace, as well. That is the reason for his sharp rejection of the temptations of Monophysitism and Monothelitism, for his critique of the background assumptions of Origenism, for the acceptance of and new emphasis on created reality as defended by Pseudo-Dionysius. Only such a metaphysic lays a foundation deep enough to bear an all-inclusive synthesis and strong enough to let different elements of Eastern spirituality be added to the structure without endangering either its cohesion or its meaning. These additional elements had, in the process, to be "retrained"—to be elevated to the higher level of a free encounter, in grace, with the God of the Bible. In the seventh century, at least, this would no longer have been possible without the powerful intermediary role of philosophy, as well as of a theology that worked with clear concepts. Syntheses between East and West based simply on a similarity of "spiritualities" or "mystical experiences" could not be achieved even then—how much less so today! So we must judge any program as inadequate that tries simply to let India and Europe encounter each other at the halfway station of Byzantine hesychasm, in the practice of the Jesus prayer and of certain bodily positions and breathing exercises—all ways in which Eastern Christianity reorientalized itself after the period of the great synthesis. Less adequate still are all attempts to introduce Indian and East Asian practices into the life of the Christian Church without any philosophical or theological justification. In the face of such naïveté

---

[51] *Mystagogia*, chap. 5; PG 91, 681A; cf. chap. 15; PG 91, 693C.
[52] Ibid., chap. 17; PG 91, 693D–696A.

—which never leads to the gaining of what is foreign but only to the loss of what is one's own—Maximus' example must serve as our inspiration: the ultimate and highest degree of reconciliation occurs only within the active range of clear, discerning, and decisive intelligence. The power of thought is the force that transforms the world.

3. The Synthesis

a. Contents and Levels

"At that moment, in which the peoples of East and West still had a history in common and were engaged in a common struggle, it was enormously significant that there was a man who could belong to and support all parties even-handedly, who could, to some degree, bring their concerns to a single head and combine the different families and methods of thought, not just superficially, but—so far as it was possible—with real depth."[53] This statement of Hans von Schubert about Maximus Confessor identifies his intellectual position and accomplishment exactly: to gather together what was divided or coming apart in the relations of East and West, and to do this "not superficially" but organically, "with real depth". Let us not spoil the sport of those who think they can find the different "sources" of every great intellectual achievement, in the assumption that what once existed separately can never be brought together organically to have a life of its own; but if they really can see no more in Maximus than a conglomerate put together from Evagrius, Gregory [Nazianzen] and Pseudo-Dionysius, in proportions that vary from work to work, why should they concede that such irreconcilable elements as Platonism and Aristotelianism could ever enter into a genuine synthesis, either—as, for example, in the work of Thomas Aquinas? Why not also cut up the work of Kant into the incompatible "sources" of rationalism and empiricism? Why not write off the synthesis of Thomas and Kant in the work of someone like Maréchal a priori, as simply a *mélange*?

This way of thinking about the figures of intellectual history is either blind to creative systematization or else assumes, without need or warrant, that two Christian ways of conceiving the universe can stand

---

[53] Hans von Schubert, *Geschichte der christlichen Kirche im Frühmittelalter* (Tübingen, 1921), 241.

in a such contradictory relationship to each other that no power of
the intelligence will ever be able to remove the contradiction by creating a higher, third possibility.[54] How ridiculous those grumblers are,
who typecast a Christian thinker with some particular label—for example, Christocentrism—and then stamp as tasteless excess whatever
they cannot arrange, in an obvious concentric way, around not simply
that theme but the very term itself. The freedom of the mind proves
itself not least in one's unshakeable ability to change perspective, to see
things at one time from behind, at another from below or from above.
It also consists in the possibility of changing one's mode of expression,
of saying the same thing in different ways, and in the ability to take the
depths of conceptual perspective into consideration so that one does
not always speak on the same level. These are not simply frivolous shell
games, meant to throw an honest citizen off his course; they are signs
of the presence of the Spirit, which blows where it will and which lets
everyone who is truly born of the Spirit blow with it (so John 3:8:
οὕτως, "in the same way"). Thinkers of the class of Maximus Confessor are not simply trivial compilers or passive reservoirs; they are
creators, who can work, surely, with traditional material but who also
know how to arrange the pieces according to their own architectural
design.

What makes Maximus a genius is that he was able to reach inside,
and open up to each other, five or six intellectual worlds that seemingly
had lost all contact; he was able to bring out of each a light that illu-
mined all the rest, leading to new connections that gave rise, in turn, to
unexpected similarities and relationships. He was a contemplative biblical theologian, a philosopher of Aristotelian training, a mystic in the
great Neoplatonic tradition of Gregory of Nyssa and Pseudo-Dionysius
the Areopagite, an enthusiastic theologian of the Word along the lines
of Origen, a strict monk of the Evagrian tradition, and—finally and
before all else—a man of the Church, who fought and who gave his
life in witness for the orthodox Christology of Chalcedon and for a
Church centered in Rome.

---

[54] Without such unconscious presuppositions, the judgment of Fr. Viller in *Revue d'ascétique
et de mystique* 11 (1930), 259—and partly also that of Fr. Hausherr, "Ignorance infinie", *Orientalia christiana periodica* 2 (1936): 351–62—would never have been possible. For another
very negative estimate of the systematic power of Maximus, see the series of articles by
M. Lot-Borodine, *Revue de l'histoire des religions* 105–7 (1932/33), esp. 536 [reprinted as *La
Déification de l'homme selon la doctrine des Pères grecs* (Paris, 1970)].

1. It would be a mistake to choose one of these intellectual worlds as the *real* one and to judge the rest by its standard. At best one can say this: inasmuch as *Pseudo-Dionysius* was historically the last and most comprehensive theological and spiritual phenomenon before Maximus, and insofar as he includes essential elements of his predecessors (Origen, Gregory of Nyssa, and Evagrius) in his own thought, in a way that both corrects and surpasses them, his insight can be accorded a certain preeminence in Maximus' intellectual ancestry. His ecstatic vision of a holy universe, flowing forth, wave upon wave, from the unfathomable depths of God, whose center lies always beyond the creature's reach; his vision of a creation that realizes itself in ever more distant echoes, until it finally ebbs away at the borders of nothingness, yet which is held together, unified, and "brought home", step by step, through the ascending unities of an awestruck love; his vision of a world dancing in the festal celebration of liturgical adoration, a single organism made up of inviolable ranks of heavenly spirits and ecclesial offices, all circling round the brilliant darkness of the central mystery —aware of the unspeakable nearness of their Source in all its radiant generosity, yet equally aware of the ever-greater distance of the "superessential", "super-inconceivable" One: this vision of reality, with something both intoxicating and religiously sober in its sacred, liturgical rhythm, could be found in such purity neither in Alexandria nor in Cappadocia, let alone in the austere deserts of Egypt or the earthy classrooms of Antioch! Yet what could be better suited for a thinker of late antiquity, struggling for an inclusive grasp of the whole, to use as the frame and the golden background for his picture of the universe? There is a panoramic sense of creation here: produced, surely, from the erupting volcano of Origen's thought, embodying Gregory of Nyssa's Faust-like drive toward infinity, Gregory Nazianzen's autumnal reserve, Basil's thorough-going balance,[55] Proclus' cosmic sense, and showing clear affinity for late Byzantium's love of liturgical display in the grand style. It is a bolt of lightning that discloses, in a single flash, the overwhelming contemporaneity of all realms of being, down to the very elements of matter themselves—of their layers and interconnections,

---

[55] One cannot deny a genuine intellectual relationship between Basil and Pseudo-Dionysius, despite all the substantial differences between them. In this one respect C. Pera is right in identifying the Areopagite with a monk of the Basilian tradition: *Revue des sciences philosophiques et théologiques* 25 (1936): 5–75. Cf. Endre von Ivánka, "Der Aufbau der Schrift 'De Divinis Nominibus' des Ps.-Dionysius", *Scholastik* 15 (1940): 386–99.

their approaches to, and descents from, the invisible peak of all things
—revealing a picture of stability and majestic peace such as has never
been glimpsed before in Christendom. Gregory of Nyssa's dynamic
insight—inspired by the Stoics—into the evolution of all things, step
by step, from the primeval potency, is turned here into a picture of
a reality that radiates outward, flows downward from above. It is not
a cosmos frozen into some kind of Byzantine icon so much as a life
that generatively streams and pulsates, like C. F. Meyer's image of the
fountain:

> The jet ascends, and falling, fills
> The marble basin's rounded palm,
> Then slips away in modest rills,
> Ruffling a second basin's calm;
> The second, likewise, must bestow
> Her riches on a lower breast:
> So each receives, to overflow
> And come to rest.[56]

Or in the image of John of Scythopolis, Pseudo-Dionysius' first commentator:

> Through the higher orders, which stand nearer God, the lower orders
> participate in the divine gifts of grace, like the overflowing basins of a
> fountain: the basins closest to the source fill first with what is poured
> into them, then they overflow and pour out their contents into the lower
> basins, in proportion to the number of vessels and to their size, whether
> small or large.[57]

From the lofty heights of this vision, the dissonances in the world
melt away into harmony for Maximus, too. "Whatever exists, has being according to a perfect law and cannot receive a better being."[58] If

---

[56] [Conrad Ferdinand Meyer (1825–1898), "Der römische Brunnen" (H. Zeller and A.
Zäch, eds. *Conrad Ferdinand Meyer: Sämtliche Werke* vol. 1 [Bern, 1963], 170). The original
text of the poem is as follows:

Aufsteigt der Strahl und fallend gießt
Er voll der Marmorschale Rund,
Die, sich verschleiernd, überfließt
In einer zweiten Schale Grund;
Die zweite gibt, sie wird zu reich,
Der dritten wallend ihre Flut,
Und jede nimmt und gibt zugleich
Und strömt und ruht.]

[57] *In De Divinis nominibus*; PG 4, 405B.

[58] *Ambigua*; PG 91, 1189B.

one wishes to conceive and describe this harmony, one's knowledge must possess, in the highest degree, that joyous calm that expresses the peace of this contemplative intuition.

> The first concern must, then, not be to speak as others speak, but to conceive of the word of truth with understanding and exactitude. . . . It is not a matter of refuting the opinions of others, but of presenting one's own; not a matter of contesting some aspect of the teaching or behavior of others that seems not to be good, but of writing on behalf of truth.[59]

If one has glimpsed the enormous cosmic game for even a moment, one knows that the tiny life of an individual person, with all its serious concerns, is only a receding figure in the dance.

> We ourselves, controlled by the imperious program of our present nature, are conceived and born like the other beasts of the earth, then become children, and finally are led from youth to the wrinkles of age, like a flower that only lives for a moment, dies, and gives rise to new life; truly, we deserve to be called God's playthings.[60]

The Areopagite's sense of the world—of existence as liturgical event, as adoration, as celebratory service, as hidden but holy dance—this is the golden background of Maximus' mental picture of creation.

2. But if Maximus is "a mystic like Dionysius", he is surely "a mystic who is also a *metaphysician*, an ascetic who has reached, through his familiarity with Aristotelian philosophy, a consistency and precision of thought that one looks for in vain in the works of the Areopagite."[61] This statement of a French patristic scholar grasps the real difference between the master and his interpreter and marks the second level in Maximus' thought. What comes explicitly from Proclus and Plotinus in the work of Pseudo-Dionysius, what gives him his Neoplatonic coloring, Maximus has abandoned. He has noticed the questionable points of the system; with unquestionable discretion, he transforms the Dionysian system of emanations into the framework of an ecclesial metaphysic. His philosophical education, his study of post-Chalcedonian Christology, not only developed his taste for a con-

---

[59] *In Epistulam Dionysii* 6; PG 4, 536C.

[60] *Ambigua*; PG 91, 1416C.

[61] J. Tixeront, *Précis de patrologie* (Paris, 1934), 395.

ceptual exactness approaching the style of geometric theorems[62]—a compression that, since Photius,[63] has often been unjustly taken for obscurity and verbosity,[64] whereas it is in fact the result of an almost exaggerated precision. It also gave him the means for overcoming the "emanationism" of Pseudo-Dionysius: the Aristotelian and Stoic conception of the concrete universal (καθόλου), which is, ultimately, also proper to Neoplatonism. In place of a merely temporary world, made for dissolution, such as is suggested in Origen and even—gently—in Pseudo-Dionysius by the Neoplatonic rhythm of the divine being's radiation and return, diastole and systole, Maximus envisages a naturally lasting cosmos as the supporting ground for all supernatural divinization. His sense of the dignity of natural being gives Maximus the key to the decisive objection that can be made against Origenism.

> If we allow souls to exist before their bodies, and see the reason for their union with bodies as a punishment for some guilt incurred as bodiless beings before their birth, then we run the greatest danger of seeing this unique miracle, the sensible world, where God lets himself be known by wordless proclamation, as simply the result of sin.[65]

Maximus can be considered the most world-affirming thinker of all the Greek Fathers; in his basically positive attitude toward nature he goes even beyond Gregory of Nyssa. While Origen considers Scripture as alone supremely normative, Maximus accepts also the natural world, contemplated in the light of revelation, as a source of wisdom. Perfect knowledge—the knowledge of the believing Christian and even the knowledge of the mystic—is gleaned from both "books" together. The "contemplation of nature" (θεωρία φυσική) and of the structures of meaning (λόγοι) hidden within it, structures that are part of every single being, becomes for Maximus a necessary step, a kind of initiation, into the knowledge of God. This contemplation does not even stop at the stars: they, too, are astrological signs of decisive events. "The stars in the heavens are like the letters in a book. Through both, people find access to knowledge of things as they are. Through letters, they

---

[62] "In the rigor of his literary form he is already a scholastic": J. Tixeront, *Histoire des dogmes*, 7th ed., vol. 3 (Paris, 1927), 188.
[63] *Bibliotheca*, cod. 191; PG 103, 645BC.
[64] E.g., Garbas, in the introduction to his translation of the *Liber asceticus* (Breslau, 1925), 6.
[65] *Ambigua*; PG 91, 1328A.

remember words and meanings; through the stars, they come to know the 'signs of the times' in an equally legible script."[66] The wise person stands in the midst of the world's realities as in an inexhaustible treasury of knowledge. No being leaves him untouched; everything provides food for his intellectual nourishment.

3. But Maximus is no worldly philosopher. From the court of the Emperor Heraclius, where he held a prestigious office, he fled across the Bosporus into a monastery. By profession, he was a *monk* and an *ascetic*. He does not contemplate the world for contemplation's sake, but because it serves as a ladder, a hoist to higher intellectual insight. He is uncompromisingly determined to reclaim the original meaning of monasticism as the "philosophic life" (φιλοσοφεῖν), and monasticism is always, in the life of the Church, a "return to the sources".[67] In searching for these sources, he could not avoid coming into contact with Origen and his most dedicated disciple, Evagrius Ponticus.[68] Viller has demonstrated the strong influence of this philosophical monk on Maximus' spiritual doctrine.[69] The practical side of his ascetical teaching, like its theoretical and mystical side, largely depends on the intellectual models and principles of the Egyptian desert hermits. From that source comes his concern for the "realization" of theoretical knowledge, for the preservation of what one has learned in living virtues, for the transformation of a merely contemplative embrace of all things into a living, concrete love.

Yes, Maximus' insistence on the ultimate interpenetration of contemplation and action begins with Evagrius; but it goes beyond him. From Evagrius, too, comes his relentlessly sober austerity, his freedom from illusion concerning the ability of the sensible world to seduce us through the eight principal vices; in his ability to describe and unmask these with psychological depth, Maximus is fully the equal of his master. If his first Dionysian trademark is an ability to play weightlessly

---

[66] Quoted by Messerschmidt, "Himmelsbuch and Sternenschrift", 68.

[67] Heinrich Bacht, S.J., "La Loi du 'retour aux sources': Quelques aspects de l'idéal monastique pachômien", *Revue Mabillon* 51 (1961): 6–25.

[68] On Evagrius' monasticism, see H. U. von Balthasar, "Die Metaphysik und Mystik des Evagrius Ponticus", *Zeitschrift für Aszese und Mystik* 14 (1939): 31–47; Karl Heussi, *Der Ursprung des Mönchtums* (Tübingen, 1936).

[69] See above, n. 8. The parallels Viller points to can be multiplied now that *De oratione* has been identified as a work of Evagrius by I. Hausherr, "Le Traité de l'oraison d'Évague le Pontique (Pseudo-Nil)", *Revue d'ascétique et de mystique* 15 (1934): 34–93, 113–70.

before God, and his second an Aristotelian ability to contemplate the world, the third trademark of Maximus must be identified as a calm freedom from all the passions that cloud or weigh down or tear apart the mind, in order to rob it of its freedom and self-possession. This calm is also his mode of entry into the mystery of God, which stands beyond the world. Only the spirit that has become pure and simple can encounter the transcendent One; the soul that has fully emptied itself, that "has no song to sing", becomes the place of revelation, the abode of the infinite God. Right through the middle, then, of the Dionysian, Aristotelian picture of a self-contained, hierarchically ordered universe cuts—straight as an arrow—the Alexandrian way of ascending from the sensible to the intellectual and ultimately to the divine world; it brings to Maximus' conception of reality the axis that holds it together and that makes its movement possible.

4. To give Maximus' three-dimensional conception of the world an unmistakable originality and unity, a fourth ingredient was needed: his polemic against the great heresies of the time, Monophysitism and Monothelitism. This polemic dominated the second half of his life and work and brought about his death as confessor of the faith. It shaped his theological attitudes to their very depths: he did not die simply for a formula, after all, but for the heart of the world. The key word of the *Chalcedonian* formula is the seed from which his understanding of reality could and did develop: ἀσυγχύτως, "without confusion".

Only here was the latent pantheism of the ancient Alexandrian Christology—an element foreign to the spirit of both the Bible and classical Greece—finally expelled. The newness of the Christian message of salvation looked for expression first in ecstatic categories, suggesting a "mixture" between divinity and humanity: a union like that of two fluids blending with each other, or better—to use the image of Gregory of Nyssa—like a drop of vinegar being dissolved in the sea. Only when such language began to be exploited by heresy did the Church come to realize—as Theodore of Mopsuestia was first to realize—that κρᾶσις, mixture, was far from the most perfect and intimate kind of union. From the moment that Chalcedon, in its sober and holy wisdom, elevated the adverbs "indivisibly" (ἀδιαιρέτως) and "unconfusedly" (ἀσυγχύτως) to a dogmatic formula, the image of a reciprocal indwelling of two distinct poles of being replaced the image of mixture. This mutual ontological presence (περιχώρησις) not only preserves the being particular to each element, to the divine and the human natures, but also brings each of them to its perfection in their very difference, even enhancing that difference. Love, which is the highest level of union, only takes root in the growing independence of the lovers; the union between God and the world reveals, in the very nearness it creates between these two poles of being, the ever-greater difference between created being and the essentially incomparable God.

Maximus defended the formula of Chalcedon, even with his blood, out of a deep insight into this difference. He knew that Christ, whom he was defending, was incomparably more unified and unifying than the Christ of the Monophysites, with his single nature. The unity of his *hypostasis*, his concrete and individual "Person", possesses its two natures both ontologically and in full spiritual freedom; by that very fact, it is far more sublime than any natural union one might imagine. This theological insight had a fruitful effect on the whole history of metaphysics. Alongside the "Porphyrian tree", which tried to arrange and elucidate all existent being in the categories of "essence" (οὐσία), as genus, species, specific difference, and individual (ἄτομον εἶδος), new possibilities now began to open up for ontological reflection. These new "categories", which could not be reduced to the dimensions of essential characteristics, point at once in the direction of the "existential" and the "personal". Both of these are implied in the new terms that came to be used: ὕπαρξις (existence) and ὑπόστασις (concrete, individual being). These are words from everyday speech, less than perfectly clear around the edges, which now groped to find a home and an exact meaning in the field of abstract thought. Maximus, who saw the words "being" (εἶναι) and "essence" (οὐσία), on the one hand, and "personal being" (ὑπόστασις) and "existence" (ὕπαρξις), on the other, as closely related, was surely far from proposing the neoscholastic "real distinction" [between essence and existence]. Still, with the appearance of a new emphasis on existence and person, alongside the classical Greek concern with essence (οὐσία), an important step had been taken in the direction of an ontology of created being. One thing is certain: that when Maximus makes ontological distinctions, he sheds a much more phenomenological light on the beings he discusses than do many of the empty distinctions of the sixth century. It requires, surely, a delicate ear for the overtones and variations of new or changing terminology to establish the exact point this philosophical development has reached in the work of Maximus. But perhaps his stage of development is more fruitful, philosophically, than the clean complacency of finished neoscholastic distinctions, which run the danger of hacking off the living sprouts of being and of destroying the mystery of a polarity that can never be seen in anything like a single, final vision.

It is enough for our purposes here simply to indicate the connection between being and person that is expressed in the word *hypostasis*. In the work of the Cappadocians, even to some degree in Plotinus, something akin to existential and personal thinking had begun to take shape.[70] But the existential element there appeared as something purely negative: amid the collapse of every concept of essence and of the order of ideas as a whole, the complete otherness of being shone through clearly. With Maximus, the outlines of a positive view of existence begin to appear. Certainly, it would have fallen apart had it not had the Cappadocians' corrective by its side—an emphasis Maximus found, in its strongest form, in the works of the Areopagite. Only to the degree that we pay attention to the reciprocity of both spheres, the mystical-negative and the conceptual-positive, do we approach the living central point of Maximus' thought. The direction in which this point must lie has already been indicated. The notion of existing "without confusion" (ἀσυγχύτως) will allow the Greek genius for clarity, precisely in this kind of reflection, to achieve a final triumph, while the notion of "individual being" (ὑπόστασις), as the contribution of Christian theology, will become, in its intellectually highest form, the necessary condition of that triumph. In the sphere of a Christian philosophy of person and existence, the clarity of the Greek grasp of the world of being was to find its final fulfillment.

b. Christ and the Synthesis

Only in this context does the remarkable, even unique historical role of this thinker become apparent. The time had come to set forth antiquity's conception of the universe in a final, conclusive synthesis. The time had come, too, to bring the doctrinal disputes about the being of the incarnate God, disputes that had torn the Church apart for centuries, to a final resolution. And why should not that decisive

---

[70] See Hans Urs von Balthasar, *Présence et pensée* (Paris, 1941), and the introduction to my translation of Gregory of Nyssa's commentary on the Song of Songs, *Der versiegelte Quell*, 2d ed. (Einsiedeln, 1954). I intend to deal later with the criticism of Walther Völker, in *Gregor von Nyssa als Mystiker* (Wiesbaden, 1955), 41 and n. 5.

christological formulation, seen in its deepest implications, also serve as the right model for the world? That, at least, is how Maximus understood it. No one could have done this before Chalcedon, and it took a further two centuries before the implications of Chalcedon had been fully thought through. Later there would be less chance of success: Scotus Erigena already stood outside Christology's sphere of influence and thought simply in metaphysical terms of the relation of God to the world. For Maximus, however, a synthetic understanding of Christ became a theodicy for the world: a justification not simply of its existence but of the whole range of its structures of being. All things, for him, had become organic parts of ever-more-comprehensive syntheses, had become themselves syntheses pointing to the final synthesis of Christ, which explained them all. One cannot avoid seeing here an anticipation of the christological conclusion of Nicholas of Cusa's *Docta Ignorantia*, or that of the young Hegel, whose philosophical notion of synthesis was a secularized derivative of biblical theology.[71]

In the course of this investigation, we will keep encountering texts that speak of the hidden immanence of the pre-incarnate Word (Logos) in all the intelligible structures (*logoi*, λόγοι) of the world. For example, Maximus says that the natural law, the written law, and the law of Christ are one and the same and that anyone who breaks any one of them sins personally against Christ and will be judged by him.[72] Although the hesychastic tradition in Byzantine spirituality was to practice the constant awareness of Jesus in a way that was ultimately mechanical, Maximus—bringing Origen's Logos-theology to its fulfillment—laid hold of all the human powers, theoretical as well as practical, speculative as well as spiritual and mystical, powers of thought as well as those of prayer, in order to find Christ in all things and to find the triune God in him.

This is why he begins "from below", in the philosophical and structural foreshadowings of the final synthesis. For Maximus, the reality of this synthesis is best conceived by the image of a right angle, in which two lines meet:

---

[71] [See Hans Küng, *Menschwerdung Gottes* (Freiburg, 1970); English trans., *The Incarnation of God: An Introduction to Hegel's Theological Thought as Prolegomena to a Future Christology* (New York, 1987).]

[72] *Quaestiones ad Thalassium* 19; CCG 7, 119, 7ff.; PG 90, 308BC.

There are a variety of angles a divinely fortified mind can use to build its towers. One kind of angle, found in the realm of nature, is the synthesis of a particular with a universal being within one identical conception of substance or of the act of being: for instance, the synthesis of individuals in the species to which they belong, or of species in a genus, or of genera in their common being. All of these come together in the same way because their poles are finite, yet these universal meanings are discovered in particular individuals in such a way that the various elements form, in their very coming together, a whole variety of different intellectual "angles". Another synthesis is that of sensible reality and mind, of earth and heaven, of what appears and what is known to be, of nature and idea. On all of this, the contemplating mind, using its inherited ability to form true intelligible explanations of every object, wisely raises a mental tower that incorporates all these angles: from these syntheses, that is, it forms an overall theory of synthesis itself.[73]

In this most general of intellectual laws, Maximus discovers the truth behind the ancient Gnostic theory of paired beings, or *syzygies*: "By syzygy, I mean the [synthesis] of theoretical and practical reason, of wisdom and prudence, of contemplation and action, of knowledge and virtue, of immediate vision[74] and faith."[75] Despite its extraordinary character, the christological synthesis is so far from being an exception that it finds confirmation of a sort in the most general laws of being. Why should we not affirm it, he asks, "since we know such a number of syntheses in which the poles are united inseparably without undergoing the slightest change or transformation toward each other"?[76] Maximus phrases this "most general law of being" as follows:

Every whole—especially every whole that is formed from the synthesis of various elements—even as it preserves its own individual identity in a consistent way, also continues to bear in itself the unmixed difference of the parts that make it up, including even the essential, authentic character and role of each member in its relation to the others. On the other hand, the parts—for all their undiminished continuity in their own natural role within the synthetic relationship—preserve the unitary identity of the

---

[73] Ibid. 48; CCG 7, 341, 178–93; PG 90, 440CD.
[74] Literally, "of vision without forgetting", a Platonic expression from Evagrius, denoting the highest level of vision, face to face. Cf. below, "The Synthesis of the Three Acts".
[75] *Mystagogia* 5; PG 91, 676A.
[76] *Epistle* 12; PG 91, 472D.

whole, which gives them a hypostatic condition of complete indivisibility.[77]

The mystery of the presence of a whole in its parts, from whose
synthesis it comes to be, is not, for Maximus, simply the object of dis-
interested contemplation. For him it is the direct way to God: "[Think
of] multiplicity in number and unity in kind: coins, pieces of silver,
obols, for instance, whose unity is one of kind—of copper or gold or
silver. Or of a multiplicity of kinds of organisms—grasses, for example
—and unity in species: all are grass. Multiplicity in species: horse, cow,
human being, intellectual being; unity of genus: all are living creatures.
Multiplicity in the product: creatures; unity in the source: God is the
cause of all."[78]

And there is more. If the members of a synthesis differ from each
other only within unity, then God himself is, in the end, the highest
synthesis, in which all differences are both formed and dissolved. "He
alone is the thought of the thinker and the content of the thought, the
word of the speaker and the meaning spoken, the life of the living and
the core of life itself."[79] If the members [of a synthesis] only have contact with each other through the unity of the whole that arches over
all of them, creatures, as such, can only be open to each other through
their transcendental identity in the unity of God. This is a negative
identity, in that all of them have their origin in nothing and have as
their one common quality the fact that none of them is God. But it is
also a positive identity, in that the one Creator keeps them in being,
one might say, through his relationship to them. Maximus expresses
this relationship in a mighty paragraph that takes the natural synthesis
of the world in God as the starting point for describing the synthesis
achieved in salvation history: the unity of all men and women in the
Church. Here it is the first part of the comparison that is relevant for
our point:

> God created all things with his limitless power, brought them into be-
> ing, holds them there and gathers them together and sets boundaries to
> them; in his providence, he links them all—intellectual beings as well
> as sensible—to each other as he does to himself. In his might, God

---

[77] Ibid. 13; PG 91, 521C.
[78] In De Divinis nominibus 13; PG 4, 405D–408A.
[79] Mystagogia, prooemium; PG 91, 664A.

draws up all the things that are naturally distinct from each other and binds them to himself as their cause, their origin and goal; and through the power of this relationship to him as source, he lets them also be drawn toward each other. This is the power through which every being is brought to its own indestructible, unconfused identity, both in activity and in being. No being can permanently isolate itself through its own particularity or through the drive of its nature toward some other end; rather, everything remains, in its very being, bound without confusion to everything else, through the single, enduring relationship of all to their one and only source. This supreme power overshadows the individual relationships that are to be seen in every individual nature, not in a way that corrupts or eradicates or terminates them, but in order to dominate and illuminate them as the whole does its parts—or better, in order to reveal itself also as the cause of the whole of things, thanks to which both the whole and the parts of the whole are revealed and come to be, while the power itself remains the radiant cause of them all. Just as the sun outshines the reality and the luminous activity of the stars, so the ultimate ground of being conceals the being of creatures: for as the parts come to be from the whole, so created things come to be from their cause and are recognized in its light, and if they are totally possessed by their movement toward this cause, through the power of the relationship itself, then they tend to cease from their own individual being. For God, who is "all in all" and infinitely exalted over all, is recognized by the pure of heart as the sole ultimate One, at the moment when their minds gather the intelligible meanings of all things together in contemplation, and grow quiet before God as the beginning and cause and end of the world's being, the undivided root and ground that embraces all things. In this same way, the holy Church of God, made in God's image, reveals the same mystery to us and brings it to reality.[80]

Here, in the end, is the inconceivable fecundity of this divine unity: on the one hand, it is the cause of the unity of all things and of their respective differences; it makes each of them an image of the divine unity and uniqueness; it is the basis of what is most personal and immediate in each of them. On the other hand, this divine unity is, in itself, the overflowing unity and root identity of these individuals, the source of their community and their loving communion. This paradox of a synthesis that unites creatures by distinguishing them and distinguishes them by uniting them—a paradox that can be found throughout the

---

[80] Ibid. 1; PG 91, 664D–665C.

whole edifice of the universe—takes its origin in the most original relation of all things: their relation to God. Maximus writes:

> The law of him who willed this unity, the law that inheres in all things as unifying power and rule, is simply this: it does not permit the individual character of either part of the unity of a person to be banished into obscurity by the natural difference between them, nor does it allow the particularity that stamps each part to lead to an overemphasis of their difference and individuality, to the detriment of the mysterious relationship naturally inherent in them that lovingly moves them toward unity. The heart of this relationship is that there is one universal presence (παρουσία) of the cause of all that is, secretly and unrecognizably binding all things together, yet dwelling in each being in a different way; this presence holds the individual parts of the whole together, in itself and in each other, unconfused and inseparable, and allows them, through this very relationship of creative unity, to live more for each other than for themselves.[81]

These texts are enough to give us a notion of the way the christological formula [of Chalcedon] expands, for Maximus, into a fundamental law of metaphysics. Illuminated by the highest level of theological synthesis—the union of God and the world in Christ—Maximus searches out the traces of the developmental principles, of the conditions of possibility of this synthesis, and in the process discovers the formal structure of all created being, even the formal structure of the relationship between the absolute and the contingent.

One must keep in mind, of course, that Maximus did not work out all the metaphysical transformations of this law of the synthetic nature of being—that he was not equipped for such an ontological project. Much, then, [in his conception of synthesis] remains unexplained. At times, the indwelling of the whole in the parts seems to be conceived as a kind of independence and freedom in relation to particular being, a transcendence of generic or individual differences; this conception is expressible in the ascetical and practical realm in terms of ethical "indifference", of imperturbability, apatheia (ἀπάθεια). At other times, the same indwelling appears more as an effective, positive act that takes control of these opposite poles, either by "grasping" them in intellectual insight (literally, in intelligentia) or by loving them in a way that recognizes and affirms their very difference. This alternating, double

---

[81] Ibid. 7; PG 91, 685AB.

form of synthesis—as *indifference* or openness toward the constituent parts and as the affirmation of their *difference*—corresponds, in the end, to the very essence of the synthesis and must not be watered down. We will meet this conceptual variability on key issues again in our discussion of aspects of Maximus' thought: in his doctrine of God and God's relation to the world, in his Christology, and in his teaching about final human fulfillment.

However one understands the structure of synthesis [in Maximus], it remains always a predominantly Aristotelian concept, even when it is pressed into service of a Neoplatonic, mystical striving toward union.[82] For in such union, too, all synthesis still preserves the basic principle that distance is the presupposition of any higher union, against any tendency toward direct juxtaposition and confusion of the two poles. Aristotelianism and the theology of Chalcedon enter here into an un-breakable alliance: they preserve the rights of *nature* against the ram-pages of an unchecked supernaturalism.

In this respect, Maximus is a real predecessor of Aquinas, anticipating his concern to preserve the essence of every thing—or better, to set each thing's integral completeness within an openness and a readiness for union that allows it to be elevated and brought to fulfillment. For both thinkers, the difference between creatures is a feature of their per-fection. Maximus speaks of a "constitutive, foundational difference" (συστατικὴ διαφορά)[83] and, in so doing, utters the decisive word against Origen. Thomas makes himself the defender of the many-colored vari-ety of beings in the world, which reflect God's beauty more perfectly in their very nonidentity than a unitary world could do.[84] So both of them conceive the relationship of nature and grace in basically the same way. The distinction they draw between the two orders, despite all their concrete mutual involvement, grows, in both systems, out of the same attitude: reverence and a sense of distance before the majesty of God

---

[82] For the difference between Maximus and Pseudo-Dionysius on this subject, see below, chap. 7, sec. 4: "The Synthesis of the Three Acts of Worship".

[83] *Opuscula*; PG 91, 249C.

[84] "A builder does not seek the same sort of goodness in a foundation that he seeks in a roof, if he is to prevent the house from falling into ruin; so, too, the maker of all things, God, would not make the whole universe to be the best of its kind if he made all the parts the same, because many levels of goodness would be missing in such a universe, and that would be an imperfection. . . . The best state for created things is the perfection of the whole, which consists in the order of the various parts": *Summa contra gentiles* II, 44 (Parma ed. 5:98–100).

(are they not both commentators on Pseudo-Dionysius, the theologian of reverence?) and reverence, too, before created nature, which is to be valued positively precisely because it is finite. "Nature", writes Maximus, "does not possess in itself the intelligible qualities of the supernatural."[85] That clearly does not prevent either Maximus or Thomas from discovering in nature an intrinsic ordering toward the supernatural, a "natural longing" (*desiderium naturale*) for the supernatural vision of God. But even in spite of this positive orientation, both preserve, in the concrete linking of nature and grace, the distinction that is itself the sign and the condition of true union and inner collaboration. Grace perfects nature in its innermost core only because it is not itself nature. When Maximus describes this union, one almost thinks one is hearing Thomas himself:

> We are not permitted to say that grace alone brings about, in the saints, insight into the divine mysteries without any contribution from their natural capacity to receive knowledge. Otherwise we would have to assume that the holy prophets could not receive and comprehend the enlightenments that the Holy Spirit bestowed on them. . . . On the other hand, they did not come upon a true insight into reality simply through the investigations of natural reason, without the grace of the Holy Spirit. . . . The point is that the grace of the Holy Spirit does not bring about wisdom in the saints without the receptivity of their intelligence, does not give knowledge without their ability to grasp the Word, does not give faith without stability of mind and the confident readiness to face the still-unrevealed future in hope,[86] does not bestow the gift of healing without a natural love for other people; nor does he give any charism at all without a capacity and a potentiality for effectiveness appropriate to each particular grace. On the other hand, man cannot attain any of the things I have mentioned by his own natural powers, without the divine power that provides them as gifts.

---

[85] *Quaestiones ad Thalassium* 59; CCG 22, 55, 159–60; PG 90, 609B.

[86] Maximus uses here, for "confidence", the famous word πληροφορία, which the Messalians and—on the orthodox side—Diadochus of Photike used for the immediate and consoling certainty of the heart, the instinctual trust of the spirit. (Cf. *Ambigua*; PG 91, 1121C: τὴν ἐν πληροφορίᾳ προθυμον πίστιν [a faith ready in confidence (*plērophoria*)]"; also *Quaestiones ad Thalassium*, prologue; CCG 7, 23, 97; PG 90, 248D.) However, the idea that supernatural faith necessarily rests on the natural capacity to believe is much older. Philo (*De migratione Abrahami* 39 [ed. L. Cohn and P. Wendland, vol. 2 (Berlin, 1897), 311–14]) knows it, Theophilus of Antioch (*Ad Autolycum* 1, 8) and later Origen (*Contra Celsum* 1, 10f.) develop it, and Pseudo-Macarius takes it from them (*Hom.* 14, 1).

All the saints show this when, after receiving their revelations, they try to clarify for themselves the meaning of what has been revealed. . . . They try to reveal revelation to themselves. For the grace of the Holy Spirit never destroys the capabilities of nature. Just the opposite: it makes nature, which has been weakened by unnatural habit, mature and strong enough once again to function in a natural way and leads it upward toward insight into the divine.

For what the Holy Spirit is trying to accomplish in us is a true knowledge of things; not as if he were seeking this for himself—he is, after all, as God, far above all knowledge—but he seeks it for us, who have need of such illumination. So also the Word became flesh, not for himself, but rather to bring the mystery of the Incarnation to reality for our sakes. For as the Logos accomplished divine works in the flesh, but not without the cooperation of a body animated by a rational soul, so the Holy Spirit accomplishes in the saints the ability to understand mysteries, but not without the exercise of their natural abilities or without their seeking and careful searching for knowledge. And if the saints have searched and sought, . . . they surely were aided in their quest by the grace of the Spirit, who spurred on their theoretical and practical reason to study and investigate these things.[87]

This text is all the more instructive in that it applies the general relationship between nature and grace to Christ and then applies Christology to that general relationship. The two approaches are complementary, and both are equally necessary. Maximus' great trust in the intelligibility of nature (λόγος τῆς φύσεως) is based on the law of synthesis, which has its supreme example in Christ, who succeeded in bridging the endless chasm between God and the creature without a confusion of natures. In this sense, the christological theme in Maximus' conception of the universe embraces the three others we have discussed: it corrects Neoplatonic mysticism, confirms the Aristotelian metaphysics, and prevents the Origenist-monastic strain from becoming simple escapism.

---

[87] *Quaestiones ad Thalassium* 59; CCG 22, 45, 28–51, 113; PG 90, 604D–608C.

4. Chronology of His Life and Work

Maximus was born in 580 in Constantinople, from an aristocratic family, and received a thorough humanistic education.[88] About 610, the Emperor Heraclius invited him to join the court, in the role of first secretary. This gave him the opportunity to form cordial relationships, often personal friendships, with the most important personalities of the empire. Later, when he was living as a monk in Africa, they often turned to him for advice on important matters; he was also always in a position to recommend friends and protégés to the court. After three or four years of service, however, he left his high position in order to enter a monastery: not one of the great monasteries of the city itself, but a modest one in Chrysopolis (Skutari) across the Bosporus. In 618, his disciple Anastasius was already with him in the monastery—the person who would accompany him throughout his life, even as far as martyrdom itself. About ten years after he became a monk, about 624/625, Maximus moved to the monastery of St. George in Cyzicus (Erdek), where he remained until the approach of the Persian army in 626. There, the first traces of his written works begin to appear. In correspondence with his friend the bishop John, at this period, Maximus roughed out the plan for the *Ambigua* (whose full title is: "Explanations of Various Difficult Passages in the Works of Saints Dionysius and Gregory [Nazianzen]")[89] and wrote his earliest extant letters to John the Chamberlain, including the famous Second Letter on love. The *Ambigua* consist of two clearly marked parts. The long second part, dedicated to Bishop John, was composed considerably earlier than the first section, perhaps about 630; there Maximus, without any concern for the Monothelite controversy, can speak of the "one single activity (ἐνέργεια) shared by God and the blessed in heaven",[90] a notion he

---

[88] As we have already remarked, we intend here only to lay out a broad outline of the chronology of Maximus' life and work. For all details we refer the reader to Polycarp Sherwood, *An Annotated Date-List of the Works of Maximus the Confessor*, Studia Anselmiana, 30 (Rome, 1952), where all earlier research on Maximus' life has been carefully reviewed and in many respects made obsolete.

[89] See Endre von Ivánka, review of P. Sherwood's *The Earlier Ambigua*, *Byzantinische Zeitschrift* 49 (1956): 411: "The work is an explanation of passages from Gregory Nazianzen and Pseudo-Dionysius the Areopagite that either seem, in their phrasing, Origenist or that could be misinterpreted in an Origenist or Evagrian sense."

[90] PG 91, 1976C.

later retracted.[91] The shorter first part was probably composed about 634 and is dedicated to a certain "holy man, Thomas".

The next ten years offer us few helpful opportunities for filling out his chronology. In 626, Maximus seems to have left the monastery of St. George to go to Africa; he may have spent some time in Crete and perhaps also in Cyprus. At Pentecost 632, we find him in Carthage; but before that date he probably spent several years in the monastery of Eukratas, in the outskirts of Alexandria, where Sophronius, patriarch of Jerusalem from 634, was still presumably abbot. Sophronius was the first to attack the Monothelite position as heretical; it was probably he who first made Maximus conscious of this new danger to faith. Maximus' Eighth Letter, written to Sophronius in the middle of 632, suggests that they had already been friends for some time.

Sophronius, long a bitter opponent of Monophysitism, began to become involved in the Monothelite controversy at about that time. Sergius, the patriarch of Constantinople, had advised Emperor Heraclius to try to work out a theological compromise, which would serve the political purpose of securing the border regions of the empire, with their Monophysite sympathies, against welcoming Persian incursions and of binding them once again to Byzantium. Sergius' suggestion was to leave the central question in the debate, the two natures in Christ, in the background, but to agree from then on that Christ possessed one single mode of activity (μία ἐνέργεια). Even before 619, Sergius had been involved in negotiations with both orthodox and Monophysite bishops; during his overseas campaigns between 622 and 630, the emperor had held several theological disputations and dialogues on the same issue. On the Catholic side, Cyrus of Phasis was convinced of the new approach, and in 630 he was given the patriarchal see of Alexandria, a position he immediately used to try and win over that city's many Monophysite Christians to reunion. In 633, an act of union was agreed on in Alexandria, which was greeted in Constantinople with great satisfaction. Even before its promulgation, however, Sophronius—who was the first to recognize its danger—personally implored Cyrus to refrain from publishing it. Since he met with no success, Sophronius traveled to visit Sergius at Constantinople —unaware that Sergius was, in fact, the real instigator of the heresy —and at least succeeded in convincing him that future official docu-

---

[91] PG 91, 33AB.

ments should not speak either of one or of two modes of activity in Christ. Sergius confirmed this compromise in a synodal letter of 634 (the *Psēphos*).

Soon afterward, Sophronius became patriarch of Jerusalem. At about the same time, Sergius sent his insidious letter to Pope Honorius, trying to induce the pope to approve the synodal letter [of 634] and its policy of silence on the subject of one or two modes of activity in Christ, on the grounds that two modes of activity might lead one to think Christ had two opposed wills, whereas his human will must obviously always have been "set in motion by God" (θεοκίνητος).[92] Honorius answered in terms that were meant to be orthodox but were easily misunderstood: he spoke enthusiastically of the unity of will in Christ (which he seems to have conceived along moral rather than natural lines, suggesting that Christ's human nature never acted on its own initiative [ὁρμή] but always under the control [νεύματι] of the Logos) and recommended Sergius' solution to both Sophronius and Cyrus. Sophronius issued his own long-awaited synodal letter in 634, in which he obeyed the letter of the pope's suggestion and avoided speaking directly of "two modes of activity" (δύο ἐνεργείαι) but in fact clearly advocated the essential difference of the "energies" in Christ, as a direct consequence of the essential difference of his natures.[93] Four years of relative calm followed this letter, until the *Ekthesis* ["manifesto"] of Emperor Heraclius, written by Sergius and promulgated in 638, put an end to the "watery union" (τὴν ὑδροβαφῆ ἕνωσιν); this document ordered continuing silence on the subject of one or two modes of activity in Christ but commanded all to teach that he had but one will (ἓν θέλημα).

The years that followed were years of open battle. Sophronius died in 637, and his place was taken by a Monothelite. Pyrrhus became the successor of Sergius at Constantinople in 638 and in a synod threatened to anathematize anyone who did not accept the *Ekthesis*. In the same year, Honorius died. His successor, Severinus, was first informed that the emperor's confirmation of his election would depend on his subscribing to that document; eventually he was confirmed, but only an early death (640) prevented him from having to take a stand on the *Ekthesis*. Whether he in fact had rejected Monotheletism before his death is unclear. John IV, who succeeded him, did so at a Roman

---

[92] Mansi 11:530f.
[93] PG 87, 3172.

synod, but the *acta* have not been preserved. At about this time, Maximus took over the leadership of the struggle against monothelitism. His main works on spirituality had already been finished; let us look briefly at them.

The *Ascetic Life* (*Liber asceticus*) and the *Four Centuries on Love*, as well as the *Quaestiones et Dubia*, seem to form the earliest group, written about 626.[94] The second collection of *Ambigua* follows these works closely (before 630): a very important point, because in it we see Maximus' theology already fully developed and balanced on all points, except for

---

[94] Earlier still, if it is genuine, would be the *Moscow Centuries on Knowledge*. The following is a list of works attributed to Maximus that are certainly not authentic and that will not be considered in this present book:

a. Five books *On the Trinity*; PG 28, 1116–1285. Cf. O. Bardenhewer, *Patrologie*, 3:60.

b. The *Loci communes*; PG 91, 721–1071. Cf. C. Wachsmuth, *Studien zu den griechischen Florilegien* (Berlin, 1882; reprint, Osnabrück, 1971); R. Holl, *Die Sacra Parallela des Johannes Damascenus*, Texte und Untersuchungen, 16/1 (Leipzig, 1886); A. Ehrhard, "Zu den Sacra Parallela des Johannes Damascenus und dem Florilegium des Maximus", *Biblische Zeitschrift* 10 (1901): 394–415.

c. The *Five Hundred Chapters*; PG 90, 1177–1392. These were first shown by Wilhelm Soppa to be a compilation of genuine works of Maximus (the *Quaestiones ad Thalassium*, *Ambigua*, and Scholia on Pseudo-Dionysius), along with some certainly inauthentic scholia on the *Quaestiones ad Thalassium*, which may be by Michael Psellos; the whole work was put together in the eleventh century, probably by Antonios Melissa. See *Die Diversa Capita unter den Schriften des hl. Maximos Confessors in deutscher Bearbeitung und quellenkritischer Beleuchtung* (diss., Dresden, 1922); the same conclusion was reached independently, and with some further development, by M. T. Disdier, "Les Fondements dogmatiques de la spiritualité de S. Maxime: Les Oeuvres de'Évagre le Pontique", *Echos d'Orient* 30 (1931): 168–78. Genuine works of Maximus here are only the first fifteen "chapters" of the first century.

d. The *Other Chapters*; PG 90, 1401–26, which were also shown by M. T. Disdier to be inauthentic and which probably were composed by Elias Ekdikos (PG 127, 1129–76; cf. Beck, *Handbuch*, 655). See "Elie l'Ecdicos et les hetera kephalaia attribués à s. Maxime le Confesseur et à Jean de Carpathos", *Echos d'Orient* 31 (1932): 17–43.

e. The tract *On the Soul*, PG 91, 353–62, an almost complete doublet of a treatise ascribed to Gregory the Wonderworker (PG 10, 1137–46; see Bardenhewer 2:327–29).

f. A large part of the scholia on Pseudo-Dionysius; see my article, "Das Scholienwerk des Johannes von Scythopolis", *Scholastik* 15 (1940): 16–38 [reprinted with corrections and additions, *Kosmische Liturgie*, German ed. of 1961, 644–72; *see* 359–87 below].

g. The hymns; PG 91, 1417–24. See Mercati, *Mélanges Bidez*, 1933/34, 619–25.

h. The *Capita practica* published by Epifanovich in his collection (nos. 56–60), which he himself has shown to belong to Evagrius Ponticus. Probably other fragments in the same collection also belong to Evagrius.

[A recently published work attributed to Maximus, whose authenticity must also be considered doubtful, is a *Life of the Virgin*, preserved only in a Georgian translation. See *Maxime le Confesseur, Vie de la Vierge*, ed. M. J. van Esbroeck: CSCO 478–79, Scriptores Iberici, 21–22 (Louvain, 1986), with French transl.]

his precisions on Monothelitism. About the same time the *Exposition of the Lord's Prayer* was probably written, as well as the *Mystagogy*,[95] which in many ways is closely related, both in tone and in content, to the *Ambigua*. In the years that followed (630 until about 634), he was probably occupied with his great work, the *Quaestiones ad Thalassium*, to which the short *Quaestiones ad Theopemptum* are stylistically related. The *Two Hundred Chapters on Knowledge* are dependent on both the *Ambigua* and the *Quaestiones ad Thalassium*; as I have demonstrated, they presuppose the existence of the latter and so must have been composed about 634 or shortly afterward.

All of these works do occasionally deal with the problem of Monophysitism in the style of Severus of Antioch but show no signs that the Monothelite controversy has begun. During the time he was writing them, as well as later, Maximus was called on to write various letters and tracts[96] about the Monophysite question. This had become an acute problem for the provincial governments in Egypt and Carthage once again, because of the flood of Monophysite refugees from the East, fleeing first from the Persian invasions and soon afterward from Islam. Even in the midst of the Monothelite controversy (641), Maximus would detect the old enemy [Severus] behind the *Ekthesis* and would write a very detailed essay against him (Letter 12).

The first traces of a position against the new heresy, stimulated by Sophronius' synodal letter, can be found in the later *Ambigua* and in a letter to Pyrrhus (Letter 19, written in 633/634). Pyrrhus had hoped to win Maximus' assent to the new terminology, and Maximus—at first in a conciliatory frame of mind—asked him to explain the meaning of the terms more fully.[97] But even quotations from the Fathers could not, in the end, convince him, "for the mystery of our redemption does not stand on syllables but on the meaning of what is said and on the reality itself." Maximus was already on the alert, and he was not too late for the fight. In the disputation with Pyrrhus, he knows the full details of the first letters that Patriarch Sergius had written to George Arsas and others years before (in 617), asking for proof-texts to support the idea of "one mode of activity". From this point (634)

---

[95] For more details, see my commentary on the *Centuries on Knowledge, Die Gnostischen Centurien des Maximus Confessor* (Freiburg, 1941), 154.

[96] Especially Letters 13, 15, and 17, and *Opuscula* 13, 17, 18, and 23. For further details, see Sherwood, *An Annotated Date-List*.

[97] PG 91, 596B.

on, his anti-Monothelite tracts follow without interruption, right up to his main polemical work, addressed to the presbyter Marinus in 645–646[98]—to whom another important essay (*tomus*)[99] had already been sent about 640.

In July, 645, Maximus' tour de force took place in Carthage: the disputation with Pyrrhus, in which Maximus showed the complete superiority of his theological art. It was not simply a matter of his great vision, standing in the background with unshakeable clarity; it was also the dialectical precision of his argument and his unquestionable mastery of the patristic tradition. In contrast, Pyrrhus appears as an intellectually sorry figure: he has no breadth or background to his vision; he plays his cards mechanically, without strategy or order, and then suddenly and meekly surrenders. It is questionable whether he was being honest at all, either here or in his subsequent recantation in Rome; it seems rather that he was simply trimming his sails, as he had always done, to suit the political winds.

Maximus left for Rome, perhaps with Pyrrhus, at a time when several local African synods were producing anti-Monothelite statements. In September 647, Emperor Constans II issued his *Typos*, which withdrew the *Ekthesis*, imposed a rule of silence also on the issue of one or two wills in Christ, and ordered that all restrict themselves to "the simple sayings" of Scripture and the Fathers. It was obviously a command that had come too late. At the end of 642, John IV's successor, Pope Theodore I (a native of Jerusalem), had begun to offer resistance to Byzantium in a way that had not been experienced for many years: he had dared to anathematize the Monothelite Byzantine patriarch Paul, who took his revenge by engineering the *Typos*. After Theodore's death, Pope Martin I presided at the Lateran synod in October 649; Maximus, now almost seventy years old, along with the Greek monks in Rome, made an enormous contribution both to its preparation and to its realization.

That the arrest of both the pope and Maximus was delayed for more than three years was due to the episode with Olympius, which we have already mentioned. After Olympius' fall from power, the emperor was free to move: on June 17, 653, the pope was taken prisoner; Maximus and his companions were probably arrested at the same time. Their first

---

[98] *Opuscula* 1–3; PG 91, 9–56.
[99] *Opuscula* 20; PG 91, 228–45.

hearing, in May 655, was held only long after Martin had been banished to the Chersonese on the Black Sea, where he died on September 26, 655. In August 654, meanwhile, Eugenius I had become pope. No one took any further notice of his sick and exiled predecessor; in fact, we know that Eugenius, in May of 655, made arrangements through his legates in Constantinople, over Maximus' head, to come to a new dogmatic agreement with the emperor's representatives. Maximus and his companions remained steadfast. The accusations of high treason against them could not be substantiated, despite the efforts of the court; they were simply pressed, therefore, to follow Rome's lead and enter into communion with the see of Byzantium. As soon as he heard of the new agreement between Rome and Constantinople, Maximus dictated a letter[100] to his disciple and companion, the monk Anastasius, which he instructed him to send on to a monastic community in Cagliari. In an accompanying note,[101] Anastasius labeled the new "doctrine of three wills" in Christ monstrous and called upon the addressees to use their influence against it in Rome;[102] they apparently did so, and the pope changed his mind. Maximus was transferred to Bizya in Thrace and underwent a second trial, aimed at persuading him to negotiate with Rome in Constantinople's interests. The old man at first welcomed his captors' feigned willingness to change direction, but as he came to see its lack of substance, he held to his own convictions. He was abused, spit upon, and sentenced to a second exile in Mesembria. After a final trial in 662, the old man—now eighty-two—and his companions were scourged, their "blaspheming tongues" were cut out from their roots, and their right hands were cut off. The companions were scattered; Maximus was sent to Lazia, on the east coast of the Black Sea. There, in solitary confinement in the fortress Shemarum, on August 13 of that same year, he succumbed to his sufferings.

---

[100] PG 90, 132.
[101] Ibid., 133; PL 79, 625f.
[102] Caspar, *Geschichte des Papsttums*, 2:579.

II

GOD

1. The Dark Radiance

a. The Dialectic of Transcendence

"A ray of darkness" (σκότους ἀκτις): this image sums up Pseudo-Dionysius' conception of God and also that of Maximus. It is a conception of God that brings to a conclusion an almost boundless tradition of Hellenistic, Jewish, and Christian thinkers, all of whom celebrated God's transcendence. The summit of all being, in the view of Plato and Aristotle, was enthroned in radiant but inaccessible light. Soon, however, Eastern mists began to gather around this Olympian peak, and it began to loom more and more steep and distant, until it disappeared altogether in complete incomprehensibility. The ever-more-transcendent God of Jewish apocalyptic, where some features of the biblical revelation [of God] exceeded their own limits; the God of Philo, exalted above the divine "powers", above the principles of intelligibility (*logoi*) and the angels, above domination and providence and goodness itself; the unrecognizable "abyss" of the Gnostics; the "superessential Father" of Origen; Plotinus' Good-beyond-all-being; Gregory of Nyssa's God, eternally beyond the reach of love and beyond the grasp of vision: all of these were steps toward the "mystical theology" of the Areopagite, who imparted to the idea of a transcendent being the final and most adequate level of expression.

But this idea of transcendence only came to be grasped effectively because the parallel notion of God's complete immanence had come to be recognized, conditioning and paving the way for his transcendence. The Stoics, and before them Heraclitus and Parmenides, had laid the groundwork for this theology of immanence. But while for these two classically opposed Presocratics transcendence and immanence came down, in the end, to the same thing—for Heraclitus the world swallows God up, for Parmenides God dissolves the world in himself—and while for the Stoics the Logos that dwells in the world could no longer gather itself together as an absolute, transcendent divine principle, Philo and (even more) the Christian Apologists began to develop a genuine sense of the dialectic between transcendence and immanence. Earlier Greek theology rested on a presumption of contradiction, which either (as in Plato) conceived the world simply as the decadent shadow of a genuinely transcendent ideal realm or else (as in Aristotle and the Stoics) saw the ideal as little more than a way of defining the borders of an absolutely real, inherently divine world; Gnostic theology could only see God and the world as engaged in a tragic, radical antipathy, even though the Gnostics tried without success to temper this opposition by generating countless intermediate beings. But the insight began to dawn, at the beginning of the Christian era, that transcendence and immanence in fact only complement one another. Even God, who is in no sense a part of the world, who is absolutely unrivaled in his power and fullness of being, must for that very reason dwell within every entity that claims, in one way or another, the name of Being. It is finally in biblical revelation that this sublime realization, that God's absoluteness and the finitude and relativity of the world do not mutually exclude each other, comes to its maturity. This sense of unity was foreshadowed in Philo's thought, a synthesis of Platonism and Stoicism against the background of the Bible, although it still threatened there to slide off in one direction or the other. But once the idea had been grasped, even the intermediaries of the Gnostic systems could take on a new, positive role: they no longer needed to be simply bridges between contradictory, hostile poles but could actually represent the ways God is near to the world and present within it—as "powers", as radiant means of involving himself in a "history of salvation". And when Wisdom, the focal point of this divine involvement in the world, finally shone forth for Christian faith as the personal Word, the human Christ, all doubts about the possibility of a reconciliation between God and the world disappeared.

The old patterns of thought, of course, did not simply disappear. They still haunt Clement's excerpts from Gnostic literature and his own theology of creation; they claim undeserved attention in the works of Origen, who sees the Divine Persons arranged in hierarchical order like emanations and who misinterprets the corporeal realm, again in Gnostic fashion, as a decline from transcendence. There are echoes of them in the spiritualizing ascetical and mystical theology of the early monks, and even the mysticism of the great Cappadocians is not wholly free of them. The fact that peace had finally been made between God and the world, however, despite these occasional stirrings of disquiet, is proved by Plotinus' vast vision of Being—only understandable in its fullness against the background of Christianity—which expressly and polemically turns against the Gnostic practice of downgrading the world. And although evil, for Plotinus, was still inextricably tied up with the material realm, Pseudo-Dionysius was able to take the further step of proclaiming peace with God even there. He brought to completion the final reconciliation between Platonism and the Stoics, between the human sense of a reality that is simply beyond the world and the vision of a world reaching out to be a perfectly ordered universe (*kosmos*) precisely in its variety, its nonidentity, its internal oppositions and relativity. Because God is endlessly distant from all things, he is near, internal to every one of his creatures—he protects, preserves, satisfies the needs of each creature in its very otherness, its difference from him. This great anonymous thinker's decisive achievement, then, was not simply negative theology—although he clearly developed it, with consummate consistency, to a point unknown before; he also recognized, with impeccable honesty, that such sytematically negative assertions about God can only stand if it is supported by a positive theology that has been thought through with equal consistency and thoroughness: that is why his God, who is nameless, possesses all the names of his works. Even greater than a God who defines himself only by his absolute otherness from the world, this God proves his very otherness in the fact that he can give positive Being to what is not himself, that he can assure it its autonomy, and for that very reason —beyond the gaping chasm that remains between them—assure it a genuine likeness to himself.

Was there still a step to take, even beyond Pseudo-Dionysius? Yes, and it was reserved for Maximus. Origen had developed a system of "intermediate beings" that went beyond Gnosticism by speaking of the forms the divine Logos has taken in the world in the course of salvation history and of the ranks of created spirits corresponding to the degree of their fall away from God; and Plotinus had added to the structure, building it into a graduated system of emanations from an original One. Pseudo-Dionysius appropriated this system in two important ways. First, he borrowed the idea of potentialities for being, which possess a kind of existence halfway between God and the world, as the basic structures of created reality: "being in itself", "life in itself", "mind in itself", and so on. As he attempts to explain them, these potentialities are, when considered as a point of origin, God himself, insofar as God's being can be shared; when considered as modes of participation, they are aspects of the world, insofar as it shares God's being. Secondly, he borrowed the idea of a hierarchy of creatures, a huge ladder—such as Philo had once described it—reaching down in unbroken continuity from the highest seraph, who stands directly before God, to the lowest worm and rock; in tune with ever-fainter echoes of the divine music, all the creatures on the ladder bow low and reach upward in an eternal game of loving condescension and yearning ascent, joined to each other by insatiable desire.

This "golden chain of being" is certainly a captivating picture: its upper end rests in God's fingers, and it hangs down unbroken to the border of nothingness, a shaft of light, spreading gradually outward and downward from the heart of its source, from pure intensity, into realms of increased shading and color but also of darkness, until in the end it disappears. Yet this conception of Being also risks the final loss of what had been achieved. It risks postponing once again the unity of a transcendence beyond all Being and an immanence within all Being, in order to make room for a struggle between Being and Nothingness (or matter), light and darkness. Of course, the themes of emanation and the hierarchy of beings, in Pseudo-Dionysius, are always subordinate to the more basic dialectic of positive and negative theology and, for that reason, are never developed to the fullest extent possible. But it is Maximus who banishes even the hidden contradictory influences of these themes and who finally reconciles the idea of a hierarchy of Being with the assumption of a structural analogy between God and the world. In fact, the emanation of "being in itself", "life in itself", and so on, disappears in his works, and they are replaced by univocal, inner-worldly universal principles, which he calls "generalities" (καθόλα). Later on, we will discuss the meaning and implications of this change in greater detail. With Maximus, too, the Pseudo-Dionysian hierarchies of the "thrice three heavenly choirs", with their liturgy, disappear, as does the ecclesial hierarchy and liturgy, arranged in a corresponding order. In their place, Maximus gives primary emphasis to the tension within the world between the intellectual and phenomenal realms, the world of thought and the world of sense. Rather than gazing upward along the straight ladder of being at choirs of increasingly heavenly spirits, to search for the Divine Reality above the highest movements of the dance, Maximus' eyes look for God in both realms of the world, in sense and intellect, earth and heaven, and meet their limit in both. Only the closure of the two, the growing reciprocity that forms the world as a whole, becomes for him the place where the Transcendent appears, visible precisely in this burgeoning immanence as the One who is wholly other.

This approach to immanence and transcendence is, of course, not without its limits in Maximus' works; that will be clear from what we said in the introductory chapter, since Origen, even more than Pseudo-Dionysius, left his mark on the underlying features of his thought. In this respect, Maximus remained a child of his time, a disciple of his master. But the fact that he was able to develop his own basic insight, in spite of such influences, makes him one of the greatest thinkers in Christian intellectual history. Ferdinand Christian Baur put his finger on the decisive point when he wrote, "Just as [Maximus] attempted to preserve the balance between Christ's two natures in the Monothelite controversy, so, too, it belonged to his style of thought to insist on the autonomy of man; this was in contrast to Platonism, which otherwise—as the Areopagite reveals—stands in a close relationship to Monophysitism."[1] For "man", here, we can simply read "world". It is also true that Maximus thus became the decisive connecting link to Erigena, in whose work the theology of Pseudo-Dionysius takes on a much more cosmological character. But while in Erigena this inclusion of the world in the divine process begins to lend an almost pantheistic tone, which threatens to overshadow the positive Christian tradition, theology remains for Maximus completely dominated by the Christian spirit of discernment between God and the world. It is not "heavenly liturgy", as it is for Pseudo-Dionysius, or "cosmic gnosticism", as it is for Erigena; theology, for Maximus, is Cosmic Liturgy.

b. The Dialectic of Analogy

The theme, then, that will be with us throughout this study is the reciprocal relationship of God's transcendence and God's immanence; from this relationship it follows that God is so completely identical with himself that he is able to form all the things that participate in him both into integral units marked off from each other by mutual

---

[1] *Die christliche Lehre von der Dreieinigkeit und Menschwerdung Gottes* (Tübingen, 1842), 268.

dissimilarity and into a whole built out of the mutual similarity of the parts.

> In that he always remains unchanged, by his own nature, and admits of no alienation from himself through change—neither a more nor a less —yet he still is all things to all, through the boundless abundance of his goodness: lowly with lowly creatures, exalted with the exalted, and the substance of Divinity for those whom he makes divine.[2]

He is like a gentle wind, which stirs through all things, imperceptible in himself yet perceived in each different creature. Elijah felt him as a light breeze, "for all feel the wind's breath: it goes through all things and is not hindered or captured by any of them."[3]

> For who could really understand or explain how God is completely in all things as a whole and is particularly in each individual thing yet neither has parts nor can be divided; how he is not multiplied in a variety of ways through the countless differences of things that exist and which he dwells in as the source of their being; how he is not made uniform through the special character of the unity that exists in things; how he offers no obstacle to the differences in created essences through the one, unifying totality of them all but truly *is* all in all things, without ever abandoning his own undivided simplicity?[4]

This, surely, was the inconceivable mystery of the divine peace that Dionysius had celebrated and that Maximus now outlined in a sharper, more philosophical way. It is the mystery of a supreme, self-contained simplicity, fully coexisting with the twofold, incomprehensible, and irreversible self-opening of this unity to both the world as a whole and the world in all its particulars. Whenever they seem about to fall on each other in open hostility, the opposing forces of the world always return, in the end, to the form of unity: the individual to the totality, and vice versa.[5] But the unity of God cannot be fully grasped, either in the pole of a particularizing individualism or in that of a faceless totalitarianism that melts all particularity down. Within the world, unity is only visible as the "fluidity of love", as the inconclusive, incomprehensible convergence of opposites. This is the way Pseudo-Dionysius

---

[2] *Ambigua*; PG 91, 1256B.

[3] Scholion on *The Divine Names* 1; PG 4, 208C.

[4] *Ambigua*; PG 91, 1257B.

[5] See the bizarre but pointed comparison used by John of Scythopolis in the scholia to Pseudo-Dionysius: *In De Div. Nom.* 4; PG 4, 269C.

had described our longing desire for God: as the melting of the individual to a fluid state and, at the same time, as the solidification of what, in that individual, is irreplaceable and particular. In the world, there is always a polarity between "participators and the participated, but that is not so in God".⁶ Yet this polarity that binds active and passive together and forces both of them into a reciprocal giving and taking, this inner movement, is the underlying rhythm of being in the world and is therefore also the precise place where God is present, where his incomparable otherness appears. All created being "moves completely or else is moved, causes or is caused, contemplates or is contemplated, speaks or is spoken, . . . acts or is acted upon".⁷ In this state of their being formed for each other, in their relatedness (σχέσις), Maximus sees the basic characteristic of all the things that exist in the world.⁸ It is not as if passivity were produced in some way by a principle opposed to God, as ancient Greek and Gnostic thought imagined—not as if it flowed out of nothingness, out of some kind of original matter that formed the underlying stuff of the world; it is also not as if beings in the world come closer to God to the degree that they lay this passivity aside and are taken up into the pure act which God is. Rather, the very passivity of creatures comes from God, is inseparably tied to their createdness, and is not pure imperfection because even being different from God is a way of imitating him. So to the degree that the creature comes closer to its own perfection, its passivity is also made perfect; and its perfection is the pure state of "undergoing God" (παθεῖν αὐτόν —that is, τὸν Θεόν),⁹ a state in which, as we will see, its "activity" is also perfected.

So God reveals himself as equally superior to the more "passive" material world and the more "active" intellectual world, regardless of the fact that the mind reflects him more brightly than does matter. His being is "absolutely inaccessible, equally so (κατὰ τὸ ἴσον) to visible and to invisible creation".¹⁰ The "difference between uncreated and created nature is infinite (ἄπειρον)"¹¹ and grows ever greater and less controllable. This is reflected in the fact that the perfection of the

⁶ *In De Div. Nom.* 4; PG 4, 252C.
⁷ *Ambigua*; PG 91, 1296A.
⁸ So *Centuries on Knowledge* I, 7; PG 90, 1085B; *Ambigua*; PG 91, 1153B.
⁹ *Ambigua*; PG 91, 1296D.
¹⁰ Ibid.; PG 91, 1288B.
¹¹ Ibid.; PG 91, 1077A.

creature can only be expressed in the paradox of its complete "disappearance" before God (as the stars disappear before the sun),[12] a process that implies at the same time its full establishment as a creature and even its "co-appearance with God".[13]

God's immanent name, then, is the name Being; his transcendent name is the name Not-being, in that he is not any of those things we can speak of as being. The second of these names is more proper to him, since such negation means a reference to God as he is in himself, while an affirmation only refers to him in his activity outside of himself. This is not contradicted by the fact that Maximus, along with the tradition reaching from Philo to Gregory of Nyssa, says we can only know God's *existence*—know *that* he is[14]—not his *essence,* or *what* he is.[15] For this "being" of God has not, in itself, any conceptual content; it lacks even the notion of concrete immediacy implied by "existence" in the created sense.[16] Thus affirmation and denial do not contradict each other here:

> Negation and affirmation, which stand in opposition to each other, are happily blended when it comes to God and come to each other's aid. The negative statements that indicate that the Divine is not "something" —or better, that tell us which "something" is not God—unite with the affirmative statements whose purpose is to say what this Being, which is not what has been indicated, really is. On the other hand, the affirmative statements only indicate *that* the Divine is, not *what* it is, and so are closely tied with the negative statements whose purpose is to say what this Being is not. So long as they are simply taken in relation to each other, then, they show the opposition we call *antithesis* (ἐξ ἀντιθέσεως); but when they are referred to God, they show their intrinsic interdependence in the fact that these two poles mutually condition each other (τῷ εἰς ἄλληλα τῶν ἄκρων κατὰ περίπτωσιν τρόπῳ τὴν οἰκειότητα).[17]

This linguistic shell game reveals, in fact, that our words only describe our creaturely efforts to speak of God and so cannot bring the

---

[12] Ibid.

[13] *Centuries on Knowledge* I, 79; PG 90, 1113 B.

[14] [In German: "nur das Da-Sein oder Dass-Sein".]

[15] *Ambigua*; PG 91, 1216B; cf. 1129A; 1288B.

[16] [German: "Denn dieses 'Sein' ist selbst kein begrifflicher Inhalt, es fehlt ihm alles Inhaltliche, das noch im weltlichen Sinn von 'Da' enthalten ist." Balthasar is playing here upon the implications of the "Da" in "Dasein", which in Heideggerian terminology is used to denote the concrete, historical existence of an individual being.]

[17] *Ambigua*; PG 91, 1288C.

One who is utterly other into our field of vision. Even negative language, which in itself—without the anchoring of affirmation—only
points into the void, does not directly lead toward the transcendent
God. He lies far beyond both modes of knowing.

> He who is and who will be all things to all—and who exercises this
> role precisely through the things that are and that will come to be—
> is in himself no part of the realm of things that are and come to be, in
> any way, at any time, nor shall he become so, because he can never be
> categorized as part of any natural order of beings. As a consequence of
> his existence beyond being, he is more properly spoken of in terms of
> not-being. For since it is indispensable for us to recognize the difference,
> in truth, between God and creatures, the affirmation of what is above
> being must be the negation of all in the realm of things that are, just as
> the affirmation of existing things must be a negation of what is above
> being. Both of these ways of speaking must, in their proper sense, be
> applicable to him, yet on the other hand neither of them—being or not
> being—can be applicable in a proper sense. Both are applicable in their
> own way, in that the one statement affirms God's being as the cause of
> the being of things, while the other denies it because it lies, as cause, so
> infinitely beyond all caused being; on the other hand, neither is properly
> applicable, because neither way of speaking presents us with the real
> identity of what we are looking for, in its essence and nature. For if
> something cannot be identified as either being or not being in terms of
> its natural origin, it clearly cannot be connected either with what is, and
> what is therefore the subject of language, or with what is not, and what
> is therefore not the subject of language. Such a reality has a simple and
> unknown mode of existence, inaccessible to all minds and unsearchable
> in every way, exalted beyond all affirmation and denial.[18]

The point of all this dialectic is first and foremost to make clear
that no neutral, common "concept" of Being can span the realities
of both God and creature; the analogy of an ever-greater dissimilarity
stands in the way, preventing all conceptualization of the fact and the
way they are. So the "not" cannot be bracketed away from "being"
for the briefest instant of our reflection: if one were to try and hide
it even for a moment when considering the essence of the creature,
it would immediately appear, with commanding force, on the side of
God. Of course, this dialectic of being and not-being preserves its life
and color only as long as we are reflecting on the relationship of God

---

[18] *Mystagogia*; PG 91, 664AC; cf. *Moscow Centuries on Knowledge* 1 (ed. Epifanovich, 33).

to the world—relationships of nearness and distance, of immanence and transcendence. As soon as the thinker tries to detach himself from these relationships and to project himself into the realm of the Absolute, everything becomes gray, every tangible shape melts away.

Dialectical movement does not grasp God. It must simply limit itself to the statement of opposites: in one and the same moment, God "goes forth out of himself and remains within himself". And even this is simply a statement about the relation of the world to God, for God only "goes forth" and "moves" in that he causes motion, God "remains in himself" only in that he causes stable identity.[19]

> God is the one who scatters the seeds of agapē (charity) and eros (yearning), for he has brought these things that were within him outside himself in the act of creation. That is why we read, "God is love", and in the Song of Songs he is called agapē, and also "sweetness" and "desire", which are what eros means. For he is the one who is truly loveable and desirable. Because this loving desire has flowed out of him, he—its creator—is said to be himself in love; but insofar as he is himself the one who is truly loveable and desirable, he moves everything that looks toward him and that possesses, in its own way, the power of yearning.[20]

Insofar as it is both eros and agapē, the divine mystery is in motion; insofar as it is loved and longed for, it moves all that is capable of eros and agapē toward itself. To put it more clearly, the divine mystery is in motion insofar as it endows beings capable of longing and love with an inner share in its own life; on the other hand, it moves other beings insofar as it stimulates the longing of what is moved toward it, by means of its very nature. Or again: God moves and is moved, thirsting that others may thirst for him, longing to be longed for, loving to be loved.[21]

This dialectic of motion and rest teaches us no more than the dialectic of being and not-being. It simply brings us, once again, back to the focal point of this polarity within creaturely existence, where the creature's precise difference from God and his precise similarity with God stand inseparably linked. For in the path of historical existence lie both the creature's powerlessness and his vitality. This is the ultimate

---

[19] See John of Scythopolis, *In De Div. Nom.* 5; PG 4, 333CD.
[20] Ibid., 4; PG 4, 265CD.
[21] *Ambigua*; PG 91, 1260C.

reason why there is, in Maximus' ontology, no absolute affirmation or
negation and why the "superessential light" remains a "dark radiance".

2. *Divine Unknowing*

Evagrius left us a saying that summarizes classical Greek teaching on
mystical knowledge, from Philo to Maximus: "God cannot be grasped
by the mind; for if he is grasped, he is surely not God!"[22] Gregory of
Nyssa and Augustine say similar things, as does Maximus: "Whoever
has seen God and has understood what he saw, has seen nothing!"[23]
Even the saints never saw God's face.[24] "[God] is rightly called 'sunlight' and not 'the sun' itself. For just as we cannot look directly into
the sun, but at best at its rays, so we can neither think of God nor comprehend him."[25] Only by recalling to our minds the great attributes
of creatures in the world does God give us hints of himself: "In himself, God is not known; insofar, however, as he is origin and end of
all things, he is the simplicity of the simple, the life of the living, the
superessential essence of essences, and finally the fulfillment of all that
is good."[26] So Maximus repeats the advice of Gregory of Nyssa: μὴ
πολυπραγμόνει, "Do not search like a busybody into what the essence
of God might be!"[27]

Even our knowledge of creatures is simply a movement from subject
to object, or from the process of thought to the thinker who sustains
it and who is never identical with the act of thinking;[28] so it is a kind
of suspension between poles that never come together in simple identity. "To comprehend accurately even the least of creatures is beyond
the power of our reason"; we understand only general qualities, never
the unique, existent subject that lies beneath these qualities.[29] In an
emotional excursus, Maximus repeats the long warnings of Basil and
Gregory of Nyssa against the childish rationalism of the Eunomians;

---

[22] PG 40, 1275C.
[23] *In Epistula Dionysii* 1; PG 4, 529A.
[24] *In Coel. Hier.* 4; PG 4, 56BC; ibid., 13; PG 4, 96C.
[25] *In De Div. Nom.* 1; PG 4, 188A.
[26] Ibid.; PG 4, 193B.
[27] Ibid.; PG 4, 192B.
[28] *Centuries on Knowledge* 2, 2–3; PG 90, 1125CD.
[29] *Ambigua*; PG 91, 1224D–1229A.

he praises the unknowability of the world and the miracles, far exceed-
ing all comprehension, that lie hidden in the unfathomable depths of
the least of its parts. Only such a sense of reverence can be the true
presupposition for knowing the far more unknowable God.

> For the divine mystery is utterly without parts, because completely with-
> out quantity, . . . without characteristics, . . . completely simple . . . and
> without distance from us, . . . without limits, because completely free
> of movement, . . . and without relatedness. That is why it is, in ev-
> ery respect, ineffable and mysterious and why it remains, for all who
> stir themselves toward it with a seemly reverence, the ultimate limit of
> knowledge, possessing really only one characteristic we can know with
> certainty: that we do not know it as it is.[30]

This lack of knowledge is not an empty indifference, not a lack of interest. It is an encounter with the inconceivable, an encounter that lies
above all conceptual knowing and becomes all the more intense, the
closer this inconceivable mystery comes. "The Divine is inimitable,
without comparison; for to the very degree that one makes progress
in imitating and comparing oneself to God, one experiences how impossible imitation and comparison are."[31] This constant balancing of
"however much" and "to that degree" (ὅσον-τοσοῦτον) reflects the
basic relationship, on the level of ideas, of God and the world. Distance grows with increasing nearness. Fear, hesitation, and adoration
grow with love. Silence increases with the progress of revelation—"that
great, echoing voice of the dark, inconceivable, polyphonic silence of
God", which man begins to perceive "through that other, buzzing,
noisy silence" of his own knowledge.[32] Once one penetrates "into the
innermost noiselessness of God",[33] the silence that lies above the inar-
ticulateness of concepts becomes the only appropriate form of praise,[34]
"pure wonder, which alone describes the indescribable majesty".[35]

And yet there is a genuine way into this mystery. The play of affirmation and negation not only engages God and the world but even
within the world engages its various levels of being. So Paul, perhaps,

---

[30] Ibid.; 1232BC.
[31] In Epistula Dionysii 2; PG 4, 529D–532A.
[32] Mystagogia, chap. 4; PG 91, 672C.
[33] Quaestiones ad Thalassium, prooemium; CCG 7, 21, 75f.; PG 90, 248B.
[34] In De Div. Nom. 1; PG 4, 192C.
[35] Ambigua; PG 91, 1244A.

was initiated into the positive qualities [of the heavenly spirits] through the negation of insight on his part, and through the ecstatic loss of his own natural condition he was able to imitate theirs. For every intellectual nature, in ways that befit its rank and capacities, is initiated into the intelligible condition and positive characteristics of the rank and essence above it, through the loss and the stripping away of itself; in this way, it comes to imitate the higher being. The affirmation of the knowledge of what is ranked above is a negation of the knowledge of what is ranked below, just as the negation of the knowledge of what is below implies the affirmation of what is above. The ultimate goal is to move on through a step-by-step process of negation to the nature and rank that, as the highest of all, is incomparably superior to all others, until one receives that reality as gift, after all the steps and powers have been left behind, in a negation of knowledge that directly involves God himself. This negation cannot be affirmed in a positive sense by any other being, since now there is no further limit or definition that such a negation can once again absorb.

So the knower mounts from level to level, "but he comes to rest (λήγει) ultimately in the ineffable, in the unthinkable, and in the absolutely impenetrable."[36] The only word that remains for this encounter is "unity", since it is no longer "thought": the soul

has nothing left to think about, after it has thought through everything that is naturally thinkable. Beyond mind and reflection and knowledge, it comes to be without thought, without knowledge, without words, and it simply rushes forward to throw itself into the embrace (προσβολή) of God and to be one with him. It thinks no more, it imagines God no more. For God is not an object of knowledge, whom the soul can objectify by some pattern of behavior; rather, it knows him through simple union, without comparisons and beyond thought—in a way that cannot be uttered or explained, and which only he knows who shares this unspeakable gift with his chosen ones: God himself.[37]

Maximus tells us no more about this "divine unknowing". But what he says is enough to let us see which of the two ways of conceiving the divine transcendence—that of Evagrius or that of Dionysius—he prefers. One must, of course, resist seeing the two as sharply opposed to each other; both are Christian thinkers and men of prayer, and neither can be accused of pantheism, despite their Neoplatonic tendencies.

[36] Ibid.; 1240C–1241A.
[37] Ibid.; 1220BC; see also *Moscow Centuries on Knowledge* 72 and 92 (ed. Epifanovich, 48, 53).

But Evagrius finds his way to God by prescinding from all sensible and
intelligible forms: a way that leads to its goal only through committed
asceticism and the consistent practice of contemplation; and that goal
is to allow the mind to emerge into the infinite, divine light of the
Trinity "free from both matter and form". The knowledge of God is
for him no longer objective consciousness; rather, the light of God can
be nothing else but what simply enfolds one, beyond all distinction of
subject and object. In its own light, the purified mind directly perceives
the radiance of the light of God. Hence, the notion of the soul as a
"divine spark" is not far from Evagrius' thought: this pantheistic image
from Stoicism becomes here a way of expressing a Christian truth.

Pseudo-Dionysius, on the other hand, emphasizes first of all the transcendence, the total otherness of God. He emphasizes it so strongly that
all the forms and realms of creation seem to be posited and explained
from the point of view of this boundless elevation of the Divine; the
highest degree of insistence that God is beyond the world becomes
the highest degree of affirmation of the world, the strongest stress on
God's immanence. Here Dionysius can clearly be seen as expressing
the final form of all Christian Platonism, while Evagrius represents
something more preliminary.

If this is true, then one can understand how Maximus can make his
intellectual home basically with Pseudo-Dionysius yet, from this home,
can draw the whole Evagrian system to himself and bring it to a fulfillment that exceeds its own capabilities. One would be wrong, then,
simply to oppose these two approaches to mysticism to each other as
if they were mutually exclusive. Even if Maximus uses the Evagrian
term ἐκδημία, "migration" from the world and from all created reality
toward God,[38] it is not entirely clear—*pace* Viller and Hausherr[39]—
that he is not using it in the Pseudo-Dionysian sense of ἔκστασις, of
"being transported beyond" all creation into the inconceivable reality
of God. Basically, Pseudo-Dionysius' dialectical language and level of
philosophical reflection is simply more fully developed, more refined
than that of Evagrius; his message is the same, as long as one agrees

---

[38] *Centuries on Love* 2, 28; 3, 20. On this term, see Sherwood's introduction to his translation
of the *Centuries: The Ascetic Life: The Four Centuries on Charity*, Ancient Christian Writers,
21 (Westminster, Md.: Newman Press, 1955), 89.

[39] See M. Viller, "Aux sources de la spiritualité de s. Maxime: Les Oeuvres d'Évagre le
Pontique", *Revue de l'ascétique et de la mystique* 11 (1930): 156–84, 239–68; I. Hausherr, "Ignorance infinie", *Orientalia Christiana periodica* 2 (1936): 351–62.

that Evagrius, too, may not be presumed a pantheist, even though the "knowledge" (*gnōsis*) of God (*theologia*) [in his system] may not be taken in an objectifying sense.

Maximus' first concern is to preserve God's transcendence. Accordingly, he stands at first, especially in his major works, completely by the side of Pseudo-Dionysius. At the end of the passage we quoted just above, he expresses the concern not to identify with God that "infinity, into which the whole movement of the world and the mind finally empties itself, where thought breathes itself away and the water we swim in drains away. For infinity is surely something that comes from God, but not God himself, who is beyond even it to an incomparable degree."[40] If Maximus emphasizes, perhaps more strongly than Pseudo-Dionysius, the ascending line from sensation to mind, from stage to stage, it is because he is more strongly influenced by the Alexandrian theology of the Logos and its sense of a transforming upward movement [toward the divine mystery]. Still, he is aware that at the end of this ascent, of these progressive revelations, the divine mystery will not be revealed—as in Evagrius' system—as the naked core of Being; rather, the bottomless abyss of divine freedom and sovereignty, and the corresponding lowliness of all that God has created, will first of all yawn before us as an unbridgeable chasm.

Of course, Maximus also encounters, in this unapproachable midpoint of being—more consciously than does Pseudo-Dionysius—the simple, original idea of the world, divested of all its robes of multiplicity: the Logos, the "dawning realization" (*cognitio matutina*) of all things. In this respect the Neoplatonic image of the center of a circle receives, in his thought, a slight twist in the Alexandrian direction. "As in the center of a circle we see the indivisible point of origin for the straight lines that go out from it, so the one who is worthy to be found in God comes to know in him all the preexistent ideas of the things that have come to be, in a simple and indivisible act of knowing."[41] In this respect, too, Maximus comes closer than Pseudo-Dionysius to Hegel's principle, "The mystical is the speculative."[42]

But even if this convergence in God of the ideas of the world does, in the end, also open up the possibility of a scientific and "system-

---

[40] *Ambigua*; PG 91, 1220C.
[41] *Centuries on Knowledge* 2, 4: PG 90, 1125D–1128A.
[42] *Philosophie der Religion*, ed. G. Lasson (Leipzig, 1927), 2:235, n.

atic" theology (and not just a theology of images and likenesses, as
in Pseudo-Dionysius); even if thought, for Maximus, always takes the
form of a quest that sweeps through all the world's realms in search
of self-forgetting union in God; even if his style of thought is thus,
necessarily, one of a progressive synthesizing of poles, tensions, limited differences, all of which—when thrown into the melting pot of
the Logos—are meant to rise from his fire as complete, simple wisdom: still he realizes, with utter clarity and certainty, not only that this
unity can never be the result of our own laborious ascent, but also that
God always remains something infinitely other than the unifying idea
of the world. Only this certainty explains the tendency of Maximus'
thought, in contrast to the oversimplifications of Origen and Evagrius,
to conceive of the particularity and mutual nonidentity of things as
something final and positive—his horror of "mixing, as the pagans do,
what ought not be confused".[43] Note how far into the realm of mystical
speculation the echoes of the Chalcedonian formula have penetrated!
The highest union with God is not realized "in spite of" our lasting
difference from him, but rather "in" and "through" it. Unity is not the
abolition of God's distance from us, and so of his incomprehensibility;
it is its highest revelation.

This is also clear in the way Maximus describes the Incarnation of
the Logos. Far from taking away our ignorance of God, the Incarnation
increases it, in that the Unknowable One has here revealed himself as
he is. It is true, certainly, that "otherwise creatures would never have
conceived of the Creator, whose nature is infinite and inconceivable."[44]
But it is still more true that

> he was not subjected to nature or made a slave by becoming human;
> rather, he has elevated nature to himself, by transforming it into a second
> mystery, while he himself remains completely inconceivable and has re-
> vealed his own becoming flesh as something beyond all intelligible being,
> more inconceivable than any other mystery. He became comprehensi-
> ble in [human] nature to the very same degree as he has been revealed
> more fully, through this nature, as the incomprehensible One. "He re-
> mained the hidden God, even after this epiphany," says the Teacher [Gre-
> gory of Nazianzen], "or, to put it in a more theological way, even *in* this

---

[43] *Ambigua*; PG 91, 1244C.
[44] *In Psalm* 59; CCG 23, 16, 242–17, 244; PG 90, 868AB.

epiphany. . . ." Even when uttered he remains unspoken, even when seen he remains unknown.[45]

In the revealing of the mystery, then, and in the experience of union, the liturgy of adoration comes to its full celebration.

3. A Thrice-Praised Unity

a. The Blighted Image

Pseudo-Dionysius had wrapped God in "holy veils" so impenetrable that the mystery of his rich inner life was almost entirely inaccessible to theological insight, however much he spoke of that mystery in liturgical terms, with a reverence that did not look for conceptual knowledge. He did this in full self-awareness, all the more so because his method of thought—inspired by Proclus—found triads everywhere, which powerfully invited the speculative mind to interpret them as traces, images, expressions of a triple mode of being at the heart of God. In contrast to the Western Christian Neoplatonism of Victorinus and Augustine, Greek thought found that the productive inner life of the three Persons withdrew more and more completely, not only from the human attempt to contemplate God in the things of the world, but also from mystical experience. While the West, trusting in the inferential ability of the created mind, dared to find the impress and the shadow of trinitarian life in all realms of the world, and later developed these traces in the rich orchestration of the Victorines' trinitarian mysticism, Eastern thought sank deeper and deeper into reverent silence before God as ultimate mystery.

Earlier, in the works of Origen and in pre-Nicene theology in general, the processions of the Divine Persons were conceived as an opening up, a condescension of God to the world: the Son, as the totality of ideas, contained in himself the possibility of multiple being; the Spirit, as "grace", could bring the world to fulfillment. Thus the great categories of being within the world—"existence", "life and rationality", "holiness"—could be interpreted as a directly perceptible reflection of the supreme Trinity. After the Council of Nicaea, which canonized the unity of God and the equality in rank of the Persons, this way of

---

[45] *Ambigua*; PG 91, 1048D–1049A.

interpretation was much more difficult to walk. The Cappadocians developed their thought on the Trinity only in polemical works directed
against Arianism; here, too, the concern was more for protecting the
orthodox formulation of faith than for commenting on its theological
or mystical importance. The important thing was to avoid all appearance of self-contradiction; the dogmatic language of tradition was like
a precious vessel that must not be shattered, because it contained an
unknown jewel. One looks in vain in the spiritual works of the two
Gregories for a genuinely trinitarian mysticism.[46] What happened in
their thinking was that the Son and the Spirit were elevated to the
level of the superessential simplicity of the Father's primordial being;
the door of that being opened for an instant, to let them both in, and
immediately shut again to guard the unsearchable mystery.

Evagrius fought passionately to keep the unity of the divine essence
and the trinity of the Persons from being understood in a numerical
sense: the *three* in God has nothing in common with the worldly number three. So he can again attribute to God the old name that Origen
had reserved for the Father: "monad" and "henad", utter simplicity.
This remains the approach of Pseudo-Dionysius. He knows that the
inner life of God is one of eternal, virginal productivity, but he has not
the slightest thought of peering curiously into the abyss. If faith did
not know of it, nothing in the orderly structure of his hierarchies or
in the structure of created spirit would betray, in his view, the traces
of this mystery.

Here as everywhere, Maximus is heir to his past. He is heir to the
Cappadocians, to Evagrius, to Pseudo-Dionysius; reaching back on his
own beyond them all, he is heir also to Origen. A love for a theology

---

[46] The arguments of Hubert Merki, O.S.B. (Ὁμοίωσις Θεῷ [Rome, 1952], 172) have
convinced me to abandon my earlier contention that the homily on Genesis 1:26 (PG 44,
1327–46) is a genuine work of Gregory of Nyssa: see my *Présence et pensée* (Paris, 1942), 139;
(English translation, *Presence and Thought* [San Francisco, 1995], 169). The homily speaks of
an "image of the Trinity" (τυπικὴ τριάς) in the three parts of the soul (sensual, emotional,
rational), as well as in the soul's role as *psyche*, *nous*, and *logos* (1337A). But Merki remarks
correctly, "Such an interpretation and application of the image-motif to the Trinity is not to
be found anywhere, even by intimation, in all the genuine works of Gregory, even though he
has many opportunities to do so" (175). The whole human person is image and likeness of
the triune God—an image that had been darkened by sin and that is restored to its original
brilliance when it is cleansed by the redemption. This motif is developed in a thoroughly
Plotinian way, in that the *unity* of the created mind remains the leading theme. Cf. Roger
Leys, S.J., *L'Image de Dieu chez saint Grégoire de Nysse* (Brussels, 1951).

that celebrates the inscrutable mystery liturgically is just as noticeable in his thought as in that of Pseudo-Dionysius, so it is not surprising to find in his work traces of the same tendency to remove the triune life of God from any sort of rational speculation. He quotes, in fact, Pseudo-Dionysius directly: "Even if the Godhead, which is exalted above all things, is spoken of in the liturgy as monad and triad, neither we nor any other being *knows* it as monad or triad; but in order that we might celebrate what is supremely one and what is divinely productive in it, in a way corresponding to the truth, we name that which is above every name with these titles."[47]

The clearest expression of this tendency is the fact that Maximus assigns the Trinity to negative theology, while he assumes that positive theology deals with the God of "salvation history", the God who rules the world by providence and judgment. In giving an allegorical interpretation of the Lord's Transfiguration on Tabor, he calls the radiance of his face a metaphor for apophatic theology, while that of his robes—along with the appearance of Moses (as "providence") and Elijah (as "judgment")—represents cataphatic theology. Referring to the first of these, he writes:

> The radiance of the Lord's face [is an image] . . . of negative, mystical theology; according to this approach, the blessed and holy Godhead is essentially and supremely ineffable, unknowable, elevated an infinite number of times beyond all infinity. It does not provide the beings below it with the least trace (ἴχνος: lit., footprint), with the cloudiest conception of itself, nor does it offer any being at all a notion—even a dark hint— of how it can be at once unity and trinity. For it is not for the creature to grasp the uncreated, nor for limited beings to embrace the unlimited in their thought.[48]

Nonetheless, the Christian knows about God's triune being from divine revelation; it is not simply revealed as a "fact" to be believed, but it is revealed already in the "facts" that the incarnate Christ is the revelation of his Father and that the Holy Spirit, who proceeds from them both,[49] is given to those who believe as the spirit who makes them holy and adopts them as children. The Christian, armed with those

---

[47] *De Div. Nom.* 13, 3 (PG 3, 980D–981A), quoted by Maximus at *Ambigua*; PG 91, 1188A.

[48] *Ambigua*; PG 91, 1168A.

[49] Maximus uses and expressly defends the idea behind the Latin *Filioque*: *Opuscula*; PG 91, 136AB.

traditional trinitarian formulas that had been gained at such a price—
"three Persons (hypostases, concrete individuals) in one essence", "a
triple mode of existence (τρόπος τῆς ὑπάρξεως) in one being"—does
not simply stand before a riddle that surpasses the world's understanding or before what is simply that mystery's "way of appearing" in the
world; rather, because the history of the triune God in the world, a
history of salvation and sanctification, is the real restoration of the creature to the Father through the Son and the Spirit, the Christian finds
himself truly "*in*" the Trinity. The Trinity "moves in the spirit that
can make it its own, whether angel or human—the spirit that searches
through it and *in it* for what it really is."[50] And if this searching mind
should attain to God, then it "shares not only in a unity *with* the holiness of the Trinity, but even in the unity that belongs to the Trinity
in itself".[51]

It would be an anachronism, in dealing with a thinker like Maximus (or with any patristic or early scholastic writer), to try to make
a distinction between philosophy and theology when the subject is a
thoughtful interpretation of God and the world and their relationship
to each other, as if to suggest that trinitarian issues are not connected to
the purely philosophical problem of positive and negative theology.[52]
The fact that Maximus grounds both the natural law and the positive moral teaching of the Old Covenant in Jesus Christ, as Word-to-
be-made-flesh,[53] excludes such an approach, as does the way he always
considers all the "philosophical" problems of the emergence and return
of the world exclusively within the concrete, supernaturally grounded
order of sin and redemption. In such a unified view of things, it would
not be at all odd or inconsistent to expect to see traces and images of
the Trinity in creatures, as part of the cataphatic stage of considering
God's appearance, even if such affirmations should be retracted and
denied later on, in the apophatic stage. Nevertheless, Maximus must
have continued to be impressed by the intellectual restraint Pseudo-
Dionysius had imposed upon himself. Other than a traditional and
hasty reference to a triad in the structure of the soul,[54] Maximus never

---

[50] *Ambigua*; PG 91, 1260.

[51] *Ambigua*; PG 91, 1196B.

[52] This is how Sherwood tries to solve the problem: Maximus, *Ascetic Life*, introduction
34, 37.

[53] *Quaestiones ad Thalassium* 19; CCG 7, 119; PG 90, 308BC.

[54] In the homily of Pseudo-Gregory of Nyssa we have already mentioned (above, n. 46), this

speaks of any "vestiges of the Trinity" in other created beings at all. Just as hastily and incidentally, another traditional motif is mentioned in only one place:[55] the conception, dear to Gregory Nazianzen, of the historical unfolding of our knowledge of the Trinity as a divinely planned pedagogical scheme.[56] This notion, too, plays no real role in Maximus' unhistorical style of thought.

To understand correctly the other texts of Maximus we have to consider, one must always keep before one's eyes Pseudo-Dionysius' dialectic of affirmation and negation, but never an opposition between natural and supernatural knowledge of God. The God who "grants to those who love him to be, through grace, what he himself is by nature" does so "that he may be fully known, yet even in that knowledge remain the fully inconceivable one";[57] this assertion is confirmed by the Dionysian way of speaking of ecstatic knowledge of God, which —like that of Maximus here—does not refer to "philosophical", but to Christian knowledge. This formulation, however, stands in the way of any systematic explanation of the processions within God (such as Western theology knows them, but which must not be implicitly projected onto Eastern theology, even as an unconscious presupposition). It is precisely the lack of a conceptual scheme for inner-trinitarian life —however much such a scheme may be, in the end, derived from the structure of created being—which prevents theological thought from following creaturely "images" any farther back than God's action in history: in other words, one is led from them to the God of revelation, but precisely not to God as he is in himself.

Only with this in mind can one make proper sense of statements such as that on Romans 1:18f., where Maximus interprets the "hid-

---

structure is expressed as *psyche*, *nous*, and *pneuma* (PG 44, 1337A); in Maximus (*Ambigua*; PG 91, 1196A) it is *nous*, *logos*, and *pneuma*, conceived as an "image of the archetype", to which, as far as possible, the creature should "conform itself". As a connecting link, Sherwood (Maximus, *Ascetic Life*, introduction, n. 170) mentions Pseudo-Eulogius of Alexandria (or Epiphanius II of Cyprus; see *Theologische Quartalschrift* 78 [1896]: 364). One should notice, also, that this mention of the triadic structure of the soul is made, not in the context of the development of this structure to its full realization, but in that of its rootedness in the unity of the Trinity; this is usually the case, when one is speaking of the creature's being made in the image of the triune God.

[55] *Ambigua*; PG 91, 1261A.

[56] *Orat.* 31, 25–27; PG 35, 160–64; *Orat.* 45, 12–13; (PG 35, 639); cf. Gregory of Nyssa (PG 46, 696–97); Cyril of Jerusalem, *Cat.* 16, 24; PG 33, 953.

[57] *Opuscula*; PG 91, 33D.

den reality of God", which is "seen by reason" in creation, first of all in terms of the eternal ideas that are "mysteriously hinted at" in creatures, then also (as Paul does) in terms of the qualities or attributes of God, "his eternal power and divinity". "In the being (existence) of things, we recognize, through faith, the true being of God"; in the articulation of essences and in their preservation, the divine wisdom; in their natural movement, his vitality. This Dionysian triad of being, wisdom, and life allows us, in Maximus' view, to gain a distant view of the triune God: not in such a way that Being would be allotted to the Father, Wisdom to the Son, or Life to the Spirit, but rather in a way that concentrates us on the Pauline concepts of the "eternal power and divinity" of God. It is, in fact, a marginal note in a strange hand that first brings to closure what Maximus doubtless intended to leave open, by connecting these concepts with the triad life-power-spirit (*zoē, dynamis, pneuma*).[58]

In the course of a great reduction of the five ways from the world to God (essence, motion, distinction, connection, affirmation) to three, then two, then one, the Dionysian triad of being, knowledge, and life once again makes a hurried appearance; it is suggested as a symbol of the Trinity[59] but then immediately disappears in favor of an increasingly strict emphasis on unity, where the person rapt in contemplation mirrors God's unity "like air communicating light". In the *Mystagogia* (chap. 5), where God's unity is presented as a goal to be approached through five syntheses or "syzygies", unity can be reached in one case under the revealing sign of the second Person and in another case under that of the third Person. One kind of unity is conformity to Christ through grace: the process by which man comes to be himself in the "place" of the hypostatic union—the coming-to-be, from the starting point of the Church, of the Jesus who already exists eternally in himself—and then the return, in Christ, of the image to its original, who is God.[60] Another kind of unity is reached through syntheses on the "practical" side of the soul, in its perfection through the Holy Spirit and in the strenuous efforts that come to fulfillment in his grace[61] (corresponding to the christological way to unity mentioned above),

---

[58] *Quaestiones ad Thalassium* 13; CCG 7, 97, 1–6; PG 90, 296CD.
[59] *Ambigua*; PG 91, 1136BC.
[60] *Mystagogia* 5; PG 91, 676BC.
[61] Ibid.; PG 91, 677C.

in which, once again, everything ends in "divinization", and so in a unity that lies beyond intelligible being.[62]

b. Hidden Fruitfulness

This God, of course, is the Christian God, not some empty and abstract, speculative unity; his mystery is pregnant with a life of ineffable fruitfulness.

> In the first (mystical) encounter, God teaches the mind, in the embrace of unity, the reality of his own monadic existence, so that no separation from the first cause may be introduced; but God spurs it on to be receptive to his divine, hidden fruitfulness, as well, by whispering quietly and mysteriously to the mind that this Good can never be thought of without the fruit of the Logos and of Wisdom, the power that makes creatures holy—both of which share in his essence and abide personally in him.[63]

This intrinsically fruitful God is not only the God of the highest goodness, as Plato conceived him, but the God of Christian love. Here erotic love and selfless charity rejoin each other at the highest level, as they do in Pseudo-Dionysius, and the generally indifferent but benevolent providence of ancient philosophy is transformed, almost automatically, to the divine love of the Sermon on the Mount, a love that shows its perfection in being directed toward good and bad alike. It is precisely this love,[64] which draws no distinctions but loves all its fellowmen equally—the distinctively Christian form of love (agapē), then, here distinctively understood as a sublimation of philosophical and contemplative desire—that is, for Maximus, the purest reflection of God, as he has revealed himself in his incarnate Son and in his Holy Spirit. So the unity that the Church realizes on earth is the first and most exalted image of God in the world, precisely as a unity of love.[65] Only this makes it understandable why Maximus sees such a distance between the "narrow, imperfect, and almost insubstantial" Jewish image of God, which, in its emptiness, "approaches atheism",

---

[62] Ibid.; PG 91, 680A–681B.

[63] *Ambigua*; PG 91, 1260D.

[64] Sherwood emphasizes this important point (Maximus, *Ascetic Life*, 29f.) Maximus is implacable in making this demand; in this respect he distinguishes himself from Evagrius, who expressly chooses a different direction (*Praktikos*; PG 40, 1252B).

[65] *Mystagogia* I; PG 91, 664D–668B.

and the Christian God, who for the first time lets his fullness shine forth.[66]

Salvation history is the appearance in time of a loving, triune God; that is why the Father and the Spirit both have a personal role in the Incarnation, even though only the Son has become human. The role of the Father is his "good pleasure", that of the Spirit his "cooperation", while the role of the Son is to "act in his own name". Nevertheless, Maximus immediately emphasizes that

> the Father as a whole was essentially present in the whole Son, as the Son worked the mystery of our redemption by becoming flesh; the Father did not himself become flesh but gave his approval to the Son's becoming flesh. And the Holy Spirit, as a whole, dwelt essentially in the whole Son, not becoming flesh himself but bringing about the mysterious Incarnation along with the Son.[67]

The triune love appears in Christ; as the love of the God who is beyond intelligible being, however, it is not accessible to our thought in any other way than through the Dionysian dialectic.

In the Christian understanding of God, too, the Trinity cannot properly be the object of "scientific knowledge" (in the classical sense of Plato's ἐπιστήμη). For to be concerned with this mystery "is not [to seek] knowledge through explanations (αἰτιολογία) that begin with the superessential cause of all things so much as it is the presentation of the reasons we have in our imagination (δόξα) for praising that cause".[68] *Doxa* here is the Platonic opposite to causal explanation, since causality in God can never be obvious or accessible to our minds. Maximus knows and expressly states that "faith is true knowledge (γνῶσις ἀληθής) based on unprovable principles, because it is the testimony to things that lie beyond both theoretical and practical reason."[69] Nevertheless—in fact, for this reason—he refuses to distinguish between an "absolute" and a "relative" order in God, even though he knows that

---

[66] *Exposition of the Lord's Prayer*; CCG 23, 51, 414–54, 468; PG 90, 892A–893A.

[67] *Quaestiones ad Thalassium* 60; CCG 22, 79, 100–105; PG 90, 624BC; cf. ibid. 63; CCG 22, 155, 167–157, 182; PG 90, 672C; also *Exposition of the Lord's Prayer*; CCG 23, 31, 87–32, 95; PG 90, 876CD.

[68] *Ambigua*; PG 91, 1036B; cf. 1364BC. John of Scythopolis takes note of the ambiguity in Pseudo-Dionysius over whether theology is or is not to be considered ἐπιστήμη: *In De Div. Nom.* 2; PG 4, 213CD.

[69] *Centuries on Knowledge* 1, 9; PG 90, 1085CD; cf. *Ambigua*; PG 91, 1053: "undemonstrable knowledge" (ἀναπόδεικτος γνῶσις).

the Persons are distinct from one another. "The three are, in truth, one: for this is their being. And the one is, in truth, three: for this is their existence. For the one divine Mystery 'is' in a unitary way and 'subsists' in a threefold way."[70]

"This is hard for our understanding", Hegel says, for the basic principle of intelligibility—the abstract unity of number—is here denied. "One applies one's finite categories, counts one, two, three, mingles with one's ideas the unfortunate form of *number*. Yet number is not the point here."[71] Maximus speaks in the same vein: "Whether the Godhead, which is exalted above all things, is praised as Trinity or as Unity, it is still neither three nor one as we know those numbers in our experience."[72] "For the threeness is not in the oneness as an accident is in a substance", and "the oneness is not conceptually distinguished from the particular individuals contained within it as a universal or a genus." "That which is completely identical with itself and without causal dependency is not mediated through relationship, like that of an effect to its cause"; "nor does the Three proceed out of the One, for the Trinity is unproduced and is revelatory of itself."[73] It is no less unacceptable, on the other hand, to think of God's unity as a "synthesis" of threeness.[74] In this way, Maximus' trinitarian theology unfolds in long, seemingly dry, and unyielding formulas, which are really dogmatic litanies inspired by the spirit of liturgy; most of them are intended, in negative terms, to prevent misunderstanding, and in positive terms they simply repeat the complete identity of One and Three, as well as the complete integrity of the three divine individuals (*hypostases*) within the one divine nature.[75] His preference is to emphasize the unity of the Persons in nature and activity and to say no more.[76]

Even in the dogmatic tracts of his middle period, when the theology of the Incarnation kept forcing Maximus to turn to the mystery of God's threeness as a way of clarifying and delineating the

---

[70] *Ambigua*; PG 91, 1036C.

[71] *Philosophie der Religion* (1840), 2:234.

[72] *In De Div. Nom.* 13; PG 4, 412C; *Ambigua*; PG 91, 1185C; 1188AB.

[73] *Exposition of the Lord's Prayer*; CCG 23, 53, 446–54, 460; PG 90, 892CD.

[74] *Mystagogia*, chap. 23; PG 91, 701A; cf. *In De Div. Nom.* 2; PG 4, 220C.

[75] *Centuries on Knowledge* 2, 1; PG 90, 1124D–1125C; *Mystagogia* 23; PG 91, 700C–701B; *Exposition of the Lord's Prayer*; CCG 23, 53, 446–54, 460; PG 90, 892CD.

[76] *Ambigua*; PG 91, 1261B–1264B.

mystery of Christ, he says no more. He does not go beyond what Gregory Nazianzen said; rather, he constantly ducks and parries, constantly draws a ring of silence around the bottomless depths of God. The only exception is when the *Trisagion*, the "Holy, holy, holy" of the liturgy on earth, compels him to allow himself a peek into heaven:

> The threefold cry of "Holy!", sung by the whole faithful people in praise of God, hints in a mysterious way at the union that is to come, our equality with the bodiless intellectual powers; as a result of that union, the single race of men, joined with the powers above in the identity of eternal, tranquil movement around God, will spend its energies blessing and celebrating the threefold face of the single divine mystery, in a threefold canticle of praise.[77]

4. Transformations of the One

a. Elements of the Tradition

New light is shed on Maximus' trinitarian theology through his philosophy of number. Not that Maximus developed such a philosophy himself, to any great extent, for its own sake, or that he made any original contributions to it. Its significance for him lay rather in a strange confluence of quite separate influences and themes, which had a fruitful effect on each other. What we are speaking about is the different ways one can approach the problem of number itself, not the interpretations of particular numbers—something, of course, that Maximus also practiced freely, without intending to introduce new themes of his own.

We can distinguish here three sets of problems, although this is not the place to summarize their complicated history. The first concerns unity and multiplicity in general. For Maximus, the basic sources of antiquity—Pythagoras, Plato's *Parmenides*, the Neo-Pythagoreans— remained outside the picture. For him, the problem was caught up in the tension between the Origenist and Evagrian model of a [human] fall into multiplicity and the Cappadocian and Dionysian speculations about unity. For both groups, unity in the highest sense was something beyond number. But while for strict Origenists, number and multiplicity was an expression of a cosmic fall from grace, so that history became a simple circular movement from unity to multiplicity to unity again,

---

[77] *Mystagogia* 19; PG 91, 696BC.

number for the Cappadocians, and even more for Pseudo-Dionysius, was an expression of the nature of created being itself. The transcendent effect of unity, for the latter thinkers, was precisely to preserve the multiplicity of the world, which hovers somewhere between the unity of partial being and the unity of being as a whole: "You will discover nothing that is not . . . what it is through the One and that is not preserved and perfected by it."[78] Maximus basically chose this second approach, even though he sometimes uses the terminology of the Alexandrians.

A second set of questions is closely connected with this: questions concerning number as movement. The Pythagoreans were aware of such a dynamic within number-series and saw them as organized in an endless "run" from the *monad* (or one) to the *myriad* (ten thousand), the point at which the original unit had reached its "fullness" and the end had come round to meet the beginning again. Philo speaks of the "race" of numbers as if it is a well-known metaphor and compares it to the race around a track within the limits of an arena. He immediately applies the image to finite being, which completes its "limited run" in moving from the original one to the ultimate myriad, both of which are God.[79] In Origen, of course, and even more clearly in Evagrius, there is also a connection between number and movement: the latter is simply the philosophical name for sin and the fall. For that reason, movement is only an unnatural condition of the creature, something that will ultimately end; the very numerical sequence strives to return to a unity that is above number. To Gregory of Nyssa and Pseudo-Dionysius, however, things appear quite different. While Gregory recognizes the finitude of material time and its circular course as essential to its nature, he sees in the created intellect a certain endless movement, which remains in effect despite and alongside this finitude. He does not equate such "finitude" with guilt, nor does he see "rest" simply as the ideal state. The ideal, rather, is a kind of paradoxical unity between rest and movement,[80] which allows both poles to find their validity and their positive meaning. With Dionysius, both centers of this tension receive their final approval, preserved in equal status by the highest unity. He asks:

---

[78] Pseudo-Dionysius, *De Div. Nom.* 13, 3; PG 3, 980C.
[79] *De Plant.* 75–77; ed. Wendland, 2:148–49.
[80] *Life of Moses*; GNO 7/1, 118, 1; PG 44, 405C.

How do things long for peace? For many beings rejoice in being different and special and seem never to want to remain in rest and peace of their own accord. But if one were to say that this is the peculiar bent of every existent being and were to conclude that no being in the world ever wants to lose its own essence, still we will see . . . even here the traces of a longing for peace. . . . And if someone were to say that everything that is moved, too, is not at rest, but that it wants to be moved according to its own particular kind of motion, this, too, is a way of reaching out for the divine peace in the universe, a peace that so preserves each thing that it never deviates from being itself . . . and continues to perform its own operation.[81]

Therefore the absolute One is of such a nature "that it produces, perfects, and preserves everything that is one and everything that is manifold".[82] Here, too, Maximus will essentially follow this second conception of movement: for him, it is always an expression of nature and of its finitude; and if he does occasionally also raise the question of the mystical and eschatological end of all movement and all limits, he does so simply as part of a search for the grace of unmerited self-transcendence toward God.

The third element in this speculation about number is inspired by Christology: more specifically, by the orthodox defense of the Chalcedonian doctrine of Christ's two natures in one person, against the Monophysites. Here Leontius of Byzantium, who was himself relying in this issue on Heraclian of Chalcedon,[83] so laid the groundwork that Maximus could repeat the essential elements of his argument almost unchanged. If one assumes two natures in Christ, the Monophysites had argued, one must divide his being in the Nestorian fashion, for it is the function of number to divide things and to keep them separate from one another. Leontius had provided the appropriate answer: in itself, number is not a reality (πρᾶγμα) at all, much less an activity. It is a "clarifying sign" (σημεῖον δηλωτικόν),[84] which on its own neither separates nor unites.[85] Its peculiar relativity (σχέσις) consists in the fact

---

[81] *De Div. Nom.* 1, 3–4; PG 3, 952BD.

[82] Ibid.; 2, 11; PG 3, 649C.

[83] See J. P. Junglas, *Leontius von Byzanz: Studien zu seinen Schriften, Quellen und Anschauungen,* Forschungen zur christlichen Literatur- und Dogmengeschichte, vol. 7, no. 3 (Paderborn, 1908), 56ff.

[84] *Adversus argumenta Severi* (= *Epilyseis*); PG 86, 1920C.

[85] Ibid., AB.

that it appears, from one point of view, to separate, while from another it appears to unite: "If one considers the units by themselves, from which a number is made up, the number is divided into these units and so broken down; if, however, one considers their totality (ὁμάδα), it is synthesized from them into one." Applied to "natures", number can display both their (relative) multiplicity and their (relative) synthetic unity; applied to the "hypostasis" [= concrete individual], it displays the sheer (numerical) nonidentity of individuals who share the same nature, without giving any hint of the "whatness" of the existing being (*hypokeimenon*).[86] Maximus made this argument his own and developed it further in his own anti-Monophysite writings. The most important point, however, is that in his works the three currents of speculation we have mentioned come together and reinforce each other, as will become clear in what follows.

b. Number and What Is Beyond

Number, in Maximus' view, is neither substance nor accident, neither quality nor quantity, but is essentially a sign, whose function is to indicate quantity.[87] Therefore, it is also not exactly a concept; Maximus calls it "rather a kind of sound and, at the same time, a predicate associated with quantity".[88] It is not a concept, because it is only joined to the expression of a concept obliquely, through the addition of [a number or] an indefinite article. If, then, every being in the world contains in itself two aspects—that of its "uniqueness", through which it stands among other beings without reference to them, and that of its "relatedness", through which it stands toward others in a relationship (σχέσις) either of connection or of separation—then these two aspects are in reality inseparable (since the whole world exists in a context of essential relationships, especially those of the universal and the particular) but are distinguishable on the level of thought. Whether we

---

[86] Ibid., 1913A–D; 1917A; 1920D–1921A. Cf. Leontius, *Adversus Nestorianos et Eutychianos*; PG 86, 1280AB. This fine sense for the difference between qualitative and quantitative distinctions had been absorbed from trinitarian theology (cf. Basil, *On the Holy Spirit* 27; PG 32, 148B). The *De Sectis* takes up Leontius' argument and again refutes the Monophysite position on the divisive character of number (PG 86, 1241D–1244D). This was the bridge that led to Maximus.

[87] *Epistles* 15; PG 91, 561D; *Epistle* 121; PG 91, 473CD, referring to Gregory Nazianzen.

[88] *Epistles* 15; PG 91, 564D.

are conscious of it or not, number accompanies every affirmation of a particular being, in that it sets up a negative boundary against some other being, positing that other being implicitly as one that is "other" than the first.

> As every difference indicates a quantity that implies some aspect of number, because it introduces the conception of *how* a thing is (for what is not quantitative is also not distinguished [from other things], because it is simple in substance and character), so every number indicates the quantity of certain different essences and is based on how a thing is (the essence) or how it exists (the individual). In this way, it introduces the distinction of subjects, but not their relatedness.[89]

The role of number is finished when it has indicated this difference. It cannot express, over and above this, the way in which difference exists concretely, its positive relationship toward others (as union), or its negative relationship away from them (as distinction).

> No number indicates the relatedness of things itself—that is, their separateness or connectedness—but only the quantity of the things spoken of. It conveys only the notion of "how many?" that is proper to quantitative language, not a conception of *how* a thing is. For how could number include the relatedness of things in itself, since that is surely prior to number and can be understood without it.[90]

"It has neither the power to unite nor the power to divide."[91]

In reality, however, things *are* essentially united (or divided). For that reason, the separate consideration of one of these two aspects, being-in-itself and being-related, always remains an abstraction—or better, a "prescinding" (*praecisio rationis*).[92] "Distinction and unity are in fact not the same thing, although they hold good for and are predicated of the same subject and are even qualities of the same subject."[93] Number, we may conclude, does not belong to the realm of "essences", "for no one has ever made use of number to define something."[94] But it also does not indicate, in any genuine sense, the mode of existence of

---

[89] *Epistles* 12; PG 91, 477A. [The words "the essence" and "the individual" in the second-to-last sentence represent von Balthasar's interpretive additions.]

[90] Ibid.; PG 91, 476C.

[91] *Epistles* 13; PG 91, 513A; cf. 473D.

[92] Κατὰ μόνην τὴν θεωρίαν τὸν ἀριθμὸν παραλαμβάνοντες: ibid.; PG 91, 477B.

[93] Ibid.; PG 91, 480B.

[94] *Epistles* 15; PG 91, 564C.

things, in either unity or separation. One can say, surely, that synthesis "makes" things one and analysis "makes" them two, but also that, on the other hand, synthesis need not eliminate the duality of the things united and analysis need not destroy the unity of the separate things. This is precisely what makes it clear that number cannot be included unequivocally either in the realm of essence or in that of existence (ὑπόστασις, ὕπαρξις). If it is simply a sign, as we have said, it is also simply an instrument: "The Fathers thought they could not find any other form of expression so well suited to denote difference. But if someone were convinced he had a more practical way, . . . we would gladly yield to his learning."[95]

To express nonidentity, one has to use one of two "signs", depending on the aspect one wants to point to. "To indicate unification, we do not use the same term of reference as we do for distinction . . . , but rather we keep the meaning of what we are trying to indicate quite separate."[96] Unity and multiplicity are equally necessary to describe created being in its peculiar ontological character of identity and difference. Maximus, therefore, emphasizes again and again that no created being is Being-as-such, but rather that it is being qualified by temporal and spatial characteristics (πῶς εἶναι), and therefore also that it is quantified being.[97] For this reason, God is not "Being" but beyond being, because being necessarily includes multiplicity.[98] Yet this "many", as Maximus explains along with Pseudo-Dionysius, is always such only because of unity.[99] And such a dialectic is possible only if multiplicity and unity are not simply juxtaposed indifferently, but if their conceptual opposition is the expression and sign of a movement, a "becoming".

In practice, Maximus understands numbers greater than one as expressing a movement of unity, just as he conceives everything that is

---

[95] Epistles 12; PG 91, 480D–481A.

[96] Ibid.; PG 91, 477C. Numerability, which reveals itself in the accidents of a subject, also applies, to a certain extent, to the ontological substance of the thing itself, but this does not mean that it destroys its unity. A parti-colored stone reveals a quantitative multiplicity, which is not only externally related to the unity of the stone's existence (μοναδικὸν τῷ ὑποκειμένῳ: 476B), as simple "appearance" (φαντασία: Opuscula; PG 91, 169B), but which is applied to that unity itself as a kind of mode of being (modus), without introducing a multiplicity of substances (485C; cf. Epistles 13; PG 91, 513D–516A). Here one can see the puzzlingly indefinite character of number.

[97] Epistles 12; PG 91, 485C.

[98] In De Div. Nom. 13; PG 4, 412C. (The attribution of this passage is uncertain.)

[99] Ambigua; PG 91, 1313A.

not divine, on the level of Being, as reality in the state of dynamic becoming:

> The myriad is the monad in movement, and the myriad without movement is the monad. . . . The end of the monad is the myriad, and the beginning of the myriad is the monad.[100]
>
> For the beginning of all nonidentity (*dyas*) is the monad, and if the monad is not without origin, it also cannot be without movement. It moves, in fact, by means of numbers; it starts from atomic units and moves toward a synthetic unity, and then—by dissolution—into atomic individuals. That is its being.[101]

The series of integers is, therefore, nothing more than the progressive synthesis of an originally simple, undeveloped unity.[102] In the section on "Being and Movement", we will attempt to show how much this movement, in the realm of simple signs, reflects the meaning of the being that is signified.

All created being is on a finite course between its origin and its end. But precisely the movement of numerical signs warns us against taking this course in too simple and too unidirectional a way. For if the series of numbers from the monad to the myriad, by means of synthesis, seems to be the dominant direction of this movement, still the reverse course, from the myriad to the monad by means of analysis, stands beside it; and this course, too, rushing from multiplicity back to simple unity, has its corresponding meaning in the realm of being itself—in fact, it often seems to be, for Maximus, the real direction of meaning in the world's history. That suggests, however, that the movement of created being is no longer discernible in an unambiguous way; it can only be conceived as a shuttling back and forth within the bounds of finitude, while genuine unity withdraws beyond the circle of creation into the realm of the inconceivable. So "every created thing has the divine and ineffable monad, which is God himself, as its origin and its end, because it comes forth from him and ultimately returns to him",[103] and so moves in a closed circle. But this is only possible because the point of contact between the unity of the atom and the unity of the great synthesis remains completely beyond all the phases of becoming.

---

[100] *Quaestiones ad Thalassium* 55; CCG 7, 489, 150ff.; PG 90, 541C.

[101] *Ambigua*; PG 91, 1185B.

[102] Σύνθεσις γὰρ μονάδος εἰσὶν οἱ εἰς πλῆθος ἀριθμοί: *In De Div. Nom.* 13; PG 4, 409B.

[103] *Quaestiones ad Thalassium* 55; CCG 7, 489, 153ff.; PG 90, 541C.

True unity is no number at all, because it contains no movement.[104] It is "neither a part nor the whole nor relatedness"; it has, as its root, "no more ancient origin, from which it takes both its motion and its unity of being". And while this genuine unity is absolute Being, no reality corresponds to the numerical unit, taken by itself. The numerical unit "does not express a reality but points in a direction".[105] It does not adequately represent either the unity of God or the unity of the creature, which is never achieved but always only in process. For if the unity of the atomic individual indicates "existence" or the "subject", such an existent subject is only found as the bearer of a necessarily generic nature; its unity is thus never separable from the manifold web of other existences and other natures. And if synthetic unity points to "essence", still no universal essence ever exists except in a series of nonidentical individuals, whose unity is divided, not by some metaphysical afterthought, but in the depths of its being, and so is robbed already there of its simplicity.

At this point, we can take a step beyond what Maximus himself said and draw the conclusion that the two real "poles" that are at stake in this dialectic of unity—"person" (existence) and "nature" (essence)—are simply abstractions, even in this pure state. For if one could think through, without contradictions, their implications as *pure* principles of Being, that very possibility would make them something absolute, not simply aspects of created being. Just as the two forms of created unity fundamentally include each other and dynamically proceed into each other—even if they do reveal genuinely different tendencies of Being-as-becoming—so the same must be said about the poles essence and existence. Both of them, too, are only identical in a transcendental "Being-beyond-being"; their disintegration on the level of Being corresponds to the realm of "distention" (διάστασις), of nonidentity, and thus acts as the root of quantity within finite being. Later, when we are dealing with Christology, we will have to investigate more closely how Maximus understands this real distinction between existence and essence.

Thus the unity that lies beyond the created world is the ultimate principle of every number: "God is the creator and the inventor even

---

[104] "Only the monad is genuinely without movement, because it is neither number nor numerable (Μονὰς δὲ μόνη κυρίως ἀκίνητος, ὅτι μήτε ἀριθμός ἐστι, μήτε ἀριθμητόν)": *Ambigua*; PG 91, 1185B.

[105] Οὐ γὰρ ὡς παραστατικὸν πάντως, . . . ἀλλ᾿ ὡς ἐνδεικτικόν: *Ambigua*; PG 91, 1185B.

of number."[106] Therefore "every number participates in unity—that is, in God. . . . Even if you begin counting with two, you at least take *one* two as your starting point." Thus it is true, on the one hand, that the transcendental unity "cannot be added, in a natural way, to another, as can the number one"; it is not affected by number at all.[107] "Neither is it the highest genus of things—for genera are necessarily subdivided into species—nor is it, in the true sense, a point or an atom, for they retain a natural relationship to other points and atoms."[108] On the other hand, this unity is so immanent in every number that one must speak, with Pseudo-Dionysius, of a "multiplication of God".[109] At this point, the whole theory of unity returns to the simple scheme of an analogy of being between God and the world: to the absolute transcendence of God and his immanence in created being. God is, on the one hand, "beyond unity";[110] on the other hand, "unity, as the cause of numbers, includes all numbers in itself in a unitary way, just as the center or point contains the straight lines of the circle."[111]

In light of this, we can better understand Maximus' reticence in attempting to grasp the Trinity conceptually. Anything one could say about it would always be based on number and could never attain the absoluteness of the Divinity or its identity of essence and being. Number is itself only a sign, not an actual conception of created being; so its application to God is doubly dark and fragmented. In the end, we can only say with Pseudo-Dionysius, "He is neither trinity nor unity."[112]

---

[106] *In De Div. Nom.* 13; PG 4, 408D. (This text, and the following six texts cited, are uncertain in their attribution.)
[107] "The One is incapable of being affected" (τὸ ἓν ἀπαθές): ibid., 412AB.
[108] Ibid., B.
[109] Ibid., 409B.
[110] Ibid., 408D.
[111] Ibid., 5; PG 4, 321C.
[112] Ibid., 13; PG 4, 412C.

III

IDEAS

1. Ideas in God: A Critique of Pseudo-Dionysius

a. The Ontological Approach

Since Philo and the Gnostics, the transcendence of the divine mystery was hedged in defensively by a kind of heavenly court of principalities and powers. In Plotinus, it was protected by the power of the Nous (Mind), which took its place firmly between the divine One and the World Soul. The holy dance of created beings around the unapproachable mystery at the heart of things was taken over from Plotinus and Philo by Pseudo-Dionysius, and with it came the step-wise "emanations" of God outward toward the world, spreading themselves out like ripples in a pond.

This theme of emanations, however, is only a secondary one in the works of Pseudo-Dionysius and withdraws into the background to make room for the graduated hierarchy of personal beings. To adapt the doctrine of the overflow of the One—first into the fundamental principles of being and life themselves, then into individual beings— as a full component of Christian philosophy, certain of its emphases had to be shifted. John of Scythopolis[1] accomplished this soon after the Pseudo-Dionysian corpus appeared. He deliberately uses the expression "ideas" and interprets them as "God's thoughts". But he is careful, too, to underline their ontological character: they are, in themselves, identical with God's essence—in other words, with Being itself —and therefore they reveal, on their own and in an archetypal way, the essential *and* existential being of creatures. These divine ideas are, in John's approach, also the fundamental principles of the world's being: "Being-in-itself", and so on. John prefers, in fact, to characterize them as the intelligible raw material (ὕλη) of things. This should not be understood, however, in a pantheistic sense, since John speaks much more clearly than Pseudo-Dionysius does of creation from nothing.

---

[1] See Hans Urs von Balthasar, "Das Problem der Dionysius-Scholien", *Kosmische Liturgie*, 2d ed. (Einsiedeln: Johannes-Verlag, 1961), 661–63 [see appendix below].

The major task in the Christian adaptation of Pseudo-Dionysius' system was already finished, then, when Maximus came on the scene. His interpretation of the Pseudo-Dionysian scheme of potential being moves in the same direction as that of John of Scythopolis but is more elaborate and more complicated. He attempts to solve the riddle of the participation of things in God's ideas from various points of view: those of philosophy, epistemology, and mystical theology.

The basis for these interpretations is the "abyss" (χάσμα) that yawns between uncreated and created nature. It can only be bridged by a free creative act of God, not through some impersonal "seepage" or—as the Origenists suggested—through the sinful disintegration of the ideal cosmos' original unity. A further implication of this assumption was that the general principles of created being could no longer simply be considered identical with God's ideas. Gregory of Nyssa had described the essence of these general principles in an original and profound way, at least as far as they concerned the whole of humanity. He interpreted the Platonic "idea" in terms of the Aristotelian and Stoic notion of the "universal" (καθόλου), which meant both the dominant unity and the ground of the being of all individuals categorized under it as well as their collective, final reality.[2] In this way, the notion of "totality" was completely transformed into a principle of created being and took on a real existence in concrete things. Maximus expands this conception, which had until then been developed only for the totality of humanity, and made it into a general philosophical axiom; he saw the basic struc- ture of the world as a dynamic tension between universal (καθόλου) and particular (καθ' ἕκαστον) being. Obviously this took away from the category of the universal the other-worldly halo that it had had as divine idea and root of the world's being. In Gregory, the "world of ideas" had, in fact, also disappeared, which resulted in various serious crises, some of them on the level of epistemology.[3] It had appeared again, however, in Pseudo-Dionysius, due to Neoplatonic influences, and Maximus retains it: the "ideas" are the basic outlines, in God, of his plan for the world, the preliminary sketch of the creature within

---

[2] See Hans Urs von Balthasar, *Présence et pensée* (Paris, 1942), pt. 1; English translation; *Presence and Thought* (San Francisco: Ignatius Press, 1995), 27–108.

[3] See E. von Ivánka, "Vom Platonismus zur Theorie der Mystik: Zur Erkenntnislehre Gregors von Nyssa", *Scholastik*, 1936, 163–95; von Balthasar, *Présence et pensée*, 140f.; English translation, 171f.

the Spirit of God, and thus something quite different, in themselves, from created "universals" (καθόλου).

Nevertheless, at this point Alexandrian speculation about the Logos intersects with a simply linear conception of the divine plan. By conceiving of the Logos—as Origen had done—both as the second Person in God and as the locus of the divine ideas, Maximus is led to conceive the world as an unfolding of the unitary divine Idea and so comes close to the idealist notion of an "economic" return of all things in the world to their Idea in God. This theme echoes at various times in Maximus' works, but it was only Scotus Erigena who was to develop it into a dominant preoccupation and wrap the Christian view of the world in the cloak of Neoplatonic pantheism—something essentially alien to Maximus' thought. Even though the formulation occasionally sounds similar, the spirit of the two systems is completely different. In what follows, we shall treat only of Maximus' doctrine of ideas and will save his theory of universals (the καθόλου) for a later chapter.

> With God, the ideas (λόγοι) of all things are firmly established; because of this, one says of God that he knows all things before they come to be, for they are in him and with him insofar as he is the truth of all things. This is true, even though the totality of things—things present and things to come—have not been brought into being contemporaneously with their being known by God; rather, according to the wisdom of the Creator, individual things have been created in an appropriate way at the proper time, in correspondence with their ideas, and receive concrete, active existence in themselves (καθ᾽ ἑαυτὰ εἶναι τῇ ἐνεργείᾳ λαμβάνῃ). For the Creator is always-existent-Being; they, however, exist first of all only on the level of possibility, not yet on that of reality. For the infinite can in no way stand on the same level of being (τῶν ἅμα εἶναι) as finite things, and no proof can show that essence (οὐσία) and the superessential share the same kind of being, or that measure and the immeasurable can be put in the same class, or that the relative can be classed with the absolute, or the being about which no categorical statement can be made with the being that is constituted by all the categories. For all created things are defined, in their essence and in their way of developing, by their own ideas (λόγοι) and by the ideas of the beings that provide their external context; through these ideas they find their defining limits.[4]

---

[4] *Ambigua*; PG 91, 1081AB.

From this passage, it is clear that God's ideas are neither identical with his essence—for they are not immediate and infinite being in the same sense as God is—nor do they coincide with the existence of things in the world (not even with universals [καθόλα]), which are their realization. This remains essentially true, even when—as we will presently see—the twofold relation of ideas to God and to the world amounts to a twofold appropriation, almost to a reductive identification.

On the one hand, we are confronted with the question of the unity of ideas in God. This unity *must* be presupposed, insofar as the origin of the plan of world history is God, who is utterly simple.

> If the highest, negative theology of the Logos is taken in its transcendent aspect, by which we can neither speak of him nor think of him but recognize that he is none of the things we know because he is above intelligible being and is not shared by any being in any way at all: that is how the many ideas of the single Logos [must be understood].[5]

In this, most elevated sense, the phrase "Be what you are", as an invitation to conform one's existent being to the idea God has of it, is identical with the call to follow the Son of God.

> The substance of all the virtues is the Lord himself, as it is written, "He became for us, from God, our wisdom, our righteousness, our holiness, and our redemption" (1 Cor 1:30); obviously, this must be understood of him in an absolute sense: he is the original wisdom, the original righteousness, the original holiness, and not in some limited sense, as we men are when someone calls one of us wise or righteous. Every human being, then, who comes to share in some virtue by firm habit, certainly participates in God, who is the substance of all virtues.[6]

Maximus thoroughly works out the implications of this thought in his theory of the immanence of the Logos in the intelligible structure of God's commandments (λόγος τῶν ἐντολῶν);[7] there is a corollary to it, also, in his conception of the "liberation" of the Logos from perceptible and even intelligible natures through "natural contemplation" (θεωρία φυσική).

But it would be a mistake, as we have already said, to emphasize this

---

[5] Ibid.; CD.
[6] Ibid.; D.
[7] For example, in the *Centuries on Knowledge*.

line of thought to such a degree that it were to take on pantheistic implications. The concentration of the ideas of the world in the Creator
does not mean the dissolution of the world into God but simply points
to the ultimate, underlying source of all intelligible multiplicity. The
relationship of the ideas to God is that of supremely free production,
not that of a necessity of nature. This becomes clear in the way that
God knows the ideas. "I do not believe", writes Maximus, "that any
reverent person should suppose that the things that were previously
contained in the endless might of God's foreknowledge as ideas, God
learns in detail through their coming into existence."[8] In this context, Maximus quotes a saying of Pantaenus, the [supposed] teacher
of Clement of Alexandria,[9] in reply to a pagan critic who argued that
God knows sensible things in a sensual way and intelligible things in
an intellectual way:

> God neither knows sensible things in a sensual way nor intelligible things
> in an intellectual way. For it is not possible that the one who is above
> all existent things should know things in a way corresponding to their
> being. Rather, we say[10] that he knows existent things as the products of
> his own acts of will; . . . for if he created all things by his will, and if
> no one will deny that one must, in all justice and piety, allow God to
> know his own will, . . . then God must recognize things as the products
> of his will.[11]

Any other solution would introduce passivity into God and, by doing
so, would commit an anthropomorphism. But that does not mean that
God only knows things in general—as the Neoplatonists assumed—
and is unaware of them in the most particular aspects of their individuality. For the idea of a thing is its "truth";[12] this is just as much the
case for particular things as for things in general. It is precisely this
movement into absolute particularity, which is realized with the final

---

[8] *Ambigua*; PG 91, 1328C; cf. *Moscow Centuries on Knowledge* 6 (ed. Epifanovich, 34): "He
himself is the one who knows all things and has precise, subsistent foreknowledge of them
before they come to be" (ἑαυτὸ γνῶσκον πάντων ἔχει καὶ πρὸ γενέσεως αὐτῶν ὑφισταμένην
κυρίως τὴν πρόγνωσιν).

[9] On the philological details of this text, see J. Draeseke, "Zu Maximus Confessor",
Zeitschrift für wissenschaftliche Theologie 47 (1904): 250–59. The passage seems to come from
Clement's work *On Providence*; cf. Stählin 3:224.

[10] Here Maximus seems to take over again and to complete Pantaenus' thought on his own.

[11] *Ambigua*; PG 91, 1085AB.

[12] Ibid.; PG 91, 1081A.

constitution of individual things, that is the real miracle of providence and the reason it is so inexplicable.[13]

Alongside this identification of the world of ideas with the sovereign will of God stands another identification that seems opposed to it: that of ideas with existent things. Here, our first task is to establish the exact meaning of this relationship. The world of ideas for Maximus (as also for the earlier Fathers) is, first of all, not at all simply a world of simple, unrealized possibilities; it is restricted to the ideas of things that exist: "The things for whose essences ideas preexist with God are those things that, in God's plan, are to come into existence."[14] Therefore the ideas are also called "divine willings", "divine predispositions". It is very significant that Maximus represents the Incarnation of the Logos and the whole historical course of the world's salvation as both a primeval idea of God and as the underlying structure of his overall plan for the world[15] and that he designates the mystery of the Cross, grave, and Resurrection [of Christ] as the basis and goal of all creation.[16]

The world of ideas, in fact, does not only have the same extension as the world of existent things; in a certain way, it is limited by these things and depends on them. After Maximus has established that the ideas of things in God are precisely the ideas of things that are to be created, he continues:

> The things that are to come into existence, however, according to God's plan, have their essential existence in such a way that they cannot turn back again, from being into nonbeing. But if things that have once come to be do not turn again, in their core of being, from existence to nonbeing, their ideas must be solid and unchangeable; they have God's Wisdom as the one and only source of their being, from which they come and from which also they have the power to remain firmly anchored in being. But if the ideas of things are firmly founded in God, then the will of God, who has created all things, must be changeless in their respect, . . . for he wills that what he has once determined, with his Word and his Wisdom, shall be forever.[17]

---

[13] Ibid.; PG 91, 1193AB.

[14] Ibid.; PG 91, 1329B; cf. John of Scythopolis, PG 4, 320BC. For Gregory of Nyssa, see *Présence et pensée*, 140f.; English translation, 171f.

[15] *Quaestiones ad Thalassium* 60; CCG 22, 73–75; PG 90, 621A.

[16] *Centuries on Knowledge* 1, 66; PG 90, 1108AB.

[17] *Ambigua*; PG 91, 1329BC.

Between the ideas, then, and the existence of things there is a certain reciprocal dependence, a sort of circular motion, which lays the foundation for existence in the idea, as God's decision, and then assures the eternal endurance of the ideas on the basis of the enduring solidity of existence itself. Maximus even attempts to explain bodily immortality through this line of thinking. Both levels of reality, ideas and existence, have their roots in the single will of God. In this view, the ideas appear, in fact, as the ultimate metaphysical grounding for existence itself, and the full development of existence through freedom and the self-realization we call virtue is, on the other hand, nothing else than the realization and attainment of the ideas.[18]

The transcendental relationship between ideas and existence thus resembles the relationship, within the created realm, between particular and universal being, although they are not exactly the same thing: in both relationships, prominent emphasis is given to the positive role of the individual thing, of existence, rather than to a Platonic overestimate of the ideal order. In Pseudo-Dionysius there is not only "being in itself", "life in itself", "similarity in itself", but also "dissimilarity in itself". The difference between things does not simply come from their inability to imitate God's self-identity; it is one of the great and positive motifs in God's creative plan. "By inequality (ἀνισότης) he means the difference that is found in every creature from all other creatures, and he emphasizes that God's righteousness has come to the defense of this inequality. It is certain that there is also a natural inequality [among things]."[19] For nonidentity, as "that which distinguishes" (ἀφοριστική), is also a constructive element (συστατική) in the world's being.[20] God "gives to all things the ability to endure and to remain both in existence and in intelligible being."[21]

We must, then, keep this in mind when, on the other side, Maximus emphasizes the absolute simplicity of the divine Word[22] and suggests the possibility of reaching, in the highest level of contemplation, the point where all the ideas of creation are united in God, as the center of all the circle's radii.[23] Dominant here is the Pseudo-Dionysian notion

---

[18] Ibid.; PG 91, 1329A.
[19] *In De Div. Nom.* 8; PG 4, 368D.
[20] *Ambigua*; PG 91, 1400C.
[21] *Opuscula*; PG 91, 36D.
[22] *In Coel. Hier.* 3; PG 4, 49B.
[23] *Centuries on Knowledge* 2, 4: PG 90, 1125D–1128A; *Ambigua*; PG 91, 1081C.

that "in divine things, the unities are stronger than the differences."[24]
So Maximus says, "Everything in God is to be considered as identical,
even if in its natural being it is not identical, for God is, in an identical
way, . . . the cause of all things."[25] The cause—but not the substance!
Therefore the final identity of things is not simply God but just as
truly their shared status as *not* being God;[26] the reduction of what is
unlike to a state of identity is not a reduction of existence to ideas, and
also not simply a reduction of the creature to God, but is, finally, the
union of all the intelligible principles (*logoi*) of the world's creatures
in the Word (*Logos*) of God, made man, who brings together in his
own free unity as an individual two different things: the identity of all
the world's ideas in God's essence and their identity with each other
as creatures (that is, in *not* being God). For this reason, the incarnate
Word—in his personal freedom and also as God's basic idea in creating
the world—is the identity of identity and nonidentity.

b. The Epistemological Approach

Along with these philosophical reflections, which try to correct what
could be interpreted as emanationism in Pseudo-Dionysius' writings,
Maximus took other steps to move beyond philosophical Platonism.

The first step was in an epistemological direction. At the end of *The
Divine Names*, Pseudo-Dionysius once again defended against misinter-
pretation his theory of potential being and explained that the primal
potencies, such as "being in itself", "life in itself", "divinity in itself",
can be understood in two ways: in terms of origin (ἀρχικῶς), they are
nothing other than God himself; in terms of participation (μεθεκτικῶς),
however, they are

> the powers of providence, which radiate outward from God, whose
> being cannot be communicated: the communication-of-being-in-itself,
> the gift-of-life-in-itself, divinization-in-itself, all powers in which things
> participate according to their natures. . . . Therefore it is said of God
> that he graciously gives being to first principles, next[27] to totalities-in-
> themselves, next to partial-beings-in-themselves, next to things that par-

---

[24] Pseudo-Dionysius, *De Div. Nom.* 2, 11; PG 3, 652A.

[25] *In De Div. Nom.* 8; PG 4, 373D.

[26] *Ambigua*; PG 91, 1312B.

[27] In his translation of this passage, J. Stiglmayr, Bibliothek der Kirchenväter, 2d series, vol.
147, reads εἴτε ["either"] instead of εἶτα ["next"], which completely confuses its meaning.

ticipate in them in a total way, next to things that participate in them in a partial way.[28]

This hierarchy of powers is Pseudo-Dionysius' last word on the essence of creation.

Maximus, however, attempts to give these stages of being an epistemological justification. If Pseudo-Dionysius calls God "pre-being" and "super-being", Maximus explains,

> he is attempting by this to explain that God's being is completely without origin and inconceivable and that he has established the general being of all things in advance, through the preliminary plan of his own ineffable knowledge. For the created mind encounters this being [of God] first of all when it is focused on some thing, and only afterward does it come to know *how* the thing is. When Dionysius speaks of being-in-itself, he is referring to being as such (τὸ ἁπλῶς εἶναι), not to being in some way (τὸ πῶς εἶναι); so later, when he speaks of life-in-itself, of similarity-in-itself, and similar concepts, he means the general character of life or life without qualification, not a life that is specifically determined in this or that way, and so on."[29]

> First of all the thing itself comes into our awareness; then, as a second step, its general concept—for instance, life or substance considered quite generally; and only after that do we grasp the particular, that is, form a concept of the individual, specific essence existing for itself, as for example an angelic or human life.[30]

All of this brings the ontological process of Pseudo-Dionysius down to a series of phases of consciousness, which begin with a general, confused first impression of reality (πρᾶγμα) and gradually grow clearer in content until they reach the full knowledge of the individual object. What flashes upon us "in an undivided way" (ἀμερίστως) "in the first encounter" (ἐν τῇ πρώτῃ προσβολῇ) is not some empty general concept of being—a contradiction in terms!—but a revelation (*logos*) concerning the Monad (περὶ Μονάδος), the unity of that being that truly is one: a *logos* that instructs the thinking mind that God and the world are undivided and so makes possible all thought of things different from God, whether they are universal or individual beings. All this is good epistemology and has nothing to do with ontologism.[31]

[28] *De Div. Nom.* 11, 6; PG 3, 856A.
[29] *In De Div. Nom.* 5; PG 4, 317C–320A.
[30] Ibid., 11; PG 4, 401AB.
[31] *Ambigua*; PG 91, 1260D.

Maximus knows another solution to Pseudo-Dionysius' problem, but he does not work it out with full consistency. This solution understands the general principles of participation, not as the elementary features of created being, but as the purely supernatural participation in God through grace, in the order of redemption. With this in mind, he distinguishes between God's "works begun in time", from which God will "rest" at the end of time, and his "supertemporal" works, which he carries on in eternity. To this second category belong goodness, supernatural life, immortality (in the supernatural sense of that incorruptibility or ἀφθαρσία which the Greek Fathers generally conceive as a gift of grace), simplicity, stability in the good, infinity, virtue, and holiness.[32] For there never was a time when God did not perform these "works", since they are part of his own essence. Here Maximus happily transposes the Platonic notion of participation, which Pseudo-Dionysius applied to created being as such, to the sphere of the supernatural—of grace. At one point, it is true, he interrupts this train of thought and includes "essentiality" (ὀντότης) among God's eternal works:[33] something that can perhaps be interpreted as meaning that he is thinking here of the absolute Being that belongs to God eternally, the sharing of which (becoming *participes divinae naturae*) is grace itself.

These three distinct ways of interpreting Pseudo-Dionysius' principles do not contradict each other. If we attempt to see them in an integrated way, it will become clear just how Maximus distances himself from all hidden forms of pantheism, ancient as well as Christian (for example, Erigena).

In commenting on Paul's phrase, "in whom we live and move and have our being" (Acts 17:28), Maximus explains that man

> *is* in God in his concern not to violate the idea of his own existence that preexists in God; he *moves* in God, in conformity with the preexistent idea of goodness that God has, when he acts virtuously; he *lives* in God, according to the preexistent idea in God of his own eternity. Insofar as he is irrevocably one with himself, even here on earth, in his integrity of action, and will be so in the world to come through the gift of divinization, he loves the ideas that preexist in God—or rather he loves God, in whom all ideas of the good are securely grounded, and embraces them tenderly. So he becomes "part of God": as one who *is*, because of

---

[32] *Centuries on Knowledge* 1, 48–50; PG 90, 1100C–1101B.
[33] Ibid.; PG 91, 1101B.

the idea of his being that is present in God; as one who *is good*, because of the idea present in God of his being good; as *God himself*, because of the idea present in God of his eternal being. He honors these ideas, he acts according to them; through them, he translates himself completely into the realm of God alone and represents and expresses only God in all that he is, so that he both is and is known to be God, by grace, and so that God, in his condescension, both is and is known to be man in him.[34]

From this passage it is clear: in God, the idea is God himself, and as man lives out his own idea, he lives himself into God and lives God into himself; in that sense, he becomes a "part of God" (μοῖρα θεοῦ). Yet when he loves his own idea, he does not, in the end, love himself —even his better self—but God. And God, who opens up to man this idea of himself as the "space" of his existence, also gives himself freely to him, in grace: man's divinization takes place through the love of God (διὰ τὸ φιλόθεον); God's hominization takes place through the love of man (διὰ τὸ φιλάνθρωπον). So the connecting link, not mentioned up to now, must finally be put into place, to anchor the whole process: "For always, in all things, God's Word, who is God, has willed to accomplish the mystery of his Incarnation."[35]

Maximus' integration contains several important principles: (1) the free origin of the ideas in God as Creator, since he is not internally compelled, on the basis of his essence, either to will to create or to form the ideas; (2) the anchoring of the idea of the world in God's prior decision—which is, as we have said, free—to divinize all creation (θέωσις) in giving it eternal existence (ἀεὶ εἶναι), an action that, against the prospect of humanity's fall into sin, takes the form of the Incarnation of God's Word; (3) the rooting of the intelligible principles (*logoi*) of all individual things, by nature and by grace, in the divine Logos, thanks to which things—even in their concrete reality —are from the start genuinely immanent in God (and therefore are akin to each other in the divine Logos), and the divine Logos is immanent in all of them. Maximus' Platonic conceptuality is radically extended by Aristotelian and Stoic assumptions: the logos of things, in natural terms, is the unchanging "law" of their behavior, variable only in their "mode" (τρόπος) of being, in the "how" of existence. Yet

---

[34] *Ambigua*; PG 91, 1084BC.
[35] Ibid.; PG 91, 1084CD.

insofar as God's providence is free, and limitlessly superior to nature, the logos or law of providence always takes priority over the logos of nature and cannot be derived from it—an anti-Stoic contention! This explains why Maximus distinguishes so carefully between "reflection on existing things" (θεωρία τῶν ὄντων) and "reflection on providence and judgment" (θεωρία προνοίας καὶ κρίσεως). But since a Christian view of reality always fixes on God's original idea, Christ, in every individual being—and will continue to gaze on him more and more —Maximus knows of no exclusively empirical or philosophical kind of reflection. Rather, all insight into being is insight into a reality that is both historical and supernatural: for historically it is the same Logos who becomes flesh in both the law of nature and the law of Scripture —in the salvation history, that is, that moves from the Old to the New Covenant. He moves along both roads toward his Incarnation.

The freedom of God's ideas opens the way for us to recognize that the existence of things is absolutely underivable from their ideas in God. Maximus, the christological thinker, is fully aware of this un-bridgeable gulf—as opposed to Neoplatonism, the Stoics, and Scotus Erigena, who nimbly dodge the problem. "Everything" comes into being "at the right time"; this is not the same as being "as eternal as its idea,"[36] and the relationship of the eternal ideas to existence in time is, within the realm of God's utterly free choice, beyond our compre-hension.[37]

This grounding of created being in the divine Logos also solved the urgent question of the "reduction" of all intelligible principles of being (logoi) to the one Logos. Here there is no reduction in the Asiatic sense of a dissolution [of beings in the divine], but rather the "unconfused union" (ἕνωσις ἀσύγχυτος) of the Christian theology of the Incarnation and of human divinization centered on Christ.[38]

---

[36] Ambigua; PG 91, 1081A; Quaestiones ad Thalassium 2; CCG 7, 51; PG 90, 272A.

[37] Centuries on Love 4, 1–6; PG 90, 1048B–1049A. This was a timely issue, since Maximus was opposing here the pagan Neoplatonism of Ammonius Hermeiou [early sixth century], who taught that the ideas in God guaranteed the eternity of the world.

[38] Ambigua; PG 91, 1077C. On this subject of logoi and Logos, see I.-H. Dalmais, "La Théorie des 'logoi' des créatures chez s. Maxime le Confesseur", Revue des sciences philosophiques et théologiques 36 (1952): 244–49.

2. Ideas and the World: A Critique of Origenism

a. Correcting the Myth

Origen's name appears in the writings of Maximus as seldom as does that of Evagrius. The master, who had so often been condemned and who now was only useful to the integralists as a straw man, had one of those names that could no longer be mentioned in support of an orthodox idea. That Maximus, however, had read him carefully, and valued and admired him deeply, is evident from his *Centuries on Knowledge*, where he once again gathered the most personal thoughts of the great spiritual writer and handed them on namelessly to posterity. He did Evagrius the same service in the *Centuries on Love*. It was chiefly through Maximus, in fact, that Origenist spirituality made its way into the Eastern tradition, as it found a home in the West thanks to Jerome, Ambrose, and Cassian.

Maximus filtered Origenism, however, and removed its poisonous fangs. His main work—the commentary on Gregory Nazianzen [the *Ambigua*]—begins almost directly with a long philosophical and theological polemic against Origenist cosmology; this polemic is perhaps the only important anti-Origenist document in Greek patristic literature[39] that rejects the doctrine of the henad with sympathetic understanding rather than with a judgment of heresy, managing instead to overcome its weaknesses from within and to detach the grain of truth from it in the process. One part of the polemic is directed against the idea that all created spirits originally existed in a stability (στάσις) centered in God, that all movement began with the fall into sin, and that that movement continues endlessly, to its own misfortune, for ceaseless new ages; the other part attempts to point out the myth's positive meaning.[40]

According to his [Origenist] opponents, then, Maximus explains, there once existed "an original henad of rational beings, as a result of which we would have had a stable and permanent existence of

---

[39] "A refutation perhaps unique in Greek patristic literature": Polycarp Sherwood, *An Annotated Date-List of the Works of Maximus the Confessor*, Studia Anselmiana, 30 (Rome, 1952), 3.

[40] *Ambigua*; PG 91, 1077B, makes the contrast clear: "Concerning the fact that the henad he prattles about does not exist . . . ; but concerning the way in which we, being sharers in God, have flowed outward from him . . ." (περὶ μὲν οὖν τοῦ μὴ εἶναι τὴν θρυλομένην Ἑνάδα . . . περὶ δὲ τοῦ πῶς μοῖρα ὄντες Θεοῦ ἀπερρύημεν . . .).

natural relationship with God; but movement is supposed to have
started, through which these rational beings were scattered into multiplicity and moved God to take the step of creating this bodily world,
with the purpose of enclosing them in bodies as a punishment of their
previous guilt."[41] Let us, for the moment, leave aside the anthropological arguments Maximus presents, following Gregory of Nyssa, against
the independent preexistence of some part of the human reality, which
surely must be regarded as an indissoluble unity of body and soul. The
main proof of the absurdity of this myth of the world's origins lies
elsewhere: the idea that creatures were originally without motion is
contradictory in itself. For the conceptions of origin and immovability
exclude one another, or rather they oppose one another without being
at all related.

> It cannot be squared with the truth to propose that becoming is prior to
> stability, since stability is of its nature without motion; but it is equally
> impossible to posit stability as the consequence of a motionless becoming
> or to equate stability and becoming. For stability is not a potential con-
> dition of becoming, . . . but is rather the end stage of the realization of
> potency in the development of created things. To put it briefly: stability
> is a relative concept, which is not related to becoming but to motion,
> of which it is the contradictory.[42]

The Origenists, then, confuse the meaning of being when they conceive of stability as the product of becoming and of movement as the
product of stability. The real direction of the meaning of being can
only lie in the sequence: becoming, movement, stability (γένεσις—
κίνησις—στάσις). For "everything that takes its being from nonbeing
is also in movement, because it is directed toward a final cause."[43] Only
when it has reached this goal, and has completed its ontologically pre-
programmed course from potency to actuality, can one speak of its
coming to rest.

The relationship of coming to be and movement, on the one hand,
and of movement and rest, on the other, is analytically true for Maximus and the basis of all created ontology.

> Before we think of any natural movement of things, we must think of
> their becoming; but movement must naturally be presupposed as prior

---

[41] *Ambigua*; PG 91, 1069A; cf. ibid., 1089CD, 1100B.
[42] Ibid., PG 91, 1220CD.
[43] Ibid., PG 91, 1069B.

to all rest. . . . Therefore it is impossible for becoming and rest to come into existence at the same time, since they are naturally separated from each other through the middle term of movement.[44]

Origenism, which proposed such a contemporaneous existence [of motion and rest], thus forces movement from its natural place and isolates it; in doing so, it exposes creation to unending restlessness and, hence, to despair. So despite its seductive mysticism, Origenist thought is basically tragic: "That spirits are so shifted about and can neither have nor hope for an unshakeable basis for remaining firm in the Good: What could be greater reason to despair?"[45] For even though "movement," and thus [the possibility of] falling away, may be conceptually compatible with really reaching the goal of the vision of God, still "if God can be abandoned once for the sake of experiencing (πεῖρα) something different, there is no adequate reason why this should not repeat itself over and over."[46]

Here is the real heart of the controversy. The metaphysics of Origen's *On First Principles* was, in reality, a metaphysics of πεῖρα: a necessary, if also a painful, "experience" of sin and distance from God. This seemed to be the only way to imbue the soul with enough of a sense of dependency, and of longing for the lost blessings it once had, to prevent it—at least for a long time—from falling away from God again. We have shown elsewhere how much this theory is influenced by Origen's intellectualism and from the old Platonic tradition of the "daimons".[47] Gregory of Nyssa took the decisive step beyond this tragic attitude when he linked movement naturally, on the one hand, to becoming, but excluded from the eternal vision of God even the possibility of a "satiety" (κόρος), of "boredom", as something unthinkable. This vision, it seemed to him, would be so utterly fulfilling that it brought with itself an eternal, blessed longing for more. Still, for Gregory eternity retained, for that very reason, a kind of kinship with the present condition of becoming; the "leap" from the one to the other was more evident in the assertion than in the reality.

---

[44] Ibid., PG 91, 1217D.

[45] Ibid., PG 91, 1069C. Augustine made exactly this point against the Neoplatonists and characterized the "eternal return" as another way of making the pains of hell eternal: *De Civ. Dei* 12, 20.

[46] *Ambigua*; PG 91, 1069C.

[47] See Hans Urs von Balthasar, *Parole et mystère chez Origène* (Paris, 1957), 113–16.

If Maximus was to reject the metaphysics of experience (πεῖρα), he also had to reveal, at the same time, the positive philosophical content of Origen's notion of permanency as well as to root out the last vestiges of the canonization of human striving from Gregory's ideal of a blessed eternal yearning.

> If they say to us that the intellects *could* have [adhered to the divine goodness], but simply *would* not do so, because they wanted to experience something different, then Beauty, in their eyes, would not be a good necessarily worth desiring simply because of itself, because it is beautiful, but would only be [desirable] because of its opposite—not as something loveable absolutely, through its own nature.[48]

Over and over, down to Hegel and Berdyaev, this speciously deep thought was to haunt Christian metaphysics: that love without pain and guilt remains simply a joke, a game.[49] Led astray through the theatrical dimensions of the Incarnation and the Cross, which exhaust the possibilities of dramatic encounter between God and the world, people think they may take what can only be beyond history and reinterpret it as a metaphysic of created being in itself. Even if Maximus himself, in other contexts, sometimes threatens to succumb to this danger,[50] he recognized it clearly here and discovered the most thoroughgoing means of overcoming it: he gave the concept of motion a new fundamental interpretation. While motion, for Origen, rested completely on the creature's undetermined freedom of will, and while this freedom, due to its extreme instability, was doomed to plunge the creature sooner or later into sin, motion for Maximus is fundamentally an orientation of nature, which as such is good. The freedom of the creature is no longer elevated to some quasi-divine height and left there completely by itself; it rests on the solid base of nature, whose previously indicated direction it simply has to realize for itself. So movement, for Maximus, is even less a matter of restless yearning than it is for Gregory of Nyssa; rather, it consists in allowing oneself to be carried by another in the depths of one's being and to be borne toward the ocean of God's rest.

---

[48] *Ambigua*; PG 91, 1069C.
[49] See G. W. F. Hegel, *Phänomenologie des Geistes*, ed. Lasson, 2d ed. (Leipzig, 1907), 13.
[50] See below, chap. 5, sec. 6: "The Sexual Synthesis".

b. The Truth of the Myth

Before we turn to describing this motion, we ought to point out the positive interpretation that the Origenist myth receives from Maximus. For him, the Origenist problem is a pointer toward the ideas: the original *henad* of the intellects is, in reality, the unitary existence of created ideas in the Logos. What man, who

> has considered wisely the beings brought by God from nonbeing into being, who has directed his soul's imagination intelligently toward the endless variety and range of natural things and has turned his questing eye with understanding toward the intelligible model (*logos*) after which things have been made, would not recognize the one Logos as a multiplicity of *logoi*, in consequence of the irreducible differences of created things, which are distinguished both by their reciprocal otherness and the unmingled identity of each with itself? And again, who would not recognize the many *logoi* as the one Logos, who through all the process of drawing all things upward (ἀναφορά) to himself remains unconfusedly himself, as the essential and individually distinctive divine Logos of God the Father, the origin and cause of all things, "in whom all things were made, things in heaven and things on earth, the visible and the invisible, thrones, dominations, principalities, and powers: all things were made from him and for his sake" (Col 1:16). For because he possessed the ideas of things from all eternity, as consistent parts of his holy will, he created visible and invisible creation from nothing, according to them.[51]
>
> The very same [Logos] is therefore, through his infinite superiority, ineffable and inconceivable in himself and exalted beyond all creation and beyond the distinctions and divisions that are valid and recognized in it; he is similarly revealed and multiplied in all the things that have their origin in him, with the degree of beauty appropriate to each being, and so he sums up all things in himself.[52]

So the problem of the original unity of the world, and of its diffraction into multiplicity, is resolved into the simple structure of analogy between God and the world.

This structure, however, contains within it a new problem: how "the idea" of the creature, as his complete perfection and integrity in God, can be related to his existence simply in and for himself.

---

[51] *Ambigua*; PG 91, 1077C–1080A.
[52] Ibid., PG 91, 1077AB.

One can (Maximus continues) call every reasonable or understanding mind, whether angel or human, a part of God, with reference to the idea according to which it was created and which is in God and with God, for that is what it is. . . . If it were to move according to this idea (*logos*), it would exist in God, in whom the idea of its being preexists as its original source and cause. And if its efforts and its longing should willingly prefer nothing to its own original source, then it would not depart from God but would rather itself be called God and a part of God because of its striving upward to him, since it partakes of him in an appropriate way.[53]

This is the curious position of the creature: that it is ontologically incapable of seeking itself and the fulfillment of its own intelligible structure without at the same time reaching out toward what is other than itself, without loving the infinite reality that lies at the root of its own radicality. So a fulfillment of the creature within the world's terms is unthinkable for Maximus; and since his thought moves, from the start, within the frame of reference of a world elevated by grace, he likes to conceive the breakthrough from the level of one's "personal" idea to that of the "idea in God" and "as God" in terms of a transition from the realm of nature, the "world", to that of grace or of God. The distance between mere "existence" (εἶναι) and "idea" (λόγος) is lessened through the realization of free intellectual acts, through which the potentiality of existence is both realized and qualitatively enhanced;[54] concrete being "draws near" to its idea through "natural motion" (διὰ φυσικῆς κινήσεως ἐγγίζοντα). Yet to the same degree that this approximation is realized, the idea vanishes into the realm of transcendence and no longer appears as a naturally attainable goal of striving, but rather as grace; the "correspondence" of concrete existence and the idea, which is impossible on the level of nature because the idea is essentially timeless and the creature essentially historical, can only come about through a completely transcendental initiative of God, in which the idea is revealed simultaneously as brought back to its ultimate root in God himself. In the sinner, who has not pursued this effort to its root, essentially the same transcendental revelation of God as his radical reality takes place; but it leads to his punishment and torment as a gap

---

[53] Ibid., PG 91, 1077BC.
[54] "Through the qualitative and quantitative motion of choice" (κατὰ τὴν ποιὰν καὶ ποσὴν τῆς προαιρέσεως κίνησιν): ibid., PG 91, 1329A.

that has not been filled and across which he can not participate in the ideal order.[55]

In the Logos, then, all the individual ideas and goals of creatures meet; therefore all of them, if they seek their own reality, must love him and must encounter each other in his love. That is why Christ is the original idea, the underlying figure of God's plan for the world, why all the individual lines arrange themselves concentrically around him. The truth of the Origenist myth thus becomes clear: the teleological goal of the world may indeed be projected backward into a prehistorical world, provided this is not taken as a real existence before our birth but rather as the ideal, timeless superexistence of all beings in their divine idea—an existence that contains in itself, by anticipation, the essence and existence of all creatures in a superessential, superexistential way.

> One Logos is many *logoi*, and the many *logoi* are one Logos. According to the creative and sustaining movement of the One outward into the world, in a way that is appropriate to God, the One is many; according to the thoughtful, pedagogical elevation of the many to the one, in God's providence, as if to the ultimate cause of all things or to the center of the straight lines that proceed out from him . . . , the many are one.[56]

So the Origenist conception of a "descent" from an original unity finds its justification, either as a primordial nonidentity between the idea in God and existence outside of God, or else through the sin—not something necessary, but a fact of history—of those creatures who "have not acted according to the idea of themselves that exists beforehand in God".[57]

This attempt to correct Origenism still does not bring us to Hegel, or even to Scotus Erigena. The rhythm of the Godhead's emergence and return is not at all a necessary, metaphysical process, contained within the very concept of God, but rests on his free decision and is controlled by his will. God himself remains, even in the emergence of the world, irreducibly absolute, "through his own immeasurable superiority the inconceivable and ineffable one".[58]

---

[55] Ibid., PG 91, 1329AB.
[56] Ibid., PG 91, 1081BC.
[57] Ibid., PG 91, 1081C.
[58] Ibid., PG 91, 1080A.

So even if God is, for Maximus, indistinguishably the origin and the end of created movement, this is no more pantheistic than his philosophy of union, which included a movement of number from the atomistic unit to a synthetic unity. What seems to be circular from God's point of view, because the beginning and the end are the same, can appear just as authentically as genuine development and movement, from the standpoint of the world: the course of loving movement toward "the ideas that preexist in God, or better: toward God himself".[59] The dimension of free self-realization allows us to pass from the state of being simple natural images (εἰκόνες) of God to an intellectual self-possession that is truly God's likeness (ὁμοίωσις), and so to fulfill the original plan of God, who created us "in the image and likeness" of himself.[60]

This entry of the world into God, however, is only perfectly achieved through the Incarnation, through the hypostatic union realized there between created and uncreated nature, by which the two of them become "one and the same" (ἓν καὶ ταυτόν).[61] Maximus expressly says that the Incarnation—more precisely, the drama of Cross, grave, and Resurrection—is not only the midpoint of world history but the foundational idea of the world itself.[62] The Redeemer is the borderline between all sensible and intellectual motion.[63] For him all the ages were established, along with everything they contain; this synthesis of God and the world is a divine idea, which is older and more deeply hidden than all things and for which everything else remains simply an approach, a means of achievement.[64] And because Maximus does not intend to demonstrate a necessity [for the Incarnation] in the metaphysical sense, but rather [to point to] the meaning of history itself—*all* history!—he also includes the historical process of sin in this supreme synthesis. Seen from God's point of view, sin and rebellion are the

---

[59] Ibid., PG 91, 1084B.

[60] Ibid., PG 91, 1084A; on this subject, see M. T. Didier, "Les Fondements dogmatiques de la spiritualité de s. Maxime le Confesseur", *Echos d'Orient* 33 (1930): 296f.

[61] *Ambigua*; PG 91, 1097B.

[62] *Centuries on Knowledge* 1, 66–67; PG 90, 1108AB. In the [modern] controversy on this subject, this text was not given sufficient consideration; see H. Straubinger, *Die Christologie des hl. Maximus Confessor* (Bonn, 1906), 126–30.

[63] *Quaestiones ad Thalassium* 62; CCG 22, 131; PG 90, 656D.

[64] Ibid. 60; CCG 22, 75; PG 90, 621B.

world's last word: they make possible the greatest conceivable work of love and carry with them God's death in the world, as the revelation of the triumphant life in which he pours himself out in response.

It is here, for the first time, that Maximus' work of correction can be seen in the full breadth of its implications. As soon as motion (*kinesis*) is no longer seen simply (in Platonic fashion) as a sinful falling away but is seen (in Aristotelian fashion) as the good ontological activity of a developing nature, the highest ideal [for existence] can also be transformed from a Gnosis that conquers the world by seeing through its reality into a loving, inclusive affirmation even of finite things. Now finitude is no longer evil; now union with God, from which we come and which, in the end, we hope to regain, no longer includes the destruction of all the boundaries between beings. This union, in fact, may not be imagined here as a concept that excludes differences but as a concrete idea that includes particularity. Synthesis, in reference to both God and man, can now be reinterpreted primarily in terms of a love rooted in freedom: both the Incarnation of the Son and his commandment of love, which brings to full realization the idea of humanity, presuppose and generate freedom.

As a result, the great Evagrian categories for interpreting the world, κρίσις (judgment) and πρόνοια (providence), have become obsolete, in their original meaning, and can be used in a new and different way. Κρίσις can now no longer mean the banishment of intellects into bodies, as the sentence imposed in response to their turning from God; πρόνοια can no longer mean the reversal of this sentence and the recall of creation to its original intellectual unity. Now, instead, the ontology of Pseudo-Dionysius can be read into these terms: κρίσις refers to the distinction of things that grounds their being and is essentially good, even a way of imitating God; and πρόνοια does not destroy this distinction in the process of drawing beings to God but gives them strength and substance, by leading creatures sunk in the worst kind of individuality to an integration willed by God and modeled after him, through the redeeming power of love.[65]

With this reinterpretation, the Origenist philosophy of "experiencing the opposite" as a way of coming to know the good is refuted

---

[65] This reinterpretation of Evagrius' terminology is especially noticeable in *Ambigua*; PG 91, 1133C–1136A; cf. below, chap. 5, sec. 4: "Existence as Contradiction".

in its demonic aspect, while its central truth is assimilated. Maximus found a means of doing this in the world view of Pseudo-Dionysius, after he had come to know it for himself and had made the necessary adjustments. By letting Origen and Pseudo-Dionysius be correctives for each other, he constructed his own philosophy of the movement of creation, which we now have to consider.

IV

THE SYNTHESES OF THE COSMOS

1. Being and Movement

a. "The Age"

The basic structure of creaturely ontology has already been described: it consists in a fundamental nonidentity of the existing thing within its own being, in an extension or distancing (διάστημα, διάστασις) that finds its expression in momentum (φορά), and more specifically in the triad of coming to be, movement, and coming to rest (γένεσις, κίνησις, στάσις). The middle concept of these three, movement, expresses the insight that although the origin and goal, the coming to be and the coming to rest, of finite being are—in themselves—identical, they are not identical *for* finite being; its extension, its becoming, forces it to achieve this identity through a process of transition. "For duality is neither infinite nor without beginning nor without movement."[1] Every creature, however, whether material or intellectual, is constructed in a polarity. If it is material, that polarity consists in matter and form; if intellectual, in its generic concept and its individual qualities.[2] It is indissolubly, but also irreducibly, both a "what", a nature, and a "who", a person. Or, if one transfers the distinction into the realm of being itself, it is both "being in general" and a certain *kind* of being. "Nothing, then, that in any way needs to be categorized as a 'what' in order to reveal its particular existence is in the true sense of the word *simple*."[3]

---

[1] *Ambigua*; PG 91, 1184B.

[2] *Ambigua*; PG 91, 1400C. The Greek here—despite the Latin translation in the Migne edition (*potestatis*)—must be ἐξ οὐσίας ("from a generic essence") and not ἐξουσίας ("of power"), as is clear from the following phrase: "the distinction is obvious . . . in the generic essence" (τῇ οὐσίᾳ . . . τὴν διαφορὰν συνεπιθεωρουμένη).

[3] Ibid. The scholia on Pseudo-Dionysius develop this theory in a particular direction. Picking up a thread in Pseudo-Dionysius, they speak of the simplicity of the pure intellect. But one must not cling literally, in this context, to terminology. These intellects are, to be sure, without matter—at least the higher among them (*In Coel. Hier.* 2; PG 4, 37B). They

With this position, Maximus took up Gregory of Nyssa's axiom that finite being is essentially characterized by *spatial intervals* (διάστημα) and, therefore, by *motion*. For both authors, finite being is essentially *time*.

To have a beginning, middle, and end is characteristic of things extended in time. One would also be right in adding to this "things caught up in the age (αἰών)". For time, whose motion can be measured, is limited by number; the age, however, whose existence is expressed by the category of "when", also undergoes extension (διάστασις), in that its being has a beginning. But if time and the age are not without beginning, then surely neither are the things that are involved in them.[4]

---

are simple insofar as they are not compound (ἀσύνθετοι): that is, their unity is not the result of a natural synthesis of body and soul (ibid.; cf. 13; PG 4, 97C: "non-compounded and immaterial" [ἀσύνθετα καὶ ἄϋλα]; In Eccl. Hier. 6; PG 4, 172C). (Maximus wrote a tract of his own to demonstrate the immateriality of some created intellects: Epistles 6: PG 91, 424f.). As a result of such simplicity, the pure intellect possesses its virtue and knowledge not, as we do, as an accident (κατὰ συμβεβηκός)—that is, as something inhering extrinsically (ὡς ἄλλος ἐν ἄλλῳ)—but rather as something proper to itself (οἰκεῖα: In Coel Hier. 13; PG 4, 97B). "There is no question there of accident and underlying subject, since all synthesis and all the unformed character of matter are there nonexistent" (In Coel. Hier. 6; PG 4, 65B). The polarity referred to here, which has no place in the being of angels, is a polarity conditioned by bodily existence. "Souls have their knowledge as something introduced from outside (ἔξωθεν), . . . but angels know through and in themselves, as a result of their resemblance to God" (In Div. Nom. 7; PG 4, 345C). The habitual characteristics of pure intellects are thus rightly called "substantial" (οὐσιώδεις ἕξεις: In Ecc. Hier. 4; PG 4, 157C), based in their own substance (ἕξεις αὐτουσιωμέναι: In Coel. Hier. 7; PG 4, 65C), since their substance is, of itself, intellectually conscious. But even if their knowledge is not "introduced from without" through sense knowledge, it is, nonetheless, still "introduced": namely, by God (ἐπεισάκτον οὖν ἔχουσιν ἐξ αἰτίου τοῦ θεοῦ τὴν νοερὰν ταύτην ἐνέργειαν: In De Div. Nom. 7; PG 4, 345B). It is "infused", as scholastic philosophy would later say. Only God has no infused knowledge (οὐκ ἐπείσακτον ἔχων τὸ φρονεῖν: In De Div. Nom. 5; PG 4, 320B), because he is himself fully actuated subsistent knowledge, without any admixture of potentiality (ὅλη ἐνεργείᾳ . . . οὐ δυνάμει)—because he alone is a knowledge that does not have an ignorance, a foolishness as its basis (πρότερον οὖσα ἀφροσύνη, εἶτα νοῦς ἐνεργείᾳ γινομένη), even as a basis that is always being contradicted (In De Div. Nom. 5; PG 4, 320B; cf. Schelling, Philosophie der Freiheit, vol. 7 of Collected Works, 465–66). If, then, the activity of pure spirits is "substantial", because they are always in a condition of realization (ἄπαυστοι ἐνέργειαι: In Coel. Hier. 7; PG 4, 68D), like a voice that cannot grow silent (ἀσίγητοι), still their unchangeableness (ἀπαράλλακτον) always depends on God's creative activity (In Coel. Hier. 13; PG 4, 101C). "By a free decision growing from their overpowering desire for God, they remain always in the firm condition of being immersed in the divine" (In Coel. Hier. 7; PG 4, 68C). "For God alone is of his very nature without motion" (In Coel. Hier. 7; PG 4, 68C).

[4] Centuries on Knowledge 1, 5; PG 90, 1085A. [Gregory of Nyssa—and to some extent Maximus—distinguished between existence in time as we know it, which is characteristic

All finite beings, whether characterized by the "time" of sensible things or the "continuity" (*aevum*) of intellectual things, share these primal ontological characteristics of the *where* and the *when*, which locate them in the universe's system of coordinates.

> We will say nothing here about the fact that the being of every thing necessarily includes a "whatness" [that is, is qualified in some way] and is not *simply* being; that is the first kind of limitation and a strong indication that there is a beginning to the being of things and of their coming to be. But who would deny that every conceivable being—except for the unique Divine Being, which lies beyond being itself—presupposes the concept of "where" in order even to be thought of and that necessarily the concept of "when" is always and in every manner identified with it. . . . They belong to those concepts that are always included with others, because the others cannot be thought without them.[5]

Time and space are, for Maximus and Gregory of Nyssa, the expression of finitude itself; they are pure limitation. Space is not fundamentally a physical or astronomical reality but an ontological category: "the limitation of the world through itself". Time is the "scattering" of being that invariably accompanies finitude. It expresses that fundamental nonidentity, for which scholasticism would develop the theory of the real distinction between essence and existence. Just as things are understood to be somewhere, "so all things are recognized as simultaneously subject to the category of 'when', precisely because they do not have their being in a simple way but in a qualified way. . . . For whatever has qualified being at one time was not, even if it now exists."[6] Thus for Maximus, as for Gregory, the notions of infinite space and endless time are contradictory in themselves. Just as the universe is determined as "a limited space", so "time is limited movement" (ὁ χρόνος περιγραφομένη κίνησις).[7]

While Maximus agrees with Gregory in deriving motion immediately, analytically, from becoming (understood as being-with-an-origin,

of material creatures and includes growth and dissolution, and the sequential existence characteristic of bodiless intellects such as angels, which they call existence in "the age" (αἰών, *aevum*). See David Balás, "Eternity and Time in Gregory of Nyssa's Contra Eunomium", in H. Dörrie, et al., eds., *Gregor von Nyssa und die Philosophie* (Leiden, 1976), 128–58; Brooks Otis, "Gregory of Nyssa and the Cappadocian Conception of Time", *Studia Patristica* 14 (Berlin, 1976), 327–57.]

[5] *Ambigua*; PG 91, 1180B.

[6] Ibid.; PG 91, 1180CD; cf. *Moscow Centuries on Knowledge* 2; Epifanovich ed., 34.

[7] *Quaestiones ad Thalassium* 65; CCG 22, 285, 533–534; PG 90, 757D.

γένεσις), and also in specifying motion as completely finite, he distances himself from Gregory by unconditionally equating motion and temporality. For Gregory, there were two kinds of creaturely motion, even if he did not put the distinction in an absolutely consistent set of philosophical terms: the essentially finite and closed cycle of movement in creation is measured by time and by "the age" (*aevum*). Even if "time" expresses more the becoming of material things, "the age" more the limitedness of the whole universe as something coming to be, still the two concepts refer essentially to the same reality. In addition, Gregory speaks of an "eternal becoming", which belongs to the intellect in its movement toward the unattainable God and which is simply endless,[8] even though the sting of despair will be removed from it in the world to come, through the spirit's immediate union with the object of its longing.

This dynamic of endless passage through and beyond the essential finitude of the creature—a dynamic that expresses for Gregory the highest nobility of the creature, its quasi-divine infinity, along with its deepest need, its endless and insatiable hunger—is missing from Maximus' synthetic thought. He takes the equation of temporality and finitude seriously. The movement of the intellectual creature is not something removed from the realm of "nature" and "the world", not a middle term between the world and God, as it is for Gregory. It is simply the consciously reflected realization of the basic structure of creaturehood itself: of its finite course from its origin, through the intervening distance, to its goal. The concept of "the age" (*aeon*) has a different meaning in Maximus' works. The *Centuries on Knowledge*, which [of course] hand on the Origenist heritage, use the word still in its older sense of "a period of history", sometimes referring to layered systems of different cosmic "durations" through which the soul must wander on its pilgrimage to God, only at last to reach the place beyond all temporality, removed from all the universe's motion, which is final and transcendent security in the Absolute.[9] But this notion is basically,

---

[8] See Hans Urs von Balthasar, *Présence et pensée* (Paris, 1942), 10–19; English translation, *Presence and Thought* (San Francisco: Ignatius Press, 1995), 37–45.

[9] *Centuries on Knowledge* 2, 85 (PG 90, 1164D–1165A), following Scripture, makes a distinction between "temporal ages (aeons)" and "other ages liberated from time (χρόνος)"; it also speaks of the "fullness of the ages", of "ages of ages (*saecula saeculorum*)", of the "age of ages (*saeculum saeculi*)", "the times of the ages", and "the races of the ages". *Centuries on Knowledge* 2, 86 (PG 90, 1165AB) repeats the Origenist exegesis of the scriptural text, "The

as the style of the *Chapters* clearly shows, a historicizing echo of Origen; it expresses Maximus' own thought only insofar as he, too—like Origen—was convinced of the finitude of all motion, both in the [material] world and in the wider realm of the *aeon*. Yet their convictions had different reasons behind them: for Origen, motion was connected with the fall, while for Maximus it was an ontological expression of created existence.

John of Scythopolis introduced a new interpretation of temporality. In his use of the term, "the age" (*aeon*) is an attribute of God himself, insofar as he alone is the origin and end of all created time;[10] the temporal being of the created intellect lies in its participation in the "eternity" of God. For the word *aeon* is derived from ἀεὶ ὤν, "ever-being", and is defined as "endless life, which is always complete . . . , without extension (ἀδιάστατος)".[11] For the creature, "the age" is identical with the final point of its own limited movement—or better, with the ecstatic moment in which its own circular movement is complete and its absolute transcendence [of time] becomes evident. Created time, in this moment, exists no more in itself—that is, in its exclusion (καθ' ὑπόβασιν) from eternity—but is restored to its original place, embedded in eternity (ἐν τῷ ἀεὶ ὄντι ἀναπαύεσθαι).[12]

Maximus subscribes materially to this interpretation, which fits well into his ontology of created being. For in the moment he moves from considering the idea and life of God to the extended, distanced, individualized being of the creature, the connection between time and eternity becomes clear: "When the age [*aeon*, eternity] ceases its motion, it is time; when time becomes measurable by being carried [thrown] into motion, it is the age."[13] But if one wants to understand by *aeon* the totality of the world's time—as Scripture does, and Gregory of Nyssa, too—a time that also includes the pure intellects, then it is "the fulfillment of time as it returns to itself (closes in on itself)", a time beyond which God elevates the creature in divinization.[14]

Lord rules . . . for the age and beyond" (Ex 15:18), and interprets this "beyond" as a rest beyond all the movements of temporality (aeons).

[10] *In De Div. Nom.* 5; PG 4, 313C.

[11] Ibid.; PG 4, 313CD.

[12] Ibid.; PG 4, 316A.

[13] *Ambigua*; PG 91, 1164BC.

[14] Ibid.; PG 91, 1377D–1380A. (Cf. *Centuries on Knowledge* 1, 70; PG 90, 1109A: "The whole universe, defined by the limits of its own intelligible principles [λόγοι], is called place

This conception of Maximus, which stresses the finitude of time and thus also the possibility of being removed from it, corresponds to [an aspect of] the spirit of late antiquity, from which the hesychastic prayer of the monks was to develop and which sought above all else, like Augustine, peace for the "restless heart" in eternal life. The heroic sense of sharing in a divine adventure, which dominates Gregory of Nyssa's conception of eternity, has given way to a liturgical attitude of silent, recollected adoration. Even so, the underlying feeling of Maximus' thought, despite its appearances, remains closer to Gregory than to Augustine. For the quieting of the heart's urgent quest does not at all have the character of self-abandonment, in Maximus, but contains in itself the full truth and positive implications of motion. Peace is not simply confirmation but at the same time a transcendence of motion (ὑπὲρ πᾶσαν κίνησιν).[15] The concepts of rest and motion, which are in themselves—that is, outside of God—opposed to each other, are, like all created antinomies, united, because surpassed, in God. "God is not moved in any way; he is also, however, in no way motionless, for such a characteristic belongs only to essentially limited things, which have a beginning of their being."[16] Gregory of Nyssa had anticipated this synthesis of rest and motion, precisely in his paradox of an eternally fulfilled—yet, in its fulfillment, eternally expanding—longing [for God]; "for this is the highest paradox of all," he writes, "how motion and rest can be the same thing."[17] He had given this paradox expression in a kind of parable, simultaneously describing the soul as an arrow shooting across the vast spaces of eternity and as resting quietly in the hands of the divine bowman.[18] In Maximus' thought, the bowshot of yearning is tamed into a metaphor of perfectly measured beauty, which brings both motion and rest together in their perfection: the archetypally Greek image of the "sacred dance".[19]

[τόπος] and time [αἰών]": πᾶς ὁ κόσμος ἰδίοις περιοριζόμενος λόγοις καὶ τόπος λέγεται καὶ αἰών).

[15] *Ambigua*; PG 91, 1221A.

[16] Ibid.

[17] *Life of Moses*; GNO 7/1, 118, 3f.; PG 44, 405C.

[18] *Homilies on the Song of Songs* 4; GNO 7, 127, 7–129, 19; PG 44, 852B–853A.

[19] *Ambigua*; PG 91, 1292C; *Centuries on Knowledge* 2, 78; PG 91, 1161C.

b. Extension

To grasp the meaning of this transcendence of self-contained temporal finitude more deeply, we must turn for a second look at the "otherness" of the creature. By conceiving the prescribed pattern of the creature's career as a circle, Maximus is brought to a deeper metaphysical explanation of the identity of origin and goal in finite existence than Gregory of Nyssa was able to give.

> All created things have their motion in a passive way, since it is not a motion or a dynamic that comes from the creature's own being. If, then, intellects are also created, they, too, will necessarily be set in motion, because they are naturally led away from their source, simply by existing (διὰ τὸ εἶναι), and towards a goal, by the activity of their wills, for the sake of an existence fulfilled by value, of well-being (διὰ τὸ εὖ εἶναι). For the goal of movement in what is moved is, generally speaking, eternal well-being (ἀεὶ εὖ εἶναι), just as its origin is being in general, which is God. He is the giver of being and the bestower of the grace of well-being, because he is origin and goal. Only motion in general comes from him, insofar as he is its origin; motion of a particular kind is directed toward him, insofar as he is its goal. And if an intellectual being will only move in an intellectual way, as befits its nature, it will necessarily become a knowing intellect; but if it knows, it will necessarily also love what it knows; and if it loves, it must expand itself in longing and live in longing expansion and so intensify and greatly accelerate its motion. . . . Nor will it rest until it comes, in its fullness, to enter into the fullness of what it loves, and is fully embraced by it, and accepts, in the utter freedom of its own choice, a state of saving possession, so that it belongs completely to what possesses it completely.[20]

Here a new triad of concepts appears, which will afterward become a main theme in Maximus' thought and which corresponds exactly to his first triad of origin, motion, and goal: being, well-being, and eternal being. The "being" that serves as origin is, first of all, pure "becoming" (γένεσις) and, as such, is the same as pure motion (ἁπλῶς κινεῖσθαι) and directionality (φέρεσθαι). To become "being", like the source it has left behind—namely, God—this "pure becoming" must be transformed into some qualitative *kind* of motion (πῶς κινεῖσθαι) and must fill the emptiness of its own existence with the full content of being (whose "transcendental characteristics", as true, good, and

---

[20] *Ambigua*; PG 91, 1073BD.

beautiful, Maximus summarizes with the adverb "well [εὖ]", meaning all that is valuable); it must realize itself through the voluntary (κατὰ γνώμην) affirmation of its own natural (κατὰ φύσιν) direction and so return, by conscious intention, to that long-abandoned source, which has always contained in itself the identity of being and fulfillment and which is for that reason absolute, eternal being.

This is also the ontological reason that the motion of the creature, although cyclical and finite, still is not shut up within itself in a sense of self-sufficiency: "No created thing is its own goal, because it is not its own origin. . . . For every self-sufficient thing is, in some sense, without origin."[21] "No creature can cease its own motion until it has reached the first and only cause, which gives to all existent things their being."[22]

"There are, then, three utterly general modalities of existence . . . : being, being good, and being eternal, . . . of which the first and the third depend simply on God, who causes them; but the second is also conditioned by our free determination and our motion and gives the two on either side of it, for the first time, their own full meaning", because being only reaches its full potentiality in self-realization, and eternal being is the expression of this fulfillment.[23] So the determination of our own "proper being" (κυρίως εἶναι), which is realized in the intellectual assent and personal "ownership" of our natural constitution, depends on this middle term (μέσον), transitory though it is.

Therefore this model of the "transcendental" realization of being[24] can also take two other forms. First, it can be expressed psychologically: here the first stage is that of potentiality, the simple "equipment" of nature (δύναμις); the second, the state of activation (ἐνέργεια); the third, that of relaxation and rest (ἀργία).[25] But this psychological pattern, in turn, points to another ontological and theological one, in which the first stage is that of pure essence or nature (οὐσία), the second the intellectual and free realization of this nature as "relationship" (σχέσις) or "intentionality", while the third stage breaks out of the boundaries of self-contained nature and is labeled "grace" (χάρις).[26] For the be-

[21] Ibid.; PG 91, 1072BC.
[22] Ibid.; PG 91, 1072C.
[23] Ibid.; PG 91, 1116B.
[24] Maximus returns to this idea repeatedly: see *Ambigua*; PG 91, 1329AB; 1348D; 1392AD.
[25] Ibid.; PG 91, 1392A.
[26] Ibid.; PG 91, 1237A.

ing that has been projected into existence cannot achieve for itself the condition of rest and full realization; it can only assimilate to itself the ontological direction of its own being, like someone rowing a boat downstream, and "increase the intensity of its movement" (ἐπιτείνειν τὸ σφοδρὸν τῆς κινήσεως) in an intellectual way.[27]

> Being in itself, then, which receives from nature only the ability to actualize its own potential, cannot at all come to full actualization without free self-determination; on the other hand, if one only possesses this natural potential, in fact, as the will to be good, one cannot possess it in its fullness unless nature supports it. The mode of eternal being, however, which certainly includes the first two, potential as well as actualization, is in no sense immanent in beings as a natural power and certainly does not follow with necessity from the free resolution of the will (for how could eternity, without beginning and without end, dwell within things that naturally have an origin and that move toward an end?). Eternal being is itself a limit.[28]

The creature is not asked to "redeem" itself but simply to "continue to make earnest efforts", to adapt itself willingly to the movement whose origin is before the creature's own being and whose goal is beyond it. Since, as a being passively in motion, it does not belong to itself, it need not trouble itself about its own perfectibility.

> What advantage—as the saints may have said, in their own private reflections—what advantage would a being have, which is not responsible for its own existence, in choosing itself as the goal of its movement, or in choosing anything as goal but God; for neither through itself nor through any other thing that is not God can it gain the slightest advantage for its own being?[29]

In acting thus, it would only raise a barrier to the meaning and flow of its existence, would remain behind itself and not make the slightest gains toward its own self-realization.

"Everything," Maximus says, "absolutely everything is in motion, . . . pure intellects just as much as rational souls that are moved by knowledge and insight, because they are not knowledge-in-itself or insight-in-itself."[30] "Intellects move in an intellectual way, material

---

[27] Ibid.; PG 91, 1073C.
[28] Ibid.; PG 91, 1392B; cf. Centuries on Love 3, 27–29: PG 90, 1025AC.
[29] Ibid.; PG 91, 1116C.
[30] Ibid.; PG 91, 1177AB.

things materially . . . , either in a straight line or in a circle or in a spiral."[31]

c. Realization and Grace

Does not this intoxication with development, however, ultimately dissolve all being in becoming? There are two elements that distinguish Maximus' approach from a philosophy of pure becoming. First, his thinking is dominated by an undiminished optimism with respect to the *reasonableness of nature's motion*, to its directedness and consequently to its correctness; this is a trust in the essential goodness of nature, which works toward reducing the difference between ontological (transcendental) and moral goodness—an approach that moves Maximus close to Aristotle and Thomas. Secondly, he sees natural movement itself, which takes its origin in transcendental reality, as being directed forward beyond itself. This raises the problem of the *supernatural*, as intrinsically connected with the problem of motion, which it supports and envelops. We must now consider these two aspects of motion in more detail.

If finite being is defined by its motion, this motion must be something natural, a part of nature (φύσις). In fact, Maximus writes, "the definition of every nature is given with the concept of its essential activity (ἐνέργεια)."[32] The essence of a thing

> is only truly indicated through the potential for activity that is constitutive of its nature (συστατικὴ δύναμις); one can correctly also call this "natural activity (φυσικὴ ἐνέργεια)." Through it the thing is primarily and most perfectly characterized, because it is a motion constitutive of species (εἰδοποιὸς κίνησις) and because it includes, as its most general characteristic, every other peculiar quality that attaches to it; besides it, there is only nothingness, . . . which has neither existence nor motion.[33]

In this perspective, a *nature* is nothing else than organized motion, as was already apparent in the parallelism of the two models, "coming-to-be, motion, rest" and "nature, potentiality, actuality". Nature is a capacity, a plan (λόγος), a field and a system of motion. One can guess how important this proposition will be for Christology: a nature with-

---

[31] Ibid.; 1072AB. On the movements of bodies, cf. John of Scythopolis, *In De Div. Nom.* 8; PG 4, 381BC.

[32] *Ambigua*; PG 91, 1057B.

[33] Ibid.; PG 91, 1078A.

out activity inevitably appears as a contradiction in itself, just as it is "impossible for there to be within the same essence and nature two kinds of existence or natural activity".[34]

Since this natural motion, however, is directed toward a goal, and since that goal cannot be anything else than God, its origin, the underlying orientation of nature must have goodness written into its being; intelligence can only have the task of translating this naturally ingrained goodness into a goodness that is consciously acquired. The borderline between natural and moral goodness thus becomes somewhat fluid. The natural motion of an intellectual being is, as we shall see, itself in some way intellectual, while even the freest act can only be realized within the retaining walls of natural motion. With this in mind, Maximus also comments on Pseudo-Dionysius' notions about the "nonbeing" of evil. Evil is neither a substance nor something that adds to substance as it is;[35] even the nature of the devils is and remains luminously good.[36] Yet "their natural activity" is still affected adversely by their wickedness of mind and weakened by it.[37] John of Scythopolis went even farther in this direction and assumed—consistently with this interpretation—some kind of weakening of their being itself.[38]

One can understand, then, why Maximus always describes the punishment of sin as a consequence of evil that is inherent in the sin itself.

> The law of nature disciplines those who use nature in an unnatural way. In the same measure in which they attempt to live contrary to nature, nature punishes those who try to abuse and corrupt it: they no longer can summon up the whole power of their nature but have lost its original freshness and so are chastened.[39]

Maximus' theory of original sin rests, as we shall see, completely on this principle; correspondingly, his positive ethics are built up more on the fundamental instincts of nature than on an analysis of the free act. "Everything that rests, in one way or another, on a natural process and cannot be entirely explained has a strong, irrefutable power as evidence for the truth."[40] The ideal, then, is the complete overlapping of nature

---

[34] *Opuscula*; PG 91, 201C.
[35] *In De Div. Nom.* 4; PG 4, 296A.
[36] Ibid.; PG 4, 293A; 288C.
[37] Ibid.; PG 4, 289D.
[38] Ibid.; PG 4, 289 A–C. (There seem to be errors in the transmission of this difficult text.)
[39] *Ambigua*; PG 91, 1164C.
[40] Ibid.; PG 91, 1192CD.

and freedom. Guilt is always something foreign to a nature that "calls all good things its own".[41]

The second problem raised by Maximus' theory of motion is that of *nature and the supernatural*. How can a being come to perfection naturally, by itself, if it is so thoroughly oriented beyond itself? And how can a being be so radically "open" without losing the consciousness of its own being in the process? In other words, does not the close parallel between the triads "nature/possibility/reality" and "being/being good/being eternal", if we understand "eternal being" as grace, cause the difference between nature and grace to disappear entirely? It would be anachronistic, obviously, to look in Maximus for the Tridentine or Thomistic teaching on nature and the supernatural. His thought concerns itself with the one, concrete order of the universe; he knows no other nature than that which has been elevated supernaturally. Like all the Greek Fathers, he has not even conceived the question of a possible "purely natural end" [for human existence]. But such a hypothesis has become questionable for us again today, so we would do well not to approach a Greek theologian with questions that make us somewhat uncomfortable ourselves. Rather, we will have to be content with finding in Maximus' works two propositions, both of which are indispensable, yet which neither he nor we can hope, systematically, to make any the less incompatible by explanation: the teleological structure of all being, and especially of conscious, finite intellectual being, and the transcendence of the very goal that this whole teleology presupposes. Even Thomas Aquinas never managed to pass beyond these two propositions in the direction of a single, coherent system.

First of all, it would be a good idea not to press the parallel between [the pairs] potency/actuality and natural motion/fulfillment in grace ("well being", εὖ εἶναι, and "eternal being", ἀεὶ εἶναι), or to look at them through scholastic eyes. The parallelism of the triads we have discovered in Maximus comes always from his urge to order and systematize ideas, which can attempt the most daring and elaborate combinations on the spur of the moment but which never ties itself down exclusively to a single scheme. A more important question is *how* he describes the transition from the realm of natural motion to that of the fulfillment and rest that are the work of grace.

This transition is essentially a passive process. Because the point of

---

[41] *In De Eccl. Hier.* 3; PG 4, 141D.

origin for being was a transcendent one, not lying within nature itself, and because this point of origin is identical with its goal, we cannot reach up to this height on our own power. "We experience divinization passively—we do not achieve it ourselves, because it lies beyond nature. For we have, within our nature, no power capable of receiving (δεκτικὴν δύναμιν) divinization."[42] Man is assimilated into God through *pathos* (πάθος), a passivity; the process is an activity only in the one who assimilates.[43] It encounters

> no faculty, of any sort, for being assimilated, because then it would no longer be grace but the revelation (φανέρωσις) of an activity latent within the potentiality of nature. Further, divinization would then no longer be a paradox (παράδοξον), if it occurred as the result of a natural capacity for being assimilated. Divinization would be an achievement of nature, not a gift of God; a person so divinized would be God by nature and would have to be called so in the proper sense. . . . And how divinization then could elevate such a person ecstatically out of himself, I fail to see, if it lay within the bounds of his nature.[44]

But this "abandonment of self" is always, for Maximus, the sure sign that the goal of motion has been reached.

> Nature, then, is incapable of conceiving what lies above nature. As a consequence, no creature can achieve divinization for itself naturally, simply because it cannot grasp God. It belongs wholly to God's grace to distribute divinization by grace, according to the measure of each being, to enlighten nature with supernatural light and to lift it above its own limitations by the superabundance of glory.[45]

Thus even in the most intimate degree of union, "the ideas of nature and grace" remain "ever unmingled with each other (οὐδαμῶς ἀλλήλοις συμφυρέτων). . . . Grace never does away with the passivity of nature."[46]

The first expression of this "passivity", appropriate to the present world, is death and decay; the second, however, is not the dissolution of the person in God but the resurrection of the flesh, through which

---

[42] *Quaestiones ad Thalassium* 22; CCG 7, 145, 28–31; PG 90, 324A.

[43] *Ambigua*; PG 91, 1237D.

[44] Ibid.; PG 91, 1237AB.

[45] *Quaestiones ad Thalassium* 22; CCG 7, 141, 91–98; PG 90, 321A.

[46] Ibid. 37; CCG 7, 249, 35–48; PG 90, 384C–385A.

the enduring difference between God and the creature is sealed. It is necessary, too, that

> the world of appearances die, just as man must, in order to rise again—transformed from old age to youth—in that resurrection which we hope will soon follow death. Then we men, too, as parts with the whole, as each a small world within a great one, will rise with it and receive the power of a never-ending incorruptibility; the body will be conformed to the soul, and material things to intellectual things, while God's power radiates over all things its visible and active presence, offering each creature in an individually appropriate way, yet to all through a share in itself, the unbreakable bond of unity for endless ages.[47]

Until that point, however, the creature is unable to make contact with its own root, "that deep and all-supplying root that sustains and bears it",[48] "for created things cannot touch the uncreated, the finite cannot touch the infinite."[49] The creature is therefore unaware of its own limits, the place where it runs into God. God alone "is the measure of things and knows the beginning and the limits of all things, because he alone is their creator".[50] The creature's movement toward its "idea", which is also its "truth", can therefore never be a direct approach, just as the movement of number from the level of distinct individuals to that of synthesis was not a direct approach to transcendental unity. The way of the creature, after all, leads—simultaneously with its growth in "perfection"—to its ever-greater recognition of itself as nothing before God, as pure passivity before free and inexplicable grace; and this knowledge itself is also a grace. But even if this seems to "shut the creature up" in itself, that shutting is also an opening, precisely because it is the work of grace. "For the power of God always opens everything, in its power to do all things."[51] In this opening, the creature understands that it cannot understand itself[52] and that it is incapable not only of conceiving God's essence but even of conceiving his existence.[53] So passivity and imperfection remain until the end:

---

[47] *Mystagogia*, chap. 7; PG 91, 685BC.
[48] *Ambigua*; PG 91, 1188C.
[49] Ibid.; PG 91, 1168B.
[50] *In De Div. Nom.* 4; PG 4, 245D.
[51] Ibid. 8; PG 4, 356C. (The attribution of the text here is uncertain).
[52] *Quaestiones ad Thalassium* 56; CCG 22, 11; PG 90, 584AB.
[53] *In De Div. Nom.* 4; PG 4, 246C (uncertain).

For anyone who is arrogant enough to think he has reached the fulness of virtue would no longer seek the ultimate source from which beauty flows; he would limit the force of his longing to himself and exclude himself from reaching the final stage of salvation: God. But anyone who remains conscious of his own natural powerlessness in the good will not tire of running, with eyes fixed on the goal, toward him who can supply his imperfection with abundance.[54]

In this radical openness to the transcendent, the world is thus indeed the "closed house" that Aristotle and Gregory of Nyssa had conceived it to be, a whole "that needs no addition and no subtraction, in order to become better."[55] And if Christ,

> as befits God, is to bring all things together and sum them up in his person, he will prove that all creation is a unity that comes together through the cooperation of its parts and draws inward on itself through the totality of its being—governed by a single, simple, in itself definite, and unchangeable idea: that it comes from nothing. In this concept, all of creation can be understood as a single, identical, and undifferentiated idea: namely, that it has nonbeing as the basis of its being.[56]

After what we have said, one will rightly understand what Maximus means when he says that God "has placed in all intellectual beings, as their hidden but primary power, the potentiality of knowing him; ever a generous Lord, he has planted in us lowly men, as part of our nature, the longing and desire for him" as well as the urge to seek for him through and beyond all creatures.[57] Whether one understands this longing as a kind of dowry of grace, or more in the direction of the Thomist "natural desire for the vision of God (*desiderium naturale visionis*)", it does not contradict what we have said above, for in no way can it reach its goal by any natural power. It does provide a bridge, however, over the apparently sharp division between nature and the supernatural, in that it conceives our fulfillment in grace as the goal of all the striving of our nature as it really is.

---

[54] *Quaestiones ad Thalassium* 52; CCG 7, 421, 103–10; PG 90, 493D.
[55] *Ambigua*; PG 91, 1176B.
[56] Ibid.; PG 91, 1312AB.
[57] Ibid.; PG 91, 1361AB.

d. Between East and West

There are clearly two concerns that move Maximus, the theologian of final goals, to insist on making this jump: his Pseudo-Dionysian, anti-Alexandrian emphasis on "passivity before God" (θεῖα παθεῖν), rooted in his consciousness of the absolute transcendence of the divine essence, and his resistance to the pagan Neoplatonism of Ammonius Hermeiou, which had previously been attacked by [John] Philoponus and Zachary [of Mytilene] but which still had its followers and which taught that the essences of things are co-eternal with God, since they are in fact divine ideas. In contrast, the Christian must hold that all created being, whether substance or accident, comes from nothing and therefore stands far below God's being in dignity; it therefore needs a free act of God's grace in order to be elevated into the sphere of his dignity and to share in his eternal life.[58]

This raises no real difficulties. At the most, one should ask whether the immanent goal-directedness of the creature, in this system, is sufficiently respected—whether, in other words, the goal of nature remains preserved also in the order of its supernatural end, if it is "absorbed" (*aufgehoben*) in the sense of being assimilated, as well as in the sense of being replaced. Up to now, we have had no reason to doubt this; it is only in our treatment of Maximus' theology of original sin that certain shadows will begin to appear in his system.

It is precisely at this borderline between the two meanings of "absorption" (*Aufhebung*) that Maximus' thinking takes on historical importance. To undervalue natural goals by absorbing them into an ultimate supernatural one is to develop the idea of the world's movement toward perfection, necessarily, into that of the total overshadowing and domination of all finite reality by God. The world's sabbath then becomes—for instance, in the *Centuries on Knowledge*—the silencing and the termination of all the purposeful activity of creatures and their utter replacement by the activity of God: God is all in all, through his presence that radiates through all. That is an Eastern, Asiatic ideal. At least, it is when it stands without further qualifications. But Maximus does qualify it, in that the glorious appearance of the Absolute, despite its gratuitousness, is in his eyes the positive goal of all created, natural, and intellectual activity and, so, the immanent fulfillment and "re-

---

[58] *Centuries on Love* 3, 27–29; PG 90, 1025AC.

ward" of such effort.[59] It is also clear that anyone who has emphasized as strongly as Maximus the priority of creation from nothing can only conceive of final divinization as a perfecting of what has been created finite. But that is a predominantly Western style of thought; Maximus stands at the point of balance between the two approaches, and it is Christology that will decide the issue.

Let us give at least a hint of the outcome: the dimension of thought that opens up here between nature (φύσις) and the concrete individual (ὑπόστασις) leads Greek thought, in a twofold yet inseparably unified way, beyond itself. Beyond nature the reality of person appears, and beyond essence the depth of existence comes into view. And as, in the extension of this intuition, which first dawned in the process of reflection on Christ, man comes to be seen as a "composite" of intellectual nature and person, so the creature in general is seen as a composite of essence and existence. In this way, person and existence are forced to draw together, and from the same depths of being—which is more than all intelligible essence—arises the invitation of a personal God to his created child, an event that belongs to another realm altogether than all the in-built natural orientations—however mystical—of intellectual beings. Even if these dimensions are not reflexively perceived by Maximus, they are, as we shall see, very much present and will reveal themselves as the background to all his speculative efforts. As a thinker between East and West, he has drawn from the mystery of Christ a perspective for the whole Christian view of the universe.

In external terms, it is the East that dominates: the thinking of an ascetic, of a monk who thinks only of God and who waits for the coming of his Kingdom. Despite all the Aristotelian categories, there is no room left for a theology of history, let alone of culture. Yet the seeds have been sown: the goal God sets for the world is now not simply dissolution in him alone but the fulfillment and preservation also of the created realm, "without confusion (ἀσυγχύτως)", in the Incarnation of his Son.

Only when we see it in this breadth can we make sense of the first of Maximus' cosmological syntheses: the synthesis between being and motion, ultimately between eternal being and the finite being that moves out from it and on toward it. This remains the basis for all the syntheses

---

that follow—their goal, their condition, and the internal form that will give shape to all the rest.

2. Generality and Particularity

a. Being in Motion

The synthesis we have just described is a genuinely transcendental one —or, if one wants to distinguish between ontology and metaphysics, a metaphysical one, which concerns the ultimate basis for created being as such. The syntheses that follow attempt rather to describe created being from within; they are, in a more narrow sense, ontological syntheses. Still, the two realms cannot be cleanly divided. An "immanent" theory of being finds its final explanation and illumination only in metaphysics, which sets created being against the background of absolute Being. And metaphysics, on the other hand, by revealing the underlying motion of the creature as such, provides the supporting explanation for the whole theory of motion and relationship within the created realm.

In fact, the ontology of created being is a study of motion. More precisely, it is the study of the relationship between rest and motion, whose balance is what defines the essence of finite being.

> The Teacher (Gregory Nazianzen) says that visible things are set in motion without disturbance, in a way that corresponds to the idea of their development. They are motionless in their nature, their capabilities, and their effects; in their place in the general order of things, in their stability of being, they never leave their peculiar natural place, never turning into other things or confusing themselves. On the other hand, with respect to increase and diminution they are in motion, by growing in quantity and quality and especially by succeeding one another, in that those that come earlier make way for those that come later. To put it briefly, all beings are constant and utterly motionless with respect to their essential concept, by which they have come to be and remain in being; but they are moving and inconstant in their accidents and relationships, through which the drama of this universe is formed and played out to its end.[60]

This balance is so mysterious that one must reckon it among the great mysteries of the world.

---

[60] Ibid.; PG 91, 1217AB.

What human being knows the essential laws of things, through which they come to be and are distinct from each other? Who knows how their natural motion, which never allows them to be transformed into each other, is related to the immovable principle of their continuity? For they come to move precisely by remaining what they are and have their motion, paradoxically, through their continuity. What can the force be that brings such opposed things together, for the continued existence of a single world?[61]

Motion and rest, then, are not external to one another but interpenetrate and presuppose each other. This became clear in our last chapter, in that the motion of the single being also comprised the basis of its indispensable peculiarity, its nature. Let us remain with this thought for a moment longer. The "motion" of a being is its way of establishing itself as a particular, existent thing; it is its self-delimitation, its way of distinguishing itself from every other nature. Certainly, this motion itself comes from elsewhere; it is not master of itself. Therefore the limitation produced by creation's motion away from the center is not pure perfection. "For everything that comes to be is in motion passively, is not its own principle of movement."[62] Nevertheless, despite the fact that its origin comes from elsewhere, this motion is an expression of the being's self-possession; for that reason, its limitation is also not pure imperfection. This positive side of finite being is expressed in a very remarkable sentence: "Whatever has no end (τέλος) to its natural activity is also not complete, not perfect (τέλειον)."[63] To wish to eliminate this finitude, under the pretext of attaining a more intimate ontological identification with the Infinite, would mean destroying the deepest meaning of the creature's being. Its perfection is reached, rather, precisely in that it preserves and emphasizes its own limits.

The indwelling presence of the divine unity in finite being, which brings it to its perfection, can only be conceived in the paradox that this unity perfects both the individuality and mutual differences of creatures and their mutual similarity within the whole universe. "Paradoxically, it reveals itself by creating distinctions (ἀφοριστικῶς), according to the ineffable way in which it makes things one."[64] It brings about both

---

[61] Ibid.; PG 91, 1228BC.
[62] Ibid.; PG 91, 1073B.
[63] Ibid.; PG 91, 1220A.
[64] Ibid.; PG 91, 1172C.

"mixture (σύγϰϱισις) and separation (διάϰϱισις)", so that "no being has the unique idea of its nature simply overruled." [65] So we are again confronted with the mysterious dialectics of unity:

> If all godly activity reveals God, whole and undivided, as present in a particular way in every existing creature, however constructed, who of us could possibly imagine and express how the whole God exists in all things, indivisible and beyond our sharing, universally but also particularly in every individual? He is neither divided into many, along with the endless variety of different beings in which he dwells as Being itself, nor is he drawn into individuality by the distinct existence of the particular thing, nor does he draw together the essential differences of things into the unitary totality of the All; but he is truly all in all things, without ever abandoning his unapproachable simplicity. [66]

Only when one has really understood and accepted this paradox can one fully understand also the mysterious character of providence, which does not stop at simply steering things "in general", but precisely pursues the individual, that which is *distinguished* from everything else, and dwells in the whole confusing particularity of the world. [67] This sheds decisive light, too, on the structure of the individual being, in which both the generic ("nature") and the particular (the "individual") together give form to the underlying unity of being yet at the same time leave it unformed. So Maximus repeatedly labels the category of difference as "constitutive and definitive (συστατιϰὴ ϰαὶ ἀφοϱιστιϰή)" [68] as something that is at once irreducibly both negative and positive.

The polarity of the singular and the universal is thus *the* structure of finite being, because it is the only possible way [for creatures] to imitate the simplicity of God without being simply God.

> The whole structure of existent things, which are not God, is polar (δυάς). So all material being is constructed in a polar way, in that it consists in matter and form (εἶδος), and so too all intellectual being, which is composed of a general essence (οὐσία) and an additional essential element that forms it specifically. For no created thing is, in the proper sense, simple; for it is not "just this" or "just that", but possesses at the same time, in a single subject (ὑποϰείμενον), both an essence (οὐσία) and

---

[65] Ibid.; PG 91, 1189A.
[66] Ibid.; PG 91, 1257AB; cf. PG 91, 1280AC; 1077C.
[67] Ibid.; PG 91, 1193AB.
[68] Ibid.; PG 91, 1400C; *Opuscula*; PG 91, 249C; *Ambigua*; PG 91, 1133CD.

a specifying, limiting difference that gives it concrete existence, forming it as a self and clearly distinguishing it from every other thing.[69]

Translated into the intellectual realm and into the activity of thought, this has immediate implications:

> Just as all thought has its designated place within an essence (οὐσία), as a quality of that essence, so it has its motion as directed toward such a qualified essence. For a completely absolute and simple thing cannot possess such a thing as thought, because thought is not absolute and simple. God, who is absolutely simple in both respects—he is both an essence without an underlying subject (*hypokeimenon*) to possess it, and thought without any object (*hypokeimenon*) to focus it—does not belong in the realm of either thinker or thought; he exists beyond both essence and thinking.[70]

Created being, then, is essentially a dynamic relationship between the unity of individuality and the unity of generality; created thinking is the expression of this same relationship on the intellectual level, as a dynamic exchange between the generic concept and the knowledge of an individual thing. Being, then, is "movement between"; only in this sense is it a *something* at rest.

b. Essence in Motion

What we have considered up to now in particular, existent individuals reappears in a similar form when we turn our attention to the "essence" of the created realm as such. This also is subject to motion —although not in the sense that a nature could ever, by that motion, leave its own specified limits. "For no nature has ever existed in the realm of the real, nor does it nor will it exist, which does not from the very beginning correspond to the concept of its own essence; it can never become, now or later, what it has not been all along." The metaphysical reason for this fact has already appeared, in connection with the world of ideas:

> Things whose ideas have received from God, along with their being, their completeness (τέλειον) do not permit of any increase or decrease

---

[69] *Ambigua*; PG 91, 1400C.
[70] *Centuries on Knowledge* 2, 3; PG 90, 1125D.

in their being; they have become what they are in accordance with their own particular idea, and they represent that idea essentially.[71]

At the heart of this developed being, however, lies also the necessity of motion.

The essence (οὐσία) of all things, in its simple sense[72]—not just the essence of things subject to (real) coming-to-be and passing-away, and which are moved in that process, but also the general essence of all things —has always been in motion and moves in the manner of expansion (*diastolē*) and contraction (*systolē*). For it moves from the most general genus, through less general genera, to the species, through which and in which it finds itself divided, and it presses on down to the most specific kinds of being, where its expansion comes against a limit, which circumscribes its being on the "downward" side; then once again, it moves from the most specific kinds of being through more and more general categories, until it is included in the most generic genus of all, and there its contraction meets its end, limiting its being on the "upward" side. Circumscribed thus from two directions, from above and from below, it shows that it is endowed with both a beginning and an end and can give no evidence at all of the idea of infinity. This same pattern is true for the (category of) quantity: not only the quantity of things that come to be and pass away, which are moved in every conceivable way with respect to growth and decline, but also totalities—beings on the level of general classes— are moved in the direction of relaxation or tension. They are specified through particular differences in a kind of "expansion" (*diastolē*) and so are limited and cannot simply extend themselves to infinity; and they also "contract" by ascending in the opposite direction and let go of their individual species, although not of their generic class. This is also true of quality: not just the quality of things that come to be and pass away, which move by change, but also the qualities of whole classes, of universals, are moved by the changing, scattering effect of their own specific differences and undergo both expansion (*diastolē*) and contraction (*systolē*). No intelligent person would say, however, that something that can be scattered and gathered again—either in concept or in reality—is simply without motion.[73]

---

[71] *Ambigua*; PG 91, 1345BC.

[72] That is, taken as the highest category of being (*ens commune*), which includes all genera and species under itself; thus not in the sense of Aristotle's "first substance" (πρώτη οὐσία).

[73] *Ambigua*; PG 91, 1177B–1180A.

c. A Balance of Contrary Motions

To answer the question of the ontological meaning of this essential motion, we must examine more closely the relationship between being in general (*katholou*) and individual being (*kathekaston*). We must understand these categories, however, from the start as ontological and not simply logical classes. This means that the *general* corresponds to a real ontological condition; it is not at all simply an "abstraction" of thought, drawn from the simple similarity of individual things. The first thing to notice is the strict opposition of the two poles, which both complement and presuppose each other.

> Universals are destroyed by transformation (ἀλλοίωσις: literally, "becoming different", "self-alienation") into individuals, while individuals are destroyed by dissolution (ἀνάλυσις: an elevating dismemberment [into universals]). The development of the one means the destruction of the other. For the reciprocal engagement of universals, from which individuals come into being, means for the former a transformation that signals the end; on the other hand, the dissolution of the connecting links that created the singular being, a dissolution that begins a process of decline toward the universal, also brings about the endurance (διαμονή) and new growth (γένεσις) of universal reality.[74]

There is, then, a strict reciprocity between both kinds of motion. Universal being, for Maximus, is in no sense simply the (higher-ranked) ground of particular being, as it would be for Neoplatonic thinking, but it is equally its effect, its result. Its changeless stability (διαμονή) is not self-sufficiency but is also something supported from below, something always newly brought into being (γένεσις) from particularity. This developing stability, however—as Maximus expressly says—is not something that happens in the order of temporal reality but occurs on the level of ideas. The dissolution of totality into existence as parts presupposes the previous dissolution of partial existence into totality, and vice versa.

> For none of the universal, all-embracing, generic beings is itself divided along with the singular, the subordinate, the particular. If something could not any longer gather together what is naturally scattered, it would no longer have the qualities of a genus but would be scattered itself and would leave behind its original monadic unity. Rather, every genus, ac-

---

[74] Ibid.; PG 91, 1169C.

cording to its own intelligible reality, dwells totally and univocally in the whole mass of what is understood under it and is recognized in every particular thing generically, as a single whole. Likewise the species reveal their identity in relation to each other when they let go of their range of differences.[75]

Universals, in other words, presuppose the "expansion" (*diastolē*) of particulars, which in turn makes possible their own "contraction", (*systolē*), "through which they first attain stability and concreteness (ὑπόστασις)".[76] They do not only presuppose this expansion but are equally the source from which particulars continually issue forth. The independence of universals has the same status and character as that of particulars; and if, in their "scattered" state, they still appear complete and undiminished in each particular thing, the particular—when dissolved into universals—must likewise remain complete and undiminished in them:

> Neither of the two harms the other by being its opposite, (neither) the tendency of parts to move toward the whole, (nor) the total identification of the universal with its parts, (nor even) the unconfused distinction of the parts from each other through the differentiating characteristic that makes each what it is, corresponding to the unconfused union [of the parts] through their simple identity in the wholes.[77]

This identity uses the whole difference of the parts, in fact, as the basis for producing unity—a "concrete" unity: "In the idea of a common essence (οὐσία, Latin: *ens commune*)" are included "the particular qualities (ἰδιώματα) of the particular essence (τῆς καθ᾽ ἕκαστον οὐσίας)".[78] This notion of the whole as a summation of particulars taken in their own right along with the notion of it as the dissolution of particulars are two different aspects of what is still a single and unitary system.

> We speak of "wholes" (πάντα) if the species and parts and differences exist in a scattered way; on the other hand, we speak of "totalities" (ὅλα) if the parts are so brought together that they form together one reality or if the species form a genus or if the points of contradiction—the poles of opposition—come to rest in harmony and mutual sympathy.[79]

---

[75] Ibid.; PG 91, 1312CD.
[76] Ibid.; PG 91, 1192A.
[77] Ibid.; PG 91, 1188D–1189A.
[78] *In De Div. Nom.* 5; PG 4, 321D.
[79] Ibid., 13; PG 4, 409A.

While the universal thus becomes a *concrete* universal (that is, itself an "individual") through the nourishing effect of the inclusion of individuals within it, the individual becomes, at the same time, a *universalized* individual through the presence of the universal in it.

> In his providence, . . . God brings about an increasing similarity between the individual and the universal, until finally he identifies the self-expressive drive of the person with the general law of intellectual being as such, by means of the instinctive drive of each individual to realize his goodness; he brings these individual drives into harmony and unity of motion both with each other and with the all, because their personal efforts are no longer focused on particular interests that separate them from the whole but are now found as the realization of a single idea in all of them.[80]

This idea of the balance and reciprocity of universal and particular is perhaps the most important in the whole of Maximus' thought. Here the old Greek suspicion of particularity, the exaggerated preference for the universal, is finally overcome. Even if Pseudo-Dionysius was an important source for this intuition—because he elevated God to an equally infinite distance (κατὰ τὸ ἴσον), as Maximus clearly puts it,[81] above all created categories, the universal as well as the individual—still his Neoplatonic tendency to conceive the universal as the independent source of the particular could only be neutralized, in the end, by an original philosophical contribution of Maximus' own. Here the fruitful effect of Chalcedon, and its emphasis on "unconfused (ἀσυγχύτως) union", is so real one can touch it with one's hands!

Maximus also found a predecessor for his philosophy of the concrete universal, as we have already suggested, in Gregory of Nyssa. Gregory, however, developed the idea simply in connection with mankind as a whole; in the process, as we have demonstrated elsewhere,[82] he regarded the individual, in an ultimately Stoic fashion, as both the cause and the effect of a concrete, global "human nature". Maximus, as a monk, seems to have emphasized this social side of the theory a little less strongly than the bishop of Nyssa, although it is certainly also present in his thought. His *Mystagogia*, for example, is almost entirely constructed on the parallel polarity of particular versus universal and

---

[80] *Quaestiones ad Thalassium* 2; CCG 7, 51, 12–19; PG 90, 272AB.
[81] *Ambigua*; PG 91, 1288B.
[82] *Présence et pensée* 19f.; English translation, 47f.

individual versus Church; his letters constantly emphasize the duty to
"universalize" one's personal efforts as a means of realizing the unity of
human beings in their identical common nature, as something willed
by God. In any case, Maximus deserves credit for giving the doctrine
of universals a general philosophical application and grounding, far beyond what Gregory had achieved.

What is still more striking, however, is the immediate similarity of
this dynamic style of thought to German idealism, and especially to
Hegel, whose underlying intuition was precisely the constantly shift-
ing interrelationship of universal and particular being. Maximus, the
philosopher of synthesis, is perhaps the only Christian philosopher who
seriously recognized the necessity of introducing motion into an ontology of (ideal) Being. For he was no more interested than Hegel
in the motion of purely theoretical, abstract concepts; both of them
were concerned with profoundly ontic, "real" processes, which could
take their place with full and equal rights alongside the movements
of historical, factual development. With both of them, ontology was
opened to a completely new dimension of development: a dimension
in which, in untroubled companionship, both motion and peace, both
"drunken bacchic revelry" and "transparent clarity and rest"[83]—the
one as movement toward individual, nonidentical being, the other as
its "immediate dissolution" in unity—blend into each other. Hegel
applies his conception, just as Gregory and Maximus had done, to the
philosophy of community:

> Reason is present as fluid, universal substance, as the unchangeable and
> simple concreteness of things; it splits into as many perfect and inde-
> pendent beings as starlight is scattered in countless points that glow
> by themselves—beings which, in their absolute independence of being
> [Fürsichsein], are not only resolved into simple independent substances
> in themselves but also for themselves. They are conscious of being such
> single, independent beings only insofar as they sacrifice their singularity
> and allow this universal substance to be their soul and essence—just as
> the universal, on the other hand, is their activity as individuals or is the
> achievement they produce.[84]

The basic insight of Maximus could not be expressed more clearly than
in this statement of Hegel. It will appear even more striking when we

---

[83] Hegel, *Phänomenologie des Geistes*, ed. G. Lasson, 2d ed. (Leipzig, 1920), 31.
[84] Ibid., 232.

come to consider his universalization of the individual through the assimilation of the intelligible meaning of creatures in "natural contemplation" (θεωρία φυσική) and through love.

In addition, Maximus also provides the weapons with which Christian philosophy must fight against the final conclusions of Hegel's thought. In his theory of ideas in motion, Maximus has only one purpose: to prove their contingence. For it is not simply "existence" that is contingent, created in finite being; the ideas, too, because of their dependence [on God], carry the stamp of createdness on their foreheads.

> Universal substance cannot be infinite, even though there are many universals. For because there are many universals, it possesses numerical quantity as a limit within itself; and this quantity circumscribes both the law of its being and of its essence, since universal substance is not absolute (that is, without relationships). It is equally obvious that no particular being can possess unlimited existence, because individual things limit each other reciprocally through the laws of number and nature. If, then, nothing that exists is without limitations, clearly everything, in a way corresponding to its nature, is specifically located in time and in place.[85]

The addition of cosmic totalities, too, can never generate something absolute, because temporality and limitation belong to them intrinsically and because they "limit each other reciprocally".[86] Even if one were to suppose that they did not simply add themselves to each other as parallel (παρακειμένην) quantitative wholes, but acted like syntheses that embraced each other (ἑτέραν ὑπερβαίνουσαν ἔχοντες),[87] the highest universal would still remain constitutionally dependent on all the particulars that were counted under it.

> For if the universals are constituted by the particulars, it is utterly impossible that they could preserve the intelligible form of their existence and continuity in themselves if the singular were to disappear. . . . For the parts have their existence in the wholes, and the wholes exist in and are constituted by the parts.[88]

---

[85] *Ambigua*; PG 91, 1181AB.
[86] Ibid.; PG 91, 1185A.
[87] Ibid.
[88] Ibid.; PG 91, 1189CD.

The world, then, is a closed unity formed by inner dependencies, and precisely in this self-contained character it is not absolute. "For the all of all things is not above the all, . . . but it possesses limitation within itself"; therefore it has its meaning and goal, not in its own generality, "but its goal is outside of itself."[89]

Being manifold, having a variety of interwoven meanings: these are for Maximus—in opposition to Plotinus and Proclus, as also to the pantheistic side of Origenism—signs of being a creature. The finite is located, along with essence and existence as a whole, on one side of the great chasm (χάσμα) that separates God from the world. And "if creatures can be numbered, they are also essentially diverse; for it is impossible that what is many should not also be diverse."[90] The Origenist idea of an absolute henad of intellects in the original state of creation contradicts at the deepest level—as Thomas Aquinas will also say—the whole structure of created being.

But the two kinds of motion—that between the universal idea and the underlying subject, which establishes the concrete individual, and that in the realm of universal meanings itself between created being in general (as the highest class of universal being) and the most restricted of species (εἶδος ἄτομον)—are not unrelated to each other. The contingence of the ideas and that of concrete, individually existing things are only the twofold expression of a single contingence: that of created being. We have already pointed out that the ideal totality of created meanings in God is just as much conditioned by its *real* totality as it is the basis and presupposition for it. As we saw in his refutation of Origenism, Maximus sees no such thing as "simple being" (εἶναι ἁπλῶς) in the world, but only being that is already marked by qualities (πῶς εἶναι) and that is therefore limited being. That is why God stands above being itself.[91]

But even the ideas have a "qualified" being, in this sense. The transition from nothingness to being, and thus also motion and limitation, belong to the essence and to the idea of the creature; that idea is therefore in itself incomplete, deficient (ἐλλιπές). Even if such a being is in a state of completeness (τέλειον), it cannot be absolutely self-limiting (αὐτοτελές).[92] Maximus has no hesitation, then, in inferring the con-

---

[89] Ibid.; PG 91, 1180C.
[90] Ibid.; PG 91, 1256D.
[91] Ibid.; PG 91, 1180D.
[92] Ibid.; PG 91, 1181C.

tingence of existence from the contingence of the essential being. For both poles—existence and essence—form, after all, a single, tension-filled unity. The contingence of the one pole is immediately obvious from that of the other.

> If, as our opponents assert, being (οὐσία) were something more excellent than the specific form (εἶδος), and if the existent thing, as they want us to believe, were able to produce or simply to possess being of itself, why is being then not even able to produce, or simply to possess, the less excellent of the two—namely, the specific form?[93]

Just as the existent subject has not produced its own existence as this (universal) kind of being, but was thrust into it (φέρεσθαι), so the universal essence has not produced its own existence in this subject—for this lies beyond its own conceptual content. Both poles thus point beyond themselves, through their reciprocal openness to each other; the whole finite, closed reality of created being itself cannot, because of this openness, be closed in the sense of being self-sufficient. Therefore the dynamism of being points once again beyond itself to God as the transcendental end of creation. The real individualizing of the world can only come from the unity that lies beyond the created order, which surpasses all forms of created unity, both that of universality and that of particularity.

3. Subject and Object

The unity of the universal and the particular was not a synthesis in the strict sense. Even if the world was the product of the interpenetration of the two, in a constant motion of expansion (*diastolē*) and contraction (*systolē*), it was this more as a *state* of interpenetration than as the *product* of two poles that actually produced it. The synthetic, in the full sense of the word, comes into view only if we leave the realm of the simple components of being and enter the living forces that have the ability to engage in the creative construction of syntheses. These forces correspond to the levels of independent being and to its increasing intellectuality; the very interiority of the process makes it possible for being to escape the abstract dialectic of the one and the many. The existentially "full" concept of universality rises above

---

[93] Ibid.; PG 91, 1181CD.

its abstract concept, insofar as it is the result of such an achieved synthesis.

> What is the idea of a universal that actively brings about, through mediation, the mutual connection of poles that are divided by their own finitude, so that it binds together the thinker and the thing thought about through the mediation of (active) thinking—through a thinking that is a unifying relationship of the separate poles and that labors to produce both the fruit of the two—which is a thought—and at the same time their integration?[94]

There are four concepts here we must deal with: the thinking subject (νοῦς), the object thought about (νοούμενον), the process of thinking (νόησις), and the result of thinking or the thought (νόημα). The last of these is the natural conclusion (τέλος) of the intellectual movement (κίνησις) of thought, which is itself an activation (ἐνέργεια) of the intellectual capacity (δύναμις) of the soul.

> The soul, which is an intellectual and rational being, thinks and ponders; its state of potentiality is the mind (νοῦς); its activation is thinking; its realization is the thought. This last is the goal and end of thinking, as well as of the thinker and the thing thought about, for it includes the mutual relationship of the poles. For as soon as the soul has come to insight, it stops thinking its thought; the process of thinking is complete.[95]

One should notice that thinking is here described as the "relationship" between subject and object; this relationship, however, is not a new, third thing alongside the poles but is simply the realization of a reciprocal directedness, an affinity for one another, an ontological relatedness that Maximus calls σχέσις and which is a fundamental expression of created existence. This "relatedness" has its roots in the spatial "distance" (διάστασις)[96] and "extension" (διάστημα)[97] of created being, bound together like poles in tension. Everything that can be included within this realm of being "moves or is moved, produces or is produced, thinks or is thought, speaks or is spoken, teaches or is taught"[98]—is, in other words, in relationship.[99] Activity and passivity,

---

[94] Ibid.; PG 91, 1228D.
[95] Ibid.; PG 91, 1220A.
[96] *Centuries on Knowledge* I, 5; PG 90, 1085A; cf. I, 7; PG 90, 1085B.
[97] *Ambigua*; PG 91, 1397B.
[98] Ibid.; PG 91, 1296A.
[99] Ibid.; PG 91, 1312BC.

being a subject and being an object, are here basically all on the same level. Even being objectified is, for Maximus, part of the way something is related: it is what specifies the thing internally, what gives it "being-for-others". The consequence of this is that God, who cannot participate in relatedness and cannot be the object of knowledge, also cannot *know* in the created sense.

> All thinking is something involving the thinker and that which is thought about. But God does not belong either to beings that think or beings that are thought about, because he is beyond both. Otherwise he would be limited: as a thinker, he would need to be related to the thing thought about, or as thing thought about he would be a natural object for the thinking mind, able to be thought about because of his relatedness. As a result, we can only conclude that God neither thinks nor is thought about but lies beyond both thinking and being thought. For both belong to the nature of creatures.[100]

The relationship of knowing that unites the creature to God is not "objective" knowledge in an inner-worldly sense, since it cannot base itself on any relatedness [to itself] in its object; it brings with itself an essentially new aspect, which Maximus calls "supposition" or "belief", but which is a kind of grasp that is sure and strong beyond all objective knowledge.[101]

Because the related subject and its object are both limited, the content that is synthesized from the two can also only be limited; thus the movement of synthesizing thought continues. Sense knowledge, in Maximus' system, has already been described as the synthetic identity of the sensing faculty with the sensible object;[102] but the result, which the imaginative process (φαντασία) produces—the sensible image (φαντάσμα) —points, as we saw, beyond itself toward a higher form of knowing. In all finite knowledge there is always a "remainder", which comes from the nonidentity of the subjective and objective poles and which remains, despite the identity of those two within the process of forming the sensible image (φαντάσμα) or thought (νόημα).

We will be on the right track if we see in this "remainder" the natural starting point of transcendental knowledge, for it has the character of a conviction akin to faith, a "positing" of what is beyond conscious

---

[100] *Centuries on Knowledge* 2, 2; PG 90, 1125C.
[101] Ibid., 1, 8–9; PG 90, 1085CD; developed more at length in 1, 82; PG 90, 1116B–1117A.
[102] *Ambigua*; PG 91, 1233D–1236A.

insight. A text that we will later have to consider more closely argues for a balance and mutual complementarity between the knowing and the trusting or believing faculties, on all levels of the life of the soul: as "theoretical and practical reason" (νοῦς and λόγος), as "wisdom and prudence", as "knowing and doing", or finally as "complete knowledge and faith" (γνῶσις καὶ πίστις).[103] In all theoretical knowing, there is present this kind of "practical" element, a conviction and a faith that does not recede as knowledge advances but that progresses in the same degree. Precisely in the highest kind of knowledge, the element of faith is of decisive importance; only through it does the absolute object of knowledge reveal itself as trustworthy, and the knowledge of it finds a solid confirmation (βέβαια πίστωσις).[104] For this confirmation is no longer derived from the "evidence" of the idea and from the concept of the "object", as is the case with the knowledge of created things.[105] But the "remainder", which already makes itself felt here, becomes a mighty force that drives the motion of thought along, until "proof from reasons" is no longer possible.

> When the soul has finally run, in thought, through all the thoughts of all conceivable sensible and intelligible objects, it takes its rest, both from all the objects it has thought about and from all thinking, as well as from its relationship to all that is relative and thinkable; for from that point on it finds nothing more to think about.[106]

This ascent of the soul is, on the one hand, a "moving through" things (in the Eastern manner), a "passage" (παρελθεῖν), because nothing can finally hold it down except the Absolute. But on the other hand, this "moving through" things is also a progressive "formation" of the knowing mind itself (in the Western manner), precisely because it is knowledge by synthesis; as we have said already, it is the continuing universalization of the knowing mind, until it reaches the full dimensions of the world's idea. We will later speak more of this formation; it will be enough here to point out that Maximus, like Hegel, likes to portray it in the image of eating, of consuming the substance of the known object. Such an "eating" of the intelligible content (λόγος) of

---

[103] *Mystagogia*, chap. 5; PG 91, 672ff.; see below, chap. 7, sec. 5 ("The Synthesis of the Three Acts").

[104] *Ambigua*; PG 91, 1124B.

[105] Ibid.; PG 91, 1364BC; *Centuries on Knowledge* 1, 8–9; PG 90, 1085CD.

[106] *Ambigua*; PG 91, 1220B.

things means inescapably, however, both a destruction, a "sacrificing" of objectivity as such (αὐτὴν μὲν τῶν ὄντων τὴν οὐσίαν κατέθυσε),[107] and also an assimilation of the object as food for the subject (τὸ νοούμενον τροφή ἐστι τοῦ νοεροῦ).

Of course, it is only in the case of a sensible object that knowledge is a kind of "destruction" of its objective independence [An-sich-sein]. But even if the knowledge of a mind cannot involve a "consuming" of the object, still this synthesis, too, contains all the positive elements that were present in sense knowledge: the termination of that state of indifferent opposition that mutually limited both subject and object before knowledge took place. What was necessary in the case of a sense object in order to end this indifference—the destruction of the objective independence of the object and its involvement in the self-conscious independence [Für-sich-sein] of the mind—becomes, according to John of Scythopolis, in the realm of minds, a perfect mutual interpenetration:

> They become mutually united to each other, without confusion (ἀσυγχύτως), because they are made in the image of God and share in the super-unitary unity of God himself, according to the level of their being. Such unions take place among incorporeal intellects, which interpenetrate each other without confusion.[108]

By sharing in God's mode of immanence, they are thus able, as he is, to be wholly in the object of knowledge and wholly one with it (and thus realize the universal side of unity) yet, at the same time, to realize mutually their self-conscious independence (that is, express the particularizing side of unity). Their mutual motions are an interplay of unity and distance, penetration and hesitation, that provides the highest example of the validity of the law of synthesis and of its way of uniting without confusion. According to Stoic physics, at least, a remote image of this can be found in the mutual and complete interpenetration of two fluids, which nevertheless do not mingle with each other (χωρεῖν δι᾽ ἀλλήλων ἀλυμάντως).[109]

In this knowledge of pure intellects, one can already see clearly the final goal and ultimate form of all knowing, toward which human knowledge, too, is under way: to know God. God, who is "of limitless

---

[107] *Quaestiones ad Thalassium* 27; CCG 7, 195, 81–82; PG 90, 356A.

[108] *In De Div. Nom.* 2; PG 4, 220D.

[109] *Ambigua*; PG 91, 1228C.

simplicity" and who stands "beyond circumscription and the circumscribed", who is "without relation", "free of time, temporal extension [the aeon], and space",[110] is therefore also the ultimate basis for
the possibility for all imperfect, created union, the final transcendental
condition of all synthesis and all identification. For this reason, Maximus—unlike Gregory of Nyssa—puts the knowledge of God beyond
all motion. If the arrival of a single act of thinking at its intellectual
content (νόημα) is in itself a "stopping" (τέλος, πέρας)—however temporary—of the mind's motion, then surely for the intellect to be filled
with its infinite object must be "an unknowing, unknowable, ineffable
union, beyond intellect, reflection, and knowledge, in simple adhesion
(προσβολή)."[111]

For God is not the relative pole of a faculty of knowing that is ordered toward him; he is therefore not, as Gregory of Nyssa would have
him, the infinitely receding goal of the intellect's eternal motion. Much
less is God, as Evagrius would have him, the most intimate spark of
spiritual life in the intellect itself. Nor is the ceasing of its motion,
then, a final return of the intellect to itself; its cause always remains
the utterly simple transcendence of God.

The possibility of forming syntheses, which is the heart of created
thinking, here comes to an end. The intellect has no further finite opposition to overcome; it is now the finite object in need of liberation.
It is taken up itself into a union that opens out from God's side, and
it flows into a reality that is unlimited.

> The end of faith is the real revelation (ἀποκάλυψις) of what is believed.
> And the real revelation of what is believed is the ineffable embrace
> (περιχώρησις) of it, which is brought about in proportion to the faith
> of each person. The embrace of what is believed is the return of the
> believer home to his origin, which is now his end. But the return of
> the believer home to his origin, as to his end, is the fulfillment of his
> longing. Now the fulfillment of his longing is the rest of the loving heart
> in eternal motion around the beloved. But the rest of the loving heart
> in eternal motion around the beloved is eternal, immediate delight, . . .
> participation in the supernatural blessings of God. And this is the forming
> of those who participate into the likeness of what they participate in; but
> such a likening consists in the actively realized (καθ' ἐνέργειαν) identity

---

[110] Ibid.; PG 91, 1153B.
[111] Ibid.; PG 91, 1220B.

of the participants with what they participate in, which comes to its fullness with the likeness itself. And this identity . . . is divinization.[112]

We have here, once again, an identity *in actu*, such as occurs in all forms of sense perception and rational knowledge; it is also an identity that lies beyond the abiding gulf of an unconfused difference in natures. The destruction of the object's independent objectivity [*An-sich-sein*] has here become its supreme affirmation and fulfillment.

4. Intellect and Matter

a. The Macrocosm

The ontology of the first two great cosmic tensions—universality versus singularity and subjectivity versus objectivity—always saw the poles of the tensions as balanced and of equal value. In opposition to Neoplatonism, Maximus emphasizes the horizontal equivalence of universal and particular. In opposition to the tendency of all Greek thought to emphasize object over subject, he stresses their equal importance on all levels of being.

This line of thought continues further, in the ontology of intellect and matter. This is a subject that has won Maximus a special place in the gallery of Christian thinkers. Here, of course, from the nature of the subject, there can no longer be any talk of a simple equivalence; in addition, the strong weight of a spiritualizing tradition worked against any tendency to put them on the same level. Nevertheless Maximus, in a mighty reaction against this tradition, was the first to draw strong and clear lines across the area under discussion. He found within the tradition itself some points of support. In Origen's cosmic symbolism there lay as yet unrealized philosophical possibilities. The Cappadocians, especially Gregory of Nyssa once again, had drawn the unity of creation, closed in on itself through its temporal extension (*aeon*), away from being considered the intellect's direct ladder of access to God; in doing that, they paved the way for understanding the intellectual and sensible realms simply in inner-worldly terms. Pseudo-Dionysius, finally, was the source of the idea that grew out of this, of a similar "distance" of the transcendent God in every principle of created being, of a God

---

[112] *Quaestiones ad Thalassium* 59; CCG 22, 53, 123–41; PG 90, 608C–609A.

who "is inaccessible to all of creation, visible as well as invisible, in the same degree".[113] The more God is seen, in fact, as wholly other, the more the intellect must give up hope of reaching him by means of a "heavenly ladder" built from the steps of the created universe—and the more the world must close in on itself, in order to become in its totality, not simply in its most noble parts, a place to praise and serve the Infinite One.

This is not to suggest one should attribute to intellect and matter the same metaphysical value. Maximus' philosophy, like his asceticism, is of course shot through with the conviction that the intellectual is superior to the material, a superiority that goes so far as to demand a strict indifference, a renunciation of all material things, in order to reach the freedom that naturally belongs to the spirit. In spite of this clear preference for the intellectual, however, there is still a perfect balance between the noble "higher" realm and the "lower" realm that is meant to serve it. The balance, however, is this time not horizontal but vertical. It is the complete correspondence and mutual orientation of "content" and "image", of "meaning" and "appearance", of the noumenal and the phenomenal realms. The whole ontological concept of the material world is exhaustively expressed in the fact that it is the likeness and the phenomenal mode of appearance of the world of intellect, while the intellectual realm has the intrinsic tendency to reveal its essence in this mirror, which is in no way provisional but has ultimate meaning. Thus a perfect mutual exchange (περιχώρησις) takes place between the intellectual and the material worlds: an insight that Pseudo-Dionysius prepared through his conception that the heavenly and ecclesial hierarchies completely mirror one another, the one on the purely intelligible level, the other on the phenomenal and material. Maximus gives to this aesthetic intuition both conceptual reflectiveness and cosmic breadth.

> This cosmos is a unity and is not divided up along with its parts; rather, precisely through its tendency to rise toward its own single and undivided being, it puts limits on the differences of its natural division into parts. So it proves that the parts are always the same as itself, even in their unconfused differentiation; that every whole dwells within every other whole; that all of them fill up the one whole as its parts and are in turn made one and are completely filled in themselves because of

---

[113] *Ambigua*; PG 91, 1288B.

the integrity of the whole. In fact, the whole intellectual world appears as mystery, expressed in meaningful forms through the whole sensible world, to those who are privileged to see it; and the whole sensible world dwells within the whole intellectual world, reduced through the Spirit of wisdom to its basic intelligible meanings. The material, that is, dwells in the intellectual in the mode of intelligible meanings, and the intellectual dwells in the material in the mode of images; but the result of both is a single world.[114]

In these statements, the Alexandrian symbolism of Origen is at once brought to its fulfillment and—through the anchoring of the intellect in the world of sense—is brought beyond itself. One is tempted to think of the philosophy of Schelling, and its identification of the All in both the real and the ideal totality of the world, a system in which the All itself appears as both origin and end product. Such notions, too, provided the starting point for the Christian aesthetic, which the Romantics and—starting afresh—Paul Claudel succeeded in developing.

b. The Microcosm

This view of the world finds its mirror image, as well as the proof of its truth, in man, as the microcosm in whom the mutual indwelling of material and intellectual come to their full realization.

For the intellectual beings, the wise man said, represent the place of the soul, as the soul represents the place of the intellectual beings; sensible things, on the other hand, contain an image of the body, just as the body is an image of sensible things. And intellectual beings are the soul of sensible things, while sensible things are the body of intellectual beings. And just as the soul dwells in the body, so the intellectual world lives within that of material things; the intellectual is equipped with the sensible as the soul is equipped with a body, and from the two together a single complete world is formed—just as man is formed from soul and body, and neither of the two destroys or lets go of the other, because they have grown together in their unity.[115]

Maximus' anthropology is the development of what is stated here as a program. The emphasis on the "essence" (οὐσία), on the "nature"

---

[114] *Mystagogia*, chap. 2; PG 91, 669BC.
[115] Ibid., chap. 7; PG 91, 685A; cf. *Quaestiones ad Thalassium* 63; CCG 22, 177, 497ff.; PG 90, 686D.

(φύσις), on the "existence" (εἶναι) of the different and irreducible parts of the human reality, which nevertheless come together in an indissoluble synthesis to form the idea of a single species (εἶδος), corresponds to this insight.[116] That is why Maximus energetically rejects the supposition of any sort of temporal priority of the soul to the body[117] or of the body to the soul.[118] The mutual metaphysical dependency of them both is so basic an idea for him that he considers both the nature (φύσις) of man and his existence as a person (ὑπόστασις) to depend on this essential unity. Origenism in all its forms—even in that abbreviated form represented by Leontius of Byzantium[119]—here receives its mortal wound.

Consistently with this position, Maximus also contradicts the hypothesis—which Thomas Aquinas would someday take up again—of the progressive development of different "souls" (the vegetative, the animal, finally the intellectual) in the development of the fetus. First of all, Maximus says, the essential motion of the seed cannot be simply a mechanical thing; otherwise its growth [into a human being] would be inexplicable. If one were to ascribe to it simply vital power (ζωτική τις δύναμις), it would doubtless form an organism but never a human body. Down to its very deepest being, the body is the expression of an intellectual soul. The theory of a progressive evolution of lower to more perfect principles of formation deserves the reproach that Gregory of Nyssa had already made against it and against the proponents of the theory of reincarnation, which Maximus now repeats: "This amounts to mixing everything up together!"[120] Instead, every finite being, throughout its development and in spite of it, possesses its own perfect idea (τέλειος λόγος) within itself from the start; through all its transformations, it never departs from that idea.[121] So while the scholastics were forced to suppose an exception from the law of the

---

[116] *Ambigua*; PG 91, 1100CD.

[117] Ibid.; PG 91, 1321–36.

[118] Ibid.; PG 91, 1336C–1341.

[119] [On the disputed question of whether and how Leontius of Byzantium could be considered an Origenist, see: Marcel Richard, "Léonce de Byzance était-il origéniste?" *Revue des études byzantines* 5 (1947): 31–66; David B. Evans, *Leontius of Byzantium: An Origenist Christology*, Dumbarton Oaks Studies, 13 (Cambridge, Mass., 1970); Brian E. Daley, "The Origenism of Leontius of Byzantium", *Journal of Theological Studies* 27 (1976): 333–69.]

[120] *Ambigua*; PG 91, 1337D.

[121] Ibid.; PG 91, 1340A.

continuity of natural principles in the mystery of Christ's Incarnation; Maximus finds there the ultimate confirmation of his own theory.[122]

The objection that the soul continues to exist without a body after death is overcome in the same way as it is by Thomas Aquinas:

> After the departure of the body the soul is not simply (and without further qualification) called "soul", but the soul of a human being—in fact, of a particular human being. For even after (its separation from) the body, its essential concept is still determined by its relationship (to the body) as to a part of the whole; only in this way is it called "human". The same is true of the body.[123]

For this reason, man only reaches perfection in the resurrection of the flesh. If "Christ sits at the right hand of God the Father, along with his body", that is the model of our hope; "we will not accept any abandonment of our bodies, however it is brought about."[124]

This underlying unity of intellect and matter, which is the basis of the species, holds true even though the elements of this unity are different, not simply in origin,[125] but even in their essence and their nature (φύσις)[126] and down to the particular ontological manner of their existence.[127]

Man, as an intellectual and material microcosm, thus appears both as the midpoint of a universe arranged in a polar pattern and as its final synthesis. Insofar as he is at the same time the subject of knowledge, through his intellect, and its object, through his body, he becomes both the world's axis and its system of coordinates, where its horizontal and vertical polarities cross. He stands in the middle, not as an independent lord; through his natural being, through his double essence, he is drawn into the internal mechanism of the macrocosm. His dual nature makes him just as passive as his synthetic character shows him to be active.

> The dependency and relationship of thinking beings to what is thought is manifold, just like that of sensitive and imaginative beings to what is

---

[122] Ibid.; PG 91, 1341AB.
[123] Ibid.; PG 91, 1101B.
[124] Ibid.; PG 91, 1324CD.
[125] Ibid.; PG 91, 1333CD.
[126] Ibid.; PG 91, 1373C.
[127] Ἄλλος λόγος καὶ τρόπος καθ᾽ ὃν γίνεταί τε καὶ ἔστι (ibid.; PG 91, 1321CD).

imaged through the senses. Man, who consists of soul and body, is just as much included in a larger whole through his natural mutual relation- ship to the two realms of creation, and through the peculiar character of his own essence, as he is a being who includes others: he is included through his intelligible way of being (οὐσία), and he includes through his intellectual power (δύναμις). By being extended, then, into these two realms through his double nature, he is able to draw both of them together to himself in a synthesis, by the means of the components of his own being. He is included among both intellectual and material things because he is himself a soul and a body; but he can include them in himself through the powers of his intellect, because he possesses reason and senses.[128]

Once again, then, the midpoint of the world is occupied by the high- est degree of limitation, in synthesis, and the unconfused mutual in- dwelling of opposites: patterns that have already appeared as the de- cisive characteristics of created being. The unity that is fulfillment, the real heart of the world, can thus only be transcendent, far from the mainstream of ordinary life [ex-zentrisch]. "God, however, is simple and without limits and lies beyond all intelligible beings, both those included in others and those that include them, . . . because he is with- out any relationships."[129]

God's transcendence is the ultimate basis for the possibility of a bal- ance and a mutual imaging of intellect and matter. The world becomes, once again, a "closed house"; it is God's mirror, in that it ceaselessly realizes, in the heart of its reality, the uncanny reciprocal reflectivity of intellect and matter. Maximus expressed this insight in a final state- ment, which may be the most astonishing thing he ever wrote—even if it is also simply the slowly ripened fruit of the whole Alexandrian metaphysical tradition:

The divine Apostle writes, "For his invisible attributes have been per- ceived since the creation of the world, intellectually grasped through creatures" (Rom 1:20). And if the things that do not appear are per- ceived through those that do appear, so too—in much greater measure —the things that do appear will be perceived through the things that do not, by those who commit themselves to the vision of the mind. For the contemplation of intellectual things, in images, through what is vis-

---

[128] Ibid.; PG 91, 1153AB.
[129] Ibid.; PG 91, 1153B.

ible *is* spiritual insight and is the understanding of the visible through the invisible. For it is necessary that both kinds of reality—which are there in order to reveal each other—always convey a true and unmistakable expression of each other and show an irreducible mutual relationship to each other.[130]

---

[130] *Mystagogia* 2; PG 91, 669D.

V

HUMANITY AND SIN

1. History and the Parousia

Up to now, we have considered the world as a piece of theater, a play of powers, tensions, and balances. But it is more than that. It is theater only because it is drama, history. The vertical dimension [of God's intervention] meets the horizontal axis of time. Doubtless, we have been moving in the world of Greek thought, specifically in that of the early Byzantine period, so we should not expect to find in Maximus an interest in the historicity of existence similar to what we find in the author of *The City of God* or even that tragic sense of becoming that dominated Gregory of Nyssa. Alongside "natural contemplation" (θεωρία φυσική), one finds here no contemplation of history. Nevertheless: although the dimension of history is completely missing in Pseudo-Dionysius, totally absorbed by the overpowering contemporaneity of the divinized cosmos, this purely "axiological" view of the whole of things takes on new life in Maximus, under the influence both of the Cappadocian mysticism of development and of the Aristotelian emphasis on the goal. The ahistorical Neoplatonic circular movement of radiation outward and return to the center—a life that flows and rests at the same time and so can almost be thought of as a vitality *within* the life of God— finds in Maximus a sharper profile: it has become the effort of creatures to move from potentiality (*dynamis*) to actuality (*energeia*), even if the goal-directedness (*entelecheia*) that governs it only becomes, in the end, what it already is and, so, brings its true origin to the light of day.

Maximus' reflection on history, then, stands in a curiously unresolved state, somewhere between a pure contemplation of natural being and a concrete involvement in the variegated, constantly changing reality of actual events. His view is dominated by the three great turning points of history's drama: first, the start of the race, as a fall from original unity—the fall which is sin; then the turning of the course, away from what was a movement toward annihilation, by God's own initiative—the Incarnation; and finally, the completion of the race, through reunification in the oneness of the original state—God's final presence (*parousia*) in the world. Even these turning-points themselves are seen less as events in temporal sequence than as essential *states* of historical existence—human existence and the existence of the world: states that mysteriously overlap each other in the temporal development of every creature and that are recognizable in the creature's life.

Maximus is not very original in what concerns the theology of the fall as a historical fact; he tries to harmonize the opinions of his predecessors. What is new in his work is the way he considers the fall as present in day-to-day experience. The parousia of Christ, as the end point of history, is of little interest to him; he looks at it almost exclusively as God's open proclamation of the new aeon, already present in a hidden way in everyday life. Even with respect to Christ, the historical person and his particular earthly acts and sufferings are of less interest for Maximus than the consideration of the inner reality of the Incarnation—one is tempted to say, its "formal structure". Although this focus is certainly influenced, to some extent, by [contemporary] disputes over the most precise way to formulate the mystery of Christ, it is also due, in equal measure, to Maximus' own intellectual tendency to conceive of phenomenal history as simply the veil over, the pointer toward, a noumenal presence. The general conception of "parousia" [God's "presence"] remains the underlying category for the philosophy of history in the Greek Fathers.

2. Paradise and Freedom

The earthly paradise only interests Maximus as the starting point of the world's history, as the place of the fall. Here, too, his gaze simply follows the direction of development: it is only by glimpsing the ultimate goal that he hopes to make contact with lost origins, never by looking backward. A text will serve to adjust our focus to his perspective: "If anyone should want to say that the tree of knowledge of good and evil was creation as it appears before us, he would not be wrong; for essentially this is what communicates to its participants joy and pain." The first human beings were supposed to nourish themselves from this tree only when they had attained the strength of contemplating nature in truth: for all who engage in genuine contemplation, this "nourishment" must lead to intellectual revelation; for all who are bound to the senses, however, it necessarily becomes a cause of falling away.

So God postponed the enjoyment of this tree, so that—as was right—
man should first, by sharing in the life of grace, become aware of his own
origin and should be confirmed in freedom from sensual drives (ἀπάθεια)
and unwavering commitment (ἀτρεψία) by the gift of immortality and
so come to share in the being of God through divinization; at that point,
he could see through created reality without danger, along with God, and
gain an understanding of it as a god, not as a man. Through grace, and
because of the divinizing transformation of his intellect and his senses,
he would then have the same insight into the essences of things that God
has: Wisdom.[1]

In this way, men would have possessed a balance in their relationships
to the intellectual and the sensible worlds, by surveying both from the
viewpoint of God's transcendent realm.

Even so: did Maximus ever lament the fact that, through the failure of
the first human beings, world history has been summoned into action?
He certainly objected to the exaggerations of the Origenists, who saw
the "experience" (πεῖρα) of evil as metaphysically necessary, in order
to attach the soul definitively to the goodness that is God. Gregory
of Nyssa's insight into the inexhaustibility of this goodness, and into
the blessed unity of an exalted yearning and straining [for God] and
the ultimate fulfillment of all desires in the act of contemplating him,
remains alive in Maximus. But what Greek Christian, since Irenaeus,
could tear free from the thought that man's way, from Adam to Christ
and on to the end of the world, amounted to a progressive unfolding
and maturing, a growth to reality, of God's "seeds of intelligibility" in
the world? (For Irenaeus and Clement, after all, Adam and Eve were
children, who hardly knew what they were doing.) Who could resist
the idea that the "fall" itself contained, at the same time, the basis of
a radical "beginning"? And would it not, in some fashion, have been
a reversal of the natural order of things if Adam, from the very beginning, had taken possession of nature simply by receiving it from
God, according to his sense of who God was? Does not man's way
lead rather *through* nature to God?

Maximus knows a second way of interpreting the fateful tree, "a
more mysterious and exalted one, which we should honor by keeping
silence about it": this is the interpretation that Gregory of Nyssa, bor-
rowing from Origen, had given. It asserts the identity of the two trees,

---

[1] *Quaestiones ad Thalassium*, prologue; CCG 7, 37, 327–30, 338–49; PG 90, 257D–260A.

the "tree of life" and the "tree of knowledge", so that access to life
was ultimately only available through knowledge of good and evil.[2] So
Maximus, good Greek that he is, sets off on the dangerous track that
he will walk to the end: the track of "gnosis".

The old interpretation of the dynamic tension between "image" and
"likeness", taken from Irenaeus and Origen, appears here again, but
now in its classical form:[3]

> Those who interpret divine sayings in a mystical way and who honor
> them, as is right, with lofty thoughts tell us that man was originally
> created "according to the image of God", so that he might be born to
> the life of the spirit in a way fully in accord with his own freedom; then,
> they tell us, he received in addition the character of "likeness", as a result
> of keeping God's commands, so that he might be, as the same man, at
> once both a creature of God by nature and a child of God by grace and
> might even be himself god, through the Spirit. For there was, for the
> human creature, only one way to prove himself a child of God, and even
> god by the grace of divinization: according to his own free decision, to
> be born first according to the Spirit, through the indomitable power that
> naturally dwelt in him to determine himself.[4]

Maximus does not mean to say here that in Adam, grace followed on
freedom. But he does seem to mean that both "trees"—the tree of
the natural world and the tree of divinization by grace—had to be offered to him together: "For he had to make a free decision whether
'to cling to the Lord and to become one spirit with him' or 'to cling
to a harlot and to become one body with her' (1 Cor 6:16f.)—the latter of which, in his blindness, he chose."[5] This description of Adam's
situation closely resembles the way Augustine interprets him: on the
one hand, there is the offer of grace (as an indispensable means of support); on the other hand, the unconditional necessity to choose between two possibilities, both of which promise to complement and
satisfy this will. For Maximus as for Augustine, freedom of the will

---

[2] Ibid.; CCG 7, 37, 350ff.; PG 90, 260Aff.

[3] It had already been thus interpreted in the anonymous tract from the circle of the Cappadocians, *Quid sit ad imaginem et similitudinem* (What "image and likeness" mean); GNO
supp. (Leiden, 1972); PG 44, 1327–46.

[4] *Ambigua*; PG 91, 1345D; cf. *Centuries on Love* 3, 25; PG 90, 1024BC; *Centuries on Knowledge* 1, 13; PG 90, 1088BC.

[5] *Centuries on Knowledge* 1, 13; PG 90, 1092D.

involves more need than independence; it is an appetite that reaches outward in search of its object (ὄρεξις ζητητική) [6] and that must take its nourishment from one of the two "trees". The one offered man "the nourishment of the blessed life: the bread that came down from heaven to give life to the world, as the true Word says in the Gospel; but the first human being did not want to take his nourishment from there." [7] If he had chosen this bread, he would have dedicated himself to the highest dependence, but precisely in that way he would have received divine fruitfulness; born from God, he would himself have been able to generate offspring in a divine way [8] and would have realized his own most deep-seated law: for the tree of life is "wisdom according to the [human] mind". [9] But he chose material nature as the nourishment of his intellect [10] and so committed himself, not to dependence on God, but to dependence on the senses and on material things.

The two "trees" thus point to the two laws, or better still to the two criteria human nature uses for evaluation.

> The two trees are, in the symbols of Scripture, our faculties that enable us to distinguish between particular things: our intellect, that is, and our senses. The intellect has the ability to discern between the intellectual and the sensible, between temporal and eternal things; it is the gift of discernment that urges the soul to give itself to some things and to refrain from others. The senses, on the other hand, have the criteria for telling bodily pleasure from pain; more precisely, they are the power of ensouled and sensitive bodies that gives them the ability to be attracted by pleasurable things and to avoid painful things. [11]

In that Maximus emphasizes human freedom of choice, as able to allow one or the other of the laws of his being to dominate, he understands original sin completely as rebellion against the higher law and, thus, as insubordination, as pride. That this upsetting of right order was also for him, as for many of the Greek Fathers, also a sin of the flesh does not contradict this principle. To follow the law of the

---

[6] *Opuscula*; PG 91, 16B.

[7] *Ambigua*; PG 91, 1157A.

[8] Ibid.; PG 91, 1348A.

[9] *Quaestiones ad Thalassium* 43; CCG 7, 295, 58–59; PG 90, 413A.

[10] *Ambigua*; PG 91, 1156CD.

[11] *Quaestiones ad Thalassium* 43; CCG 7, 295, 40–48; PG 90, 412D.

body[12] means "to turn the eyes of the intellect from the light",[13] to place enjoyment (*frui*) above use (*uti*).[14]

> For certainly God created these things and gave them to the human race for their use (χρῆσις). And everything that God made is good and was intended for us to use well. But in our own weakness and fleshly attitudes, we have preferred material things to the commandment of love.[15]

This "other" love, however, which Augustine calls "concupiscence", consists for Maximus and his contemporaries of two inseparable, almost equally emphasized elements: love for bodily things and egoism. It is really the love of self (φιλαυτία).[16] The tendency of intellectual self-seeking to slip into the region of baser sensuality, this necessarily downward movement, is for Greek monastic theology more than simply a consequence and sign of all sin; it is its very essence. As a distortion of order, however, it is "the attempt to take control of things without God and before God and not according to God".[17] This comes down to giving an intellectual nature sensible, temporal, transitory food to nourish its being and, so, to poison it at its root, to hand it over to death. For the opposite of what Adam hoped for was bound to happen: instead of the intellect assimilating the world of sense to itself, which could only have happened according to God's order and plan, the sensible realm took over the intellect. "[Adam] handed all of nature over to death, to be gobbled up by it. That is the reason that death lives through this whole span of time and gnaws away at us as if we were its meal; we never manage really to live, constantly consumed by death in our transitoriness and decay."[18]

---

[12] *Ambigua*; PG 91, 1092D.

[13] Ibid.; PG 91, 1156C.

[14] [Von Balthasar here employs a distinction developed and emphasized by Augustine; see, for example, *De doctrina christiana* 1, 4.]

[15] *Liber asceticus*: PG 90, 916D–917A.

[16] Irénée Hausherr, *Philautie. De la tendresse pour soi à la charité selon s. Maxime le confesseur*, Orientalia Christiana Analecta, 137 (Rome, 1952).

[17] *Ambigua*; PG 91, 1156C.

[18] Ibid.; PG 91, 1157A.

3. Passivity and Decay

The place to which our guilt has banished us is "the present world of transitoriness and of the mutual corruption of things into each other".[19] But is not this transitoriness, from another point of view, a natural law of things? May one trace it back so exclusively to an original sin?

> The true Word, (Maximus writes), teaches us mysteriously that man, master of the whole visible world by the grace of God, his Creator, perverted the natural tendencies of his intellectual being by misusing them and diverted his instincts to what was unnatural; as a result, he drew down on himself and on this whole universe the present order of change and corruptibility, according to the just judgment of God.[20]

Death and corruptibility depend, in a mysterious way, on a first sin. "Through sin, this cosmos became a place of death and destruction",[21] the realm of the πάθη.[22] *Pathos* and death are connected by definition. "I repeat what the great Gregory of Nyssa taught me: only when man fell away from his perfection were the πάθη introduced since they grew in the nonreasonable part of his nature."[23] Maximus follows Gregory down to the last implications: only under this new law, which did not hold at the beginning, did a way of procreation come into effect that is

---

[19] *Quaestiones ad Thalassium* 62; CCG 22, 125, 175–77; PG 90, 653A.

[20] *Epistles* 10; PG 91, 449B.

[21] *Quaestiones ad Thalassium* 65; CCG 22, 255, 86–88; PG 90, 740B.

[22] Everyone knows how untranslatable this word is; it runs the gamut from active emotional "passion" (affect, affection—in the direction of either anger or desire) to a suffering susceptibility, a "passivity" in the face of a situation that forces itself through the defenseless sense faculties. That these two poles of the concept of *pathos* are so indissolubly one— much closer than in the French word *passion*, where "affect" and "suffering" branch off from one another almost as if they were two different meanings of the same word—says more about Greek and patristic thought than whole books could hope to explain. Much as the Stoic, even Platonic, origin of this confusion was neutralized by the Fathers where possible —neutralized by Maximus in that he usually contrasts *pathos*, as "a sinful addiction", with a neutral expression for "sensibility" ("the part of the soul capable of being affected": τὸ παθητικὸν (μέρος) τῆς ψυχῆς) —the word always remained a threat, even a danger, because at its root is the identification of sensibility and passivity. Therefore, if the ideal of the intellect was action and activity, the way to the true subject was to free oneself from the senses (the destruction of the "passions"). Cf. section 5 of this chapter, "The Dialectic of Passion", and the *Centuries on Love*.

[23] *Quaestiones ad Thalassium* 1; CCG 7, 47, 7–10; PG 90, 269A.

naturally (φύσει) connected with both fleshly desire and death.[24] "For
the original will of God (προηγούμενος σκόπος) was that we should not
be born in the way of this transitory world, by physical copulation;
only our transgression of the law introduced marriage."[25] In this way,
conception is really connected with the "law of sin",[26] which now
dwells in the body.

Is this not, however, a contradiction? If the πάθη first arose in Adam's
body as a consequence of sin; if another, spiritual means of reproduction existed first, in place of fleshly procreation—a means that did not
have decay and death as its logical counterpart; if Adam's body was not
put together out of the usual qualities and elements (such as cold and
warm, moist and dry), but consisted in a restful and unchanging state
of consistency, "without accretion or diminution", in a "graced condition of immortality and incorruptibility"; if Adam was not in any sense
bodiless, but lived in a finer form of corporeality, without ignorance
and so without changing opinions (γνώμη) or supporting skills (τέχνη):
how could he have felt the law of sensuality or observed it in preference to the criteria of the intellect?[27] Indeed, Maximus assumes Adam's
union with God was so exalted that it was a direct (οὐδὲν μεταξύ) vision, even higher (ὑπεράνω) than the contemplation of God through
created things (φυσικὴ θεωρία). With such an exalted conception of
the original state of humanity, must not the whole biblical reality of
Paradise descend to the level of weak symbolism? We have already seen
that the tree of Paradise, for Maximus, is pure imagery,[28] as are the ser-
pent[29] and Adam's nakedness.[30] Does this not mean that the situation
of [original] glory, as it is described, is completely a myth, as it was for
Gregory of Nyssa? Not a myth, of course, in the sense of a fictional
untruth, but in the sense of a prehistorical or metahistorical reality, of
which the historical situation of the first humans was only a reflection
in the world of phenomena. We have attempted elsewhere to show that
Gregory of Nyssa's statements, with their apparent contradictoriness,

---

[24] Ibid., 61; CCG 22, 91, 109ff.; PG 90, 632B.
[25] Quaestiones et Dubia 3; CCG 10, 138, 3–5; PG 90, 788AB.
[26] Quaestiones ad Thalassium 49; CCG 7, 369, 305; PG 90, 457D.
[27] Ambigua; PG 91, 1353A–D; 1348A.
[28] Quaestiones ad Thalassium, prologue; CCG 7, 37; PG 90, 257CD; ibid., 26; CCG 7, 183;
PG 90, 348D; ibid., 64; CCG 22, 189; PG 90, 696A.
[29] Ibid., 63; CCG 22, 151, 100f.; PG 90, 669B.
[30] Ambigua; PG 91, 1353B.

can be reconciled only in this sense.[31] Maximus enumerates the two great attempts of previous thinkers to solve the question: the Origenist approach, according to which the ideal, metahistorical state of the first creatures means a heavenly, incorporeal existence, from which souls fell into earthly bodies through sin—a conception that Maximus rejects on ontological as well as anthropological grounds[32]—and Gregory of Nyssa's approach, according to which God created the consequences of disobedience—sensuality, and especially sexuality—along with human nature, in his foreknowledge (κατὰ πρόγνωσιν) of sin.[33]

But while the attempted solution of Gregory of Nyssa is more or less a rough compromise between Origen's mythic structure and the historical approach of the Antiochenes and Irenaeus—a compromise that tries to solve the riddle of the fall with the paradox of a "reciprocal causality" (that is, the consequence of sin is also its cause)— Maximus goes a step beyond Gregory and approaches the theory of Scotus Erigena, for whom the creation and the fall are conceptually distinct but factually simultaneous. "Together with his existence (ἅμα τῷ εἶναι)",[34] "together with his coming to be (ἅμα τῷ γενέσθαι)",[35] "man leaves his own origin behind through sin" and "turns his mind toward sensible things". Gregory of Nyssa loved to look back to the place of our origins in Paradise, as if it were the true and somehow historical homeland of the human race. For Maximus, the bronze doors of the divine home are slammed remorselessly shut at the very start of our existence; there remains only the dimension of the future, of development and of realization, at whose end—like that of an enormous arc—our point of origin can be reached again at last.

> In looking for his end, man meets his origin, which essentially stands at the same point as his end. . . . For we should not seek our origin, as I have said, as something that lies behind us; rather we should seek out ways toward the goal that lies before us. It is through his end that man

---

[31] Hans Urs von Balthasar, *Présence et pensée* (Paris, 1942), 41–61; English translation, *Presence and Thought* (San Francisco: Ignatius Press, 1995), 71–87.

[32] *Ambigua*; PG 91, 1325Dff.

[33] Ibid.; PG 91, 1104AB.

[34] *Quaestiones ad Thalassium* 59; CCG 22, 61, 262; PG 90, 613C.

[35] Ibid., 61; CCG 22, 85, 13; PG 90, 628A; see *The Ascetic Life: The Four Centuries on Charity*, trans. P. Sherwood, Ancient Christian Writers, 21 (Westminster, Md.: Newman Press, 1955), 64.

comes to know his lost origin, once he has realized that he must not look for his origin to find his end.[36]

4. Existence as Contradiction

The face of original sin has changed once again. The act of turning from God toward the sensible world, which is simultaneous with our coming forth from God, has now become the natural, yet also the sinful starting point of mankind's long, painful search for God.

> By experiencing pain (because of material, perishable nature) and by being damaged by it, the soul is meant to come to a recognition of God and to a realization of its own dignity and, through God's kindly providence, to attain to the right attitude toward its body and itself.[37]

Through the "confusion" of material nature, through its "chaos", providence wisely steers "our unreasonable desires for what lies before us" into a right order once again. In the end, there are no longer two laws that rule the human heart, but concretely only a single love and longing, which moves forward by the detour of worldly love—our own providentially guided mistake—and gradually finds its way to God and to itself:

> When God created human nature, he did not equip its sensate faculties immediately with lust and pain but gave to the intellect a certain capacity for pleasure, with which it should be capable of rejoicing in him in an ineffable way. The first man turned this capacity—I mean the mind's natural longing for God—toward sensible things as soon as he was created, and so, from his first conscious moment on, an unnatural pleasure drew him toward sensible things, through the medium of his sense faculties. That is why he who cares for our healing, providentially but to some extent also as a powerful act of retribution, added pain to pleasure. Through pain, the law of death was wisely allowed to take root in our bodily nature. In this way, God put a limit to the frenzied and unpredictable drive of the mind toward sensible things.[38]

The contradiction implied here comes to its painful climax when our sensuality is seen and affirmed, not simply as the result of the fall

---

[36] *Quaestiones ad Thalassium* 59; CCG 22, 61, 268–63, 276; PG 90, 631D.
[37] *Ambigua*; PG 91, 1104B.
[38] *Quaestiones ad Thalassium* 61; CCG 22, 85, 8–21; PG 90, 628AB.

—foreseen by God—but also as very much part of our nature; but taking this statement seriously can then also lead us toward a way out of the contradiction.

It is only in a late letter—his great theological epistle of 641 against Monophysitism, addressed to John the Chamberlain—that this natural aspect [of sensuality] becomes fully clear. Here man appears as "a synthetic nature", consisting of body and soul as parts that not only came into existence together but "necessarily embrace and interpenetrate each other".

> For the soul did not take possession of the body by its own free decision; rather, it is also possessed by the body (ὑπ' αὐτοῦ κρατουμένης). The soul does not bestow life on the body freely, but simply because it happens to exist in it and naturally (φυσικῶς) shares in its passivity and pain, because of its innate capability to receive these things (δεκτικὴ δύναμις).[39]

Maximus adds another nuance, by labeling this natural reciprocity of body and soul in our "synthetic nature" a contribution to the beauty of the universe—something that is understandable only if it is not directly connected with sin.

Should one say that Maximus, in this text, is recanting the earlier statements he made in his principal works? Or should we say instead that he has not so much recanted them as brought them to a climactic point and sanctioned the pure contradiction [implied in them], by ultimately identifying the aspect of nature with the aspect of sin? Neither conclusion would fit comfortably with the mentality of this thinker, whose underlying tonality is never contradiction but always the reconciliation of opposites in a higher level of insight. Thus one should rather suppose that he himself must have conceived this last-quoted passage as the way out of a tragic view of the universe—once again inspired, to a significant degree, by christological reflection. (The "synthetic nature" is described in order to distinguish it from the "synthetic person" of the Redeemer, which is rooted in his free choice.) The good Creator, then, created a good nature, for the passivity of the body-bound soul originally contains nothing sinful; it was this natural constitution that led the soul, without any necessity, to sin. Maximus wanted, in other words, to distinguish the stage of nature from the stage of sin on the

---

[39] *Epistles* 12; PG 91, 488D. Sherwood, in his translation of *The Ascetic Life*, 35, directed my attention to this text.

speculative level, although he normally saw them, in their concrete objectivity, as inseparably intertwined. From this living unity he drew the necessary conclusions for Christology and anthropology, just as God himself created this nature concretely "in the foreknowledge of sin" (*praeviso peccato*).

In any case, one cannot deny[40] that here some shadows of Platonism are darkening the Christian view of the world that Aristotelianism had brightened; a feeling about creation is accepted and propagated here that has influenced both the Byzantine Middle Ages and the "Sophianism" of modern Russian religious philosophy. The "Sophia" that Bulgakov sees as a remarkable intermediate being, hovering between God and created nature—one face turned toward eternity as everlasting creaturehood, as a superessential yet passive, feminine world of ideas, the other face turned toward the world as its source and root: this "Sophia", to which Böhme, Schelling, Baader, and Soloviev pay their respects, flows down to them, through Byzantium, from ancient Platonic and Gnostic springs. A certain ineradicable mistrust for an autonomous, objective nature, which exists prior to all participation in grace and which is not only spiritual but corporeal—a mistrust, in fact, for the fundamental analogy between God and the creature— has always characterized Eastern thought and has led it to feel primordially related to all forms of self-transcendence, absorption, release of the finite into the infinite. This is the common heritage of everything [in Eastern spirituality] from distant Asia to Neoplatonism: a religious thought that bears the double stamp of sensing both the impersonal nature of reality (and that therefore has a tendency toward monism) and the tragic destiny of the world (and that therefore tends to identify sin with finitude). Maximus made it his project, not only to escape from these Eastern patterns through turning toward the personal thinking of the West, but also to illumine Eastern thought as a whole, in a redemptive way, with a personal Christology. This elevating clarification of the impersonal, lifting it into the personal sphere, means lifting an enormous weight. It is no wonder if the faces of corrupt-

---

[40] Even Sherwood (*Ascetic Life*, 65f.) admits he cannot suppress "three suspicions", all of which confirm my view: (1) the suspicion that the passions were given to nature, according to Maximus, because of the sin that was to occur; (2) the suspicion that the soul in itself is, all protests notwithstanding, independent of the body and that its endowment with sensation has something to do with the fall; (3) the suspicion that sexuality, especially, is for Maximus intrinsically associated with sin.

ibility keep appearing through the sunlight, demonic faces that have the same features even in the Christian and non-Christian thought of modern Russia; for Asia is not redeemed once and for all, nor easily, nor through a single person, nor even through a single age. This remains the constantly new, constantly challenging task of Europe, both classical and Christian—a task against which its actual achievements must be measured, weighed, and often found wanting in substance.[41]

Maximus was not the first to engage in this gigantic undertaking of redeeming Asiatic thought. Origen himself, as well as Evagrius, had really aimed at nothing else. They could not and would not content themselves with drawing an external contrast between the religions of the world, based on natural instincts, with supernatural Christian religion. They had to make the contradiction their own, in order to clarify it from within.

For Origen, Gregory, and Maximus, the world of sensible appearances, with its suffering and death, is inseparably both a punishment and a gracious gift of God. According to Origen, who praises the beauty and order of this sensible world fairly frequently, the world nevertheless remains, as a whole, the consequence of the sin of intellectual beings. Yet this is not its immediate consequence; rather, God devised the wide range and variety of different beings in the world, which comprise its harmony, as the "good" image, the best possible "expression" of creation's original turn from unity and of the various levels to which creatures fell. So the creation of the world, according to Evagrius, is inseparably both "judgment and providence" (κρίσις καὶ πρόνοια);[42] so, too, in the anthropology of Gregory of Nyssa, the sexual organs are both a (precreated) consequence of sin and a means of limiting the self-destructive tendencies of creation and providing for the continuity of the human race. Likewise, in Maximus the sensible world takes on this double character, of being at once the good, even the best creature made by God and of being nevertheless reshaped in its inmost being by the human weakness resulting from the fall.

If one interprets [the religious thought] the East as a unitary and cohesive phenomenon—if one interprets it independently from Christianity and in its difference from Christianity—one must say: the rhythm

---

[41] See Thomas Ohm, *Asiens Nein und Ja zum westlichen Christentum* (Munich: Kösel, 1960).

[42] See my articles, "Metaphysik und Mystik des Evagrius Ponticus", *Zeitschrift für Aszese und Mystik* 15 (1939): 35f., and "Die Hiera des Evagrius", *Zeitschrift für katholische Theologie* 63 (1939): 86–106, 181–206, esp. 103f. passim and, most particularly, 195.

of such a view of the world, considered with utter consistency, can only be an ecstatic, even an irrational, purely emotional one, because the object of its final affirmation is simply identical with the object of its decisive renunciation—because it is not some accidental aspect of its nature but its very essence that bears in itself the brand of both grace and condemnation. The enthusiastic delight in the world that characterizes Gregory of Nyssa's essay *On the Creation of the Human Person*, standing alongside his spiritualizing flight from the senses, anticipates both Alyosha Karamazov's enchanted gesture of kissing the earth and his angelic, other-worldly nature. This rhythm is necessarily misleading, because it seems, in its very breadth, to divide up reality exhaustively into its "heights and depths". But precisely this alternation from pole to pole, this apparent reconciliation of extremes by brusquely slapping them together, conceals the "truth" of created reality: a truth based on the fundamental measure and distance that is the basis of created nature in itself. To have grasped this, even before Christianity, was the charism of the Greeks, the birth of Western culture; and it was precisely this insight that was given credibility by Christianity—here bearing within itself its Jewish heritage—and that was finally sealed in the relation of humanity to God as children to a Father.

This excursus has been a necessary preface to interpreting rightly Maximus and his anthropology against the wide context of Eastern thought. His teaching on the original state of man stands in the Eastern, Gnostic tradition: in the flash of a moment, creation and the fall, [the soul's] emergence from its origins and its turn from the world of intellect to the world of "appearances", are fused into one; in the same instant, its mythical, supernatural "home" in God and its earthly Paradise, overshadowed from the beginning by the sin that is to come, spring apart from one another. What gives Maximus a particular place in this tradition has appeared already, over and over: his movement toward a clarified conception of nature, toward assuming the fundamental innocence of the creature, and so toward an eternally positive sense of the creature's entire constitution as intellectual and sensual, body and soul. This approach grew out of a double root, which was single, at least, in its Hellenic origins: Pseudo-Dionysius' sense of distance from an eternally unapproachable, superessential God and the Aristotelian and Stoic sense of the self-contained unity of the corporeal and spiritual world.

If it is plain that the doctrine of man's original state, for Maximus, almost comes down to an understanding of man's present condition, one must also recognize, at this point, that he tries to understand this human condition—between damnation and grace, between Paul's two "laws"—as man's *concrete* situation, not so much as his metaphysical structure. In this sense, the rhythm of contradiction between sensuality (or sexuality) as "sin" and as "nature", even as "gift", is softened to a peaceful phenomenology of man's concrete state, wherein God draws good out of sin and is able to turn every aspect of darkness into light. Here Pseudo-Dionysius' sense of God's remoteness from all the world's contradictions and of his consequent immanence and nearness to each of its contradictory poles can be a wonderful means of untying the tragic knots that complicate the heritage of sin. The interplay of the destructive and purifying forces of suffering and death, conception and childbirth, coming to be and passing away, seems from this viewpoint no longer to be the irredeemable curse of existence but a dramatic dialogue between human defiance and divine mercy, played on the stage and in the language of created and redeemed nature.[43]

5. The Dialectics of Passion

Maximus' theory of πάθη points to the struggle necessarily to preserve nature in its pristine condition. The two aspects of πάθη—its origin in nature and in sin—tempt us to separate them. So Maximus' definition of the "law of sin" is as follows: "Its power rests in a condition of our will that is contrary to nature, which introduces into the passive side of our nature a 'pathological' condition (ἐμπάθειαν ἐπεισάγουσα) of either slackness or overexcitement."[44] So *pathos*, on the one hand, is rooted in a natural capacity (the "passible", παθητόν) but is caused, on the other, by a free decision of the will. Correspondingly, the first human beings are seen as having chosen "the law of the first creation",[45] physical

---

[43] This same attitude is expressed by Gregory of Nyssa in the idea that coming to be, passing away, and death are in themselves grounded in the *nature* of the creature and, therefore, that they can only be considered as "punishments" in the light of the graces of Paradise. See *On the Creation of the Human Person*, passim.

[44] *Ambigua*; PG 91, 1044A.

[45] Ibid.; PG 91, 1276B. On the question of whether the sin of Paradise was sexual, see F. Asensio, "Tradicion sobre un pecado sexual en el paradiso?" *Gregorianum* 30 (1949): 490–520; 31 (1950): 35–62, 163–91, 362–90; for Maximus, 375.

procreation, of their own free will, as a possible realization of their
sensual nature. But this is precisely how sin itself could be "rooted in
the bosom of nature"[46] and "stain" this nature as guilty through and
through, like a dye that seeps through everything and colors it all.[47]
Nevertheless, this law is something that has "affected us from without", and that cannot accompany us into eternal life,[48] however much
it is burned into our nature here below as a "necessary accompani-
ment" (ἀναγκαῖον παρακολούθημα), of which our nature—even at its
most purified—cannot rid itself.[49]

In their natural aspect, as "natural impulses" and "satisfactions", the
πάθη are "not blameworthy",[50] but simply the spur to actions that in
themselves guarantee the continuation of nature.[51] So it is symbolically
significant that the rite of circumcision had to disappear in the New
Covenant: "No natural thing is unclean if it has God as its Creator."[52]
True circumcision is only the cleansing of those passions that prevent
the true fruitfulness of the soul.[53] In this cleansing process, the πάθη
of the soul are helpful and useful (καλὰ γίνεται καὶ τὰ πάθη): covetousness becomes yearning desire (ἔφεσις ὀρεκτική); love of pleasure becomes a taste for divine grace; anxiety becomes a healthy, cautionary
fear; sadness becomes heartfelt repentance. "All these things are good
through the use made of them by those who know how to train their
thoughts for the service of Christ."[54] The "tension" (τόνος) released
by the irascible part of the soul, the "longing" of the desiring part,
communicate themselves, by a kind of sublimation, to the "intellect
as a whole";[55] there is a "wise desire", just as there is a "reasonable
anger".[56] If all these drives are naturally implanted in animals, they
could not be reprehensible (ὡς φυσικαὶ οὔτε κακαί).[57] The love of God

---

[46] Quaestiones ad Thalassium 61; CCG 22, 85, 19; PG 90, 628B.

[47] Ibid., prooemium; CCG 7, 23, 114; PG 90, 249A.

[48] Ibid., 55; CCG 7, 489, 139–42; PG 90, 541B.

[49] Ibid.; CCG 7, 487, 126–27; PG 90, 541A.

[50] Ibid.; CCG 7, 487, 123ff.; PG 90, 541A.

[51] Ibid.; CCG 7, 489, 132f.; PG 90, 541AB.

[52] Ibid., 27; CCG 7, 201, 164–66; PG 90, 357D–360A.

[53] Ibid., 48; CCG 7, 343, 227f.; PG 90, 441C.

[54] Ibid., 1; CCG 7, 47, 18–49, 33; PG 90, 269B.

[55] Exposition of the Lord's Prayer; CCG 23, 58, 539ff.; PG 90, 896C.

[56] In De Div. Nom. 4; PG 4, 292C.

[57] Ibid.; PG 4, 296B. This doctrine of sublimation is worked out with particular clarity in
Centuries on Love 3, 67, 71, 98.

itself has its root and foundation in our capacity to desire and in our courage.[58] "The soul makes use of its desires in order to long for the things it seeks and uses its anger and courage to keep them and to care tenderly for them."[59]

Nevertheless, although *pathos* may be the root of the highest abilities of our intelligence, on its own ground it cannot simply be translated into a positive intellectual value—into "innocence". Even if it is not strictly reprehensible (ἁπλῶς κακόν), still it stands in a hidden and indestructible relationship (πρός τι κακόν) with that sensual egoism (φιλαυτία) that acts as the basis of sin. "It is clear: if someone is in love with himself [that is, has φιλαυτία], he has all the passions (πάθη)."[60] Even if such self-seeking is natural for animals, it cannot be so for an intellectual being, who is made to know God and so is subject to a second, intellectual or spiritual law alongside the law of his own sensual well-being, by means of his openness to the divine. The ontological duality of human nature is translated, of necessity, into levels of knowledge and action. "Man is composed of a soul and a body; thus he is moved by a double law, the law of the flesh and the law of the spirit."[61] "For reason and sensuality are naturally active in opposite ways, because their objects are in the highest degree different and dissimilar."[62] Even before it becomes real, then, evil lies potentially in the nonidentity of the reasonable and nonreasonable parts of man, to the extent that the operative law of the latter can only be subjected to the former by the former's active intervention but is not subject to it by nature.[63]

Does this not lead us back to Gnosticism, even to Manichaeism? Are not disharmony and sin identified here with being itself? Maximus gives a tentative answer to the charge, without offering a final solution. The scholia on Pseudo-Dionysius, first of all, often emphasize strongly that matter is perhaps "nonbeing" in a relative sense but in no sense the origin or focal point of evil. The fact that the demons are

---

[58] *Quaestiones ad Thalassium* 49; CCG 7, 355, 68ff.; PG 90, 449B.

[59] Ibid., 55; CCG 7, 491, 176f.; PG 90, 544A.

[60] *Centuries on Love* 3, 8: PG 90, 1020AB; *Epistles* 2; PG 91, 397Aff.

[61] *Quaestiones ad Thalassium* 33; CCG 7, 229, 26f.; PG 90, 373C. In this parallel of body-soul and flesh-spirit (with "spirit" understood as "mind", νοῦς, as well as πνεῦμα—) lies the "original lie", or at least the gaping danger, of Eastern religious anthropology.

[62] Ibid., 58; CCG 22, 33, 103–6; PG 90, 596D.

[63] So also John of Scythopolis, *In De Div. Nom.* 4; PG 4, 276C.

bodiless is sufficient proof of this.[64] If the πάθη are to be considered
the immediate symptoms of evil in man, it is necessary to make a clear
distinction between the loss of moral equilibrium and the natural consequences of this disturbance—between "voluntary sin" and "physical
sin". "The judgment, then, on Adam's voluntary sin was the transformation of his nature in the direction of passion, corruption, and death,
. . . toward physical sin."[65] In the same sense, Maximus distinguishes
between the "curse" that is the immediate ethical effect of sin and
the "curse" that is its natural punishment,[66] or between "temptation"
as sensual desire, which gives rise to sin, and "temptation" as a trial,
which punishes sin by causing suffering.[67] This distinction is made in
light of the Incarnation: the Redeemer was able to take the "physical"
side of our punishments on himself without any shadow of voluntary
sin and, so, became "sin" and a "curse" for us.[68] But how are these two
sides related to each other? Can they be separated so easily? Maximus'
philosophy of the sexes offers an answer to the question of how they
are one.

6. The Sexual Synthesis

The focal point of the whole question of *pathos* seems, in fact, to lie
in the phenomenon of sexuality. Two elements combine in the central
sin of self-love: egoism and passionate, fleshly lust. All sin is a renunciation of the lordship of God, a desire to be on one's own, and in that
very act—in the case of humans, at least—a descent into sensual self-
indulgence.[69] But concealed in these two elements lies also the inner
contradiction of sin, which will immediately appear as their built-in
punishment. In sensual pleasure, the human spirit seeks a self-centered
substitute for giving itself to God; this alternate gift of self thus isolates
the person in his egoism, rather than uniting him with the beloved. Sen-

---

[64] Ibid.; PG 4, 297C.
[65] *Quaestiones ad Thalassium* 42; CCG 7, 287, 58, 69; PG 90, 408CD.
[66] Ibid., 62; CCG 22, 123, 137ff.; PG 90, 652C.
[67] *Exposition of the Lord's Prayer*; CCG 23, 72, 800ff.; PG 90, 908BC.
[68] *Quaestiones ad Thalassium* 42; CCG 7, 285–87; PG 90, 405C–408D (referring to 2 Cor 5:21 and Gal 3:13).
[69] Ibid., 58; CCG 22, 31, 78f.; PG 90, 596B; the statement is limited, of course, by the adverb "almost" (σχεδόν).

sual lust "divides the unity of human nature into a thousand pieces,[70] and we, who all share the same nature, mindlessly tear each other into shreds, like wild beasts".[71] Self-love has even divided the one God into a multitude of idols, just as it tore nature apart and "turned our capacity for anger toward each other into something bestial, for the sake of our sensual desires".[72] This "deceptive and corrupting love",[73] this "much-indulged, much-repressed sensuality"[74] gradually hollows out our flesh—"the flesh of all men and women is a valley, worn away by the constant flow of passion"[75]—and ends "in the disgust that follows and that obliterates the whole state of mind that has gone before".[76]

But this outbreak of pain is influenced so little by external sources that one must rather see it as implied in the first stirring of sensual desire. "For mingled into sensual desire is the torment of pain, even when, through the overriding power of passion, it seems to lie hidden in those who are dominated by it."[77] And if this torment is also sometimes described as an additional punishment for the misuse of our natural drives,[78] still the punishment also consists, on the other hand, in the deformation of nature itself: "Nature punishes people who seek to do her violence, in the same degree as they indulge in an unnatural style of life; her punishment is that they no longer have ready, natural access to the full powers of nature. Their natural freshness is diminished, and so they are punished."[79] Death itself, the end of these torments and their effect (ἐν οἷς καὶ ἐξ ὧν ὁ θάνατος),[80] is nothing else but the natural (φυσικῶς) unfolding of their reality.[81]

But now that these two citadels—sensual desire and death—have been raised against one another, we are swept into the implacable dialectic of historicity. "In seeking to avoid the burdensome experience

---

[70] Reading in the Greek τμήματα, "parts", rather than τιμήματα—, "honors".

[71] *Quaestiones ad Thalassium*, prooemium; CCG 7, 33, 269–72; PG 90, 256B.

[72] *Epistles* 28; PG 91, 620C.

[73] *Quaestiones ad Thalassium* 49; CCG 7, 359, 157; PG 90, 453A.

[74] Ibid., 48; CCG 7, 323, 171–72; PG 90, 428B.

[75] Ibid.; CCG 7, 319, 107ff.; PG 90, 425A.

[76] *Epistles* 28; PG 91, 617C.

[77] *Quaestiones ad Thalassium*, prooemium; CCG 7, 33, 260–62; PG 90, 256A.

[78] Ibid., 61; CCG 22, 85; PG 90, 628B.

[79] *Ambigua*; PG 91, 1164C.

[80] *Quaestiones ad Thalassium* 61; CCG 22, 85, 24; PG 90, 628B.

[81] Ibid.; CCG 22, 87, 26ff.; PG 90, 628D.

of pain, we fall into the arms of sensual desire . . . , and in struggling
to soothe the anguish of pain through pleasure, we only strengthen
its case against us, in that we are incapable of having pleasure apart
from torment and tedium."[82] "Fear of death"[83] is the hidden thorn
that drives us to try to make our nature eternal by procreation; from
this source, however, only another victim of death can be produced.
This is the tragedy that lies beneath every worldly care:

> For since the whole nature of corporeal things is transitory and is con-
> stantly ready to be dissolved, one may try any way one likes to make
> it stand firm, yet this will only strengthen its transitoriness. Against our
> will, we must always tremble for what we love, and contrary to our
> desires we must unconsciously come, through the things we love, to
> share in what we do not love at all, yet what is intrinsically connected
> with natural impermanence.[84]

The built-in sadness of sexual desire is nothing else than the dark contradiction one senses in sexuality.

> Since (physical) evil entered human nature through an act of transgres-
> sion, and the passionate aspect of birth through sin, and since through
> the passionate aspect of birth, which depends on sin, the first transgres-
> sion remained in force, there was no hope of redemption. Nature was
> indissolubly chained, through the bonds of retribution, to its own free
> will. For the more nature rushed to assure its own continuity through
> procreation, the more it became entangled in the law of sin, because the
> first transgression remained alive in nature's passionate aspect.[85]

Between "fear of death" and "slavery to sensual desire through love
for life", the circle is inescapably closed;[86] the perpetuation of life, for
which man strives, is in fact a perpetuation of death.[87] Doubtless we
have entered an Eastern sanctuary here: the Buddha's teaching, too,
grew out of this powerful experience; the circling wheel of births and
deaths is a tragedy, in itself beyond redemption. "All life is a mixture of
desire and pain",[88] because "death dwells potentially in all coming-to-

---

[82] Ibid.; CCG 22, 89, 94–91, 100; PG 90, 629D–632A.

[83] Ibid.; CCG 22, 95, 191–94; PG 90, 633D.

[84] Ibid., prooemium; CCG 7, 39, 372–79; PG 90, 260C.

[85] Ibid., 21; CCG 7, 127, 19–27; PG 90, 313A.

[86] Ibid.; CCG 7, 131, 83–85; PG 90, 316B.

[87] *Epistles* 7; PG 91, 437C–440A.

[88] *Quaestiones ad Thalassium*, prooemium; CCG 7, 35, 293f.; PG 90, 256D.

be, as a judgment on nature";[89] [nature is] cursed ground, a "desert",[90] "unfruitful soil, from which one reaps with much pain and sorrow and with very little joy".[91]

In this perspective, does not the sexual act, even marriage, become a sin? Not at all, Maximus replies: "If marriage were reprehensible, so would be the natural law of reproduction, and if this natural process were reprehensible, then obviously we could rightly blame the Creator of nature, who invested it with this law of reproduction. How then would we refute the Manichees? . . ."[92] Something that is naturally good or indifferent, however, can still be imposed on us as a "punishment",[93] and can surely become the external sign, the guilty mark of our internal, sinful will, as well as bringing about a crippling attachment of this will to its object. In this sense, sexual desire and the passions might be considered a "sacrament of sin", in that even here an external gesture, in itself neither good nor evil, has become an "efficacious sign" of sin.

But even if this adhesion [of sexuality to sin] "is a punishment of a just God", is it not still something good, since it comes from God and realizes a potentiality of nature itself? Is it not at least an "educational" process?[94] An experience we are allowed to have "so that through the suffering that this present life offers . . . we might finally learn how much damage the love of that life brings about, and how much more we are helped through distance from it than through involvement in it?"[95]

The role of sexuality, however, is not exclusively this somewhat negative one. It is also an educational process as a positive mode of union. The sexual synthesis is the first level of the progressive syntheses by which the world is unified and brought to its perfection in the unity of God. In [the relationships of] a sexually divided humanity, the differentiation and multiplicity of the world, which has progressed to an extreme degree, takes its first turn toward unity; man, after all, through his capacity for unity (ἡ πρὸς ἕνωσιν δύναμις), is the world's natural

---

[89] Ibid. 47; PG 90, 424B. [This reference appears to be incorrect. See, however, *Quaestiones ad Thalassium* 61; CCG 22, 95, 180–84; PG 90, 633C.]

[90] Ibid., 47; CCG 7, 317, 68; PG 90, 424B.

[91] Ibid., 5; CCG 7, 65, 12–14; PG 90, 277C.

[92] *Ambigua*; PG 91, 1340B.

[93] Ibid.; PG 91, 1348A.

[94] Ibid.; PG 91, 1317D.

[95] *Epistles* 10; PG 91, 449CD.

mediator with God (φυσικῶς μεσιτεύων). For that reason, man was also
the last to be created, because he is the center of the world, in whom
the multiplicity of beings, beginning in the nonidentity of the human
sexes, can gradually begin to come together again in unity.[96] In this
union lies a first, still confused hint and representation of the unity
and unifying love of God, even though it may be misused and twisted.

> Although it may be misunderstood, man seems to have access to some-
> thing good, to find the possibility of union, in the tender love of a com-
> rade in mortality; and even if this love is itself open to corruption, still
> it is a distant, weak echo of the love of God and embraces a phantom
> only because of the Good. . . . Through the very form of unity and love,
> man already possesses a shadowy share in the Good.[97]

The real meaning of fleshly desire thus becomes clear: "The basis
of the evil in debauchery lies in the irrational excitement of desire.
Desire itself, however, is a beneficial force: it allows the rational being
to long for the true good, which is above, and gives irrational beings an
instinct for what tends toward self-preservation."[98] Certainly, in man,
who is at once both intellectual and sensual, desire must accomplish
both goals at once: physical union comes to its fulfillment precisely
by liberating the intellectual drive toward unity. "For it is impossible
that people come to real moral unity who are not first united in their
dependence on God."[99] The savage, predatory aspect of sensual desire
thus comes, not from within itself, but from a lack of this harmony
with the true and only principle of unity, God. Yet even in such a state
of internal division—as Pseudo-Dionysius had already observed—the
still-glowing sparks of the divine are not completely extinguished; as
John of Scythopolis commented, "Even quarrelsome and unreliable
people are moved by shadowy images of a love for peace; for they are
driven by their passions, and in trying ignorantly to satisfy them, they
believe they are moving toward peace."[100]

This shadow of peace, however, is not the real thing. The double
law [of desire] in man remains, on the human level, always a tragic dualism. "Since it is impossible that the mind should make contact with

---

[96] *Ambigua*; PG 91, 1305AB.
[97] *In De Div. Nom.* 4; PG 4, 281AC. (The attribution of the text here is uncertain.)
[98] Ibid.; PG 301BC.
[99] *Epistles* 2; PG 91, 396D.
[100] *In De Div. Nom.* 11; PG 4, 397D.

the intellectual things of its own kind in any other way than by contemplating the sensible realities that serve as intermediaries between them", and since these seduce the mind to remain with them through the pleasure they give, the mind reaps, with this pleasure, "the sorrow and the lash of conscience"; if, on the other hand, the mind "tears apart the surface appearance of visible things", the result, "along with intellectual joy", is "sadness of the senses, which are deprived of their natural object".[101] So in Maximus' thinking, too, in the midst of Christian values, the heroic Platonic ideal of an "undying battle" between appearance and idea makes its appearance, as man's ultimate situation. "This, perhaps, is the reason that the present anomalous situation has been allowed to prevail: that the power of the spirit, which prefers virtue before all other things, might be displayed in us."[102]

This tragic loss of balance in man is not fate, however, but a sign of inherited sin. It is clear that this cannot be conceived simply in terms of "physical evil": in the element of "punishment", which condemns us to keep seeking the infinite and the timeless in places where there can only be new decay, one sees clearly the features of a kind of "guilt" that accompanies this tendency and that—"in us, without our consent" (in nobis sine nobis)—has put our will in chains. Here Maximus' instinct, which we have pointed out before, to make immediate applications of ontological situations in the ethical realm once again comes to light. The ontological tragedy of our human subjection to two laws —explained by Platonism through the simple fact of the duality of body and soul and by Christianity through a primeval disturbance of the world's balance and order—is immediately translated into moral tragedy. To the extent that this tragedy precedes the free decision of man and is rooted in his natural constitution, he cannot rid himself of it. The solution of the contradiction can only be awaited as a gift of God: as given with that peace in which all the world's conflict is resolved and has been resolved since the beginning.

Maximus develops his doctrine of the Incarnation with almost geometrical strictness on the basis of the anthropology of original sin.[103] The Incarnation must be the reconstitution of the state—whether it is understood historically or mythically and metahistorically—in which

---

[101] Quaestiones ad Thalassium 58; CCG 22, 33, 111-35, 135; PG 90, 596D-597B.
[102] Ambigua; PG 91, 1105B.
[103] See fragment 9; ed. Epifanovich, 28.

man was incorruptible (εἰς ἀφθαρσίαν ἀποκατάστασις).[104] It must restore the balance again, by bringing the proud intellect low and by lifting up the flesh that had been hollowed out by passion and death.[105]

In order to break through the dialectic of sin, two conditions were
required: a death that was not the natural punishment for sinful *pathos*[106]
and, therefore, also a virginal birth. Gregory of Nyssa had already
sketched out these requirements in his *Great Catechetical Oration*, and
many Monophysites exaggerated them into a metaphysical necessity,
which incidentally included also a denial of the immaculate conception
of Mary.[107] This was not part of Maximus' intention; the "necessity"
he speaks of is nothing but the inner cohesion of the divine plan of
salvation, read phenomenologically from the facts of sacred history.
Only when the tragic elements in his cultural tradition run the risk
of gaining the upper hand does he himself sink into this kind of pes-
simism. Monophysitism remains a marginal danger zone, for him as for
all theology of an Alexandrian orientation. Yet his Christology, with
its strong emphasis on a theology of two natures and two wills, will
contribute the decisive counterweight to this anthropological danger.

The "necessary" way to salvation, clearly revealed in the human condition itself, thus demands an inner, radical overcoming of this condition through a free acceptance of "physical evil" and death, independent of any natural compulsion.[108] This is impossible for a normal
human being; thus a superhuman human being (ὑπὲρ ἄνθρωπον ἄνθρωπος)[109] is necessary, whose more-than-human aspect will be just as
real and just as effective as his humanity. Such a person would have to
take upon himself the whole "transgression of Adam's voluntary sin",
the whole of physical evil,[110] but through the innocence of his suffering would let the judgment [on humanity] become a judgment on the
judgment itself (κατάκρισιν κατακρίνῃ),[111] "a genuine cursing of the

---

[104] *Quaestiones ad Thalassium* 42; CCG 7, 287, 34; PG 90, 408A; cf. ibid., 26; CCG 7, 185;
PG 90, 349BC; ibid., 64; CCG 22, 173–75; PG 90, 684AB.

[105] Ibid., 47; CCG 7, 319–21; PG 90, 425A–D.

[106] Ibid., 61; CCG 22, 87; PG 90, 628C–629A.

[107] See Julian of Halicarnassus, fragments 17, 20, 29, 71, 82, 85: in R. Draguet, ed., *Julien
d'Halicarnasse et sa controverse avec Sévère d'Antioche sur l'incorruptibilité du corps du Christ* (Louvain,
1924), *Juliani fragmenta*.

[108] *Quaestiones ad Thalassium* 63; CCG 22, 97, 211–15; PG 90, 663C.

[109] *Ambigua*; PG 91, 1056A.

[110] *Quaestiones ad Thalassium* 43; CCG 7, 287, 58f.; PG 90, 408C.

[111] Ibid.; CCG 7, 289, 69; PG 90, 408D.

curse".[112] Maximus always describes Christ's death as a judgment on sin[113] and thus as the real judgment on the world itself, even though it remains hidden. In this death, judging and being judged coincide. And thanks to this death, the same process also takes place for the individual Christian. In the second birth of baptism, suffering and death lose their sting, because baptism, as an effective sign of Christ's death, takes away the guilt of the first birth and restores the original, spiritual birth from and in God that Adam had spurned.[114] The necessity of death for the sinner is surpassed through his own free choice of this death [in Christ].[115]

> And since it is not possible to complete a life without death, (the Christians) created, as a death for this life, the renunciation of every concern for the flesh, through which death made its way into our life, so that by inventing a death for death they might no longer live for death; by dying they have gained power in the death that is "precious to the Lord", in the death that truly puts an end to death, so that they might let corruptibility itself fall into corruption.[116]

Through this death, the real reproductive power of the soul is finally released;[117] the soul is now not only begotten and born itself in the Spirit,[118] as at the beginning,[119] but it now even conceives and bears the eternal Word in its bosom, "where Christ mystically wills to be born again and again, becoming flesh through those he has redeemed and making the virgin soul that bears him into a mother".[120] The soul becomes a mother passively, as the one who constantly "receives and bears" [him], as a "receptive bosom"; it does so actively by "nourishing the Logos with the breasts of contemplation and active virtue".[121] So it is by fulfilling the mystery of sexuality that the soul goes beyond it.

The sexual synthesis, then, remains, for Maximus as for most of

---

[112] Ibid., 62; CCG 22, 123, 129; PG 90, 652B.
[113] Ibid., 61; CCG 22, 95, 197; PG 90, 633D; ibid. 63; CCG 22, 173, 443-44; PG 90, 604A; CCG 22, 177, 474; PG 90, 685B.
[114] Ibid., 61; CCG 22, 91; PG 90, 632C; CCG 22, 95; PG 90, 633D.
[115] *Ambigua*; PG 91, 1157D.
[116] Ibid.; PG 91, 1157C.
[117] Ibid.; PG 91, 1364D.
[118] Ibid.; PG 91, 1348A-C.
[119] *Quaestiones ad Thalassium* 61; CCG 22, 97, 230; PG 90, 636C.
[120] *Exposition of the Lord's Prayer*; CCG 23, 50, 397-400; PG 90, 889C.
[121] *Epistles* 19; PG 91, 592AB.

the Fathers, too overloaded by the tragedy and the despairing dialectic of original sin to find a positive place among the syntheses achieved by Christ. "For in Christ Jesus there is neither male nor female" (Gal 3:28). Certainly, the unity of man and woman retains, in his thought, that reflective glimmer of God's own unity in love that Pseudo-Dionysius had also found there. But Maximus is not able to admit that sexuality has a final and fulfilling meaning; here the tradition of Eastern thought retains the upper hand. The verse of Paul we have quoted, which refers primarily to the sexual act, Maximus understands extensively, taking it to include all sexual difference; as a logical result, this cannot be included in the "likeness" to God referred to in Genesis 1:27—not in the realm of personal relations, first of all, but not even in the bodily realm. Maximus put the responsibility for this approach on Gregory of Nyssa. But if the personal synthesis of the sexes is swept aside, there is no way to conceive the sexual synthesis as rooted in the synthesis of Christ; metaphysics, at this point, must systematically take on a monastic character! It is therefore no accident that in Maximus' great syntheses, no exalted place is reserved for Mary as the New Eve, the Bride of Christ.[122]

Sexuality [for Maximus] is too closely bound to time and corruptibility,[123] and they are too closely bound to sin. If, in the Gnostic view of the original state of things, man came into existence as fallen—and therefore as sexual—from the start, then Christ's work is necessarily more than the restoration of the original state, which itself belongs in the "first age of creation (aeon)."[124] In fact, his achievement becomes itself, by a synthesis of the unspoiled state of Paradise and our present mortal condition, a higher, third condition:

> In that [Christ], through his own person, united the two opposed realities perfectly, . . . he effectively removed the weaknesses of both sides: the second, dishonorable state he made into the source of salvation and renewal for the first and honorable one, while he made the first the

---

[122] Maximus was not unconscious of doing this; he rejected the exaggerated devotion to the Mother of God current in his own time and was accused of being against Mary. See *Acta Sanctorum*, August 3 (1867), 107. Cf. J. A. Jungmann, "Die Abwehr des germanischen Arianismus und der Umbruch der religiösen Kultur im frühen Mittelalter", *Zeitschrift für katholische Theologie* 69 (1947): 49.

[123] *Exposition of the Lord's Prayer*, CCG 23, 51, 403–14; PG 90, 889D.

[124] *Quaestiones ad Thalassium* 54; CCG 7, 459, 275ff.; PG 90, 520C, with the explanatory scholion no. 18: ibid.; CCG 7, 475, 152–55; PG 90, 532C (where it is scholion 22).

justification and excuse for the second. . . . He made procreation into
the redemption of created existence, by paradoxically restoring the incorruptibility of creation through human vulnerability (*pathos*); but he
made creation the justification of procreation, by sanctifying its vulnerable aspect through creation's own innocence.[125]

---

[125] *Ambigua*; PG 91, 1317A–C.

VI

CHRIST THE SYNTHESIS

1. Setting the Question

The figure of the redeemer stands in the center of Maximus' theology. In step with the process by which Maximus the Monk changed into Maximus the Confessor, the perspective of his Christology changed, as well: the Alexandrian cosmic Logos, with his predominantly Eastern appearance, took on ever more human and evangelical features. Maximus' breathtaking duel with the Monothelites, which reached its peak in his disputation with Pyrrhus at Carthage in 645, forced the mystic —to his own saving benefit—to take seriously and to apply, in all its consequences, the formula of the Council of Chalcedon, which asserts the "unconfused" (ἀσυγχύτως) character of the two natures of Christ and which prevents any dissolving of the human substance in God.

Even so, we have already shown in the introductory chapter that the Chalcedonian formula dominated even Maximus' early, mystical writings. "Synthesis", not "confusion", is the first structural principle of all created being. His early explanations of Gregory Nazianzen [the *Ambigua*] brought to full expression this incomparably bold application of a theological truth to philosophical, ontological, and cosmological thought. In this respect, too, Maximus looks straight in the eye of Hegel, who clearly derived his synthetic way of thinking from the Bible—more precisely from the anthropological antitheses of the Old Testament and from that between the Bible and Hellenism, as well as from the reconciling synthesis of Christ, understood principally from a Johannine (and thus, in effect, from an Alexandrian) perspective. The difference is that the theological starting point in Hegel is kept in the shadows, while in Maximus it remains luminously open; everyone recognizes that his ontology and cosmology are extensions of his Christology, in that the synthesis of Christ's concrete person is not only God's final thought for the world but also his original plan.

If we have mainly been trying, up to now, to point to this synthetic structure from its philosophical side, it seems time to consider it in its historical and objective starting point: in the central synthesis

between God and world, grace and nature, that is realized in the hypostatic union of Christ. Here the [synthetic] principle finds its justification; for only when Christ appeared did it become irrefutably clear
that the creature is not simply pure negation with respect to God and,
thus, cannot be saved simply through mystical absorption in God, but
rather—however much he is elevated to share in God's being, however
much he dies to the world—the creature is saved only in the express
preservation and perfection of his nature.

In the conceptual material it employs, Maximus' Christology is *not*
"a new creation". Just as the early aspects of his speculation on the
Logos depended—even so far as verbal citation—on Origen, so his
later christological speculation is founded on the Neo-Chalcedonian
theology of the sixth century, especially on that of Leontius of Byzantium, as well as on the inspiration Maximus received from Sophronius,
with whom he spent some time, living with him in the same African
monastery about 630.[1] But Maximus not only corrects and deepens,
in many respects, the dry and often aimless speculation of the Neo-
Chalcedonians and develops and extends theologically the dogmatic
exposition of Sophronius; his great achievement remains his choice of
christological terminology as the cornerstone of his understanding of
the world. Here his vision parallels that of the greatest Christian minds
—Augustine in his battle against Donatus, Thomas in his dispute with
Averroes—in understanding how to transform an apparently immediate situation in the history of ideas into a question of universal relevance, how to make a particular attack on Christianity into an occasion
for developing a view of the faith's entire structure.

Even the reverent tone with which Maximus treats christological
questions alerts us to his awareness, not just of being in a wearisome
contest of words, but of standing before the central mystery of the
world. "Of all divine mysteries, the mystery of Christ is the most sig-

---

[1] On the relation between Leontius and Maximus, see V. Grumel, "L'Union hypostatique
et la comparaison de l'âme et du corps chez Léonce de Byzance et saint Maxime le Confesseur", *Echos d'Orient* 25 (1926): 393–406. Maximus never mentions Leontius by name,
yet Leontius' direct, or at least his indirect, influence on Maximus is beyond any doubt
(Grumel, "L'Union hypostatique", 400). On the objective connection between Sophronius
and Maximus, see C. Hefele, "Sophronius und Maximus über die zwei Willen in Christus",
Tübinger theologische Quartalschrift 37 (1857): 189–223; there is nothing on the influence of
Sophronius on Maximus, but simply an analysis of both the synodal letter of 634 and of
the disputation at Carthage of 645. There is not much more in Straubinger, "Die Lehre des
Patriarchen Sophronius von Jerusalem", *Der Katholik* 87 (1907): 81–109, 175–98, 251–65.

nificant, for it teaches us how to situate every present or future perfection of every being, in every kind of intellectual investigation."[2] The "ineffable manner of union" of the two natures in Christ is, in the end, beyond comprehension. "For who could know how God takes on flesh, yet remains God? How he, while remaining true God, still is truly a human being. . . . Only faith understands this, by paying silent homage to the Word of God."[3] If, in fact, our reason is ordered toward created, natural things, how could it help but be puzzled, when it discovers this same nature translated into another, supernatural manner of being? And if this manner of being is divine, although God stands in contrast to everything created, how could this unity *not* appear to be a contradiction?

> For the superessential Word, who took on himself, in that ineffable conception, our nature and everything that belongs to it, possessed nothing human, nothing that we might consider "natural" in him, that was not at the same time divine, negated by the supernatural manner of his existence. The investigation of these things exceeds our reason and our capacity for proof; it is only grasped by the faith of those who reverence the mystery of Christ with upright hearts.[4]

Faith alone sees, in the mirror of Christ's creaturely appearance, the uncreated face of the eternal one.

And yet this vision inflames all our desires to know and to see. The mysterious oscillation between the light and the mirror, between what sanctifies and what is sanctified, between truth and image, immediacy and concealment, which flickers through the relationship of Christ's two natures, allows the mystery of the world to appear, concentrated in the midst of these two things, as in an enormous magnifying lens. The borderline between appearance and reality must become palpable here, if it is to become so at all. Here is the joint of the compass, whose one leg points to the world while the other rests in God. Through the Incarnation, the Lord became "his own precursor".[5] He became, as Maximus puts it (bringing an Origenist idea into sharp focus), "his own image and likeness; he was able to point from himself to himself and to lead all of creation upward through himself, as he appeared in

---

[2] *Ambigua*; PG 91, 1332C.
[3] Ibid.; PG 1057A.
[4] Ibid.; PG 91, 1053CD.
[5] Ibid.; PG 91, 1253D.

the world, to himself, who is utterly hidden and who can never appear."[6] So Christian love can never cease examining, over and over, the mystery of this being who is two yet one, never cease questioning his "supernatural physiology" (τὸ μέγα τῆς ὑπερφυοῦς Ἰησοῦ φυσιολογίας μυστήριον).[7]

The way to the mystery has been designated, since Ephesus and Chalcedon, by negative markers: it can only lie somewhere between Nestorius and Eutyches, between a theory of two persons and a theory of one nature. The goal was to avoid "division" (διαίρεσις) and "fusion" (συναίρεσις) with equal care.[8] It was not simply that Eutyches had united the natures "too much" and Nestorius "too little", but that they divided them and united them in the wrong way; they did not understand in what unity really consisted. Their mistake was to look for the synthesis on the level of nature itself and then to describe it as a synthesis of natural powers (Nestorius) or as a natural union (Eutyches). A solution to the problem was impossible as long as one was unable to recognize any other dimension of being than that of "nature" or "essence"—the dimension considered by ancient Greek philosophy. For the result of this one-dimensionality was the conclusion that all "essence" (οὐσία, φύσις) possessed reality in itself, or was at least the key element, the structure, the law of some really existing thing.

The way from this one-dimensional space to the full development of a second dimension in scholastic ontology is a long and tortuous one. The discovery of the new dimension, one that begins in the non-identity of abstract and concrete being, of essence and existence, as the fundamental objective state of every created reality, is the product of the Christian consciousness, which was the first to notice the relation between God the Creator and the radical contingency of the world. It was in this same relationship, too, that the full conception of personal being, in its metaphysical implications, was discovered: as the ultimate seat of God's sovereign freedom, on which all the "that" and the "what" of the creature depends, and consequently—since the creature is an image of God—as the ultimate center in the creature's

---

[6] Ibid.; PG 91, 1165D.
[7] Ibid.; PG 91, 1052B.
[8] *Opuscula*; PG 91, 88B.

being, beyond all "nature" and "essence", of the power freely to be, which is at the same time the center of radical dependency on God.

Even if the relationship of these two pairs—essence and existence, being and person—still remained objectively unexplained [in Maximus' work], it is at least clear that in a time of philosophical transition these two polarities had to stand in the closest touch with each other. Both were expressions of a single basic insight—one that still needed conceptual clarification—into the insufficiency of a closed system of essences and natures. The christological disputes, which had largely been caused by the unavoidable complexity and contextual variation of the concepts of ancient philosophy as they lost their systematic stability and began to interact with each other, made an enormous contribution to the illumination of this new, Christian philosophical world.

Dogmatic formulations, in fact, are often a step ahead of the full philosophical "ownership" of a new way of thinking: with the assurance of a sleepwalker, the Church coins a formula that only later on reveals all the dimensions of its meaning. What an act of daring it was for the Council of Ephesus, faced with a choice between two equally vague and inexact formulas, simply to decide for the less inauthentic one, the one with the more adequate perspective! What an act of daring, again, it was for the Council of Chalcedon to interpret the formula of Ephesus ("one nature", μία φύσις)—against all apparent logic, which lay on the Monophysite side—in what seemed to be the opposite direction from the implications of its own wording! And what an act of daring, yet again, was the Neo-Chalcedonian rereading [of the Chalcedonian formulation], incorporating the whole Christology of Cyril into the framework of Chalcedon, in order both to assimilate the heart of the Monophysite intuition and to overcome its objections [to the Council]! Words that had had, for centuries, their own clear definitions—or at least their own popular, if confused, associations—were forced now to grow beyond their natural ranges of meaning, in order to help sketch in the outlines of something new. Maximus' own Christology still stands in this twilight; but through all the fluidity, the stress and strain, of his attempts at clear formulation, hints of an overall sense of direction begin to appear that reveal the intuition of a genius and that are well worth sympathetic interpretive description. Many of the descriptions that have been given [in the past] leave the impression that the debates about the being of Christ were simply a verbal joust—ghosts clanking their chains!—without vital implications for our own time. In the presentation that follows, I hope to convey a different impression. Much that Maximus said about the form of Christ seems all too abstract; other things seem inexact, and still others seem long since to have become common Christian parlance. Still, his synthetic thought, taken as a whole, remains a classic example of Christianity's lively struggle to give expression to the world's central mystery.

The union of God and the world in Christ could not be adequately expressed simply in terms of an essentialist philosophy. If its "natural" and "ontological" aspects were emphasized (as "union of essences" [ἕνωσις οὐσιώδης] or "union of natures" [ἕνωσις φυσική]), the consequence was the mixture of the two poles in a new "essence" (οὐσία, φύσις). But if one hoped to avoid this kind of mixture, the only alternative seemed to be the accidental, extrinsic, "moral" union of an "intellectual relationship" (σχέσις) between the two natures.[9] Certainly, both the Eutychian and the Nestorian position saw part of the truth.[10] But the level on which they came into conflict cannot itself be the context of a real solution—it can only be the scene of an empty dialectic of thesis and antithesis. For the synthesis one is looking for here stands in constant danger of degeneration: either through the separation of its two halves (ἐξ ἡμισείας μερίζεσθαι)[11] or through homogenization into a kind of "balance" (ἀντίρροπον)[12]—becoming an "intermediate" thing (μέσον, μεταίχμιον),[13] which, because of its very neutrality, can neither unite nor really penetrate its two poles (μηδετέρα φύσει τῶν ἐξ ὧν ἐστι κοινωνοῦν). The solution of the Monophysite Severus [of Antioch], who proposed simultaneously both a natural union and a natural difference of the poles, can only lead to open contradiction, if pushed to its limits (σφᾶς αὐτοὺς μετὰ τῶν οἰκείων ἀνατρέποντες);[14] the only way to prevent this would be to take the natural union seriously, but then the union would destroy the inner independence of the poles once again and would end in a docetic denial of the truth of the Incarnation.[15]

If the two great heresies thus mark off the way in a negative sense,

---

[9] Ibid.; PG 91, 56C.
[10] Ibid.; PG 91, 44B.
[11] Ibid.; PG 91, 76A.
[12] Ibid.; PG 91, 113B; cf. the note of Combéfis.
[13] Ibid.; PG 91, 121C.
[14] Ibid.; PG 91, 208D.
[15] Ibid.; PG 91, 225A.

Christian speculation on the divine Trinity, which had already been amply developed, pointed out more positively the direction in which to go. For it was here that the notion of person had first been securely established. In the midst of the complexities of the christological debate, Maximus always took his refuge in trinitarian theology. Against the argument of Sergius, who argued from an understanding of Christ's personal unity to the strict unity of his personal activity and will, Maximus repeatedly countered with an appeal to the doctrine of the Trinity: Sergius' thesis leads to three wills in God. At first, perhaps, this appeal to the internal relations in God to shed light on the being of Christ may seem less than convincing. Are not the relationships between nature and person in God essentially indescribable? Do not these concepts have a completely different meaning there, one we can hardly guess at? In his disputation with Maximus, Pyrrhus does not miss the opportunity of pointing this out: "The Fathers developed these ideas in the context of the doctrine of God, not in that of Christology. Therefore it is not a sign of intellectual honesty to use for Christology what they intended to say of the Trinity and to try to prove a contradiction in this way."[16] But Maximus was more far-sighted: in fact, the two questions are not unrelated to one another. The Logos, having once become human, still remains, as Logos, one of the three who are God, and therefore a proposition in Christology may not contradict a proposition about the Trinity.[17] What little insight we can gain by distinguishing between nature and person in God is enough, thanks to the deep interweaving of the two sets of problems, to require us to make an analogous distinction in Christ. For if the Incarnation produced a synthetic *nature*, the Son would no longer be of the same nature as the Father, and we would have been forced, without realizing it, to become Arians![18] The Trinity, too, would have expanded into a Quaternity;[19] and the nature of such a Christ would be totally different from our human nature,[20] so that it would not be able to redeem us. Sergius' misleading conclusion, that "the number of wills determines the number of willing subjects", itself leads—in its

---

[16] *Disputation with Pyrrhus*; PG 91, 348C.

[17] Ibid.; PG 91, 348C–350B.

[18] *Opuscula*; PG 91, 85B and 116AC.

[19] *Ambigua*; PG 91, 1058C. On tritheism in the sixth century, see Maximus, *Centuries on Love* 2, 29.

[20] *Epistles* 13; PG 91, 520C.

implications—either to Arius or to Sabellius: to a distinction in nature between the Divine Persons or else to a dissolution of the Persons in the undifferentiated unity of the divine nature.[21] A "personal will" destroys the very notion of the divine nature.[22]

One may not seek [for clues to the mystery of Christ], then, in the direction of "a composite thing";[23] the mystery is not to be found in the realm of "things" at all. "The mysterious manner of identification" (ὁ ἀπόρρητος τρόπος τῆς συμφυΐας)[24] raises us above the level of parts. But here the real difficulty arises: if the unity that results is not a "third thing", comprised by the parts—because Christ is no one else but the "hypostasis" of the parts[25]—how can this hypostasis be distinguished from the parts themselves? How can one define and verbalize what does not belong to the essential order?

The need to exclude the Nestorian and Monophysite solutions introduces, first of all, two arguments that limit the problem. Against Severus, one had to defend the position that the Unity [of Christ] is *free*, not the end product of a natural process, yet that it still does not cease to be a "physical" union—a union, that is, on the level of being. It is his own personal achievement (αὐτουργία).[26] Against Nestorius, on the other hand, one had to show that this free, spiritual achievement is an "ontic" and not just a "moral" union (οὐσιώδης, κατ' οὐσίαν), yet that it need not be for that reason a "natural" one (ἐν οὐσίᾳ).

Still, these arguments do not go very far. One had to find a category that would add the further tone, or dimension, of existence, without affirming a qualitative difference in the existing essence. Since Amphilochius and the Cappadocians, the term "mode of existence" (τρόπος τῆς ὑπάρξεως) had been used to suggest this of the Trinity. Could not this term be transferred to the christological problem? Does not a similarly phenomenological view of the appearance of Christ really invite us to do this, since we see in him a being whose whole bearing—down to the least word and gesture—reveals a human nature, but one that has been translated into a wholly different manner of existing?

---

[21] *Disputation with Pyrrhus*; PG 91, 289D.
[22] Ibid.; PG 91, 313C.
[23] *Ambigua*; PG 91, 1057A.
[24] Ibid.; PG 91, 1056D–1057A.
[25] Ibid.; PG 91, 1044D.
[26] Ibid.; PG 91, 1049D.

Everything that is truly human can be found in this new manner of existing,[27] yet none of it is any longer "simply human" (ψιλὸς ἄνθρωπος)[28] or "only human" (ἁπλῶς ἄνθρωπος),[29] but it appears as mysteriously "inhabited" (τῷ ἐνοικεῖν) by another.[30] This "indwelling" is perceived at once as the most interior and intimate relationship possible (οὐδὲν ἐνικώτερον), in which [God] is tenderly concerned to preserve all that is human and natural and to heal it (οὐδὲν σωστικώτερον).[31] Thus it is this "new manner [of being]",[32] this "divine mode",[33] this "way of existing thus and no other way" (τοῦ πῶς εἶναι τρόπος),[34] this new quality that has no effect on quantity,[35] that promises to show us the way to the unity we are looking for.

From all this it will already be evident that the paths of thought Maximus has begun to follow do not lead at all in the direction of the existential, in the modern sense of the term. Unity of consciousness[36] is not the foundation of hypostatic unity; for this reason, we will have to be very careful in using the word "person". The *hypostasis* is, first of all, a concept taken from formal ontology. Nevertheless, the questions asked here do lead us beyond the realm of ancient Hellenic thought. The real distinction between essence and existence is already the implied foundation of this Christology, and its concepts are moving toward this invisible point of convergence, without yet standing expressly under its normative power. In this sense, surely, the problem of "existential" categories, in all its cloudy urgency, has already been implicitly posed here. With these late Greek thinkers, the clear geometric field of [earlier] thought is already in the process of becoming "spherically bent";[37] concepts have begun to spread beyond their old meanings, and a new, "existential" meaning often expressly crops up

---

[27] *Opuscula*; PG 91, 77AB.

[28] *Ambigua*; PG 91, 1048B.

[29] Ibid.; PG 91, 1048A.

[30] *Opuscula*; PG 91, 108B.

[31] *Ambigua*; PG 91, 1044D-1045A.

[32] Ibid.; PG 91, 1052A: τὴν καινότητα τῶν τρόπων.

[33] Ibid.; PG 91, 1053CD.

[34] Ibid.; PG 91, 1053B.

[35] Ibid.; PG 91, 1057A.

[36] As F. Loofs would occasionally show of Leontius of Byzantium: *Leontius von Byzanz und die gleichnamigen Schriftsteller der griechischen Kirche*, Texte und Untersuchungen zur Geschichte der altchristlichen Literatur, vol. 3, nos. 1-2 (Leipzig, 1887), 72, 778.

[37] See my *Apokalypse der deutschen Seele*, vol. 1 (Salzburg/Leipzig, 1937), 419.

alongside the original, classical one. Often the change can only be noticed in the usage, the tone, the broad context of a word.

Obviously one must ask: Is this twilight not, on the other hand, the most normal of situations for human thought? A clear distinction between the essential and existential realms would presuppose that this underlying distinction within created being is completely graspable on the conceptual—which is to say, the essential—level; for the creature, this would be an intrinsic contradiction and would split what is actually a living tension into a fossilized parallelism. The mystery does not admit of a clean solution; rather, it reveals its own character as mystery precisely to the degree that our thought struggles to engage it. The Christology of Maximus and his contemporaries stands squarely in the midst of this struggle and deserves its place in the history of thought as a serious attempt to draw closer to the mystery.

It may be useful now to begin [our exposition of Maximus' synthesis] by assembling the basic concepts and explaining their meaning for Christology.

2. The Terminology

For Aristotle, the highest and most comprehensive category of being was *ousia* (οὐσία), the existing essence. Both aspects—existence and essence—come together in the *ousia*, in his view; the clearest indication of this is that form, by being the form of matter, also gives matter existence. Originally, then, *ousia* is used indifferently with regard to the pair, essence and existence, and this remains basically true even after Aristotle. Maximus uses *ousia* in the twofold sense, corresponding to the usage in the works of Leontius [of Byzantium]. The first meaning of the word—which should not be confused with the Aristotelian "second *ousia*", or universal essence, for which later on the term *physis* will become standard—includes *that which is*, as the highest ontological category. *Ousia* thus includes under itself all species and individuals.[38]

---

[38] So Leontius observes that *ousia* by itself (ἁπλῶς) indicates existence (ὕπαρξις), under which all being falls; but it does not indicate the "what" or the "how" (τὸ τί ἢ τὸ πῶς): PG 87, 1921C. Cf. Maximus, *Quaestiones ad Thalassium* 48; CCG 7, 341, 178ff.; PG 90, 440D. [For a discussion of Leontius of Byzantium's christological vocabulary and its ontological and theological significance, see Brian E. Daley, " 'A Richer Union': Leontius of Byzantium and the Relationship of Human and Divine in Christ", *Studia Patristica* 24 (Louvain, 1993): 239–65.]

For Maximus, general logical classes are, at the same time, ontological wholes (καθόλα). Thus *ousia* is not for him—any more than it was for the Cappadocians, who introduced the word into their trinitarian speculation—simply a universal concept; rather, [it suggests] the real totality to which the universal concept refers, including its subdivisions and individualities, which for him can only conceptually be distinguished from the whole. This notion of *ousia* as a concrete totality is threatened by the tendency—brought on by Christology—to emphasize the importance of the *hypostasis* (see below), which tends increasingly to slip free from the ontic grasp of the *ousia; ousia* does not, however, thereby simply become a purely abstract concept.[39] But while Leontius includes God within the category of *ousia*, Maximus —true to his teachers Origen[40] and Pseudo-Dionysius[41]—places him beyond it: God is not *ousia* but stands above *ousia*.[42] In this way, Maximus declares *ousia* to be both the most generic and the most ontically real degree of unity in created being.

In a second sense of the word, *ousia* is for Maximus—as for Leontius —more or less a synonym of nature, *physis*, and denotes the individual or particular nature (οὐσία καθ᾽ ἕκαστον).[43] As soon as we focus on this particularity itself, however, and define it in an isolating way, as "the being of things that exist on their own" (οὐσία τῶν καθ᾽ ἑαυτὰ ὑφεστώτων), the meaning becomes less clear. For it might well seem as though the heart of the "particular *ousia*" consisted in this particular way of being-on-one's-own. On the other hand, there is a general law among created beings (which Maximus, a theologian, will apply even to God), that an individual nature, as nature, is never identical with its own individuality—in other words, that a nature can never be limited to a single "example".[44] The phoenix, which is supposed to be the only individual bird in its species, is therefore intrinsically impossible, in Maximus' view—a contradiction in itself. All nature is universal (γενική), all particular *ousia* is, as such, still generic (εἶδος ἄτομον); the

<hr>

[39] *In De Div. Nom.* 5; PG 4, 321CD.
[40] *Contra Celsum* 6, 64.
[41] *In De Div. Nom.* 1, 1; 13, 3; etc.
[42] So John of Scythopolis, *In Coel. Hier.* 2; PG 4, 41A. Maximus repeatedly calls God "beyond being" (ὑπερούσιος): *Ambigua*; PG 91, 1036B; 1081B; 1224B; etc. Cf. *In De Div. Nom.* 1; PG 4, 188A: "God lies beyond all being" (πάσης γὰρ οὐσίας ὑπέρκειται ὁ Θεός).
[43] *Ambigua*; PG 91, 1228D; *In De Div. Nom.* 5; PG 4, 321D.
[44] *Opuscula*; PG 91, 517D–520C.

being-on-one's-own that breaks through every universal class is simply
not to be found in this order of being.

But once the particular being (καθ' ἕκαστον εἶναι) and being-on-one's-
own (καθ' ἑαυτόν εἶναι) are recognized not to be the same thing—even
though, in the concrete, there can never be an *ousia* that does *not* exist
on its own—does not a distinction between the two appear possible, at
least as something that can be thought of? [Can one not imagine it] in
the sense that while *ousia* is not necessarily broken up into these particular, unique individuals—and no others—simply because it takes on
particular being in the process of creation's "expansion" (*diastolē*), at
least this uniqueness is brought to *ousia* from "outside", [that is, from
some other ontologized source]? To try to think this way allows the
real difficulty of the problem to emerge. *Ousia* of that kind would be
"universal", without necessarily being the genus (εἶδος) of *this* unique
being that exists on its own, but simply the genus of particular beings. *Ousia, eidos, physis*, in any case, ultimately find themselves forced
into the same field of meaning by their contrast with the element of
being-on-one's own: into the field of "essence".[45] Over against them,
we enter the field of actual existence.

Next to *ousia* is the concept of "being" (*einai*, εἶναι). Usually it is used
rather inexactly; materially, at least, it has the same conceptual content[46]
as *ousia* (which is, after all, etymologically derived from it).[47] Still, it is
clear that *einai* emphasizes the existential aspect of being. We saw earlier
that Maximus rejects the idea of a "being" that is not, at its root, also
"being of a certain kind" (πῶς εἶναι)[48]—unless it is an idea in the mind
of God, who is beyond being. God himself is above being,[49] which is
intrinsically and essentially temporal,[50] derived,[51] caused, divided into
multiplicity.[52] In this sense, all created being is always colored by some

---

[45] Ibid.; PG 91, 264B: "Nature contains simply the intelligible character of genus" (ἡ μὲν
φύσις εἴδους λόγον μόνον ἐπέχει); PG 91, 488B: οὐσία and φύσις are identical, and an aspect
of them is being a genus (εἶδος).
[46] Cf., for example, *Epistles* 12; PG 91, 485CD.
[47] *In De Div. Nom.* 13; PG 4, 412C (attribution uncertain).
[48] *Ambigua*; PG 91, 1180C–1181A.
[49] *In De Div. Nom.* 1; PG 4, 188A.
[50] *Ambigua*; PG 91, 1180B.
[51] *In De Div. Nom.* 1; PG 4, 185D–188A.
[52] Ibid., 13; PG 4, 412BC.

qualitative characteristic. Even if the intellect, in the fundamental activity of thought, encounters "being in general", it immediately has to add qualifications to this generality if it is to grasp it as something real.[53] Maximus would have had difficulty conceiving created being and the real distinction between existence and essence in terms of the image of a metaphysical "composition", since he seems to imagine the interpenetration of the two poles as implying even a mutual conceptual indwelling. So he likes to identify the "intelligible structure of being" (λόγος τοῦ εἶναι), the intrinsic rationality and luminosity of "being", with *ousia* [οὐσία] or "essence";[54] he says that Christ united in his own person "the two distinct intelligible structures of being (λόγοι τοῦ εἶναι) of his parts",[55] and suggests that the elements of a generic or specific being are united "according to the same structure of being" (κατὰ τὸν αὐτὸν τοῦ εἶναι λόγον).[56] He even seems to be playing at times with the tension between *ousia* and being, as when he says:

> The fact that soul and body are two beings, as soul and as body, with regard to the intelligible structure of their essences (εἶναι δό κατὰ τὸν οὐσιώδη λόγον), is not the reason that they are always also different essences with regard to the intelligible structure of their being (ἄλλην οὐσίαν κατὰ τὸν τοῦ εἶναι λόγον).[57]

Occasionally, "being" (εἶναι) appears as a contrasting appendage to "subsisting" (ὑποστῆναι); when it does, it is meant to emphasize, in contrast to ὑποστῆναι, the existence of something from the viewpoint of its essential character.[58] Nevertheless, the etymological family *einai* points in the existential direction. One feels this especially when it is applied to "stages of being", which represent a single essential idea in various modes of ontological realization—life, for example, in things that "simply" live, in things that feel, that reason, that know by intuition;[59] or similarly, freedom [in its various degrees of realization].[60] If these concepts do not have an identical name (οὐχ ὁμονύμως λέγεται)

---

[53] Ibid., 5; PG 4, 31/D.
[54] *Mystagogia* 23; PG 91, 700D–701A.
[55] *Epistles* 12; PG 91, 488A.
[56] *Quaestiones ad Thalassium* 48; CCG 7, 341, 181f.; PG 90, 440D.
[57] *Epistles* 12; PG 91, 488BC.
[58] Ibid.; PG 91, 468B.
[59] *In De Div. Nom.* 5; PG 4, 313B.
[60] *Disputation with Pyrrhus*; PG 91, 324D–325A.

in their different stages of being, this is not primarily a question of "essential" differentiation but rather one of an increase in the "intensity of being" (πλέον ζῆν . . .).[61]

Hypokeimenon [ὑποχείμενον, "underlying subject"] is used relatively seldom by Maximus; he takes the term as an established concept, without analyzing it further. It denotes the concrete, existent bearer of the qualities that determine *what* a thing is.[62] As in the realm of essential being "every created thing is composed of essence and the qualities that are [accidentally] added to it",[63] so in the realm of being as such it is composed of essence (*ousia*) and its bearer (*hypokeimenon*), which are only identical with each other in the case of God.[64] This last remark makes it clear, however, that *hypokeimenon* does not mean the same thing as *hypostasis*; it is obviously more a point of reference for the logical predication of nature than it is an ontological reality.[65] Nevertheless, even this dimension of nonidentity points toward the central riddle of the tension between essence and existence: even if the concrete bearer of an essence is "defined on the basis of the general, common characteristics",[66] which have the ability to mark it out more and more clearly, and especially on the basis of its manner of behaving,[67] still it can never be completely transformed into its own essential characteristics.

> To come to a perfect knowledge of things, it is not enough to name a list of characteristics that pertain to it—being a body, for example, or being born, passing away, or whatever else may be gathered around the central subject (*hypokeimenon*). The underlying subject (*hypokeimenon*) of these qualities, the basis on which they stand, must be pointed out in its essential character, should we want to bring the object of our thought into full and perfect identity with sense data. For we must either name it a man or a cow or a horse, which are all not simply *body*, but bodily

---

[61] *In De Div. Nom.* 5; PG 4, 313B.

[62] *Ambigua*; PG 91, 1225A.

[63] *Centuries on Love* 4, 9: PG 90, 1049B.

[64] *Centuries on Knowledge* 2, 3: PG 90, 1125D.

[65] See the text cited in n. 64, where the *hypokeimenon* of thought—in the sense of "object", "focus"—is mentioned in the same breath with the *hypokeimenon* of the essence.

[66] *Epistles* 13; PG 91, 528B.

[67] "The definition of an object lies first of all in the concept of its essential activity; if this is destroyed, the subject (*hypokeimenon*) also necessarily disappears": *Opuscula*; PG 91, 201AB; cf. 200B.

things, not coming-to-be and passing-away, but *things* that come to be and pass away.[68]

We do not get much information on *how* we are to arrive at this knowledge, since Maximus never develops his epistemology. It is clear, though, that ecstatic experience and the vision of God bring us beyond the duality of *ousia* and *hypokeimenon* and also give us an insight into what such knowledge involves, if only as something we have already left behind us and therefore as no longer relevant.

Hyparxis (ὕπαρξις), "existence", had for a long time been the technical term for the being of the Persons in God, especially in the phrase "manner of existing" (τρόπος τῆς ὑπάρξεως). Still, the fact that Maximus contrasts God's "triple manner of existing" not only with the "singularity of his essence" but also with the "intelligible structure of his being" (λόγος τοῦ εἶναι)[69] shows that the development of philosophical concepts did not always keep pace with those of theology. The unspecific character of *being* (εἶναι), which reaches from the pole of essence (οὐσία) to the pole of existence (ὕπαρξις), does not let the really decisive contrast come to light.[70] Certainly, the passage we have just referred to intends to emphasize the absolute unity of essence and existence in God and even hints that God's essence only comes to perfection (τέλεια οὖσα) from the tri-hypostatic existence (τρισυπόστατος ὕπαρξις) itself. Consequently, Maximus can also insist on a strict correspondence, even in creatures, between unity of essence and unity of existence, since a unified essence, even if it is a composite unity, cannot possess several existences,[71] even though the existence of the whole does not imply some new, third thing over and above its parts.[72] The existence of parts that are ordered to each other is precisely an existence that is homogeneous in them all; thus the whole created world, insofar as it is a single totality, has an "undifferentiated identity of existence".[73]

---

[68] *Ambigua*; PG 91, 1225BC.

[69] Ibid., PG 91, 1400D 1401A.

[70] In *Mystagogia* 23 (PG 91, 701A), the "manner of existing" (τρόπος τῆς ὑπάρξεως), and also the "concrete individual" or *hypostasis* (ὑπόστασις), are contrasted with essence (οὐσία), which is itself explained as "the intelligible structure of being" (λόγος τοῦ εἶναι).

[71] *Opuscula*; PG 91, 201C.

[72] Ibid.; PG 91, 117C.

[73] *Mystagogia* 1; PG 91, 665A; cf. *Opuscula*; PG 91, 265D, where "nature" (φύσις) is defined as "the particular kind of existence proper to the whole" (ἡ ποιὰ τῷ παντὶ ὕπαρξις).

222   CHRIST THE SYNTHESIS

Hypostasis[74] (ὑπόστασις) is the great shibboleth and controversial term of Christology. First of all, it has the same meaning as *prosopon* (πρόσωπον,

---

[74] We will draw our explanation of this central concept from the fullness of its developed meaning, which it finds in Maximus, where the various streams of earlier tradition flow together. On the history of this term up to Chalcedon, see especially M. Richard, "L'Introduction du mot 'hypostase' dans la théologie de l'incarnation", *Mélanges de science religieuse* 2 (1945): 5–32, 243–70 (also in M. Richard, *Opera Minora*, vol. 2 [Louvain, 1977], no. 42); A. Grillmeier, *Jesus der Christus im Glauben der Kirche*, vol. 1; English translation, *Christ in Christian Tradition*, vol. 1 (Oxford, 1975). After Chalcedon the fate of the word was determined by the two Leontii. Moving beyond the Cappadocian distinction—of basic importance for the history of the concept, but insufficient and misleading in itself—which used *ousia* to mean "general essence" (originally understood in a Platonic, concrete sense) and *hypostasis* to mean "individuality", Leontius of Byzantium introduced "being-for-oneself" (τὸ καθ᾽ ἑαυτό) into the definition of *hypostasis*, a great step forward but one that brought with it the risk of depersonalizing *ousia*. The relationship of *hypostasis* to the existing substance is missing in Leontius of Byzantium (cf. M. Richard, "Le Traité 'De Sectis' et Léonce de Byzance", *Revue d'histoire ecclésiastique* 35 [1939]: 700 [also in Richard, *Opera Minora*, vol. 2, no. 55]). He simply makes the negative observation that the natures (φύσεις) that come together in a *hypostasis* do not complete each other in the process of forming an essential whole (*Contra Nestorianos et Eutychianos* 1; PG 86, 1280A). Leontius of Jerusalem was the first to introduce the paraphrase "a standing under one" (ὑφ᾽ ἓν στάσις: PG 86, 1816A; cf. 1529CD) and meant by this an existential unity of different substances that together result in a single, indivisible thing (κατὰ τὸ αὐτό . . . ἓν μόνον ἄτομον), which does not need to belong, as such, to the realm of essences but which rather is held together through the act of existence, the ὕπαρξις. "Standing under one" means, then, that essences have here come under the domination of the unifying One of Being. This liberating view is confused in Leontius of Jerusalem, in that he discovers this mode of unity on all levels of nature, down to inanimate things, and does not see the incomparable relationship of the intelligent person to the act of being. Only such a recognition can open the way to a speculative solution. But the convergence of both nuances, that of "being by itself" (καθ᾽ ἑαυτό) and that of "standing under one" (ὑφ᾽ ἓν στῆναι) points toward that speculative goal. Maximus himself remains within the process of forward-looking convergence. (Cf. M. Richard, "Léonce de Jérusalem et Léonce de Byzance", *Mélanges de science religieuse* 1 [1944]: 35–88 [also in Richard, *Opera minora*, vol. 2, no. 59]). And the treatise *De sectis*, which puts the dimension of existence in the foreground, is also historically correct in identifying this as the original intention of Cyril [of Alexandria]: [union] "in hypostasis" (καθ᾽ ὑπόστασιν) means [union] "in existence and in the things themselves" (καθ᾽ ὕπαρξιν καὶ αὐτῶν πραγμάτων) and is predicated "simply of existing things" (ἐπὶ τῶν ὄντων ἁπλῶς) which suggests also the word's other sense of singularity (PG 86, 1252BC). Besides this, the *De sectis* expressly connects the traditions of the two Leontii in 7, 2, where it states the double meaning of *hypostasis*: "being in itself" (lit., "simply being", ἁπλῶς ὄν) and "being for itself" (lit., "being by itself", καθ᾽ ἑαυτὸ ὄν). The same is true for *enhypostaton*: PG 86, 1240CD.

[For a more recent and historically more precise discussion of the meaning of *hypostasis* and other terms in Leontius of Byantium, Leontius of Jerusalem, and the *De sectis*, see A. Grillmeier, *Jesus der Christus im Glauben der Kirche*, vol. 2, pt. 2 (Freiburg, 1990), 196–210; English translation, 186–200.]

[which means] "mask", ["role"], "person")[75] and denotes the three "Persons" in God;[76] it thus is the reality that is described and expressed as a "manner of existing" or "mode of origin".[77] In its root meaning, and even in the created realm, "hypostasis" is an essence's (ousia's) "being-for-itself" (καθ᾽ ἑαυτὸν): what distinguishes a concrete being from others of the same genus (εἶδος).[78] So it answers to the question "Who?" (τόυ τίνα τῆς οὐσίας ἐμφαίνει), in a broad sense;[79] it is the indicator and affirmation of a subject, an "I" (τοῦ τινός ἐστι δηλωτική).[80] In a broad sense, I say, for the hypostasis is the ontological subject of the ascription of an essence, not the consciousness of such a subject; animals, plants, even stones each have their hypostasis, in Maximus' view.[81] "As activity is referred back to the actor, so nature is referred back to the hypostasis":[82] the relationship of "rootedness" ["In-den-Grund-Gehens"] expresses both kinds of connection. This relationship is surely similar, on the one hand, to the limitation of a general concept in a particular individual; it is a matter of focus.[83] But on the other hand, such a narrowing of essence is of a different order than that "contraction" (systolē) that was described in connection with universal and particular being. There, all that was at issue was various more abstract or more concrete ways of "being". Here, on the other hand, the concentration is tied to a "having",[84] to a way of being the possessor of essential being. This relationship is the reason that it is, on the one hand, "impossible to think of a hypostasis without a nature"[85] and that no nature, on the other hand, can simply coincide with its hypostasis. Both concepts necessarily exclude one another, even in God.[86]

Hence the difficulty of giving a definition of hypostasis. For much as it seems, at first, that it would be enough to define it as an "individual form" (ἄτομον εἶδος), by means of the essence and all its particularizing

---

[75] Epistles 12; PG 91, 469D; Epistles 15; PG 91, 545A.
[76] Mystagogia 23; PG 91, 701A.
[77] Opuscula; PG 90, 60C.
[78] Epistles 15; PG 91, 557A.
[79] Opuscula; PG 91, 201A.
[80] Ibid.; PG 91, 264B.
[81] Epistles 15; PG 91, 549C.
[82] Opuscula; PG 91, 200D.
[83] Ibid.; PG 91, 265D.
[84] Ibid.
[85] Ibid.; PG 91, 264A.
[86] Epistles 15; PG 91, 549C.

characteristics—since these clearly distinguish the individual from the universal aspects of a generic nature[87]—still in reality it contains, even beyond this, that active, functional process of "ownership" that is necessary if a concrete individual is to result.[88] Thus it is quite conceivable that a hypostasis should not be, as such, an "individual form" (ἄτομον εἶδος), insofar as that remains a category in the realm of essences.[89] Conceived in this way, of course, hypostasis would defy all proper definition, which—as we have mentioned—always moves from the more general level of being to the more particular.[90] Must not the hypostasis, then, *as such*, not always defy definition? Certainly, it is always incarnate in a nature, it is always "essentialized" (ἐνούσιον); but it is not limited to being a "mere property" (ψιλὸν ἰδίωμα) of nature. It would be much truer to say that nature is *its* property, *its* possession. Certainly, too, one can further distinguish among individuating characteristics, between "essential qualities" (ποιότητες οὐσιωδεῖς), which mark off the levels of specific being, and "hypostatic qualities" (ποιότητες ὑποστατικαί), which refer to the individual as such: the shape of one's nose, for instance, or the color of one's hair.[91] But these last remain only the sign, the indication of a being-for-itself that lies behind them; they do not belong themselves to the ontological order. In the end, only number remains to express the pure difference of hypostases.[92] Yet what could be less suited to express what is precisely the unique, unmistakable character of a being? We have already made the point, in any case, that number of itself is only a "sign" and does not touch on any reality directly or with conceptual content.

For these reasons, the hypostasis can only be described by approach-

---

[87] *Opuscula*; PG 91, 152A.

[88] Ibid.; PG 91, 152B: "Gathering, . . . dividing off" (συνάγουσα . . . τέμνουσα). It is important to notice here that the Cappadocians defined "hypostasis" in the Trinity, not just in terms of "individual characteristics", but above all in terms of the manner in which each Person has his origin: "unoriginateness" (ἀγεννησία) for the Father, "generation" (γέννησις) for the Son, "proceeding forth" (ἐκπόρευσις) for the Spirit. These are the ways in which each Person "has" the common reality [of God]. Here, in absolute Being itself, essence is transcended on the level of the "Person", the manner of existing, as the way in which being is possessed (τρόπος τῆς ὑποστάσεως: see Gregory of Nyssa, *Adv. Apollinarium*: GNO 3/1, 223, 30–224, 5; PG 45, 1256B.

[89] *Opuscula*; PG 91, 201D.

[90] Ibid.; PG 91, 204A.

[91] Ibid.; PG 91, 248Bff.

[92] Ibid.; PG 91, 152B, D.

ing it from two directions, which mutually complement each other: from that of nature and its ever-more-narrowly circumscribing qualities (that is, from the viewpoint of the being, which the hypostasis "has") and from that of the act of coming to possess this nature. Maximus puts both definitions alongside each other. "Hypostasis is being that stands apart, consisting on its own. For one defines hypostasis as the essence plus its individuating characteristics, distinguished from other (things) of the same essence through number."[93]

It is well known, however, that "hypostasis" originally had the general meaning of "subsistence", "existence". This usage continued in the verb "subsist" (ὑποστῆναι),[94] and in the adjective "anhypostatic" (ἀνυπόστατον) or "nonexisting",[95] as when it is said of evil that "it has no concrete (hypostatic) existence" (ὑπόστασιν οὐκ ἔχει).[96] This original sense still echoed in the technical use of the term to mean "being-for-oneself" or "being-on-one's-own": the mysterious point at which all the essential characteristics of a thing are concentrated and bound together appears quite automatically to be the most "concrete" aspect of a nature—which is, of itself, abstract and shared by an indefinite number of individuals—and thus as a thing's "existence". But one should not forget that in Maximus' time, "essence" (ousia) and "nature" (physis) themselves do not have a consistently abstract meaning and thus cannot be taken as the simple opposites to the existing thing. The ancient Greek identification of essence and existence is still quite alive in both notions.

So one sees even here a kind of pattern of interference appearing between theological terminology and its reflective philosophical development. It is even possible, as we have already indicated, that theological polemic's immediate need for precise terms, even for slogans, occasionally causes it to run ahead of philosophical reflection and so to threaten philosophy's slow maturing to fruitfulness. Still, this need for conceptual clarity [in theological language] remains a powerful driving force for philosophy and opens up approaches and questions that it would not have discovered on its own. Here is where one discovers the realm of tension between existence and idea. The structural relatedness of essence and its concrete bearer opens up one's view of

---

[93] *Epistles* 15; PG 91, 557D.
[94] *Disputation with Pyrrhus*; PG 91, 308D–309A.
[95] *Ambigua*; PG 91, 1261D, 1349D.
[96] *In De Div. Nom.* 4; PG 4, 304D.

the nonidentity of the order of being and the order of existence. This nonidentity is certainly not yet thematic—it is significant that the relationship between "underlying subject" (*hypokeimenon*) and hypostasis is not further explained by Maximus; yet precisely this intermediate stage between a pagan philosophy of identity and the later, scholastic "real distinction", which attempts to separate the poles in an overly facile way, is fruitful for the history of ideas.

The tension is expressed in a sentence in which the scholiast on the polemical writings comments on one of Maximus' ideas: "Nature is that which was 'created according to the image', the plan of being (λόγος). The hypostasis is that which was 'created according to the likeness', historical life (βίος)".[97] For a long time, "image and likeness" had been the shorthand labels for the abstract outline, the "projected" nature of the creature, on the one hand, and the concrete, free self-realization and appropriation of this nature, on the other.[98] But *plan* and *life*—the great poles of all created being—never let themselves be conceived as "parts" of this being, in the sense of a metaphysical "composition". For every plan is, of its very nature, the plan of a life, and all life is the vitality of a plan. "A hypostasis without nature is not even conceivable (οὐκ ἐστι νοῆσαι)."[99] The dimension that opened up through this fundamental tension is, rather, expressed in the command, "Become what you *are*"; for that reason, it can only consist in a progressive realization (in Newman's sense of "realize") of the one in and through the other. The "image", freely brought to completion and appropriated, is as such the "likeness", yet the two cannot be identified.

For such a growth to be possible, a fundamental, reciprocal indwelling [of the two elements] is required:

> The fact that no nature is without hypostasis does not make it into a hypostasis but rather into something hypostatized (ἐνυπόστατον), so

---

[97] *Opuscula*; PG 91, 37BC.

[98] Cf. *Centuries on Knowledge* I, 13; PG 90, 1088BC: "He added to what was natural beauty a goodness of free choice that realized his likeness" (οὗτος τῷ φυσικῷ κατ᾽ εἰκόνα καλῷ προσέθηκε τὸ καθ᾽ ὁμοίωσιν γνωμικὸν ἀγαθόν). Cf. *Centuries on Love* 3, 25; PG 90, 1024BC. M. T. Disdier, "Les Fondements dogmatiques de la spiritualité de s. Maxime le Confesseur", *Echos d'Orient* 29 (1930): 296–313, considered the distinction between image (a natural similarity, with the capacity for moral perfection) and likeness (similarity as a human, free, yet divinely graced resemblance to God, which was lost in Adam and given again in Christ) as the basic structural principle of Maximus' spirituality.

[99] *Opuscula*; PG 91, 264A.

that it should not be conceived simply as a property that can only be distinguished [from the hypostasis] in thought, but rather is recognized as a form (εἶδος) in actual fact (πραγματικῶς). Even so, the fact that a hypostasis is not without its essence does not make the hypostasis into an essence, but shows it to be essential (ἐνούσιον); it should not be thought of as a mere quality [of a nature], but must be seen as truly existing together with that in which the qualities are grounded [that is, with a nature].[100]

The result of this mutual indwelling is that every hypostasized nature is also existent nature (τὸ ἐνυπόστατον δηλοῖ τὸ ἐνύπαρκτον) and as such is endowed with a whole field of activity and of self-realization (ἐνεργόν, ἐνεργητικόν).[101] On the other hand, every essentialized hypostasis is the realization of a "plan of nature", and, thus, of a rational order of being that is accessible to reason; it is not unrelated to nature, then, as if it were some irrational "existential" element.

This is the way Maximus answers the weighty proposals of the Monothelites. What is more personal in man, they asked, than that ultimate center of freedom: the will, from which the first stirrings and abilities of nature come forth and by which they are ultimately mastered? This freedom, Maximus answered, is, at its root, a freedom of human nature itself; only its concrete realization, its "liberation" by appropriation, is the work of the person, and it is there that freedom comes into its own.

The concept of a *"freedom* of nature", which was to play such a large role in the Monothelite controversy, is bound up, then, strictly and consistently, with the conception of the hypostasis.[102] To act and to achieve reality is the work of nature; it is only in the manner, the "how" of realization that the hypostatic comes into its own. This head start of nature is, in the creature, the real clue to its "givenness", its creature-hood. In Christ, however, this self-contained aspect of the natural becomes precisely the condition of his genuine hypostatic union. "Does it not, then, depend completely on the will of the Logos, who is united with the flesh," Pyrrhus asks, "that this flesh is moved?" "When you speak that way," Maximus replies, "you tear Christ in two!"[103] For

---

[100] Ibid.; PG 91, 205AB.
[101] Ibid.; PG 91, 205B.
[102] *Opuscula* PG 91, 49A; 137AB.
[103] *Disputation with Pyrrhus*; PG 91, 297A.

then Christ's human nature is simply an extrinsic instrument, a marionette moved from some transcendent, "hypostatic" point.

Here, then—and only here!—the most dangerous tendency of patristic Christology is defeated: the *logos–sarx* (Word–flesh) model, which
sees the Word expressing himself in a vital, personal way through the
instrument (*organon*) of flesh that he controls and enlivens, bypassing
or simply overwhelming the rational soul. This model was developed
by Arius, Athanasius, and Apollinarius (if in varying nuances). It was
not really abandoned by Cyril [of Alexandria] and was reawakened in
a whole range of forms, after the defeat of Antiochene Christology,
by the Monophysites and Neo-Chalcedonians. With Maximus and his
intellectual victory over monenergism, it was not only Alexandria that
won the day, *able* now to say what it had always wanted to say but
had never had words to express; it was also Antioch, for whom justice
had now been done—despite all the condemnations of the past—and
whose stammering tongue had been loosened.

Nature, moved by the divine hypostasis, does not simply act passively,
[Maximus argued against Pyrrhus,] any more than the nature of any
ordinary person does when he acts personally. But if anyone wants to
assure the highest possible level of unity [in Christ] in a Monophysite
and Monothelite way, through simple passivity [of his humanity], he
"tears Christ in two".

It seems appropriate to set in this broad context Maximus' principle
that in all action the basic activity (*actus primus*) belongs to the nature, the express realization of the activity (*actus secundus*) to the person.[104] We can guess at the deep perspectives that will open up here
on the figure of Christ, who "possessed the ability to will as a man,
but this ability was moved and shaped by his divine will":[105] who had
the [natural human] ability to will, in other words, which in its realization developed, not in the direction of becoming its own [human]
hypostasis, but toward that of God [the Son], without however ceasing
to be a genuinely human ability. Here again we find in Maximus that
optimism about [created] nature that would never think of opposing
freedom, as arbitrary decision, to nature, as mechanical determinism,
in a nominalistic way; rather, Maximus allows freedom to be rooted in
nature and to grow from it. This unity of natural freedom and personal

---

[104] Ibid.; PG 91, 292D–293A; *Opuscula*; PG 91, 48AB.
[105] *Opuscula*; PG 91, 48A.

freedom raises the creature, in a certain sense, above the opposition of necessity and freedom and allows it to be, in some degree, somewhat like God.

> If you call the power of willing natural (Pyrrhus objects), and everything natural occurs with an unforced necessity, then how can someone who thinks of Christ's willing as the work of his nature not end by necessarily removing from him every free impulse? (Maximus replies:) Not only the divine, uncreated nature but the intellectual creature as well has nothing in himself that is controlled by necessity. For the naturally rational being possesses, as a natural capacity for action, rational intellectual life, which we also call the will of the intellectual soul. As a result of this life, our thinking and reflecting is grounded in our willing (θέλοντες λογιζόμεθα), just as our willing and deciding is grounded in our thinking (λογιζόμενοι θέλοντες βουλόμεθα).

After Maximus develops this notion of the mutual interplay of willing and intellectual thought, he concludes: "There is, then, no compulsion in the nature of intellectual beings."[106]

Once again, this insight meant both the conclusion and the exclusion of a long struggle, a long danger that had come to a head in Origen but had continued to rage ever since: freedom is not identical with the ability to choose between good and evil; otherwise, the fall of the creature could be expected to occur with a diabolical necessity! Christ's freedom reveals to Maximus the mistake in this concept of freedom—just as *our* freedom in Christ had revealed it to Augustine. Free self-determination toward every good thing by following the law implied in one's status as God's image, in obedience to the flow of one's own natural movement toward God: there, in Maximus' view, is where the personal freedom of the creature must come to its lived reality.[107]

So, around the central notion of *hypostasis*, Christology comes to form a unified whole with Maximus' broader philosophy. A final remark seems in order: the new dimension now open to philosophy,

---

[106] *Disputation with Pyrrhus*; PG 91, 293BC.

[107] Polycarp Sherwood, in his translation of *The Ascetic Life: The Four Centuries on Charity*, Ancient Christian Writers, 21 (Westminster, Md.: Newman Press, 1955), 55f., has explained this in an illuminating way. Also Charles Moeller, "Le Chalcédonisme et le néo-chalcédonisme en Orient de 451 à la fin du VIᵉ siècle", in A. Grillmeier and H. Bacht, *Das Konzil von Chalkedon: Geschichte und Gegenwart* (Würzburg: Echter, 1951), 1:714, points to this development of our notion of freedom through Christology and adds, as a personal note, "I believe that this is a crucial point!"

between essence or nature and existence or person, forces the first of those poles, with a certain inner consistency, toward an abstract mode of being, to the level of mere "possibility". If it is incorrect to assert, with Harnack and Loofs, that Gregory of Nyssa, Leontius of Byzantium, and, according to some, even Maximus[108] did not recognize an individual human nature in Christ, but only the general essence of humanity, which includes all individuals—an opinion that today no longer needs refutation—still there is undeniably a certain orientation here toward an abstract way of conceiving both essence (*ousia*) and nature. With Gregory, this tendency is balanced off against the idea —Aristotelian, Stoic, and Neoplatonic in pedigree—of the "concrete universal in the object" (*universale [concretum] in re*), which only in this concrete form was conceived as being at once both prior to and subsequent to the object (*ante et post rem*).[109] In Maximus, a similar concreteness survives in his view of the universal, thanks to his concept of general being (*katholou*). But he does raise the problem whether Christ, when he took on "our nature", also drew "our natures"—considered as individual—into the hypostatic union.[110]

We have already met the concepts of *enhypostaton* (ἐνυπόστατον) and *enousion* (ἐνούσιον), "hypostatized" and "essential" [being]. Junglas has shed a good deal of light on the history of the first, more important notion, which comes out of Neoplatonism.[111] At first, the word

---

[108] See Hermann Weser, *Sancti Maximi Confessoris praecepta de incarnatione Dei et deificatione hominis* (diss., Berlin, 1869), 19ff.: Christ was not an individual but possessed human nature in general.

[109] Cf. my *Présence et pensée* (Paris, 1942), 27; English translation, *Presence and Thought* (San Francisco, 1995), 53f.

[110] *Disputation with Pyrrhus*; PG 91, 305Cff. See also what we have said above concerning *ousia*.

[111] J. P. Junglas, *Leontius von Byzanz: Studien zu seinen Schriften, Quellen und Anschauungen*, Forschungen zur christlichen Literatur- und Dogmengeschichte, vol. 7, no. 3 (Paderborn, 1908), 148–62. Moeller, "Chalcédonisme", 1:706; cf. 685, 692, 706) confirmed the conclusions of Junglas. In the historical note, n. 74 above, on *hypostasis*, we mentioned that the *De sectis* 7, 2, expressly gives a twofold sense for the word: just as *hypostasis* can mean "being" (in itself) or "being-for-oneself", so *enhypostaton* [can have two meanings], as is even clearer in its contrasting term, *anhypostaton*: "not being at all", as opposed to "being in something else" (like an accident in a substance): PG 86, 1240D–1241A). The second sense of *anhypostaton* in the *De sectis* corresponds to the only meaning of *enhypostaton* in Leontius of Byzantium (PG 86, 1277D; 1300BC). The difficulty in Leontius does not come from this useful term but from the fact that he has transferred to *hypostasis* the idea of "being-for-oneself" from

had the same general sense of "existence" that was conveyed by *hypostasis* and *hyparxis*; in Christology, it emphasized the true reality of the human nature [of Christ], in contrast to a docetic "lack of existence" (ἀνυπόστατον [more precisely: lack of independent existence]) and "lack of essence" (ἀνούσιον). The word "enhypostatic" could, at that period, signify both the reality of nature and that of person. Only in the course of the christological controversy, and clearly since Leontius [of Byzantium], did the word [*enhypostaton*] come to mean that intermediate grade of existence between nonbeing (or accidental being) and full, hypostatic existence. Junglas finds a correspondence for this theory in the idea of Porphyry, handed on by Nemesius,[112] that an *ousia* can enter into the being of another, higher *ousia* as a part of it, without losing anything of its own nature and perfection. Porphyry is thinking of the body and soul of man, which remain undiminished in the totality of [human] nature. This example was to play a considerable role in Christology.

Maximus retains traces of the older usage, as when he speaks of the Father's Word as "essential and hypostatized" (ἐνούσιος καὶ ἐνυπόστατος).[113] Still, one should translate ἐνυπόστατος here not so much by "genuinely existing" as by "hypostatized into [the divine being]". This is proved in another passage in the *Ambigua*, where Maximus

---

Aristotle's definition of *substance* and that he therefore implies that no genuine philosophical distinction is possible any longer between substance and accident, both of which have their reality in the hypostasis. Another difficulty that ensues is that the *enhypostasia* of Christ's humanity in the divine Logos is reduced simply to being one case among many—which would have suited the Origenist Leontius perfectly. See on this subject M. Richard, "Traité 'De Sectis' ", 695–723, esp. 704f.; "Léonce et Pamphile", *Revue des sciences philosophiques et théologiques* 27 (1938): 27–52, esp. 32–33 [also in M. Richard, *Opera Minora* (1977), vol. 3, no. 58]. All of this shows that sixth-century theology in general no longer relies on genuine ontological thinking and, with its arsenal of concepts, can at best provide material for later thinkers. In relation to the overemphasis on the hypostasis, which in Leontius remains an abstract subject of predication (*hypokeimenon*), Maximus is the first to attempt to restore the importance of the self-conscious, free nature and, thus, is the first to create the conditions for a genuine philosophy of person, insofar as this is distinguishable from the whole ontological order.

[112] PG 40, 604.

[113] *Ambigua*; PG 91, 1077D. The Synod of Antioch, held against Paul of Samosata in 260, used similar language about the reality of the Logos "as a living and concretely real activity" (ὡς ζῶσαν ἐνέργειαν καὶ ἐνυπόστατον) (Mansi 1, 1036B). John of Scythopolis refers to the ideas, in Plato's sense, as "concretely real patterns" (παραδείγματα ἐνυπόστατα: *In De Div. Nom.* 5; PG 4, 332C) and to the angels as "concretely real activities" (ἐνέργειαι ἐνυπόσταται: *In De Div. Nom.* 4; PG 4, 240C).

refutes the theory that the unity of God's being is prior to the three Persons and naturally develops into them ("so that it is naturally distributed by moving into multiplicity": ἵνα χεθῇ φυσικῶς εἰς πλῆθος ὁδεύουσα). Rather, "the unity is the hypostatized being of the consubstantial Trinity" (ἐνυπόστατος ὀντότης τῆς ὁμοουσίου Τριάδος), just as, in the same way, the Trinity is not the synthesis of three units but "the essentialized existence of a monad that is three hypostases" (ἐνούσιος ὕπαρξις τρισυποστάτου μονάδος).[114] In another place,[115] Maximus names the second and third Person in God "of the same substance and enhypostatic" (ὁμοούσιος καὶ ἐνυπόστατος) in the goodness of the Divine Being. Ἐνυπόστατος has thus, in his doctrine of the Trinity, a twofold sense: it designates both the utterly personalized manner in which God's being exists and the way in which the being of the Divine Persons is rooted in the being of God.

In Christology, the meaning is still more restricted. "The fact of not being 'unhypostatic' (ἀνυπόστατον, without concrete existence) does not thereby imply that something *is* a hypostasis, any more than the fact that no body is without form implies that every body, as such, *is* form."[116] This same consideration arises, in the order of being, in connection with the word "essentialized" (ἐνούσιον).[117] Apart from their high theological importance, both concepts are also very useful for philosophy in its attempt to shed light on the "space" between the two "poles" of essence and existence: they offer a means of describing those steps and forms of being that result from the dynamic interpenetration of the elements of created being. This same indwelling of the hypostasis in a nature, through which the hypostasis is "essentialized" (ἐνούσιον), is what allows the nature to become "hypostatized" (ἐνυπόστατον) without causing the two poles to become identified. Maximus gives two examples of such an indwelling.

Something is called "enhypostatic" if it never subsists on its own but is discovered in other things, as for example the species in the individuals that are included in it, or else something that is synthesized with another, essentially different being in order to give rise to a totally new totality. The (part) is distinguished, then, in the same degree, from the things

[114] *Ambigua*; PG 91, 1036B.
[115] Ibid., PG 91, 1250D.
[116] *Opuscula*; PG 91, 204AB.
[117] Ibid.; PG 91, 205A.

that share the same essential class through its limiting characteristics (for example, the humanity of Christ from that of other human beings), as it is hypostatically united and identified with the thing with which it forms a synthesis.[118]

Both possibilities concern the same ontological situation: in the first case, a universal essence is "hypostatized" in the individuals that belong to it through their nature (each of which then becomes at once both an "individual form" (ἄτομον εἶδος) and an "essentialized hypostasis" (ὑπόστασις ἐνούσιος); in the second, however, the essence hypostatizes itself in a "foreign" hypostasis, and then the individual characteristics (ἰδιώματα)—those "essential" marks that indirectly reveal the hypostasis—must be seen as related to that "foreign" hypostasis.[119] One could say the same thing of the concept "essentialized" (ἐνούσιον). Both notions, which allow us to think of interpenetration without mixture, serve to illuminate Maximus' greatest preoccupation, that of "unity without confusion" (ἕνωσις ἀσύγχυτος). They are the material from which the "preservative synthesis" (σύνθεσις σωστική) becomes possible.

With three words that express this *synthesis* we can bring our roll call of concepts to an end. The first, *synthesis* (σύνθεσις) itself, had for Maximus a different sound from what it has for us. It is extremely imprecise and can denote every type of combination, starting with the most extrinsic—a pile of stones, for example—continuing through all types of mixture (for example, of fluids), and reaching to the highest forms of union. *Synthesis* conveys, then, less the active achievement of uniting two things by putting them together than it does its passive result, which remains indifferent with regard to that achievement.

The act of combining appears more clearly in the word *henōsis* (ἕνωσις), "union", although this, too, can often be used in the same sense as *synthesis*. Its result is unity (ἐνότης), which—apart from God—comes into being from "the coming together of several things into one".[120] Two things are required for a genuine union: true unity and the preservation of the elements that have come together. The more

[118] *Epistles* 15; PG 91, 557D–560A.
[119] A passage that has almost the same content and is clearer is *Opuscula*; PG 91, 149BC; cf. ibid.; PG 91, 261–64.
[120] *In De Div. Nom.* 1; PG 4, 189AB (John of Scythopolis).

234 CHRIST THE SYNTHESIS

these two are realized at the same time, the more perfect the union. According to Stoic physics, the mutual inherence of parts is realized in the corporeal realm when bodies are able to interpenetrate each other without being diminished in themselves (χωρεῖν δι' ἀλλήλων ἀλυμάντως).[121] This principle can be applied metaphorically in a number of ways: for example, in referring to the unification of the four Gospels in a single spiritual law, by which they are "united without being confused, distinguished without being separated";[122] it is also used for the four elements [of the physical world], which form a single universal substance.

Amidst all the technical aspects of applying this principle, Maximus does not forget that synthesis remains the great mystery and miracle of created being, something that can never be wholly penetrated by the mind.[123] Even so, it remains the fundamental law of all created reality, the principle to which all things point. For nothing that is in any sense composite can possess a being that is original; all is necessarily secondary, derived.[124]

All of this warns us against taking the third expression that Maximus uses so often, *tautotēs* (ταυτότης), "identity", "self-sameness", in an overly literal way. It can be used to express the unity of the parts in a universal being (*katholou*, καθόλου) that is still somewhat independent from them and that exists prior to the movement toward unity (ἀπαράλλακτον ἐν ὅλοις ταυτότητα: "the unchanging sameness in totalities");[125] it can also be used to denote the kind of union that results from them (ἑνίζεται ταυτιζόμενον: what "is united by becoming an identity").[126] In this latter sense, "the composite hypostasis draws the natural distinctness of the poles in themselves together, into a strict identity."[127] In describing more closely this identity of different elements in the principle of unity, Maximus emphasizes especially the important concept of the invariability (ἀπαραλλαξία) of the parts,[128]

---

[121] *Ambigua*; PG 91, 1228C.
[122] Ibid.; PG 91, 1245Aff.
[123] Ibid.; PG 91, 1228D–1229A.
[124] Ibid.; PG 91, 1184BC; cf. on this point John of Scythopolis, *In De Div. Nom.* 8; PG 4, 372B.
[125] *Ambigua*; PG 91, 1189A.
[126] *Epistles* 15: PG 91, 560A.
[127] *Opuscula*; PG 91, 204A.
[128] "Sameness (ταυτότης) is an invariability, by which the character (λόγος) of what is sig-

which convey of themselves this negative condition of possibility for their positive identification. This description allows us to identify a certain amount of room for different grades and forms. Thus Maximus speaks of identity in attitude and will (κατὰ τὴν γνώμην ταυτότητα) [129] among those who love each other, of the identifying force of love itself (κατὰ μίαν ταυτότητος δύναμιν), [130] of the identity of a whole in its parts, [131] of the identity of a hypostasis in its natures [132] (which is "a perfect identity" [133] through the absolute unity of the hypostasis). Ultimately, Maximus even speaks of an identity between God and the creature, which is realized from within the analogy between them both and which is an "identity in difference" (ἡ ταυτότης ἐν ἀμφοτέροις τῇ ὁμοιότητι διάφορος). [134] This final identity is the result of our being made like God by grace (ὁμοιωθέντας τῇ κατὰ δύναμιν ἀδιαιρέτῳ ταυτότητι); [135] because it is a gift, it always remains within the limiting borders of participation, a "similarity" and a "communion" (δι' ὁμοιότητος κοινωνία καὶ ταυτότης) [136] through which we belong to the family of God, who alone is truly an identity. The identity of the world, however, seen in itself, always depends on the identity of its not-being-God, [137] and thus on its yearning movement toward the identity of God in himself (ταυτότης κινήσεως). [138]

3. The Synthetic Person

The word study we have just completed gives us ready access to the most central mystery of Maximus' conception of the world, a mystery that holds within itself the solution of all the world's riddles: the unification of God and world, the eternal and the temporal, the infinite and

---

nified includes what is univocal (μοναδικόν) everywhere and is not marked by any kind of difference" (ταυτότης δέ ἐστιν ἀπαραλλαξία καθ' ἣν ὁ τοῦ σημαινομένου λόγος τὸ πάντῃ κέκτηται μοναδικόν, μηδενὶ τρόπῳ διαφορᾶς γνωριζόμενον) (Epistles 15; PG 91, 561A).

[129] Quaestiones ad Thalassium, prolegomena; CCG 7, 19, 51f.; PG 90, 245D.
[130] Epistles 2; PG 91, 404B.
[131] Epistles 13; PG 91, 521C.
[132] Ibid.; PG 91, 521B; Opuscula; PG 91, 61C.
[133] Opuscula; PG 91, 73C.
[134] In Eccl. Hier. 4; PG 4, 153A.
[135] Mystagogia 13; PG 91, 692D.
[136] Ibid. 24; PG 91, 704D.
[137] Ambigua; PG 91, 1312B.
[138] Mystagogia 1; PG 91, 665A.

the finite, in the hypostasis of a single being—the God who became man. This is a solution that only leads us deeper into mystery, and all Maximus' efforts at shedding light on it are more ways of rejecting incorrect theories and points of departure than they are an actual clarification of the being of Christ in itself. If he forges precise concepts, in the relentless zeal of his theological warfare, and hammers them into the minds of his hearers and readers with a kind of feverish intolerance, still even in this apparent "rationalism" the central function of both his dogmatic statements and their theological interpretation is obvious: they set out the limits of the mystery, they point from the farthest edges of what is sayable into a region no one may enter, and they reveal themselves, paradoxically, as more reverent, even more "existential" ways of thinking than those of the heretics, whose intellectual brilliance may at first appear more profound and more "religious". The very abstractness of Maximus' Christology has its ultimate, positive foundation in this reverence. He "interprets" only so far as his office of "protecting" demands.

Still, it is part of the protector's fate that he is often pushed, as a thinker, against his will, out of the safe arena of dogmatic formulas into a region of dusky, hand-to-hand combat with the enemy, where he must undertake daring feats of thinking, combining, and intellectual groping on his own; this is not done simply for the pleasure of empty speculation but in order to defeat the enemy with his own weapons on his own ground. Maximus dared to venture into the darkness of this hand-to-hand combat, since he could not speak authoritatively in the name of the Church, as could his friend Sophronius the bishop. He "had only a personal authority to rely on; his statements have only as much weight as he can give them by argument. . . . Sophronius can be satisfied with laying out the 'that' and the 'what' of truth, but Maximus must reveal also the 'how' and the 'why'."[139] The concepts that remained underdeveloped in his philosophical repertoire, concepts that he was forced to work with as a child of his time, necessarily left their effect at decisive junctures and added to the darkness. But it remains the achievement of the "Confessor" to have pushed the borders of what was sayable farther out into the darkness of mystery. A certain lack of clarity in philosophical reflection (visible especially in the hovering of the concept of hypostasis somewhere between "existence" and "per-

---

[139] Straubinger, "Die Lehre des Patriarchen Sophronius", 91.

son"), and a certain, correspondingly exaggerated clarity—and thus abstractness—in the formulas he does use, should not prevent us from seeing beyond these things into a passionately felt intuition, at once genuinely philosophical and genuinely Christian.

a. Parallels in Creation

Like most theologians before him, especially Leontius [of Byzantium], Maximus begins his attempt to shed light on the unity of the divine and the human in Christ with the parallel of the *unity of body and soul* in man.[140] Two "natures" are here ontologically united and interpenetrate each other without becoming confused, to bring into existence a single hypostasis [concrete individual] and "person". Orthodox and heretics alike agreed on the meaning of this comparison, to the extent that it was rooted in a moderately Platonic way of seeing things, which recognized in both elements of man a relative independence (and did not see them, as Thomism later would do, as related according to the model of actuating form and purely potential matter). Understood in this way, the comparison seemed to clarify a number of issues.

First of all, it seemed illuminating to recognize that man is, on the one hand, "nothing else" but soul and body, but that, on the other hand, to the degree that he is their *unity*, he is more than the sum of his parts taken in themselves. This double nature of the union of soul and body is the decisive issue for Maximus. The whole, he boldly proclaims, is "nothing else" but its parts: it has "no other natural existence" (ὕπαρξις).[141] Rather, it *is* the "existence" of its parts. The totality is nothing else than the pure mutual indwelling of the parts, their element of identity that overrides all their divergence.[142] The whole is the "hypostasis" of its parts (in the twofold sense of their person and their existence) and, so, their unity.[143] In this sense, the human

---

[140] For the history of this problematic analogy, see Grillmeier and Bacht, *Chalkedon*, 1:133, 447–51, 473, 705f., and other references in the index, 3:917, col. 1. Its ultimate source is Apollinarian. [See now F. R. Gahbauer, *Das anthropologische Modell: Ein Beitrag zur Christologie der frühen Kirche bis Chalkedon* (Würzburg, 1984).]

[141] *Opuscula*; PG 91, 117D.

[142] Ibid.; PG 91, 521BC.

[143] "The natures, of which he himself was the hypostasis, . . . of which he himself was the unity" (τὰς φύσεις, ὧν αὐτὸς ὑπόστασις ἦν . . . ὧν αὐτὸς ἕνωσις ἦν): *Ambigua*; PG 91, 1044D; cf. *Opuscula*: PG 91, 36BC: "He was their hypostasis, . . . he was their unity" (ὧν ὑπῆρχεν ὑπόστασις, . . . ὧν αὐτὸς ἕνωσις ἦν).

nature of Christ, simply by having its being in the Logos, also had its existence and its personality in him.[144]

To understand the full meaning of this doctrine, one has to keep in mind what we have said earlier about the mutual indwelling of the totality (καθόλου) and the part (μερικόν). The totality exists, the theory runs, only in its parts and is genuinely their product; but the parts also exist only in their whole, which is no less truly their foundation or cause. To convey unity, nonunity has to be preserved; to balance the tension, the poles have to be kept intact. "If the poles are denied, there is no longer anything in the middle."[145] From this axiom one can understand the constantly repeated formula, used both for man and for Christ: the parts "from which and in which and as which man exists",[146] and Christ, "who subsists from them and in them and as they".[147] Outside this threefold relationship there is nothing else (οὐχ ἕτερόν τι),[148] and between the relationships themselves there is strict equivalence: "Christ is also *in* the things *from* which he exists, and he *is* the things *in* which he exists."[149] The hypostasis is, without distinction, the product of the union of its parts and the existence of that unity in the parts that it produces and sustains in being. There is a completely reciprocal relationship of cause and effect:

> As the one is produced from the two (that is, as the one individual is produced from the two natures, as a totality from its parts, with respect to the hypostasis), so through the one as a totality both parts (with respect to nature) are formed as a duality.[150]

Thus: "[The one is formed], not just from (the parts), but *as* the parts, and not just as the parts, but also *in them*, just as the totality is from its parts and in its parts and is the totality because of the parts."[151] The implication is ultimately that the relationship of the whole to the parts is of equal value to the relationship of the parts among themselves:

---

[144] "Taking both its being (τὸ εἶναι) and its subsistence (τὸ ὑποστῆναι) in him, God the Word" ('Εν αὐτῷ Θεῷ καὶ Λόγῳ καὶ τὸ εἶναι καὶ τὸ ὑποστῆναι λαβοῦσα): *Epistles* 11; PG 91, 468AB; cf. 560C.

[145] 'Αποφάσει τῶν ἄκρων οὐδέν ἐστι μέσον: *Disputation with Pyrrhus*; PG 91, 348A.

[146] *Epistles* 12; PG 91, 488C.

[147] *Epistles* 15; PG 91, 573A.

[148] *Opuscula*; PG 91, 121D.

[149] Ibid.; PG 91, 224A.

[150] *Epistles* 12; PG 91, 493D.

[151] Ibid.; PG 91, 501A.

If, then, the hypostatic identity of the totality with relation to its own parts—or, to put it more precisely, if the reciprocal identity of the parts, with respect to the synthesis of the totality that results from them—is preserved intact, it is also clear that the parts will in no sense be different from one another, insofar as the one hypostasis comes to its realization from them.[152]

In this way, a unity is formed—an identity, even—which could not be more complete οὐδὲν ἑνικώτερον), even though it can itself subsist only through the absolute preservation of the particular being of its parts (οὐδὲν σωστικώτερον).[153]

All this may seem very abstract and unpromising, but the constant repetition of this, the most universal law of being, remains nonetheless the great achievement of Maximus the Confessor. Not only did he construct here an apologia for finite, created being in the face of the overwhelming power of the transcendent world of ideas; the application of this principle to the relation between God and the world, in the hypostatic union, finally assures the world itself—even in, and precisely because of, its difference from God—a permanently valid claim to being and to a "good conscience". Sophronius had already emphasized this positive aspect of finite reality when he emphasized that Christ "has always retained, and will retain for the unbounded ages of eternity", his "undiminished nature", the "circumscription of his body", the "concrete form" of his human "appearance".[154] This is not so astonishing in the anti-Origenist Sophronius; but its importance is all the greater in Maximus, in that he here provides the counterweight to his own Alexandrian instincts.

Nevertheless, one must ask whether anything was really achieved for Christology with this adoption of the syntheses of cosmological and anthropological philosophy. The cosmological synthesis of the totality and its parts presupposed that the parts are, in some sense, of equal value and so has little to offer for the synthesis of absolutely unequal parts—divinity and humanity—in Christ; in addition, its adoption as a christological model could appear to be a clear victory of Antiochene Christology. The body-soul model, on the other hand, if used without further clarification, would lead directly to Monophysitism, since man

[152] Ibid., 15; PG 91, 562B.
[153] Ambigua; PG 91, 1044D–1045A.
[154] Sophronius, Epist. synodica; PG 87, 3173AB.

is obviously *one* nature, even if composed of two (quasi-)natures. With this line of thought, Severus[155] seemed to have won the day: even if the one nature, produced by a unity of body and soul, also has the status of a hypostasis—and this is how Cyril had understood the "single nature" (μία φύσις)—still it must be a "nature" (φύσις) in order to effect a unity that is not simply moral (ἕνωσις σχετική) but ontological (ἕνωσις φυσική).

b. From Leontius to Maximus

Leontius of Byzantium was the first to apply his acumen against this conclusion. Through his use of the concept *enhypostaton* as an intermediate level of being between natural being and hypostatic being, he was able to drive a wedge into Severus' line of argument. But his Origenism[156] forced him to define the human soul, which preexists independently as a bodiless substance, in thoroughly Platonic fashion as an "incorporeal, immortal being".[157] Soul and body, considered in themselves, are therefore [for Leontius] "complete substances", which are not fundamentally required by their nature to bring each other to completion (as the Aristotelian definition demands);[158] they are only considered "incomplete" in relation to the single hypostasis.[159] The union of the two should thus not be traced back to a natural dynamism toward unity but simply to the positive will of God (which is essentially a decision to punish).[160] Considered by himself, man should not be called "a nature"; this is only correct to the extent that one is considering him as a representative of a species (εἶδος), whose abstract common character-

---

[155] See Joseph Lebon, "La Christologie du monophysitisme syrien", in Grillmeier and Bacht, *Chalkedon*, 1:441–50.

[156] See F. Loofs, *Leontius von Byzanz* (Leipzig, 1888) 3:274–97; M. Richard, "Léonce de Byzance était-il origéniste?" *Revue des études byzantines* 5 (1947): 54f.; C. Moeller, "Chalcédonisme", 1:638f. [See now also B. E. Daley, "The Origenism of Leontius of Byzantium", *Journal of Theological Studies* 27 (1976): 333–69; and "What Did 'Origenism' Mean in the Sixth Century?", in G. Dorival and A. le Boulluec, eds., *Origeniana Sexta* (Louvain, 1995) 627–38; Grillmeier, *Jesus der Christus*, vol. 2, pt. 2, 403–40; English translation, 385–410.]

[157] PG 86, 1281B.

[158] [For Aristotle, the soul is] "a primary, inherent orientation of a natural body" (Ἐντελέχεια πρώτη σώματος φυσικοῦ).

[159] Leontius of Byzantium, *Contra Nestorianos et Eutychianos*; PG 86, 1281C.

[160] Leontius of Byzantium, *Epilyseis*; PG 86, 1940B. [Leontius himself nowhere suggests that the embodiment of the soul is a punishment.]

istic consists precisely in this thoroughgoing composition from "two natures", body and soul.[161] In that union, of course, a single hypostasis arises from what was before two separate hypostases, which saves the unity of the person; the body, indeed, still remains a nature but is no longer an independent hypostasis—it is enhypostatized.[162] But after death, body and soul again become fully independent hypostases, just as they remained independent natures in the state of union.[163] If one applied this conception of man to Christology, one ended up with a seemingly simple formula: the unity of Christ could be conceived as a purely hypostatic one, in two natures that remain what they were; in fact, the independent preexistence of the soul, which is not intrinsically affected by union with the body, could provide an excellent parallel for the unchanging continuity of the divine nature and person in the hypostatic union. But the disadvantages of the formula far outweighed the advantages. Not only did the hypostatic unity of Christ lose its character of mystery and become just one case among thousands, but the denial of a genuine natural union in man was also a dangerous and unjustified concession to the Monophysites: the [putative] similarity in structure between human existence and Christ could only confirm them in their error. The whole difference now was restricted to the fact that Christ could not be called an example of a species and, simply *for that reason*, provided an example of "a person" and not "a nature".[164]

Maximus, in contrast, needed only to remember his own polemics against the Origenist idea of preexistence in order to find the way to correct Leontius' speculation and make it into an efficient weapon against the Monophysites. Leontius had the right idea when he recognized the difference between Christ and human nature in the fact that the latter is a *species*. The communality of generic form is the sign that the unity of body and soul is not *simply* a matter of hypostasis; the mark of the latter, surely, is being-for-oneself, not-being-universal. Maximus

---

[161] Leontius of Byzantium, *Contra Nestorianos et Eutychianos*; PG 86, 1289D–1291B.

[162] Ibid.; PG 86, 1277CD.

[163] Leontius of Byzantium, *Epilyseis*; PG 86, 1941D–1944A.

[164] "The fact that this composite matches a multitude of like beings does not bring about any new composition within itself and only constitutes, in fact, an accidental difference from the composite person of Christ—a difference that does not weaken the basis of comparison in any way". (V. Grumel, "L'Union hypostatique", 398). This is the reason that the author of the *De sectis* had already given up the anthropological argument. See Richard, "Le Traité 'De Sectis' ", 706f.

concedes even more to Leontius, in admitting that this nonhypostatic character of the human unity is not so much derived from "nature" as such as from the "species": the soul, in fact, retains its own "essence" even in its unity with the body, and remains different from it "according to its essential principle" (κατὰ τὸν οὐσιώδη λόγον).[165]

c. The Free Synthesis

Nevertheless, Maximus does not adhere strictly to this terminological pattern, and for serious reasons. For Leontius, generic reality was little more than a logical predication based on a similarity among individuals. For Maximus, the philosopher of universal being (katholou), it is an ontological state. Man is not only a synthetic person but also a "synthetic nature",[166] because he is inserted, as a member of a species, into a cosmic context; he is an "element" of the world, he is "dependent" on a thousand threads of influence and destiny, he is "passive" —in short, he is not simply a person. In this respect, "he has nothing more than the other generic beings, which are found within the whole of nature."[167] It is no accident that the solemn Stoic term "catholic" nature, universal nature (ἡ καθ᾽ ὅλου φύσις), appears in this context: a term that suggests the greater unity of the world, from which the thousands of individual beings are constantly being produced, in order to dissolve into it once again. For even this natural coming to be and passing away make man into a being of "species" and "nature". The connection of body and soul is, in the strict sense, a "bond", even a natural, physical necessity (ἐξ ἀνάγκης εἱρμῷ τινι φυσικῷ);[168] being a person is, in this view, only the product of an impersonal process —is something "projected" rather than self-determining. The mutual indwelling of body and soul is not only a sign of freedom, but at the

---

[165] Epistles 12; PG 91, 488B.

[166] Ibid.; PG 91, 488D.

[167] Ibid., 13; PG 91, 517AB.

[168] Ibid., 12; PG 91, 489B. Leontius had already noticed this "necessity", but because of his Origenist conception of the soul he could only see it as an extrinsic necessity, caused by God. In his view, the soul—as distinguished from the divinity—is in itself passive and capable of undergoing influences from without, because it is finite; but this passivity is not, in itself, a potential orientation toward a body (PG 86, 1284D–1285A). Without going into the philosophical background, Sophronius, on the other hand, had strongly emphasized this natural necessity as "imperious, necessary, involuntary" (τυραννικῶς, ἀναγκαστῶς, ἀβουλήτως: PG 87, 3173D).

same time a sign of "necessity": the soul that possesses the body is also put at its mercy. "The soul possesses its body, without itself willing it, and is likewise possessed by it; it gives the body life, without choosing to, simply by being within it; it shares naturally in its vulnerability and its pains, because of the passivity that is intrinsic to its nature."[169]

This passivity has its basis in the absolute contemporaneity of soul and body, which expresses their intrinsic and mutual metaphysical orientation toward each other.[170] The final reason that neither the soul can have existed before the body nor the body before the soul lies in this decisive need each has for the other, a need that rules out any semblance of a free and arrogantly self-determining union. The unity that they are forced to create exceeds the powers of both; it is required of them by a higher power: the species, "nature as a whole". Therefore the individual, even as a person, always remains a member and a complementary part of a whole (εἰς συμπλήρωσιν,[171] εἰς ὅλου τινὸς κατ᾽ εἶδος συμπλήρωσιν[172]). "Every synthetic nature has its origin in the contemporaneity (of its parts) and in its involuntary being (ἀκούσιον), for it exists as something created, circumscribed by space and by its own world."[173]

This necessary cohesion, however, is precisely what *cannot* be said of Christ. He did not come "to bring completion to a class, as part to a whole".[174] His two natures are not, in any sense, "contemporaneous"; his hypostasis does not owe its existence to natural development (γένεσις), but to a free, unforced assumption (πρόσληψις) of the human. "The one who was before all the ages—or better, the very Creator of the ages—came down among us men by his free choice and without compulsion; he emptied himself and made himself human, not to bring the universe to completion, but to raise it up in renewal."[175] Even if it

---

[169] Epistles 12; PG 91, 488D. Sherwood, as we have mentioned, has already pointed out that Maximus offers a solution to the problem of the dialectics of *pathos* in this text of 642: if the soul is already passive through its composite relationship to the body, then not every aspect of our sensible vulnerabilities need be due to sin (*Ascetic Life*, 66).

[170] Ambigua; PG 91, 1321D–1341C.

[171] Epistles 13; PG 91, 517A.

[172] Ibid.; PG 91, 529D.

[173] Opuscula; PG 91, 64D. This is Maximus' most profound definition of the essence of all composite nature (its "definition and structure and law" [ὅρος καὶ λόγος καὶ νόμος]: Epistles 13; PG 91, 517B).

[174] Epistles 13; PG 91, 529D.

[175] Ibid.; PG 91, 517B.

is metaphysically impossible for a created individual to exist without belonging to a species—the mythic phoenix, for example[176]—Christ, as a hypostasis, is not affected by this law: he is, in this sense, neither an "individual" (ἄτομον), because they are always included in a genus, nor a genus (γένος), because they always include many individuals.[177]

A hypostasis, then, can be termed "composite" for either of two reasons: first, insofar as it is produced by the synthesis of two natures and thus is "composed" as the "identity" of two poles; or second, insofar as it is itself also a "nature" and so is in turn included in a higher species —such as man, who belongs to the class of "rational animals".[178] On this point, Leontius had been right. [So Maximus writes:]

> What exists in common among all the members of a class is designated primarily (προηγουμένως) by the common element of essence or nature, which is found in every individual. Being composite, however, is common to all the individuals included under the title of a composite nature. Therefore composition, in the individuals included under this name, indicates primarily the nature, not the hypostasis.[179]

If such a common nature is lacking, however, there is no reason why it should not be an instance of the first alternative and the hypostasis itself be called, in the primary sense, "composite". Let us examine this alternative more closely.

Maximus' explanation of man's composite character rests on the constant parallel between "physical" synthesis (body and soul) and "metaphysical" synthesis (the individual being and the generic nature). This comparison is deliberate; there is a factual identity between the formation of the human hypostasis (from the synthesis of its "physical" parts) and the formation of the human individual as a member of a class.[180] Yet the being, on the other hand, that marks off the person as such and that which designates him as member of a class are not actually distinguished from each other. So we see here, once again,

[176] Ibid.; PG 91, 520AB.
[177] Ibid.; PG 91, 529A.
[178] Ibid., 12; PG 91, 489CD.
[179] Ibid., 13; PG 91, 528B.
[180] "By the simultaneous conjunction of soul and body to form the [human] species . . . [we encounter] that which is the same in essence (ὁμοούσιον) [and] . . . different in hypostasis (ἑτερουπόστατον)" (κατὰ τὴν ἅμα πρὸς εἴδους γένεσιν ψυχῆς τε καὶ σώματος σύνοδον . . . τὸ ὁμοούσιον (καὶ) . . . τὸ ἑτεροϋπόστατον) Epistles 15; PG 91, 553B; cf. Epistles 13; PG 91, 529B.

the convergence of the concepts of existence and person in the one concept of the hypostasis. The same natural synthesis brings about the coexistence of the two "physical" parts [of the person] and the unity of the hypostasis.[181] The hypostasis reveals itself (χαρακτηρίζεται) indirectly in the realm of essential characteristics, through the indissoluble synthesis of the individual qualities of soul and body; for this reason, it can be described as a synthesis of the individuality of both parts.[182] Yet it is already clear that these essential specifications are not enough to define the hypostasis itself. In addition, they must be transferred to the level of existence; or, to put it a different way, one must attempt to express the synthesis of two modes of existence (τρόπος τῆς ὑπάρξεως) in the single mode of the hypostasis—one must attempt to form a "synthetic hypostasis".[183]

The difficult aspect of the case of Christ, then, is to exclude the first of the two perspectives we have just described [that is, the synthesizing of essential characteristics] when dealing with the convergence of the notions of person and existence. The "physical" merging of the divine and human natures does not lead to a "metaphysical" composition. The reason, as we have already mentioned, lies in the fact that the two parts are neither both produced nor contemporaneous. It is not a "passive" synthesis.[184] The eternal existence of the divine

---

[181] "By the convergence [of the parts] toward each other, which comes into play along with their very existence, the designating characteristics are created for the one hypostasis that comes into full being from them both" (κατὰ τὴν ἅμα τῷ εἶναι πρὸς ἄλληλα σύνοδον ποιεῖται χαρακτηριστικὰ τῆς ἐξ αὐτῶν συμπληρουμένης μίας ὑποστάσεως) Epistles 15; PG 91, 552C.

[182] Ibid.; PG 91, 552CD.

[183] The origin of this terminology is in "neo-Chalcedonianism". As Richard showed, Leontius of Jerusalem was its principal user, in the interests of Justinian's political attempts at union (Contra Nestorianos 1, 24; PG 89, 1492B; 1528B; etc.; see Richard, "Léonce de Jérusalem", 58f. Justinian himself uses the formula fairly often (E. Schwartz, Drei dogmatische Schriften Justinians, Abhandlungen der bayerischen Akademie der Wissenschaften, NF 18 [Munich, 1939], 16, 18, 76, 86); in doing so, he shows a conciliatory attitude toward Severus, who prefers to speak of synthesis but for whom "one synthetic nature" (μία φύσις σύνθετος) and "synthetic hypostasis" (ὑπόστασις σύνθετος) are identical formulas (see J. Lebon, "Christologie", 1:472f., 486f.). Theodoret had rejected the formula (Grillmeier and Bacht, Chalkedon 1:185, n. 14). But all the neo-Chalcedonians use it, following the emperor's example: for example, Eulogius (PG 86, 2944B). The Fifth Council, too, adopts Justinian's formula of a "union through synthesis, or in hypostasis" (ἕνωσις κατὰ σύνθεσιν ἤγουν καθ᾽ ὑπόστασιν): Mansi 9, 377; DS 424f.). The word does not occur in Leontius of Byzantium: his system did not need the help of such terminology.

[184] Ἀπαθῶς: Epistles 13; PG 91, 532A.

Logos excludes any kind of natural synthesis: taking on a human nature is not a natural way of completing the divine nature. Christ is, then, as a "composite hypostasis", utterly unique (μονώτατος),[185] and it is precisely this uniqueness, beyond all nature, that allows him to share natures with the Father, on the one hand, and with man, on the other; it proves that his unity is purely on the level of hypostasis. While in man the capacities of soul and body are ordered to each other and correspond to each other, all such inner correspondence is impossible between the natures of Christ.[186] But precisely this noncorrespondence is God's unique way of divinizing humanity. For this is the way human nature can participate in the hypostasis of God [the Son] without compromising its own natural integrity; human nature's hypostasis can be the Logos himself (ταὐτὸν ὑπάρχει κατὰ τὴν ὑπόστασιν),[187] because this divinizing hypostasis confirms and preserves it in its essential humanity (παγίαν ἐργάζεται τήρησιν).[188]

d. Christology of Essence and Christology of Being

None of this solves the great riddle of how this "synthetic" person is itself to be conceived. It is helpful, in this regard, to distinguish between the aspect of essence and that of existence.

For the *aspect of essence* man provides a parallel. The body and the soul each have certain individuating characteristics that distinguish them from other bodies and other souls. The result of the combination of these characteristics, according to Maximus, is the uniqueness of the [human] hypostasis.[189] This must also be true of Christ.

> The hypostatic characteristics (ἰδιότητες) of both parts, which form, in their synthesis, the whole Christ and which exist in addition to the common natural characteristics [of the individual], form, all together, that distinguishing mark of the parts that sets apart the one hypostasis that all of them comprise as a unity. . . . I call this hypostasis "common", because it appears as the one, completely unique (ἰδικωτάτην) result of the synthesis of the parts. Or better still: it is the one hypostasis of the

---

[185] Ibid.; PG 91, 532B.
[186] "In no respect does he have analogous . . . potentialities" (κατ᾽ οὐδένα λόγον ἀναλογούσας ἔχων . . . δυνάμεις): ibid.; PG 91, 532B.
[187] *Opuscula*; PG 91, 152A.
[188] *Epistles* 14; PG 91, 536B.
[189] Ibid., 15; PG 91, 552CD.

Logos, who is the same before and after the union—before it, without created effect, simple, free of all composition, but after it (. . . without any change) truly composite.[190]

All we can do, then, is to recognize the paradox that the hypostasis of Christ is at once thesis and synthesis, at once simple cause and composite effect. Maximus leaves nothing to be desired in clarity:

> In those qualities through which the flesh of Christ distinguished itself from other human beings, it did not distinguish itself further from the Logos; on the other hand, in those qualities through which it distinguished itself from the Logos, it did not distinguish itself from the rest of us. In those, however, through which it distinguished itself from us, it preserved the union, or, better, the identity, with the Logos in the hypostasis.[191]

The same is true in the nature of God: what distinguishes the Logos from the Father is, in the state of union, no longer itself distinguishable from what distinguishes the incarnate Logos from other human beings.

With this technical description, formal Christology reaches its apex. Maximus is not afraid of formulating this bold statement with clarity. The aspect of the hypostasis as product and result of unity must not be overshadowed by its aspect as causal being. The two parts bring the hypostasis [or person] to its completion (πρὸς ἓν ἄμφω συντελεῖν πρόσωπον),[192] and the latter results from their combination (εἰς μίαν ὑπόστασιν σύνοδος)[193] in the way a whole results from its parts (ἐκ τούτων ὡς μερῶν ὅλον).[194] In truth, what results is "a single synthetic hypostasis",[195] which is, in fact, surprising enough (παράδοξον).[196] For how shall we conceive God's characteristic of unchangeability, before and after the union, as compatible with a hypostasis that is the synthetic result of this very union? How can the Logos be at one time both the subject of the synthesis and its product?[197]

---

[190] Ibid.; PG 91, 556CD.
[191] Ibid.; PG 91, 557A.
[192] Ibid. 12; PG 91, 469D.
[193] Ibid.; PG 91, 484A.
[194] Ibid.; PG 91, 488A.
[195] Ibid.; PG 91, 489BC.
[196] Ibid., 13; PG 91, 517C.
[197] "It is united to itself" (πρὸς ἑαυτὸν ἥνωται): ibid., 15; PG 91, 556D.

The question only comes to its real point with the *aspect of existence*. The aspect of essence, as a unity of individual essential characteristics, could present only an indication and a proof (γνώρισμα) of the hypostasis, not the hypostasis itself.[198] Here, on the other hand, two "modes of existence", destined to be united in a single existence, meet and interpenetrate each other. At this point, the constant ambiguity of the concept of hypostasis, which means both individual person (καθ᾽ ἑαυτόν) and existence (ὕπαρξις), becomes openly problematic. Maximus' way of dealing with this question comes very close to the later solution of one school of Thomists, first formulated by Capreolus and revived by Maurice de la Taille:[199] the *act* of being, really distinct from the being's *essence*, bestows on it also a unique and unmistakable personality. The actual being of [Christ's] human nature, in Maximus' terms, is as such the reality of the Logos as a Divine Person, since it exists "through him and in him" (ὡς δι᾽ ἐκεῖνον καὶ ἐν ἐκείνῳ).[200] This explains why the human nature of Christ, despite its integrity in the order of essences, is still not a human person. It exists and attains its own synthetic unity from the divine reality of the second Person of the Trinity. It is therefore not without hypostasis (ἀνυπόστατος), but it is *only* made real by being included in that reality (ἐν-ὑπόστατος), not by being a hypostasis on its own.

In this connection we must not forget that the scholastic or Thomist position presupposes the real distinction of essence from existence, something Maximus never succeeded in recognizing clearly for himself. One need only recall those texts [cited before] that described the mutual inherence of nature and person as the complete, reciprocal dependence of *logos* and *bios*, of the plan of being and its realization in life: such a polar, dynamic interpenetration is a different kind of tension from that of the "real distinction", as it is normally understood. The development of the intelligible structure (*logos*) of being in living existence seems, too, to lead necessarily to the supposition of a human hypostasis. Put a different way: it is impossible, in the end, to carry through a clean distinction between individualizing characteristics in the order of essence and those in the order of person, because such a

---

[198] Ibid.; PG 91, 556C.
[199] "Actuation créée par Acte Incréé", *Recherches de science religieuse* 18 (1928): 253–68.
[200] *Opuscula*; PG 91, 61B.

clean distinction simply cannot be drawn between the "order of being" and the "order of existing".[201]

If this makes a smooth, academic solution impossible, still the convergence one senses in Maximus of supersubstantial being and person remains an important directional indicator: being, as the pure reality of a referential participation in God is also, beyond all individuation of essences, the sphere in which an intellectual substance is called into existence by immediate, personal intimacy with God, and invited to become a person. It is, for that reason, the sphere in which—in the depths of the mystery of God's own freedom—the one who is called can also be, at some point in history, the one who himself calls: in which the answer to the primeval Word calling us forth can, at some point in history, be brought to a fulfillment beyond its own creaturehood and become that primeval Word itself. This is only possible because the primeval Word is, within the trinitarian reality of God, always an answer to the call of the Father and can therefore—within the economy of salvation—include and bring to fulfillment all the personal reality of creatures as responses to that call in his own primeval answer.

All of this certainly continues the direction of Maximus' Christology. It only presupposes that one detach the concepts purposefully from their undifferentiated philosophical and theological usage and set them in a context derived exclusively from revelation. In such a context, hypostasis would then no longer be useable simply as a general category of created being (as it was in the sixth century, when every created essence had its hypostasis) but would have to be limited first of all to human, intellectual persons; further, one would have to resist the temptation simply to subsume the hypostasis of Christ univocally under a concept of person formed in this way.

One can and one must, however, assume a dynamic relationship between the Divine Person of Christ and his divine nature, a relationship that is analogous to that between a human person and his intellectual, human nature. And if this Divine Person should also enter into this kind of relationship to a human nature, he can really be called a *synthetic person*—not in the sense of being a passive product of two natures that

---

[201] We have spoken of this in a number of places in our *Apokalypse der deutschen Seele* (Salzburg, 1937–39). See especially the chapters on Goethe (1:407f.), on Husserl (3:111 and esp. 125–26.), Scheler (3:144–45, n.) and Heidegger (esp. 3:261f.).

have simply come together, but rather in that the divine Person realizes
this unification in and through himself, in the highest freedom, so that
he is called "synthetic" in the sense of being the cause of synthesis.

But is this really what Maximus is thinking of? Is it not rather something else, something quite the opposite: Is not the person itself that
which is synthesized? But if so, then synthesized from what—and how?

e. Beyond Antioch and Alexandria

The solution is not simply to point out that the human nature [of
Jesus], by its assumption into the Logos, is "hypostatized into" his
hypostasis,[202] for this being-in-another is always described as the result
of hypostatic unification, not as the unification itself in its process of
realization. It is also not enough to point out that Maximus was never
willing to suppose the slightest temporal interval between the creation
of the human nature of Christ and its unification with the Logos[203]
and that therefore this nature never had any other existence except that
"in" the Logos;[204] what is at stake here is not a question of fact but
a question of being. And the passages that force themselves on our
attention in this question of being are precisely the texts that speak of
a synthetic hypostasis.

Leontius considered as a possibility (not as a reality) the case of a
human being who was first simply human and was later able to be
hypostatically united with God. "For not the *time* of unification, . . .
but the mode of union" was for him the crucial issue.[205] For him, it
was simply a matter of seemliness that Christ's humanity did not exist
before the union. This speculation stands, once again, in full accord
with the Origenism of Leontius. As an experiment, one might try to
attribute such a conception to Maximus, too. This would mean: the
human hypostasis would be synthesized with the divine hypostasis in
a single "synthetic person", but the divine hypostasis would be unable
to undergo any change in this process of union. The synthesis, as a
result, would be able to proceed only if the human hypostasis were

<hr/>

[202] *Epistles* 15; PG 91, 557D.
[203] Ibid.; PG 91, 560BC.
[204] Ibid.: "finding its hypostatic reality in him [the Logos] and receiving through him the
growth of its being" (ἀλλ' ἐνυπόστατος ὡς ἐν αὐτῷ καὶ δι' αὐτὸν λαβοῦσα τοῦ εἶναι τὴν
γένεσιν).
[205] Leontius of Byzantium, *Epilyseis*: PG 86, 1944C.

in some way or other to disappear, be absorbed; one could thus still speak formally of a synthesis, but in fact all that would remain would be the Divine Person it "produced" and the human nature that had been "hypostatized into" this divine nature.

Can this experiment of thought, which Maximus never expressly articulates himself, still shed some light, perhaps, on his final conception of the problem? The synthesis that emerges if we make this supposition would ultimately be nothing else than the existential counterpart to what Maximus himself described as an essential synthesis of individual characteristics of being in a comprehensive individuality. Yet in one way or other, after all that has been said, one cannot escape this existential perspective: what is at stake is the unification of *two ways of being*—"the two different intelligible structures of being of the parts" (ἄμφω τοὺς τοῦ εἶναι τῶν μερῶν διαφόρους λόγους).[206]

The Monothelites thought they had discovered a simple solution: synthesis through a "prevalence" or "domination" (κατ᾽ ἐπικράτειαν) of the divine will (and being) over the human. Maximus will have nothing to do with this solution, for it presupposes, as he perceptively remarks, a passivity even in the prevailing part. "The prevailing element is also conquered by what it conquers—only to a lesser degree", just as gold, when mixed with a little ore, remains gold but is simply less pure.[207] Yet Maximus himself had once defended the same theory, inspired by a saying of Gregory Nazianzen ("the more powerful is dominant" τοῦ κρείττονος ἐκνικήσαντος), before the Monothelite controversy had grown so serious: "Through the dominance of the more noble part, the Logos assumed flesh into his hypostatic identity and divinized it."[208]

In saying this, Maximus should not be branded a latent Nestorian; he would have been the first to disown all "doubling of person" (δυάδα προσωπικήν).[209] But the concept of a "synthetic person" leads to such a pattern of thought when viewed from an Antiochene perspective. Certainly, one must immediately exclude all thought of quantitative equality;[210] but the challenge then is to deal squarely with the paradox that the same reality is both part and whole, cause and effect. Both

---

[206] *Epistles* 12; PG 91, 488A.
[207] *Opuscula*; PG 91, 64AB.
[208] *Ambigua*; PG 91, 1040C.
[209] *Epistles* 12; PG 91, 556D.
[210] *Opuscula*; PG 91, 64B.

find themselves united in the mystery of Christ: "For he, who was the only one to possess real *Being*, received from his supreme power the possibility of *Becoming* what he was not, without change or confusion, and of remaining both of them: what he was and what he became."[211] So the original christological formula [of the fifth century] remains in force: [Christ's two natures are the elements] "from which—in which —which" [he is]. Is this a way of watering down the inconceivable mystery of how Christ can be fully human without being a human person? The latter, after all, is not simply excluded here but is itself also absorbed into the hypostatic synthesis. For if God reveals himself as in no way changed, even after the synthesis, he is nevertheless no longer "just God" (γυμνὸς Θεός). It is at this point in Christology, in fact, that the riddle of the analogy of being in general appears in its sharpest form: it is not true that through the existence of the created world "more being" has come into existence than was there when God existed "alone".

The whole christological tradition of the Church—of Antioch and Alexandria alike—was aimed at making this point. Theodore of Mopsuestia, the first opponent of radical Apollinarianism, defended the unity of being and person [in Christ], despite all the lasting difference of his natures, in the genuine fragments of his *De Incarnatione*—those not tampered with by Apollinarian sources. His proof of the difference of his natures was that, in the abstract, God can exist without man, just as man can exist without being united with the Godhead; the unity [of Christ], on the other hand, he conceives in ontic terms, by analogy with the unity of body and soul, without being able to specify more closely in metaphysical categories the relationship of what is ontically one and what is naturally two.[212]

Cyril of Alexandria is very close to this in his main formulation. He, too, does not want to divide Christ's hypostases or natures after the union, since an "unconfused convergence of hypostases" has taken

---

[211] *Epistles* 16; PG 91, 577B.

[212] M. Richard, "Hypostase", 21–29. Just as for Theodore the human soul can exist without a body after death and still, in union with the body, comprises only *one* human being, so the divinity of Christ has its own hypostasis and still forms one single hypostasis with his humanity. Richard traces the undeniable inconsistencies in Theodore's system back to the fact that no other developed conceptual system was available to him but that of the Apollinarianism he was rejecting.

place,[213] which principally prohibits us from speaking of the characteristics of the united natures in any other way than as of the "one nature and hypostasis of the incarnate Word". Although the "things" unified remain distinguishable, the object of attribution is a single thing.[214] One may ask whether the ontic unity is not emphasized more strongly in Theodore's works than in those of Cyril, who is centrally concerned with the "communication of idioms". With both authors, the terminology varies between ontic and personal modes of expression, neither of which reaches speculative clarification; both authors remain caught up in the abstract dialectic of "one" and "two"—urged on them by their Platonizing anthropology. Apollinarius' dynamic solution is shut off from them both.

That dynamic aspect emerges again in the works of Severus and ultimately demands to be taken into account in the christological synthesis. With Maximus, due attention is paid to the real concern of the Monophysites, who explained their rejection of a synthesis of two balanced natures completely in terms of the activity of the divine Logos, as it takes possession [of a human nature]. This activity revealed the personal, hypostatic side of the ontological event at the root [of Jesus' existence] through the paradox of a real movement on the part of a God who nevertheless remains beyond change.[215] On the other hand, the aspect of a hypostatic synthesis of two natures, not of equal value yet both preserved in their peculiar identity—a union that serves as the model of all cosmological and anthropological synthesis—can also not be eliminated from Maximus' view; this is the reason why the notion of "absorption" has little chance of success, in Maximus' mind. If we attempt to bring these two aspects together, we can make the following concluding remarks about the formal structure of Maximus' Christology.

It is certainly the Word becoming flesh, considered "from above", who is the power behind the synthesis; he is this power, both in his freedom as a person and in the absolute reality of his divine being that is inseparable from that freedom. These two dimensions must always

---

[213] Ἀσύγχυτος τῶν ὑποστάσεων σύνοδος: PG 76, 408B. It is understandable that Cyril could speak just as easily of one nature as of two, especially after the Letter of Union of 433.
[214] See Richard, "Hypostase", 243–52.
[215] See Lebon, "Christologie", 1:431f.

be taken together, for it is not simply a person who becomes human, but—through that person—really and truly *God*. The Person of the Redeemer is both the divine act of being and the unlimited personal freedom of the Son; both of them, as a unity, form the synthesis, and so both also give hypostatic form to the synthesis' human side, without being "confused" with it.

If one considers the synthesis "from below", one can distinguish three aspects:[216]

a. The synthesis of body with soul. This also comes about within the absolute Person; therefore it is a characteristic (ἰδιότης) of the essence of this flesh to be determined and supported by divine freedom and so not to be at the mercy of the inbred πάθη that are, for the rest of us, our destiny. All the genuine suffering [of Christ] is ultimately under the control of a divine core of freedom and, thus, receives a personal character that is missing from all other human flesh. In all of this, the existential aspect is evident: the whole physical chain of events is translated into a divine "manner of being" (ὁ ὑπὲρ φύσιν τρόπος),[217] without doing any violence to [human] nature.

b. The synthesis of soul with body. This likewise comes about within the absolute Person, within its being and its freedom; therefore it is an essential characteristic (ἰδιότης) of this soul to be, in its own human freedom of will, an expression of the freedom of God's personal and essential (natural) freedom. Its free conformity to the free control of the Logos is true natural freedom of will (θέλησις), because the Logos, as God, is the ultimate ground and justification of all the intelligible structures (*logoi*) of created natures; yet it lacks all our indeterminate groping and dithering guesswork about the right way to act (γνώμη), a characteristic that once again relieves the God-man of the human corruption we have all inherited, without touching the core of his humanity. In this connection, one might wish to ascribe more darkness and suffering to the soul of Jesus than Maximus himself is inclined to do, for the distinction between the "passivities of dishonor" (πάθη τῆς ἀτιμίας), which are not simply a part of nature but "disfigure" it, and those that form part of our punishment (πάθη τῆς ἐπιτιμίας), which Christ could take upon himself, is a fluid one: it is part of the style and

---

[216] We anticipate the next section, where the terminology used here will be explained more fully.

[217] *Disputation with Pyrrhus*; PG 91, 300A.

taste of the individual theologian to draw the line as he sees fit.[218] A different question is how far that process goes, which Maximus calls the "assimilation" (οἰκείωσις) of even the dishonorable sufferings and corruption of fallen humanity by the divine physician; here it is once again essential to make it clear that the passive, unfree suffering of the soul of Christ, like that of his body, is rooted in the free and active core of the divine hypostasis, which also determines *how* it experiences these things. His spontaneous *willing* to be human and to suffer is precisely what holds his human nature together as such and saves it from any transformation into being naturally divine; at the same time, it is also what gives to it the supernatural "manner" that distinguishes it from all other, purely human persons, who always simply "emerge" in a generic way, as we have seen, from the synthesis of body and soul.

c. The synthesis between human nature, as a whole, and the Divine Person [of the Son] becomes clearer, in Maximus' approach, in that nothing here need be absorbed or overshadowed any longer. The tension within the human subject between nature and person has become the "space" between a Divine Person and human nature; one can and must speak now of a "synthetic person" only inasmuch as what is characteristic (ἰδιότης) of the essence and the existence of human nature, in body and soul, is due here simply to the fact that the person who "owns" it is not a human person but a divine one. The synthesis of the person, then, consists only in the fact that the positive subject— the Divine Person, who is God in very essence—has the freedom to be himself even outside himself: that is, in the created realm.

This concluding assault on Severus really includes all the essential concerns of Alexandria and Antioch, even of Apollinarius. As we have portrayed it here, it already makes use of the results of the Monothelite controversy, which must still be explained in detail in what follows.

---

[218] See J. Ternus, "Das Seelen- und Bewußtseinsleben Jesu", in Grillmeier and Bacht, *Chalkedon*, 3:114. Undoubtedly through a misprint, Ternus has here confused the two Greek terms.

4. Healing as Preservation

a. The Exchange of Properties

The Monophysite controversy had a dangerous postlude: Monothelitism. Here the problem was pursued into its farthest corner: the focus of the question was no longer that of natures in general but the more narrow issue of their most "personal" expressions and abilities. In this way, the debate took, at the same time, a turn toward the concrete. It was no longer the formal relationship of nature and person that stood in the foreground but the living exchange (ἀντίδοσις) of them both, realized in the drama of the Incarnation and its catastrophic climax, the Savior's Passion. This turn from formal ontology to its concrete and lived experience, from *logos* to *bios*, was destined to become also the acid test of Christology.

Maximus builds his whole doctrine of salvation, with great consistency, on the basis of his formal Christology. There the unconfused but continued existence of the two natures provided the foundation for the decisive synthesis. This preservation of the human nature put it, by itself, in the position to place all its positive content, undiminished (ἀνελλιπῶς πάντας τοὺς φυσικοὺς λόγους), at the service of unification,[219] as building blocks for the great bridge between God and the world. "Precisely *because* Christ was the mediator between God and man, he had to preserve completely his natural kinship with the two poles he brings together, by being them both himself."[220] This does not imply any kind of natural communication between the two: "nature and nature do not share a common nature."[221] "For it is not by denial of opposition, as some think, that a mediating position is affirmed."[222] In fact, what happened is something unexpected, yet perfectly logical: in the synthesis, the mutual difference of the poles is precisely what is underlined and confirmed, "each rather confirming the other by means of each other" (δι᾽ ἑκατέρου δὲ μᾶλλον πιστούμενος θάτερον).[223] It is only then, when God and man come closest to each other and meet in

---

[219] *Ambigua*; PG 91, 1037A.
[220] *Epistles* 11; PG 91, 468C.
[221] *Opuscula*; PG 91, 108C.
[222] *Ambigua*; PG 91, 1056D.
[223] Δι᾽ ἑκατέρου δὲ μᾶλλον πιστούμενος θάτερον: Ibid.; PG 91, 1056A.

a single person that it becomes obvious before our very eyes that God is eternally, irreducibly other than man and that man may therefore not seek his salvation in a direction that implies an abandonment of his own nature.

For this reason, Chalcedon's great word was "save" (σώζειν): the preservation of the peculiar character of both natures.[224] All the great defenders of the Council made use of it, Leontius[225] as well as Sophronius.[226] For Maximus, this word becomes the most central concept in the whole order of redemption, for it unites in itself both aspects of Christ's saving work: healing and rescue, on the one hand, and preservation and confirmation, on the other. Insofar as nature is elevated by grace, it is also strengthened and brought to fulfillment within itself. Through man's participation in God, mankind—man's creatureliness —itself is perfected. The unity of God and man "is achieved through the preservation [of differences], guaranteed by guaranteeing *them*. For the unification of the two poles comes to full realization to the exact degree that their natural difference remains intact."[227] Only if Christ retains his full relationship with his divine Father and his human mother is he "completely of the same substance with things above and things below".[228] By bringing back human nature from the brink of destruction, by rescuing it (διέσωζε),[229] he reclaims it from the self-alienation of its sinful desire to "be as god" and presents it to itself (τὴν φύσιν πρὸς ἑαυτὴν ἀποκαθίστησιν),[230] returning each one of us to ourselves (ἡμᾶς ἑαυτοῖς ἀποδιδούς).[231] For "he did not come to undermine the nature that he himself, as God and Word, had created."[232] This preservation is realized through the unification of human nature, in the highest degree, with the God who produces and affirms it; by being divinized, the world is perfected as world. So the world is given to itself, each of us is given to ourselves, when God gives himself to the world and to

---

[224] DS 302.
[225] E.g., PG 86, 1281A; et passim.
[226] PG 87, 3169C. For Dionysius, see chapter 1 above (introduction).
[227] *Opuscula*; PG 91, 96D–97A.
[228] Ibid.; PG 91, 209C.
[229] Ibid.; PG 91, 60A.
[230] *Exposition of the Lord's Prayer*; CCG 23, 34, 135; PG 90, 877D.
[231] *Ambigua*; PG 91, 1060B.
[232] *Opuscula*; PG 91, 77C.

us in Christ: when "he makes of [the world] a new mystery"[233] and presents both it and us to himself (διδοὺς ἡμᾶς ἑαυτῷ).[234]

One must not, then, any longer misunderstand the abiding distance between the natures, as if there were between them only an extrinsic relationship of parallel existence. In the hypostasis of Christ, both have reached the stage of "strict identity",[235] which results, in the two natures, in a lively interpenetration and growth toward each other (πρὸς ἀλλήλας συμφυΐα καὶ περιχωρήσει),[236] a mutual exchange of properties, such as happens between fire and the glowing iron within it.[237] One may indeed speak, with the Cappadocians, of a kind of "mixture of the two natures",[238] with the result that one can no longer talk of "pure difference" (ψιλὴ διαφορά),[239] but one must see here the foundation of an intimate community of being and of shared operation (συνεργάτις σάρξ).[240] This symbiotic interpenetration is the basis for the possibility of an "interconnected exchange" of the names that belong to the two natures; thus one can "call God one who suffers"[241] and man "Son of God" and "God". But this application only rests on the (ontological) identity of the hypostasis and thus can come about only through it and in it as its medium.[242] This medium connects the natures in itself but also keeps them apart, so that it is only possible to predicate one nature's qualities of the other indirectly (οὐ κυρίως).[243]

This synthesis and its effect—a kind of indirect identity of God and man—remains the world's supreme miracle, for it incarnates within itself the most decisive "contradictions".[244] Because it cannot be self-contradictory, however, these contradictions must be both preserved and overcome within it. Their elimination is not simply a matter of two opposed existent things encountering each other in some third be-

---

[233] *Ambigua*; PG 91, 1049A.

[234] Ibid.; PG 91, 1060B.

[235] Ibid.; PG 91, 1053B.

[236] *Opuscula*; PG 91, 88A.

[237] Ibid.; PG 91, 189D.

[238] *In Epistula Dionysii* 4; PG 4, 533C.

[239] *Epistles* 12; PG 91, 473A.

[240] *Opuscula*; PG 91, 85D.

[241] *Opuscula*; PG 91, 121A.

[242] *Ambigua*; PG 91, 1044Bff.

[243] Ibid.; PG 91, 1068ff. Leontius had already taught the *communicatio idiomatum* with complete clarity: PG 86, 1285C; 1945CD.

[244] *Opuscula*; PG 91, 109C; ibid.; PG 91, 193A–C.

ing, where the nonidentical are united. For the hypostasis is not simply a "third being" with relation to the natures; as a divine hypostasis, it is one with absolute Being and immanent within it, and, through this unity of being, human nature has its hypostatic existence in the Logos. Thus the mutual indwelling of natures, for all its indirectness, becomes an ontological unity of the highest order and accomplishes both a transformation and an assimilation of its two components.

Death and suffering belong of necessity to human nature in the concrete, as an expression of its weakness and abandonment. Through the Incarnation, however, they become at the same time a kind of freedom, an expression of power.[245] On the other hand, the unity of God's freedom and power with human suffering and death achieves that divine annihilation (κένωσις) which subjects God to what is not God. The result of both is redemptive suffering: "He suffered, if one may put it this way, in a divine way, because he suffered freely."[246] In the identity of divine annihilation and a superhuman way of suffering, the unity of opposites becomes reality. For the self-emptying of God is that "supremely endless power"[247] which is, at once, freedom and love and which makes it possible for God "himself to become, through his endless longing for humanity, naturally and in very truth the object of his own desire".[248] He achieves this without compromising his own enduring freedom, for this "self-emptying, achieved for our sakes",[249] is itself only the pledge and the revelation of a "majesty that commands infinity".[250] This place of God's self-emptying is precisely the place of his holiest divinity, of love's highest freedom: a freedom that stands at once beyond both "natures", makes both into an expression and sign of itself, and is genuinely capable of achieving a "coincidence of opposites", in the sense of Nicholas of Cusa. Everything, then, can be predicated of this supreme focus of freedom: "the ability to suffer and freedom from suffering, uncreated and created being, limitation and

---

[245] "Indeed, in his power he has made the sufferings of nature into works of free choice" (ἀμέλει ἐξουσίᾳ γνώμης ἔργα πεποιηκὼς τὰ πάθη τῆς φύσεως): *Ambigua*; PG 91, 1053C.

[246] Ibid.; PG 91, 1056A.

[247] Ibid.; PG 91, 1053C.

[248] Ibid.; PG 91, 1048C.

[249] *Opuscula*; PG 91, 120B.

[250] Ibid.; PG 91, 120A.

freedom from limitation, the earthly and the heavenly, the visible and the spiritual, the conceivable and the inconceivable".[251]

> (Here) we are amazed at how finitude and infinity—things mutually exclusive, which cannot be combined—can be identified in him and can mutually reveal each other. The unlimited is circumscribed by limits in an ineffable way, while the limited unfolds, beyond its own nature, to meet the measure of infinity.[252]

This supreme paradox of a hypostatic center of freedom that is both in and beyond all natures—a center of freedom that is the fulcrum of the world's whole history—acts also as a corrective to concepts that may appear all too "physical" or "ontological" in the soteriology of the Greek Fathers. With Maximus, the principal weight no longer lies on Christ's acquisition of a complete human nature, its immediate and "automatic" delivery from sin, and its divinization, as was so clearly evident in Athanasius and the Cappadocians; rather, it lies at the ultimate center of hypostatic existence, where freedom, love, and being are one.[253]

b. The Meaning of the Doctrine of Two Wills

It was to this peak [of Christ's existence], however, that the last heresy of patristic Christology had also fled for refuge: *Monothelitism.* Everything seemed to favor equating this supreme personal freedom with Christ's single "hypostatic will". Does not the analogy of man support such an identification, asked Pyrrhus, since, in spite of the duality of his natures, man realizes, through them both, a single, unified, and free activity? Against even the apparent luminosity of this "personalist" philosophy, Maximus holds fast to his sober principles: an intellectual nature is defined by its self-determination (αὐτοκίνητον) and its freedom (προαίρεσις). An axiom presented itself from the ontology of things in motion: all things resemble each other in at least this respect, that none of them is the other, each of them is unlike the rest; "difference is constitutive and definitive of being" (διαφορὰ συστατικὴ καὶ

---

[251] *Opuscula;* PG 91, 120C.

[252] *Epistles* 21; PG 91, 604BC.

[253] This is especially well expressed in the *Liber asceticus;* PG 90, 916D–924C. Weser is incorrect in suspecting Maximus of having a "mechanical" soteriology: *S. Maximi Confessoris,* 22.

ἀφοριστική).²⁵⁴ But for this limitation also to imply a positive foundation for being, it may not simply be imposed from without; it must flow from the actual being itself, as its effect and its definition. By its activity, finite being defines (literally: de-fines) itself.²⁵⁵ Natural freedom cannot be established any more deeply than in this ontology of finite being. Man, then, certainly possesses a single freedom of willing, but precisely insofar as he is not simply a single hypostasis but also a single nature (κατ' εἶδος μίαν ἐνέργειαν).²⁵⁶

One must, then, hold firmly to two levels of doing and willing in Christ, which are bound together only in the unity of his hypostasis, not in a unity of nature. Nestorius attempted to find the unity in the *object* of [Christ's] two ways of willing. He rightly saw that their unity of object did not at all presuppose a unity of will. Pyrrhus, then, could not be allowed to reason from the unified activity seen in Christ's deeds to a unity of nature. If one looks more closely, in fact, this unified activity reveals its twofold cause.²⁵⁷ When Christ walks on the water, his strides as such are a human act, but his striding over water is superhuman. In a single thrust with a red-hot sword, I can still distinguish in the wound what is the effect of cutting and what of burning. So everything that Christ does is both human and superhuman at the same time; but the superhuman in his actions in no way destroys what is purely human, genuinely human. Christ has, not a "spiritual existence", but in every way a completely human one and, as such, an existence that is divinized; in fact, the divinity of his action finds its ultimate guarantee in the intact and undiminished authenticity of his humanity. Precisely his speaking, breathing, walking, his hungering, eating, thirsting, drinking, sleeping, weeping, worrying are the decisive places where the divine makes its appearance. Here the principle of "just as far as" (μέχρι-ἕως) must be strictly applied:²⁵⁸ just as far as the decisively human remains in force is as far as God appears. Or to put

---

²⁵⁴ *Opuscula*; PG 91, 249C.
²⁵⁵ "Motion is a power that creates form, that forms the definition of the subject, that constitutes and limits all its characteristics (κίνησις δύναμις εἰδωλιώδ, ποιοῦσα τοῦ ὑποκειμένου τὸν ὁρισμόν, συστατική, περιεκτικὴ πάσης ἰδιότητος): ibid.; PG 91, 201A. "For the definition of a thing is most properly the intelligible principle (λόγος) of its essential potency" (Ὅρος γὰρ τοῦ πράγματος ὁ λόγος τῆς οὐσιώδους δυνάμεως κυρίως ἐστίν): ibid.; PG 91, 200B; cf. 21C. The best commentary on these sentences is Paul Claudel's *Art poétique*.
²⁵⁶ *Disputation with Pyrrhus*; PG 91, 336C.
²⁵⁷ Ibid.; PG 91, 241BC.
²⁵⁸ *Opuscula*; PG 91, 97A.

it more sharply: just as far as the two wills remain themselves, unconfused, is as far as they can be united in a single (μοναδικῶς)[259] activity.
This unity, then, is "organic interpenetration",[260] and one may call it
"theandric activity"[261] on the basis of its indivisibility,[262] or even—
using his opponents' formulation—"a single activity", if one understands this as referring, not to the nature, but to the hypostasis.[263]

The example of man, which Pyrrhus offered, can even be reversed
and used against him. Is not a dualism possible (δυϊκῶς ἐνεργεῖν) even
in the human activity and will that are naturally one, so that we can, for
example, at the same time say one thing and be thinking of something
else? It is said of Moses that even while he spoke to the people, he
continued to converse with God.[264]

The struggle with Pyrrhus reached its climax in the former patriarch's final argument. "If there is only one acting person, so there is
only one activity: that of the one person!" Maximus replied: "Does he
have two natures? Yes or no? If yes, then there are also two activities."
Pyrrhus: "But from the fact that he acts in a twofold way (δυϊκῶς) one
cannot conclude that he has two activities. Rather, since he was but
one single actor, he can only have had one single activity." Maximus:
"What was this activity? Was it divine or human?" Pyrrhus: "If we
can call the activity of divinity and humanity in Christ single, we are
not speaking of his nature but of the manner of union." Maximus:
"That is pointless. This activity must come from a nature, either the
divine or the human."[265] One can see that the argument is ultimately
circular; the final reply cannot push the problem forward any farther.
Two ultimate conceptions of the person are on a collision course here.
For Pyrrhus, person can represent only an irrational dimension, beyond
everything natural. He wants to preserve its absolute spontaneity and
self-affirmation through negations. Thus, in many respects, Monothelitism is a precursor of the personalistic nominalism of the late Middle
Ages and modern culture. For Maximus, on the other hand, person is

---

[259] *Ambigua*; PG 91, 1044D.
[260] "Growing together, by a unitary interpenetration" (συμφυῶς κατὰ τὴν ἑνιαίαν περιχώ-
ρησιν: *Opuscula*; PG 91, 232A.
[261] *Ambigua*; PG 91, 1056BC.
[262] *Opuscula*; PG 91, 100D.
[263] Ibid.; PG 91, 101B.
[264] *Disputation with Pyrrhus*; PG 91, 337CD.
[265] Ibid.; PG 91, 340A–341A.

the realization, the concrete living out, of a rational nature; and because every realization points back to a real source, it is the original, functional center of the rational nature itself, the radiant inner expression of its being. This dynamic, actualizing aspect of being is only something "irrational" in the eyes of a narrow rationalism; for those who grasp it more deeply—as Aristotle, Thomas, and Hegel were able to do—it is that which makes being itself real.

The inner logic of Monothelitism shows that Maximus, too, despite what seems like "naturalism" in his thought, has seen more deeply. The tendency to conceive of the person irrationally may have come from the effort to think "existentially", "personally"; but it leads to a lifeless style of thought. Nature, robbed of the inner dynamic of its own purposefulness for the sake of the [freedom of the] person, descends to being a marionette. The consistent conclusion of this subtle, intelligent heresy was a new kind of docetism and, so, the denial of the ultimate basis of the Christian message. One cannot elevate the "personal" into a "system", but must always contextualize it as one of the given aspects belonging to and revealed by "nature".[266]

c. The Drama of Redemption

The last remaining step is to apply the [christological] doctrine Maximus developed to the drama of redemption. The deepest reason that Christ must possess a creaturely freedom belongs to salvation history: the healing of nature demands a descent to that tragic point in man, where sin, as opposition to God, has come into its own.[267] For sin to be overcome from within, it had, in some way or other, to be found "within" Christ. But how could he "be made sin" (2 Cor 5:21) without committing sin himself? How could he live through and represent in his own person the tragic opposition between man and God without himself being torn apart by that opposition?

---

[266] We have already indicated that Maximus' doctrine of the hypostasis is not without its defects. Besides the sharp contours of his theoretical conception, he may also be lacking in a certain sense for the ultimate urgency of the problems, which may be part of the reason for the much-criticized "abstractness" of his explanations. But it would be unfair to demand of a seventh-century Greek a Scotist understanding of the issues. It is enough that he has already anticipated the decisive insights of St. Thomas Aquinas and that the modern problem of the person can take his thought as the foundation for further development, without any necessary discontinuity of thought.

[267] Opuscula; PG 91, 157AB.

We are already familiar with the difference between "physical" and "moral" sin. The former designates the whole range of vulnerabilities that fundamentally characterize nature, insofar as they are punishment for sin. By taking them on himself without having deserved them, Christ breaks the magic circle of lust and death.[268] Like a consuming fire, he burns out the reserves of concupiscence from human weakness[269] and eradicates the note of condemnation in death.[270] He had to possess those natural vulnerabilities (πάθη) which—even though connected with sin—are so deeply rooted in the core of nature that they seemed to have become part of its very constitution. Christ's terror in the Garden of Olives was a sign of such vulnerability. "There is nothing blameworthy in the fact that the flesh does not want to die. That is part of nature."[271] And nature here means, not simply a blind, vital drive to stay alive, but intelligent willing.

For in an intellectual being, natural desire (θέλημα φυσικόν or θέλησις) is always, at its root, an intellectual desire (θέλημα λογικόν).[272] This must be understood, first of all, as an undifferentiated basic faculty, not directed to any particular object (ἁπλῶς), not yet qualified through a particular act of the will (ποιὰ θέλησις) to become a "directed desire" (βούλησις). This latter fixes its gaze on an object as desirable—first of all, of course, simply on the level of imagination (ὄρεξις φανταστική), without any particular attention to its attainability or unattainability.[273] Only when the mind turns to ways and means does the "directed desire" become a considered plan or "choice" (βουλή or βούλευσις).[274] First of all, this means excluding the unattainable; but most of the time, the way to the realization of desire is beyond our view, because of the limitation of our knowledge, and the outcome of our action is uncertain. This is the decisive situation of man: his quest, his reaching out for what he desires, is able to bring the object of his desire into view but cannot integrate it so clearly into the system of created causes and effects that the will's prior choice could ever simply reach out to its own

---

[268] *Quaestiones ad Thalassium* 21; CCG 7, 129; PG 90, 313B.

[269] Ibid.; CCG 7, 131, 72ff.; PG 90, 316AB.

[270] *Ambigua*; PG 91, 1041C.

[271] *Opuscula*: PG 91, 164B.

[272] *Opuscula*; PG 91, 21D; cf. ibid.; PG 91, 12C: "He desires by means of the senses and the mind" (κατ᾽ αἴσθησίν τε καὶ νοῦν ὀρέγεται).

[273] Ibid.; PG 91, 31B.

[274] Ibid.; PG 91, 16B.

effective fulfillment. Thus his searching and investigating result first of all in his "deciding to do" something, as a directional determination of the heart (ὄϱεξις ἐνδιάθετος)—a "setting-out", which includes just as much "preconceived opinion" as it does an objective response to the object. Maximus calls this complex state, which corresponds to something very real, γνώμη;[275] it is the immediate ground from which the will's free decision (πϱοαίϱεσις) springs. The decision-making process, therefore, in the human consciousness, rests on the double situation of naturally having to will, on the one hand, and of not being able to see all the possibilities, on the other. Freedom of choice is not a pure perfection: it is limited by the double bind of being forced by one's created condition to make a choice, in order to realize one's being, and yet of having to choose something whose implications one does not fully understand.

But to return to Christ: What shape, in his case, do the psychological phases of willing take? His fear of death is a natural drive and, at the same time, something intellectual, "for there must necessarily be a correspondence between nature and the direction of our intellectual energies, and nature must possess the drive not to die but to cling to this present life."[276] On the other hand, Christ's divine will wished for death. Was there not, therefore, a contradiction between the two wills?

It is important to distinguish sharply here, first of all, between two kinds of opposition (διαστολή): simple or contrary opposition (ἐναντίωσις) and contradiction (ἀντικεῖσθαι). The first of these is the opposition we find between the world of the senses and that of the mind, the second that between life and death. But surely it is impossible, Maximus argues, that there should be a contradiction between two natures as such, for everything natural comes from a single common source, God;[277] therefore they cannot eliminate each other as contradictories can, which belong only to the qualities of natures and not to their reality itself. But Christ's fear of death comes into play within the sphere of the purely natural, as something placed in nature by God himself (even if it is one of the punishments for sin). It is therefore an ordered, not a disordered, fear; the latter is only possible on the

---

[275] On the development of this concept in Maximus, see Sherwood, *Ascetic Life*, 55–63.
[276] *Opuscula*; PG 91, 224C.
[277] Ibid.; PG 91, 212CD.

level of γνώμη.[278] But γνώμη is impossible in Christ, because it rests on uncertainty about ends and means and thus involves a kind of groping and searching. This gnomic willing, which "especially belongs to the person and the hypostasis",[279] could not occur in Christ, since there was no room in his single divine hypostasis for wavering and hesitation. In fact, we must go a step farther and say that his whole natural range of drives, the "givenness" of his human existence, had always to be embraced and supported by the undiminished freedom of his person, that it was thus "freely permitted for our sake".

> For in Christ what is natural does not precede what is freely willed, as happens with us; rather, just as he truly hungered and thirsted, but did not hunger and thirst in the same way [as we do], but in a way above what is human because it was free, so he also genuinely experienced fear of death, but a fear that was above the human.[280]

His natural fear of death was itself supported by his underlying hypostatic freedom, which supported his whole nature. His hypostatic identity, therefore, bears and results in the natural opposition of the two natures, and in its supreme personal disponibility [to the Father's will] it dissolves the opposition between them to the same degree that it brings it into being.

The result of this freedom, however, is only redemption from the punishment of sin in nature, not an "overcoming" of sin itself. And are not our vulnerabilities so intrinsically interwoven with sin that there is always an immediate danger of passing from one to the other, so that Christ would seem automatically inclined to move from a simple opposition [between his natures] into mortal contradiction? And did not Christ take on such an intrinsic unity with human nature that he could not have remained unacquainted with this secret depth of the human soul, its revolt against God? Did he not have to have this "experience", too, just as he lived through the experience of our vulnerability (τὴν πεῖραν τῶν παθημάτων)?[281]

Maximus answers these questions by his theory of "appropriation" (οἰκείωσις) within salvation history. This can take two forms: an "appropriation by relationship" (οἰκείωσις σχετική) and an "appropriation

---

[278] Ibid.; PG 91, 193A.
[279] Ibid.; PG 91, 192BC.
[280] *Disputation with Pyrrhus*; PG 91, 297D.
[281] *Opuscula*; PG 91, 117A.

by nature" (οἰκείωσις φυσική). The former comes into being through conscious acts; so, for example, if we love each other, we can communicate our actions and our sufferings and can identify with those of another, although we are not ourselves actually doing or undergoing the same things.[282] The latter, on the other hand, is an ontological (οὐσιώδης) appropriation, which makes the assimilated object part of our very being. Now it is clear that Christ, who possessed our nature ontologically as his own, had our natural human capacity to will in himself in the same way that we do and put it to use (ἐτύπωσεν).[283] But since he could not make our sinful manner of willing his own ontologically, he assimilated it to himself through "relative appropriation".

> Our vulnerabilities (πάθη) have two aspects: that of punishment and that of guilt. The former is characteristic of our nature as such; the latter simply disfigures it. The former was freely and ontologically taken on by Christ along with his human existence; through this act, he gave strength to our nature as it is and freed it from the curse that lay on us. But he made the latter aspect his own in the course of salvation history, through his love for humanity, in that he took it up to destroy it, as fire consumes wax or the sun the mists of the earth, so that in its place he might bestow on us his own blessings.[284]

Christ achieves this second identification in his role as head of the Mystical Body,[285] by which he stands in a loving and therefore sympathetic relationship with the actions and sufferings of all his members.

But may one call this last kind of "appropriation" purely "relational", and see it as excluding all ontological communication? Christ's union with human nature, after all, is itself ontological, and original sin is situated precisely in the universal reality of this nature, as such. In his *Disputation with Pyrrhus*, this universality is clearly expressed: through his subjection to the will of the Father, Christ did not make only his own humanity subject [to him], but humanity in general[286]—all of humanity, even and most especially that element in it which had not been subjected already (ὃ ἡμέτερος ἀνυπότακτος τρόπος).[287] He repre-

---

[282] Ibid.; PG 91, 220B.

[283] *Disputation with Pyrrhus*; PG 91, 305B.

[284] *Opuscula*; PG 91, 237B.

[285] Ibid.; PG 91, 237A.

[286] *Disputation with Pyrrhus*; PG 91, 305C.

[287] *Opuscula*: PG 91, 237B.

sents our rebellion in himself (τυπῶν τὸ ἡμέτερον),[288] as an actor represents a character on the stage. In this way, he did not make his own only what is naturally ordered in us but also our ability to choose freely (προαίρεσις).[289] Now the full implications of his struggle on the Mount of Olives become clear. The "stage", on which both wills appeared like dramatic figures, was his person, identical with them both: his person, which he exposed to contradiction for our sakes, in order to destroy the contradiction within his very self. "Not as I will, but as you will": even though the will of this "you" was already one in being with the will of the eternal Son, it now became no less the will of this "I". So he "does violence to his own will"[290] in order to subject it fully to the Father.

Once again it is clear how Christology, if expressed in secular terms, leads to dialectic but in its theologically genuine form overcomes dialectic. If the hypostatic "I" were simply determined by its natures, what Hegel says would have to be right:

> Both of the two extremes are that one "I", the one forming the relationship; and the act of holding them together, of establishing the relationship, is itself the thing that struggles with itself in unity and that unifies itself in struggle. To put it another way: I am the struggle, for the struggle is precisely that resistance that is not an indifference of one to the other as simply being other but the interconnectedness of them both. I am not one of those caught up in the struggle, but I am both of the struggling parties and the struggle itself. I am fire and water and the contact and unity between the things that simply flee from each other.[291]

To the degree that the questionable aspects of Maximus' philosophy of sexuality, which we have mentioned, also indirectly cast their shadows on his Christology—insofar as our fallen, vulnerable nature is in some way also essentially a sinful nature—the danger is not fully neutralized even here. But Maximus has made every possible effort, precisely in his Christology, to keep all real contradictions, all the dialectic and all the demonic aspects of our existence, far away from the existence and the being of Christ. A chasm separates him from Hegel. For with Hegel, the struggle is itself the basis of synthesis; but with

---

[288] Ibid.; PG 91, 84BC, 196D.

[289] Ibid.; PG 91, 29C.

[290] Ibid.; PG 91, 81B.

[291] *Religionsphilosophie*, 1, 2d ed. (1840); ed. H.Glockner, vol. 15 [reprint, Stuttgart, 1959]), 64.

Maximus, everything depends on a prior, unconstrained, free act of the person who steers the struggle from above and on the voluntary character of that person's "ineffable self-immolation".[292] The opposed will is, from the start, already in submission: "Not as I will, but as you will." If sin makes any entry at all on this internal stage of the God-man, it is only, so to speak, as an empty shell, which has already poured out its sinful contents.

The inevitable question is how this struggle, already decided beforehand, can still be called serious. If [Christ's] human nature has no process of choice, no γνώμη, no indecision, does it not also fail to merit its crown?

Maximus refuses to attribute γνώμη to the human nature of Christ. For, on the one hand, this process has its origin in a darkening of human insight into what is truly good, both as end and as means; thus it is a sign of weakness that does not pertain to Christ.[293] On the other hand, γνώμη is the way a hypostasis lives out and realizes its natural striving and willing;[294] it is "the will with particular qualifications".[295] Thus it cannot be absent from Christ unless its place is taken by a perfect hypostatic realization of human nature. If γνώμη means the personal realization of freedom as something imperfect, groping, and therefore needing to choose, then Christ "must possess a natural relationship with and assimilation to the Good, simply through his being —through his divine mode of existence";[296] thus he must realize in himself, in a surpassing way (eminenter), the dimension of perfection in γνώμη.

In fact, Maximus always describes the healing of the human γνώμη as a return to a natural rightness, which consists in the unfolding of the natural capacity to will according to the norm of the will of God.[297] The possibility of choosing is thus less a perfection than it is the inevitable experiencing [Not-Wende] of a natural necessity. In the five proofs for the freedom of the will that Maximus offers to Pyrrhus, it is

---

[292] Ambigua; PG 91, 1048C.

[293] Opuscula; PG 91, 56B; Disputation with Pyrrhus; PG 91, 308D–309A.

[294] Opuscula; PG 91, 192BC.

[295] Ibid.; PG 91, 21D; Disputation with Pyrrhus; PG 91, 308C.

[296] Disputation with Pyrrhus; PG 91, 309A (reading τῷ θεϊκῶς ὑποστῆναι).": "in that he subsists in a divine way").

[297] Exposition of the Lord's Prayer, CCG 23, 35, 150–53; PG 90, 880A; Ambigua; PG 91, 1044A.

always simply the self-determination (αὐτεξούσιον) of the intellectual nature, its independence and its self-possession, that is demonstrated. This quality is equated with the possession of intellect and reason itself.[298] And since intellectuality is a gift of nature, freedom must be such a gift as well. Self-determination (αὐτεξούσιον) and intellectual willing (θελητικόν) are the same thing.[299]

This does not prevent the faculty of willing, in the creature, from being a dynamic striving toward a goal,[300] ultimately a reaching through all partial goals toward God. For this urge is itself a free movement, even though it is also a given. In any case, Maximus is thinking here, in the first instance, only of freedom from imposed necessity (οὐδὲν ἠναγκασμένον ἔχει).[301] Ultimately, however, there is no hiatus between natural will and personal will. He explains to Pyrrhus at great length that the virtues are nothing else than genuine, developed nature itself (φυσικαί εἰσιν αἱ ἀρεταί), insofar as it is alive and efficacious. In this context, he repeats a basic teaching of Evagrius: nature as such is the Good.[302] The goal of all asceticism is, in the end, to clear away the obstacles to this natural spontaneity.[303] So the central theme running through Maximus' whole thought reappears here once again: the Good is nothing else but the act of being. Being proves its power as the Eternal Good by letting itself unfold in the world as good things and so manages to attain eternal validity as its ultimate justification and its graced fulfillment (εἶναι—εὖ εἶναι—ἀεὶ εἶναι). The "space" that in us comes between possibility and habitual condition, on the one hand, and realization and action, on the other, is a space of "tension", not a real break.[304]

All of this lessens the difficulty seemingly implied by the fact that in Christ there is no γνώμη and no free choice in the human sense. Since every created nature can only be conceived of as one that dynamically develops toward a hypostasis, in a hypostasis, and as a hypostasis, the imperfect stage of having to choose must surely be present in Christ,

---

[298] "That which is . . . naturally rational is naturally self-determining" (τὸ . . . φύσει λογικὸν καὶ φύσει αὐτεξούσιον): *Disputation with Pyrrhus*; PG 91, 304B–D.

[299] Ibid.; PG 91, 301C.

[300] Ibid. 317C.

[301] Ibid. 243B.

[302] PG 40, 1240A, etc.

[303] *Disputation with Pyrrhus*; PG 91, 309B–312A.

[304] Ibid.; PG 91, 324D–325A.

too—though surely as something already surpassed. His incomparable "merit" consists precisely in the fact that he has always moved beyond any vacillation with respect to the Good, in the perfection of his formed decision and in his submission to the will of God. The drama on the Mount of Olives is the ultimate price and the ultimate proof of this obedience.

"Physically", the "appropriation" of our rebellious will, and the healing that results from it, has saved the human race by restoring to it an incorrupt, naturally functioning faculty of self-determination. This "physical" redemption, however, is a wholly "spiritual" drama: the life-and-death struggle of the natures of God and the creature on the stage of the most exalted hypostasis. So it demands of us our intellectual involvement, our participation, by entering with the Redeemer into that identification of God's "self-annihilation" with the human willing that is itself a constitutive part of the hypostasis of Christ: of Christ, namely, as head of his Mystical Body.

5. The Syntheses of Redemption

The Garden of Olives, where the cosmic struggle between the nature of God and the nature of the world took place within a single soul, is not only the center of Christ's work but also the core of the syntheses that were intended to achieve the redemption of all creation by drawing it step by step toward God. In his vision of these syntheses, Maximus brings to its completion the Alexandrian idea of the *regressus*, the reentry of the creature into God. In Origen's thought, this return is conceived in the image of a gradual ascent of the soul to ever more spiritual levels of being, under the guidance of the Logos, who is constantly changing himself into ever-higher forms:

> And perhaps just as there were steps in the Temple, on which one mounted toward the Holy of Holies, so the Only-begotten of God is himself all the steps we need. . . . The first and lowest, so to speak, is his humanity; we step across that and make our way through the rest of his states of being; he is the whole way up the stairs, so that we might ascend through him who is also an angel and the other powers.[305]

---

[305] Origen, *Commentary on John* 19, 1; PG 14, 536CD.

In Maximus, this pattern of a direct ascent is contrasted with another pattern, that of synthesis, which corresponds to his basic conception of the tension and polarity of created being. By doing this, Maximus essentially captured the vision of the Alexandrian master and brought it into a Christian perspective on the world.

Christ has become, through the depth and the divine manner of his suffering, "founder of the mysteries" (τελετάρχης) and "sun of all the ages",[306] under whose beams the world's harvest gradually ripens toward unity in God. This is the *mysterium magnum* of which Paul speaks.

> This is the great and hidden mystery. This is the blessed end, the goal, for whose sake everything was created. This was the divine purpose that lay before the beginning of all things. . . . With this goal in mind, God called the natures of things into existence. This is the limit toward which providence and all the things it protects are moving, where creatures realize their reentry into God. This is the mystery spanning all the ages, revealing the supremely infinite and infinitely inconceivable plan of God, which exists in all its greatness before all the ages. . . . For Christ's sake, or for the sake of the mystery of Christ, all the ages and all the beings they contain took their beginning and their end in Christ. For that synthesis was already conceived before all ages: the synthesis of limit and the unlimited, of measure and the unmeasurable, of circumscription and the uncircumscribed, of the Creator with the creature, of rest with movement—that synthesis which, in these last days, has become visible in Christ, bringing the plan of God to its fulfillment through itself.[307]

According to this text, there is no doubt that Maximus—in contrast to John Damascene[308]—would have placed himself on the side of Scotus, without a second thought, in the [later] scholastic controversy: not redemption from sin, but the unification of the world in itself and with God is the ultimate motivating cause for the Incarnation and, as such, the first idea of the Creator, existing in advance of all creation.[309]

---

[306] *Ambigua*; PG 91, 1356Cff.

[307] *Quaestiones ad Thalassium* 60; CCG 22, 75, 32–56; PG 90, 621AB.

[308] *De fide orthodoxa* 3, 12; 4, 4; PG 94, 1228–29, 1108.

[309] On this point, Wagenmann (*Realencyclopädie für protestantische Theologie*, vol. 20, pt. 1, 129–44; cf. vol. 9, pt. 2, 430–43) is probably right, against Straubinger (*Die Christologie des heiligen Maximus Confessor* [Bonn, 1906], 126, 130). Only if one disregards Maximus' most typical features as a theologian and a mystic can one consider his philosophical anthropology as the center of his world view. In this latter approach—which does not, however, provide an objective picture of his thought—man moves in Christ's place to the center of creation, while the Redeemer is demoted to being the auxiliary instrument of human salvation.

But of course the presupposition of that scholastic controversy, which begins with an order of being—a world free from sin—that is only possible, never historically real, is far from Maximus' thought. For him, the "preexistent will" of God is identical with the realm both of "ideas" and of "possibilities"; the order of essence and the order of fact, at this highest point, converge into one.

Maximus can never have enough of praising "all the different syntheses between diverse creatures that are realized through Christ".[310] In that the Redeemer has defeated the hostile powers of the air, he reestablishes the continuity between heaven and earth "and proves that heavenly and earthly beings join in a single festive dance, as they receive the gifts that come from God". For "through the blood of his cross [Christ] establishes peace, both for the dwellers in heaven and for the dwellers on earth" (Col 1:20); "human nature now praises the glory of God with one and the same will as the heavenly powers." And "after Christ brought his historic work of salvation to completion for our sakes and ascended along with the body he had assumed, he united heaven and earth through himself, connected sensible creation with the intellectual, and so revealed the unity of creation in the very polarity of its elements."[311]

More specifically, there are five great syntheses that lead to this unity. Christ "unites man and woman, . . . unites the earth by abolishing the division between the earthly paradise and the rest of the inhabited globe, . . . unites earth and heaven, . . . unites sensible and intelligible things, . . . and ultimately—in an ineffable way—unites created and uncreated nature".[312] These syntheses will be developed more broadly in another context. The first, in the realm of sexuality, overcomes the curse resulting from sin in a first glimpse of distant unity: "In Christ Jesus there is no longer male or female" (Gal 3:28); here the power of procreation returns to that original fruitfulness of the spirit which existed in advance of sin. This first synthesis thus presupposes the realization of the second, which Christ indicates in his words from the Cross, "Today you will be with me in Paradise" (Lk 23:43); the earth that was cursed and the Eden that preceded it have become one, and "the whole earth is made holy again through his return, through death,

[310] *Quaestiones ad Thalassium* 48; CCG 7, 333, 66f.; PG 90, 436A.
[311] *Exposition of the Lord's Prayer;* CCG 23, 33, 116–20; PG 90, 877AB.
[312] *Quaestiones ad Thalassium* 48; CCG 7, 333, 67–335, 78; PG 90, 436AB.

into Paradise." The inaccessible land of our yearning has become an earthly reality, to the degree that the earth moves through death into its sinless condition. "Because our earth was no longer, for him, a different reality from Paradise, he appeared to his disciples on it once again, after his Resurrection, and associated with them, so showing that from now on the earth was one, united with itself."[313] Before his eyes, "the earth was no longer split into different regions but brought together for him, since he could no longer allow that any of its regions should be deprived of contact with the rest."[314]

Then "he ascended into heaven" (Acts 1:9–11) and so united the heavenly spheres with the earth, thus proving "that all of sensible creation is a unity in the intelligible order. The particular aspects, the differences that divide it, receded in him into the background."[315] But his Ascension did not cease at the visible heaven; "he ascended beyond all the heavens" (Eph 4:10) and finally united spirit and matter, by bringing a material body and a soul into the company of the angelic choirs. So he brought all of creation together;[316] and what is thus united he offers to God as he "stands before the Father" in his own totality: "gathering the universe in himself, he reveals the unity of all things as that of a single person", the cosmic Adam. For he possesses, as God, "a body and its sensations, and a soul like ours, and an intellect, through all of which he binds together all the parts" into wholes and is able to unite them, in turn, in a single, supreme totality.[317] And while Christ thus subjects himself, as the universal human being, to the Father, "he unites created nature to uncreated nature in love—O miracle of God's tender kindness toward us!—and reveals that both, through the relationship of grace, are now but one single reality. The whole world now inheres (περιχωρήσας), as a totality, in the whole of God, and becomes everything that God is, except for the identity of his nature; in place of itself, it now receives the totality of God."[318]

In this way, Maximus has built the Alexandrian doctrine of divinization into his own theory of syntheses by removing its Neoplatonic and spiritualist sting. In the form in which he presents it, there is not the

---

[313] *Ambigua*; PG 91, 1309AB.
[314] Ibid.; PG 91, 1305D.
[315] Ibid.; PG 91, 1309BC.
[316] Ibid.; PG 91, 1309C; 1308A.
[317] Ibid.; PG 1312A.
[318] Ibid.; PG 91, 1308C.

slightest danger of pantheism. It is, of course, true that Scotus Erigena must have built his own system directly on texts such as this. But the pantheistic tones that he added to it through his theory of four natures are not present in Maximus. The East's instinct for divinization is held in check here by the Chalcedonian term "unconfused" (ἀσυγχύτως).

~

The syntheses realized by Christ are the plan for those others that the world and every individual, by the grace of Christ, must realize in themselves. So it remains for us to consider, in a final chapter, the syntheses that Christ brings to fulfillment in and with us, his members. Put this way, this theme includes what one might call Maximus' "spirituality": his ascetical and mystical teaching.

It seems appropriate to present the spiritual highlights of his view of reality by drawing on the works in which Maximus is at his most original—the *Questions to Thalassius*, the *Ambigua*, the *Mystagogy*, the *Exposition of the Lord's Prayer*, the letters—rather than the works in which he is mainly concerned with working out his own adaptive assimilation of the spiritual tradition: the two collections of *Centuries*. One cannot make the distinction too sharply, for Maximus is always making use of the whole tradition and is always a creative adapter—often in a very quiet way, but precisely then at his most effective! Nevertheless, the shape of the spirituality of the first group of works is completely his own, whereas in the second he is reworking what has been shaped by others. For this reason, we must interpret the second group in terms of the first.

VII

THE SPIRITUAL SYNTHESES

1. Christian Realization

The life of the Christian is to imitate the life of Christ. Christ "loved us more than himself," since he chose the darkness of the Incarnation in preference to his life in the primordial light of God. Thus the Incarnation became the measure and the law for every kind of love in this world, and our love must form itself after that model.[1] While the Origenists conceived of the "experience of suffering" (πεῖρα) as the necessary way through the darkness of opposition, the way that first allows the divine light to shine on us as something eternally desirable, Maximus proposes a new kind of "experience of suffering": the experience of Christ, which certainly also leads the Christian who shares in it down the dark path of distance from God, but which does so in a different spirit.

> In this sense, it seems to me, he who is Lord by nature has honored obedience and has obtained experience of it through suffering: not simply to save and to preserve his own, by cleansing all of nature from wickedness, but also to find out for himself what it means for us to obey. He, who includes all knowledge in his very nature, learned through the bitter experience of our suffering what it is to be human, in order to know how much could be demanded of us and how far one must be lenient with respect to that perfect obedience, through which he habitually leads those who are predestined for salvation to the Father. . . . O great and truly awful mystery of our salvation! For just as much is asked of us as was asked of him, insofar as he was human by nature; but we are forgiven in the measure that he, by union, was human in a superhuman way.[2]

We are drawn, then, into the law of the Incarnation, yet without exhausting the full measure of Christ's experience.

---

[1] *Epistles* 44; PG 91, 644AC.
[2] *Ambigua*; PG 91, 1045AB.

Rather, our narrow measure is plunged into the overflowing measure of Christ, to the degree that we are the occasion and the place of God's Incarnation, as it continues to be realized in mystery through the course of time. For "God always wills to become human in those who are worthy."[3]

> God has become a beggar through his imploring condescension for our sakes, compassionately taking the vulnerability (πάθη) of each of us upon himself and *suffering in a mysterious way, because of his love, until the end of time*, according to the measure of the suffering of each individual.[4]

We find, then, that each side lovingly draws the other into its own suffering.

> Every individual who believes in Christ is nailed to the Cross with Christ, according to the measure of his own strength and the type and condition of his virtue; *at the same time, he nails Christ to the Cross with himself*, precisely in that he is crucified with Christ in a spiritual way.[5]

The Incarnation—put more sharply, this means the descent into suffering, the Cross, and the grave and the resurrection of the creature who has been burned out in death and so has become transparent for God—is thus the final form of the world, the one that reshapes all other natural forms. Everything takes its decisive meaning and its ultimate justification only from here.

> The mystery of the Incarnation of the Word contains in itself the force and meaning of all the challenging puzzles and symbols of Scripture, as well as the significant content of all visible and intelligible creatures. Whoever understands the mystery of the Cross and the grave has grasped the essential content (λόγος) of all the things we have mentioned; and whoever, in addition, has been initiated into the mysterious meaning and power of the Resurrection knows the primordial (προηγουμένως) purpose for which God created the universe.[6]

The mystery of supernatural life, far from being thrown over the world as something foreign and purely "historical", is rather something that

---

[3] *Quaestiones ad Thalassium* 22; CCG 7, 143, 103f.; PG 90, 321B.

[4] *Mystagogia* 24; PG 91, 713B.

[5] *Ambigua*; PG 91, 1360AB. Outside of Origen (see my *Parole et mystère chez Origène* [Paris, 1957], 130) and Pseudo-Macarius (see volume 1 of *The Glory of the Lord* [San Francisco, 1982]), this kind of mysticism of suffering, which reminds us of Pascal, does not exist in the East.

[6] *Centuries on Knowledge* 1, 66; PG 90, 1108AB.

involves and transforms all natural being down to its deepest foundations—as precisely the final, utterly decisive form of being must do.
The law of Christ, despite its historical character, is a cosmological
law. So Maximus can dare to express himself in sentences that perhaps summarize his doctrine of the Incarnation most deeply and most
boldly:

> Everything visible needs the cross—needs a condition that holds in check
> our appetite for the sensible things that the world itself has produced; but
> everything intelligible must descend into the grave—into the complete
> motionlessness of our intellectual response to the world. For if not only
> that sensible appetite but also our natural activity and stimulation in re-
> sponse to all things is eliminated, then the Word arises by himself alone,
> as if from the dead, and includes and possesses in himself everything that
> takes its origin from him, even though no single thing is related to him
> by natural connection or relationship. For it is by grace, not by nature,
> that the elect attain salvation.[7]

This mighty cosmological change of course, however—this transformation of all things from being "in themselves" by nature to being
in God by grace—like death itself, which is the inner content of the
change, only comes about at that pivotal point where grace and nature,
heaven and earth are in contact: in the hypostatic synthesis of God made
human. To enter into this synthesis and share in it, however, means
to "eliminate" nature in its pure state, with Christ and by his power,
and to transform what was only compulsion, punishment for sin, and
indeliberate passion into a free act, free suffering. For "what normally
moves our wills to make a decision, Christ has shown, in his own life,
to be set in motion by himself."[8] This transformation is what we have
traditionally called "mortification": "to change into a voluntary act of
virtue" what was one of the involuntary results of sin;[9] "freely chosen
death to self" and, thus, victory over death through the anticipation of
death;[10] "freely chosen acquiescence" in the extremes [of our suffer-
ing], in shame and mockery, and thus an inner freedom with respect to
the opposites that naturally affect us—blame and praise, poverty and
riches, friendship and enmity.[11] Love, humility, continence, patience

---

[7] Ibid., 1, 67; PG 90, 1108B.
[8] *Ambigua*; PG 91, 1053C.
[9] Ibid.; PG 91, 1373A.
[10] Ibid.; PG 91, 1157D.
[11] Ibid.; PG 91, 1205AB.

are all names for this single attitude,[12] through which nature "lays aside
its irrational motions" and "returns to the greatness and beauty of its
original condition".[13] In this death to self, however painful it may be,
one can already sense the freedom of the resurrection; in fact, it is
the mystical anticipation of the resurrection. And so Christian joy can
break forth in the midst of death:

> It seems to me that nothing prevents man from rejoicing in whatever
> he finds painful. For while he is sad at the troubles caused by virtuous
> living in the flesh, he rejoices in his soul because of that same virtue,
> because he sees, as something already present, the beauty and dignity of
> what is to come.[14]

In the end, Maximus praises a "voluntary poverty" in outward things[15]
and external obedience[16] as the best means to gain this inner freedom.

This death of the human person, however, is never an arbitrary act
of taking power into one's own hands to make oneself God; it all turns
on the hinge of the Incarnation. This is expressed in a great formula of
proportionality: the *tantum-quantum* of all salvation history, and so also
of individual perfection. We are under obligation, insofar as Christ is
human; we are set free, insofar as he is God. Here the "blessed con-
version" is realized,

> which makes God human through the divinization of man and makes
> man God through the humanization of God. For the divine Logos, who
> is God, wants to see the mystery of his Incarnation brought to realization
> constantly, and in all of us.[17]

> For we say that God and man have chosen each other as a model and that
> God has made himself human for man's sake precisely to the degree that
> man, empowered by love, lets himself be divinized for God's sake; and
> we say that man is taken up by God, in the Spirit, into realms beyond
> all conception,[18] to precisely the same degree as man allows God—who
> is by nature invisible—to appear through his own virtues.[19]

---

[12] Ibid.

[13] *Quaestiones ad Thalassium* 26; CCG 7, 185, 220ff.; PG 90, 349AB.

[14] Ibid., 58; CCG 22, 37, 160–63; PG 90, 597D–600A.

[15] *Opuscula*; PG 91, 69BC.

[16] Ibid.; PG 91, 452AB.

[17] *Ambigua*; PG 91, 1084CD.

[18] I read here "beyond conception", "unknowable" (ἄγνωστον) rather than "knowable"
(γνωστόν), since the sense of the passage requires it and the old Latin translation [of Scotus
Erigena] supports it.

[19] *Ambigua*; PG 91, 1113BC.

Man has become God to the degree that God has become man, for he [man] has been led by God, through the stages of divine ascent, into the highest regions to the same degree that God has descended down to the farthest reaches of our nature, by means of a man and through a destruction of his own self that nevertheless implies no change.[20]

That cosmic law of expansion and contraction, *diastolē* and *systolē*, which we mentioned earlier, is thus now translated into the terms of salvation history and receives here its final meaning: God gathers us all together into unity with himself, for his own sake, to precisely the same degree as he has spread himself out, for our sakes, in the law of his condescension.[21] Thus self-annihilation is a mutual process, yet it rests, by its very nature, on the utter priority of God's own self-emptying. Man "is changed into the Divinity through the destruction of his passionate susceptibilities, to the same degree that God's Logos willingly gave up his own sheer glory and in truly becoming man annihilated himself by entering the transforming process of salvation history."[22]

The almost geometrical precision of this motif, which continually reappears, is sufficient proof of how much the entire realization of our salvation turns on the hinge of the Incarnation. The openness of the supreme hypostatic will of Christ determines the tremendous equilibrium between God and the world, like the tongue on the balance of a scale. So we are not surprised to see the principle of this openness or "indifference", become—as ἀπάθεια, as inner freedom—the dominant factor in the whole spiritual fulfillment of man. This occurs not simply in the sense we have already described, as an entering into that stage of Christ's supreme freedom through a voluntary and loving process of dying to the things of the world; it also appears, more expressly, as a stage of indifference *beyond* the polarities of this world, which—although irreconcilably opposed in themselves—reveal from these distant heights, accessible only to love and freedom, an inner complementarity and reconciliation in Christ.

Indifference and continence, which in Christian Platonism carried strong overtones of flight from the world, thus receive another coloring here that is more world-affirming. By choosing to free himself from dependency on individual, limited creatures, and by making the ascent

---

[20] Ibid.; PG 91, 1385BC.
[21] Ibid.; PG 91, 1288A.
[22] *Exposition of the Lord's Prayer*, CCG 23, 32, 102–33, 106; PG 90, 877A.

for the sake of Christian love, the believer distances himself from all things; yet in the very process he also forces each individual creature to yield its internal, eternal meaning, which remained hidden so long as he regarded it from close by. Only now is it possible to distinguish the conditional from the unconditional, to survey the connections of conditions among themselves, to realize a synthesis of opposites. Indifference, for Maximus, is the highest possible degree of openness to the world, conceived in the terms of Eastern monastic self-denial; thus it is a way of making classical *apatheia* an instrument for the Pauline idea of overcoming the world by becoming "all things to all creatures". This domination of the world through *apatheia* is not an apostolic idea but a "Gnostic" one; it is wholly realized in the interior, invisible space of the soul. It is the reshaping of the world through loving knowledge, a way of making its supertemporal meaning available for the intelligent creature's one great sacrifice to God. It is the daily contribution of the Christian to the world's eschatological renewal and to the building of the heavenly Jerusalem, in which there is no longer a temple because God has become present everywhere, and God's overpowering brilliance outshines all created light as the sun outshines our own little candles of the night. This ideal of an active share in the transformation of the world into the new age is Maximus' highest, most positive conception of Christian action.

Here once again, Maximus can clearly be seen as a thinker standing between East and West. By elevating both the contemplative quest for freedom from desire, characteristic of Buddhism and Gnosticism, and the drive to construct a titanic synthesis, characteristic of Hegel, into Christian love, Maximus finds the "higher midpoint" for both approaches. Like the Buddha, he calls for an attitude toward creatures that has freed itself from self-seeking, from passion, from worldliness, but he interprets it in a Christian way as the love demanded by the Sermon on the Mount, a love like God the Father's for all creatures, both good and evil. Like the Buddha and Hegel, he calls for a power of the critical and synthetic intelligence that comes within a hair's breadth of pure idealism, but he situates it, too, within the sustaining power of love: more precisely, in the redeeming love of Christ, whose self-emptying indifference and conceptual openness are revealed to be—far more deeply than with Hegel or in the abstract quest for Nirvana—the almighty power that preserves the individual and personal by elevating it into the divine. This mighty fusion of Asia and Europe, which subjects all speculative power to the law of self-emptying revealed in the Incarnation, was achieved by Maximus in full consciousness of what he was doing; it allowed him, in a feat of ultimate daring, to surpass and so to overcome two opposed brands of pantheism—that of India and China, which dissolves all things in God, and that of Hegel, which constructs God out of all things. He can speak the language of both extremes at the same time, because the "higher midpoint" between both has become a real event for him: the unification of the cosmos in the God who has become human. He can speak quite expressly of a *construction of God* in Christ, in the sense that through the incorporation and initiation of the Christian into him, Christ (and, with Christ, God) is himself being built into reality;[23] on the other hand, he can speak of a *resolution of things* into God,[24] which does not mean their destruction so much as their absorption into the Sun that illuminates all things.[25]

One should not suppose that Maximus always, or even usually, develops his descriptions of the spiritual syntheses of the world expressly in terms of freedom from the vulnerabilities of the senses (*apatheia*). To assert this would be to try to systematize his thought beyond what is due, to do violence to its loose ends and fluid elements. Yet simply the fact that in all realms of created being he recognizes two ultimate areas of meaning, which do not behave simply as levels or degrees but also as two equally valuable, equally powerful poles in tension with each other, helps us to realize that we can approach their synthetic unity only through a position of indifference and distance—a position that allows us to suspend their limited opposition and to let them be elevated, at the same time, into a positive reconciliation. Such indifference, however, is in fact related to *apatheia*, even if that relationship remains unspoken; and *apatheia* can play the role in Maximus' thought that it does only because it conforms to the deepest structure of his thought.

The texture of the spiritual syntheses [Maximus envisages] is so manifold, so changeable, that it would be impossible and also pointless to

---

[23] Cf. the texts we have already cited: *Ambigua*; PG 91, 1288; *Exposition of the Lord's Prayer.* CCG 23, 32ff.; PG 90, 877A; also *Mystagogia* 5; PG 91, 676B ("Jesus . . . completed through me": Ἰησοῦν . . . συμπληρωθέντα δι᾽ ἐμοῦ, etc.), and *Centuries on Knowledge* 2, 25, on the state of "equality with Christ" ("isochristism").

[24] *Centuries on Knowledge* 2, 74; PG 90, 1160A.

[25] *Ambigua*; PG 91, 1156AB.

try to present all their interconnections. Here, as everywhere, Maximus plays a good deal with traditional patterns of thought, as if they
were established cadences and themes; his originality is not so much
in the content of his thought as in the personal élan, the rhythm, that
constantly recurs in his richly orchestrated symphonies. Our purpose
here can only be to emphasize, from all this rich complexity, the most
typical and frequent themes, which appear otherwise [in patristic lit-
erature] only in more or less modified forms.

There are four such themes. First, the subjective synthesis, which
unites the soul in itself, precisely in the inner tension of its powers. Secondly, the synthesis of objective revelation, in which natural and supernatural revelation come to form a single whole. Thirdly, the liturgical
synthesis, in which the two great responses of the world and mankind
to that revelation become one: sacramental liturgy and the theological
liturgy of our knowledge of God. And finally, the concluding subjective synthesis of knowledge and action.

After all of this, we will have to consider once again the question of
what synthesis is—or, to put the same thing another way, the question
of what transcendence is. In doing so, we shall attempt to clarify the
puzzling relationship between indifference and love; and we shall also
attempt to shed some light on the final critical moment of this theology
that stands between Eastern and Western thought.

2. The Synthesis of the Three Faculties

Let us be honest from the start: the first of these great syntheses is
the most difficult to explain, because it is the one most clearly and
emphatically under the influence of Origenistic and Evagrian thought.
It is constructed on the assumed equivalence of the intellectual and the
sensible worlds—or, to put it in psychological terms, of the balance
between sensation and thought. Yet it is clear from the beginning that
this balance can never be conceived in the sense of an equivalence of
value, considering how near to impossible it is ever to assume equal
value between soul and body in a conception of the universe that is
under the influence of Platonic and Aristotelian thought. The most
one can expect is a sense for the insufficiency of pure thought, and for
the dependency of thought on the sensible world, that goes beyond
both Origen and Evagrius.

The foundation for such a view was already laid in that great law of "reflecting realities" expressed in the *Mystagogia*, according to which whole and part, idea and individual, ultimately the whole intelligible world and the whole sensible world, are formed in each other and with relation to each other.

> For the totality of the intellectual world appears mysteriously in sensible forms, expressed through the whole sensible world, to those who have the gift of sight; and the whole sensible world dwells within the intellectual, simplified by the mind into its meanings by the formative process of wisdom. . . . For the ability to contemplate intellectual realities through sensible ones, by analogy, is at once intellectual insight and a way of understanding the visible world by means of the invisible. It is necessary, surely, that both of these realms—which are ultimately there in order to reveal each other—should possess a true and unmistakable impression of each other and an indestructible relationship to each other.[26]

This paragraph, which recalls for us the metaphysics of the whole and the part, would be enough in itself to purge Maximus of any reputation of unworldly spiritualism. Precisely as a mystic, he understands the limitations of pure thought, which of its own power embraces its object only through abstract concepts, not on the basis of experience. Origen and his disciples, of course, and later Gregory of Nyssa, Pseudo-Macarius, and Diadochus of Photike, spoke of an intellectual and spiritual brand of sensibility[27] that was needed in order to enliven the poverty of abstract thought and bring it to full flower, through experiential contact with an intelligible or mystical object. In Platonic thinking, this "divine sensibility" remained ambiguous: one might conceive these "senses" more as fallen intellectual intuition, alienated from itself—so especially the homilies of Pseudo-Macarius—or one might interpret them as standing in irreconcilable opposition to intellectual knowledge. Both approaches to understanding the world can be found in Origen, who understands the "spiritual senses," on the one hand, as the ("normal") development of a living faith, but who considers spiritual and physical senses, on the other hand, as irreconcilable: where the spiritual eye is open, the physical eye must close.

Maximus speaks positively, first of all, in a traditional way—like Macarius and Diadochus—of the "spiritual senses": if a person has

---

[26] *Mystagogia*; PG 91, 669CD.
[27] Cf. *The Glory of the Lord*, vol. 1.

them, he "realizes" in an experiential way the mystical content of the
liturgy,[28] the true meaning of Jesus' gift of himself in the Eucharist[29]
—not by exaggerating the external liturgy, but through a concurrent
"divine perception" (αἴσηθσις θεῖα) that is aware of the intelligible content *in* the symbolic ceremony.[30] This is true, even if later the liturgical
act of shutting the doors is interpreted as the closing of the senses,
insofar as they are open to distraction from without.

A certain countercurrent to such thinking is set in motion by Pseudo-
Dionysius; for this "higher sensibility" (αἰσθάνεσθαι ὑπὲρ αἴσθησιν)[31]
cannot simply be a further development of intellectual thought as such.
The notion of transcendence formed in the school of Pseudo-Dionysius
can only conceive of the ultimate reality, and our experience of it, as lying beyond all this world's tensions, even the tension of sense and mind.
Both phenomena and noumena need the "cross" and the "grave";[32] the
mind no less than the senses must let go of all natural operations and
all stimulation from within. The ultimate "experience" (πεῖρα), then,
is beyond both intellect and senses; but for that very reason both of
them offer a positive, if insufficient, analogy for transcendental reality.
Indeed, sense knowledge can even seem, for a moment, to be nearer
the truth:

> The direct experience of something puts an end to the concept that in-
> tends it; the perception of the same thing makes further reflection about
> it pointless. I call experience, however, fully realized knowledge itself,
> which becomes real when all conceiving has come to an end; but per-
> ception is the very participation in the known object that is revealed to
> us only when all thinking has come to an end.[33]

Experience and perception, here, are contrasted with conception and
thought; the latter two have a reference (σχέσις) to, and so also an
express distance from, the object on which they are based, while the
former suggest a realized participation (μέθεξις κατ᾽ ἐνεργείαν).

The one kind of knowledge, which depends on concepts and thought,
has the power to awaken a longing for knowledge that is fully realized

[28] *Mystagogia*; PG 91, 704A.
[29] *Quaestiones ad Thalassium* 36; CCG 7, 243, 30–245, 44; PG 90, 381B.
[30] *Mystagogia*; PG 91, 700B.
[31] *Centuries on Knowledge* 2, 74: PG 90, 1160A.
[32] Ibid., 1, 67; PG 90, 1108B.
[33] *Quaestiones ad Thalassium* 60; CCG 22, 77, 84–90; PG 90, 624A.

in participation; the other, fully realized kind, which makes possible an awareness of what is known through an experiential sharing in it, eliminates the knowledge that relies on concepts and thought.[34]

In this connectedness of thought and experience—even if the notion here refers first of all to the transcendent experience of God and not sense experience—lies the dependence of all thought on a fundamental contact with reality.[35]

---

[34] Ibid.; CCG 22, 77, 71–76; PG 90, 621D.

[35] John of Scythopolis' scholia on Pseudo-Dionysius sketch out an interesting metaphysic of the thinking mind, which moves in a similar pattern: "If the mind wishes to think, it descends below itself, down into individual thoughts. For thoughts are below the one who thinks them, precisely in that they are thought and bounded [by the mind] and are clearly a scattering and division of the mind itself. For the mind as such is simple and without parts, but thoughts are countless and disorganized and are forms, as it were, of the mind. The unification of the mind, however, is called . . . the movement by which it raises itself up to what lies above it; [this occurs] when it concerns itself with contemplating God, by leaving behind all sensible and intellectual reality, and even its own movement, in a process of ecstasy" (In De Div. Nom. 7; PG 4, 344A). At first sight, these words seem self-contradictory. For at first thoughts are presented as "below" the mind, then the mind—in its discursive role—is considered as standing below its object. For the moment, it may be enough simply to read on. John says of pure spirits that they do not think discursively, as we do. But our mind "descends down into such considerations, [beginning] from divided [things], that is, from elements of knowledge derived from the sensible world and pointing us beyond themselves (διεξοδικοί)". The mind of pure spirits, however, "collects thoughts of particular species and of what is multiple—that is, of material things—in an immaterial way, and considers all of them in simplicity" (ibid.; PG 4, 344D–345A). In this way, human thought corresponds to a descent and an ascent. The mind, which in itself is pure unity, does not know of itself but needs to go out of itself in order to know and to descend below itself in order to gather experience in the sensible realm. On the other hand, this abstract unity of the beginning stage is itself described as a distinction (from its object) (ibid.; PG 4, 396A); thus the departure of the subject from itself is also a departure "from multiplicity", [a movement] that is capable of directing itself, along the circuitous ways of assimilating the "multiple" world, toward an experience that is above logic. As a middle path between two kinds of experience, thinking is itself a *way*, a means of transition; the twofold movement of descent and ascent is simply the twofold aspect of a single reality. "For the mind, which descends into reflection, is in a way divided and needs to undertake a process of consideration that moves through many analogies in order to represent [to itself] what is thought . . . , for it is characteristic of the soul to ascend above what is foreign to it" (ibid., 4; PG 4, 257BC). It is the circular movement of the mind: "In knowing, the mind turns back on itself, no longer scattered outside itself, but united with itself through precisely that by which it turns and returns to itself"—i.e., through its object (ibid., 7; PG 4, 396A). In this circular pattern of thinking, the human soul imitates the intuitive gaze and unity of the perfect spirit. "To a certain extent, their souls are made worthy and imitate the angels in this; if they pack together their thought of manifold things into unity, then they possess all things together in unity, yet unconfusedly

Non-experiential knowledge of God—knowledge that contemplates God in the mirror of his creatures—has as its overall purpose to awake in us a desire for mystical participation;[36] but it is also designed to purify the soul in a positive way and to prepare it for the transcendental experience and contact that imply "the elimination of all [intellectual] activity bound to matter, both sense perception and intellectual judgment".[37]

On the other hand, the facts force us to put intellectual knowledge closer to mystical experience than sense knowledge is. By emphasizing this superiority, one necessarily draws closer to the pattern of ascent: from body to mind to God. This corresponds to that simplest of Platonic conceptual structures, which dominates the whole picture of the world in Origen and Augustine: body below soul, soul below God. Or, put more boldly: what the soul is for the body, God is for the soul. Maximus considers this double relationship of subordination to be simply a given of nature.[38] Yet his consciousness of God's ever-greater transcendence, beyond all our efforts to know, cuts directly across this pattern of ascent; and with that consciousness stands the insight that neither sense nor mind is even remotely capable of the highest degree of knowledge. The mind is so far from being even latently divine that its own activity veils the reality of God more than it reveals it. "The knowledge of things does not reveal the unknowable reality of God, nor does it pave the way for its appearance; rather, it seriously conceals and obscures it."[39]

From this perspective, Maximus occasionally praises the intellectual side of transcendental experience at the expense of the "sensible" or intuitive;[40] at other times—less frequently—he praises the higher "sensibilities" at the expense of discursive thought.[41] Both are able to point only indirectly at the transcendent vision of God. A further and very

---

distinct from each other" (ibid.; PG 4, 345C). So thought and sensation have a similar role in this circular movement. "The circular motion in the Good is eternal: moving out of itself to the intellectual and sensible, and turning again toward itself, without ever standing still or ceasing altogether" (ibid., 4; PG 4, 268B).

[36] *Quaestiones ad Thalassium* 60; CCG 22, 77; PG 90, 621D–624A.

[37] *In De Div. Nom.* 1; PG 4, 204C.

[38] *Centuries on Love* 1, 83; PG 90, 1009CD.

[39] *In Myst. Theol.* 2; PG 4, 424C; cf. John of Scythopolis on *De Div. Nom.* 1; PG 4, 210C.

[40] *Liber asceticus* 24; PG 90, 929C; *Quaest. ad Thalassium* 47; CCG 7, 313; PG 90, 421C; *Ambigua*; PG 91, 1145C, 1300A, etc.

[41] *Quaestiones ad Thalassium* 60; CCG 22, 77; PG 90, 621D–624A.

clear sign of this is the paradox that this vision involves at once the ultimate activation of the human mind, namely, its immediate participation in its object, and also its ultimate passivity with respect to the Transcendent, what is sometimes called "undergoing the divine" (παθεῖν τὰ θεῖα). The *Disputation with Pyrrhus* led to this insight as its conclusion: the human nature of Christ is not, according to Maximus, purely "passive", simply because it is wholly under God's power and Lordship; God's activity makes itself felt precisely in and through autonomous natures.[42] But even this activity of the created realm, which Maximus draws from dogmatic Christology (not from mystical theology), is an expression of the unconfused distance between the divine and the human, even in the highest degree of union: a distance such as Pseudo-Dionysius' conception of "passive" ecstasy, on the other hand, presupposes. In this twofold sense Maximus corrects the Evagrian conception of mystical union, which endangers both the basic structure of analogy and the ever-increasing distance between God and the creature.

Ultimately, the mystical ascent of the soul is realized and anticipated, in Maximus' thought, by the great syntheses of Christ himself. As we have seen, these first bring together [the extremes of] the natural world within man, then unite earth with Paradise, heaven with earth, and ultimately everything intelligible and spiritual with sensible and material reality. It is only this total world, knit together from opposition and in opposition, that is united with God himself.[43] Even if the divine pole is, in the final synthesis, endlessly superior, still the whole sensible and intellectual world is part of that synthesis, without any omissions. A hint of this can be found in the doctrine we have already mentioned, that the soul remains just as intrinsically oriented toward its body, even after death, as the body is toward it and that therefore the final perfection of knowledge and experience can be expected only when the whole range of sensible and intellectual capacities is restored.

To anticipate this total condition, in which the complete transcendence of the mind toward God is united with the complete synthesis of the tensions of life in the world, is Maximus' idea of human perfection. There are, Maximus says in one passage, "three basic movements of the soul": intelligence (νοῦς), discursive reason (λόγος), and sense

---

[42] *Disputation with Pyrrhus*: PG 91, 349C–352B.
[43] *Ambigua*; PG 91, 1306–9.

perception (αἴσθησις).[44] The first of these is described as the place of pure encounter with the God who is beyond the world; the second, as the capacity to recognize the unknown God from his works as their cause, through acquainting oneself with their meanings and making them one's own; the third, finally, as the point of contact with external things, from which our senses extract these meanings by a kind of analogy. The perfect person, then, is able "to connect sensation with intelligence through the mediation of reason", and so to include the contents of sensation in the mind's own supreme unity. But this elevation into unity does not at all mean that the sensible disappears in the process; rather, the natural multiplicity and universality of the human essence finds its perfection there. "For [since the saints] received a soul from God that included in itself intelligence, reason, and sensation, . . . they considered it as obvious that they were not to use these capacities for themselves but for the God who gave them, through whom and from whom all things came to be." This "turning toward God" of every single capacity, however, produces automatically that hierarchical order that connects the three powers together like a chain held from above. This sense of hanging "from above", in fact—rather than being overwhelmed by the transitory and limited multiplicity of the world —is the decisive meaning of "spiritualization" and of turning to God. So the world of human capabilities develops with new vigor, but now in the direction of grace's descent to nature:

> The intelligence busies itself with God alone and with his excellences; . . . reason is the interpreter of these things intelligence comes to know, sings their praises, and reflects on the ways that lead to them through a process of unification; the senses, finally, ennobled by the action of reason, reflect back the powers and activities scattered throughout all creation and announce, as far as is possible, the meanings of things to the soul.

This world, newly unfolding from above and brought into its final order—a world that has risen again, divine in form, from the mystical death of sensible and the mystical burial of intellectual things—is the

---

[44] For what follows, see ibid.; PG 91, 1112D–1116D. The translation of λόγος by "reason" (in more or less the Kantian sense) seems justified here by the context. In other places—for example, in the *Mystagogia*—λόγος has the special meaning of "practical reason", in contrast with γνῶσις as "theoretical reason". Since all these distinctions are fluid in Maximus, it is always the context that must give the decisive interpretation of the meaning.

eternal sacrifice offered by the created intellect to God. This is the way the circular movement of the cosmos ultimately comes to be reconciled with its repose in the Absolute, so that both motion and rest form a single, "identical, endless, motionless movement around God".[45]

3. The Synthesis of the Three Laws

a. Nature and Scripture Grounded in Christ

Until now, we have been considering the unification of the world's polarities in its subjective aspect, as the tension and interpenetration of sensibility and intelligence. But this approach must be supplemented by the synthesis of the objective modes of God's appearing in the world: in nature and in history. Maximus emphasized and developed this synthesis with particular care and reveals here in unparalleled depth his breadth of spirit, open to everything that is meaningful and beautiful. Far from offering a theology and a mysticism alienated from the world, he rediscovers here the tradition of genuine Hellenic humanism.

At the most general level, there are three sets of laws in the world. "By general laws, I understand the law of nature, the written law, and the law of grace."[46] The first is engraved in nature—not simply in the human soul, but in the whole cosmos and in every one of its parts. Through the contemplation of nature ($\theta \epsilon \omega \varrho i \alpha \ \phi \upsilon \sigma \iota \varkappa \acute{\eta}$), the wise person acquires a natural knowledge of God, of his righteousness, wisdom, and goodness, and this knowledge is in the true sense a kind of "vision", a "contemplation". While this first law seems to be expressed, one might say, in the "body" of creation, the second, written law regulates —even grounds, so to speak—its "mind". It contains the documentation of God's history with the human race: in a certain sense the pure and abstract norm for the creature's intellectual and spiritual behavior.

Now this contrast, derived from Paul himself, is current in all of patristic literature; it belongs, certainly, to the basic principles of both the Origenist and the Augustinian views of the world. Once again, however, Maximus' distinction lies in the fact that he does not simply set the written law above the natural, as those two thinkers do, or consider it as a second, intermediate step between nature and the

---

[45] Mystagogia 19; PG 91, 696C.
[46] Quaestiones ad Thalassium 64; CCG 22, 233, 732f.; PG 90, 724C.

revelation of Christ; rather, he presents the natural law and the scrip-tural law, revelation in nature and revelation in history, as a tension between poles of equal value that mutually complement each other. The third law, which Christ gives and embodies, brings both of them to fulfillment and final unity, in that it simultaneously removes the limitations of both.

Insofar as the first two laws are to be taken as preludes to the law of Christ, one may speak of a triple embodiment of the Logos.

> That the Logos becomes concrete and takes on a body . . . can be under-stood as meaning, first of all, that he who is simple in his own essence and without body, who nourishes the divine powers in heaven in a spir-itual way corresponding to each of their ranks, has deigned to take on concrete bodily form by coming in the flesh . . . and to open up for us, appropriately, in ringing words and parables, a knowledge of hidden, holy things that surpasses all power of words to express. . . . Secondly, we can understand it as meaning that he has wrapped and hidden himself mysteriously, for our sakes, in the essence of things and can be spelled out analogously from every visible thing as if from letters—as a whole, in his fullness, from the whole of nature, and undiminished in each part; . . . in the varieties [of nature], as one who has no variation and is always the same; in composites, as one who is simple, without parts; in things that at some time must begin, as the one without beginning; the invisible in the visible, the ungraspable in tangible things. Finally, we can understand it as meaning that he also willed to incorporate himself in letters and deigned to be expressed in syllables and sounds for our sake, since we are slow of intelligence. The purpose of all of this is to draw us after him and to gather us together in his presence within a short space of time, having become one in spirit.[47]

In the fullness of these three embodiments, Christ, the Logos, is the unique and universal law of creation; he is the world's judge, to whom God has handed over all judgment. He is

> present to all things from within, . . . whether through nature or posi-tive law or grace. . . . For the Logos of God is the Creator of all nature, every law, every bond, all order; he is the judge of all things that have a nature and a law and relationships and order, and without promulga-tion by the Word there is no law. So if someone is judged within the law,

---

[47] *Ambigua*; PG 91, 1285C–1288A.

he is judged at the same time in Christ; if he is judged outside the law, nevertheless, he is judged in Christ. . . . In Christ, then, . . . the natural law, the law of Scripture, and the law of grace all come together as one.[48]

This comes about expressly through the fact that the first two laws are proved equally valuable in the third.

> If he will walk the straight road to God without error, man, I say, stands in absolute need of both the following things: insight into Scripture, through the Spirit, and a natural contemplation of things that conforms to the Spirit. So anyone who desires to become a perfect lover of perfect wisdom will easily be able to show that both laws are of equal value and equal dignity, that both of them teach the same things in complementary ways, and that neither has any advantage over the other or stands in the other's shadow.[49]

In the one image of the Transfiguration of Christ, his radiant face refers to the law of grace, which is no longer veiled in any way; the transformed, shining robes, however, refer at once to the letter [of Scripture] and to nature, both of which have become bright and translucent in grace.[50]

The relation of simultaneous immanence and transcendence between the law of grace and those of nature and Scripture is something so fluid that it can only be conceived, one might say, in movement or in transition. First of all, it is impossible to conceive of it as remaining on the level of the first two laws, since the third has been revealed as the fulfillment of their meaning. And every attempt to "prescind" from a synthesis with them is in itself a positive rejection.

> Pilate is the type of the natural law; the crowd of Jews, [that] of the law of Scripture. If someone has not raised himself above both laws through faith, he will be unable to perceive the truth that lies beyond nature and words but will crucify the Logos himself, by regarding [the Gospel] as a scandal, like a Jew, and as foolishness, like a Greek.[51]

> Whoever lives his life in Christ has moved beyond the righteousness of both the positive law and the law of nature, as the divine Apostle suggests in his words, In Christ there is neither circumcision nor uncircumcision;

---

[48] *Quaestiones ad Thalassium* 19; CCG 7, 119, 18–30; PG 90, 308BC.
[49] *Ambigua*; PG 91, 1128CD.
[50] Ibid.; PG 91, 1128AB; 1160CD.
[51] *Centuries on Knowledge* I, 71; PG 90, 1109AB.

by circumcision here he means to signify the righteousness of the law;
by uncircumcision, natural rightness.[52]

Attitudes that cling simply to the verbal meaning of Scripture, like those
passionate ways of looking at the visible world that cling to sensible
reality, are both truly scales on the eyes of the soul, preventing it from
moving on to the precise word of truth.[53]

But the very possibility of a spiritual, and thus of a fully adequate, fulfillment of the laws of nature and Scripture suggests already the presence of a higher, spiritual law, hidden within them and revealed, at
the same time, in their observance. For the meaning of every single
natural thing (λόγος τῶν ὄντων) and the meaning of every positive law
and commandment (λόγος τῶν ἐντολῶν) is, as we have seen, an incarnation of the one divine Logos; its pure fulfillment, therefore, is at the
same time a realization of one's own nature, of one's own law, and a
realization of the Logos in the world.

If we are willing to see "history", the temporal order of salvation, reflected in Moses and "nature", the cosmic order of salvation, reflected
in Elijah, then their appearance alongside the transfigured Christ on
Tabor has a precise significance. For they show "that all things that are
under God and that came to be from God—namely, the nature of things
and time—come into our view as beings alongside God when God
truly appears (insofar as he *can* appear) as their cause and author".[54] But
this appearing is, at the same time, a disappearing, a being-dissolved in
Christ, as Origen suggested in his interpretation (not repeated by Maximus) of the detail that when the disciples lifted their eyes again, Jesus
stood before them alone. Maximus himself developed this interplay of
revealing and concealing in a paragraph of the most daring speculation:

Both laws revealed and concealed the same Word at the same time. . . .
For just as when we call the words of Holy Scripture the garments [of
Christ], but think of their meaning as [Christ's] body, and so conceal him
with the former and reveal him with the latter, so also, if we designate
the forms and shapes of the things we visually imagine as garments, but
think of the intelligible identity according to which they were created
as flesh, we again conceal with the one and reveal with the other. For

---

[52] Ibid., 2, 62; PG 90, 1152BC.
[53] Ibid. 2, 74–75; PG 90, 1160BC.
[54] *Ambigua*; PG 91, 1164A.

the Creator and lawgiver of all things, invisible by nature, is concealed whenever he appears and appears whenever he is concealed.

When he appears, he must appear in some kind of appearance (φαινό-μενος); but every appearance conceals what is essential. Far better, then, "to bring what is hidden to appearance by *dissolution* [*Aufhebung*]", in that we pass by all merely symbolic images and "are borne upward, away from letters and externally appearing things, to the Word him-self—better this, than that we transform this self-manifesting [Word], through our concrete *affirmation* [*Setzung*], into something that conceals itself"! Otherwise, we might become "murderers of the Logos", ei-ther "in the manner of the Greeks, who served and reverenced creation and neglected the Creator", or "in the manner of the Jews, who only looked at the letter and so exaggerated the meaning of bodily reality". "For the letter, when loved for its own sake, tends to kill, in the lover's mind, the word of meaning hidden within it; so the beauty of created things, if it does not lead the mind to praise the Creator, tends to rob the beholder of intellectual reverence."[55]

In this double relation of transcendence, both laws are equal, even "identical with each other in their mutual relationship: the written law is identical with the natural, insofar as it includes the natural so far as possible, and the natural with the written, insofar as it creates the at-titude that enables one to accept the written."[56]

> The natural law is identical with the written law, if it is wisely translated into a variety of concrete symbols in the realm of action; on the other hand, the written law is identical with the natural, if it is conceived in a simple, unitary way by holy people through virtue and wisdom in word and understanding and so loses its metaphorical quality. The holy people mentioned in the law are an example of this: the Spirit drew away the covering of letters like a veil, and they found themselves in possession of a natural law that had itself become spiritual.[57]

One penetrates to the fruit within only if one does not linger stub-bornly over the skin; if one wants to grasp the "body", one must nec-essarily let go of the "garments". The Word himself, after all, said, " 'Is not the soul worth more than food, and the body more than its clothing?' Otherwise, we will suffer the same disappointment as the

---

[55] Ibid.; PG 91, 1129A–1132A.
[56] Ibid.; PG 91, 1129B.
[57] Ibid.; PG 91, 1152A.

Egyptian woman who was consumed with passion for Joseph but could only grasp hold of his clothing", which he left in her hand as he fled. For if we do not "touch the Logos with the blessed groping of the spirit", but wish to lay hold of his visible body, we must hear the same warning as Mary Magdalen, "Do not cling to me."[58] "The Lord flees from the touch of such a person, for his own good, since in him he cannot yet ascend to the Father."[59]

> If one wishes to seek God reverently, one must be careful not to let oneself be bound by any external word, so as not to lay hold unwittingly on what surrounds God, rather than God himself, . . . while the Logos slips away from the spirit, which had hoped to seize him along with his garments.[60]

> In those who interpret the Word of God in simply a fleshly way, the Lord does not ascend to the Father. In those, however, who seek him in the spirit, by contemplating exalted thoughts, he does ascend to the Father. He descended to earth for us out of his goodness; let us not hold him here below by force, but let us ascend along with him to the Father on high.[61]

We must "not prevent him from leaving the world once again, in a mysterious way, and returning to the Father".[62] For if it is true of the whole world of appearances that "All things grow old, as a garment" (Ps 102:26), then we must let the whole world go its own way, before its eternal transformation becomes possible, according to the other words of Scripture, "Like a garment you change them, and they will be changed" (Ps 102:26).[63]

Through nature and through Scripture alike, our task is to "reach out for the Spirit". This "reaching" means neither holding nor letting go, but a yearning quest and a hesitant touching of what we seek.

> The characteristic feature of one who is groping for something is the ability to make distinctions. So anyone who goes through the symbols of the written law with a spiritual sense and considers the external, natural

---

[58] Ibid.; PG 91, 1132B–D.

[59] *Centuries on Knowledge* 2, 45; PG 90, 1145A. Cf. *Quaestiones ad Theopemptum*; PG 90, 1400BD.

[60] *Centuries on Knowledge* 2, 73; PG 90, 1157C.

[61] Ibid., 2, 47; PG 90, 1145B.

[62] Ibid., 2, 94; PG 90, 1169B.

[63] *Ambigua*; PG 91, 1132D–1133A.

appearance of things with insight; anyone who can make the necessary distinctions with regard to Scripture, nature, and himself—discerning in Scripture the letter from the spirit, in creation meaning from appearance, in himself reason from sense—and who can lift the spirit out of Scripture, meaning out of creation, and reason out of his own consciousness and then bind them inseparably with each other: such a person has found God![64]

b. Relation between Natural and Biblical Law

Until now, we have mainly considered the presence of the third, synthetic law from the viewpoint of the dissolution of the two inner-worldly laws. Yet we have already seen that the revelation of the third brings the first two to a mutual interpenetration within their own dynamic trajectories of meaning and so fulfills their potential. It is time now to develop this perspective and so to come closer to the meaning of both natural and positive law in themselves.

First, we must consider the relationships between the natural law and the Scriptural law. The most striking thing here is the place accorded to the natural law. We are far from Augustine, even from Origen; the dominant mood here is a Hellenic—more exactly, a Stoic—confidence in nature, such as one finds most readily in Basil or Gregory of Nyssa. And one must not forget that none of these Fathers, including Maximus, imagines *physis* (φύσις, nature) and *nomos* (νόμος, law, Scripture) as contrasting with each other along the lines of a natural and a supernatural order of creation. Even if *nomos* stands first of all for Old Testament revelation and *physis* for what has been revealed to the whole human race, putting even the pagans under a law, the contrast here—if one must use modern categories—is at best that between a predominance of the supernatural, on the one side, and of the natural, on the other. (In this way of thinking, Maximus occasionally draws an oversimplified contrast between the "law of nature" and the "law of the Spirit",[65] and opposes the natural law as "literal sense and appearance" to the law of Scripture as "secret meaning".)[66] In general, however, the two are rather related as the law of being, both natural and supernatural, to positive law and, in the most general sense, as

---

[64] *Quaestiones ad Thalassium* 32; CCG 7, 225, 17–24; PG 90, 372CD; cf. ibid., 39; CCG 7, 261; PG 90, 393AB; *Mystagogia* 7; PG 91, 685D–688A.

[65] *Quaestiones ad Thalassium* 63; CCG 22, 171, 401–3; PG 90, 681BC.

[66] *Ambigua*; PG 91, 1129B.

God's twofold revelation in the world and in history.[67] And it is quite clear from Maximus' whole treatment that even the contemplation of nature (θεωρία φυσική) can be genuinely and fruitfully carried out only in the light of grace.

Maximus describes the core of both laws as follows: the natural law, engraved in the hearts of all men and women, forces us to recognize the unity of human nature in all individuals, to reverse the fragmentation and alienation of men that has its origin in sin, and to see spontaneously in each person a member of the same human family. Identity of nature demands identity of conduct and constitution, including in turn a deep-seated concord in habits and way of life. This, in turn, ultimately leads the human mind and consciousness to make a natural translation of this natural bond of union into a freely chosen unity and agreement ("bringing everyone, in one attitude of mind, to one intelligible form of nature" [κατὰ μίαν τὴν γνώμην ἄγων τοὺς πάντας πρὸς τὸν ἕνα λόγον τῆς φύσεως]). Love of self, in the divisive sense—φιλαυτία—is thus founded not on nature but on sin; it conceals and hinders the law of nature. The saying of the Lord, "Whatever you want people to do to you, do it similarly to them", expresses the most general law of nature: a benevolent righteousness.

On the other hand, the written law is, in its most fundamental sense, a law of fear and, so, a law of obedience demanded from above; it restrains self-interest through a thoroughly ideal order of righteousness, but it also gradually impresses a sense for what is right on nature, through this strict training, and with such an instinct for what is appropriate gently leads it—step by step—from fear to love, which is "the fullness of the law". So love incorporates the natural law, but on a higher level. The natural law is the realization of the natural meaning of being (λόγος φυσικός), which has taken our sensible faculties under its control through moral training, in order to remove the irrational impulses that divide beings that are naturally tied together.

The written law, or rather the fullness of the written law, is the realization of the natural meaning of being, accompanied by a new spiritual motivation for action: care and support for our fellow members of the human race. So it says, You should love your neighbor as yourself, and not simply Behave toward your neighbor as toward yourself. The first

---

[67] This becomes clear when Moses is allied with "time", Elijah with "nature": ibid.; PG 91, 1164A–D.

rests on simple communality of being with the other members of our race, the second on concern for their spiritual welfare.[68]

Nevertheless, once Maximus has expressed this superiority of the positive law over the natural law, he seems to reject nothing *more strongly* than "Jewish" narrow-mindedness, which can also reappear, from time to time, in the Church of Christ and which,

> through its adherence to the mere letter of the law, does not hesitate to despise or to manipulate natural laws and implications. For no one who is satisfied with an exclusively bodily observance of the law can realize, at the same time, the meaning and intellectual demands of nature, since signs and symbols cannot be identical with being itself.[69]

For this reason, "the law, taken in a purely material sense, is reprehensible; the Jew is a fanatic if he thinks he can honor God in a purely material way."[70]

> If we consider things spiritually, it will become obvious that by means of the contemplation of nature on the high plane of wisdom, the written law is completely abolished, in the sense of a material connection of the service of God to signs and symbols. Where should we look for the circumcision of the flesh, then, if the law is understood spiritually? Where are the Sabbaths and the new moons? . . . For if we consider things from the standpoint of nature, we recognize that perfection cannot consist in the elimination of that pristine quality of nature, which comes, after all, from God. It is not an artificially disfigured nature that can bring about perfection; . . . let us not consider some human procedure as more effective than God himself in sealing our righteousness.[71]

> It is not because God willed that men should venerate particular days that he included among his commandments that they should honor the Sabbath itself and the new moons and feasts. Otherwise he would be encouraging us, in his commandments, to honor the creature instead of the Creator; days would then necessarily appear as naturally holy and, so, worthy of adoration. Rather, he wanted to teach us in this commandment that he himself is to be honored, in the sign and image of days. For he himself is the Sabbath, in that he is the life-giving rest of the soul

---

[68] *Quaestiones ad Thalassium* 64; CCG 22, 235, 768–76; PG 90, 724C–725B, supplemented by 725D.

[69] Ibid., 75; CCG 22, 259, 155–261, 160; PG 90, 741D–744A.

[70] Ibid.; CCG 22, 305, 827–829; PG 90, 772B.

[71] Ibid.; CCG 22, 277, 443–279, 459; PG 90, 756AB.

after the labors of the flesh and its restorative power in the struggles for righteousness. He himself is the Pasch, as the one who frees those who languish in the bitter chains of sin. He is himself Pentecost, as the beginning and end of all things, as the Logos, in whom all things are naturally grounded.[72]

Let us not focus here on the questionable element, the apparent abolition of all ritual symbolism; it is obvious that Maximus is thinking only of the external liturgies of Jewish observance and not of the rites of the New Covenant, which in fact he expressly defends and retains in his *Mystagogy*. The point here is the typically intermediate position of the "contemplation of nature", and of the assimilation and fulfillment of its law, between the positive law of Scripture and the law of grace. "The contemplation of nature stands in the midpoint between signs and truth." Its role is "to reveal the wisdom hidden, in a mysterious way, in the letter".[73] This "mediation of natural contemplation" through the spiritualization of matter is nothing else than the means given by God to man for "seeing essences", for "abstracting" meaning out of signs—the capacity of internalizing the external, of seeing what is scattered as a unity. There is no other way to move from the letter to the spirit:

> For if someone should want . . . to move directly toward the beauty of intelligible things, according to the Spirit, without having recognized beforehand, in a natural way, the dissimilarity of signs and symbols with the divine and intelligible realm, he would not be able at all to extricate himself from the dazzling variety of bodily things in the world of images.[74]

In other words, the essential "spiritualization" is just as much a process of nature as a gift of grace. "Everyone who does not recognize the spiritual meaning of the Holy Scriptures holds the natural law in contempt, on the one hand, as the Jews did, and misconceives the law of grace, on the other."[75] An incident in the Scriptures teaches us this same point: King Saul, symbol of the positive law, has sinned; but the punishment for his sin, a famine, will affect the land only after his death. What does this mean?

---

[72] Ibid.; CCG 22, 283, 502–13; PG 90, 757BC.
[73] Ibid.; CCG 22, 273, 373–75; PG 90, 752A.
[74] Ibid.; CCG 22, 271, 343–49; PG 90, 749C.
[75] Ibid.; CCG 22, 265, 247–67, 250; PG 90, 745D.

As long as the time of fleshly service of the law continues, the lack of spiritual wisdom is not felt; that only happens at the time of the gospel of grace. If, then, after the kingdom of the letter has passed, we do not understand all of Scripture in a spiritual way, we must necessarily suffer hunger, because we are not being nourished in the Spirit by the mystical ministry that alone is appropriate for Christians. But if, following David's example, we become reasonable and seek the face of the Lord, it will be clear to us that we have lost the grace of wisdom because we have not used the natural meanings contained in things in order to ascend in spirit to a mystical vision, but remain bound by the merely bodily viewpoint of the letter of the law.[76]

A final perspective fills out what we have just said: Christ and the law of grace imply the recapitulation of the holiness of all people— even of those who lived in a way pleasing to God before the law of the Old Covenant. They knew "God only from worldly creation", and from their understanding of his providence lived virtuous lives. So "they always naturally anticipated the written law within themselves, in a spiritual way", and can be held up as an example to those who live under the written law.[77] Here again, "nature" is given equal rank with "the law".

c. The Essential Points of Tension

After this description of the mutual relationship of "nature" and the positive "law", our task now is to look more deeply at the essence of both poles in the tension. From what has been said, one might guess that the pole "nature"—not so much in its practical, ethical aspect as the "natural law" (νόμος τῆς φύσεως), but in its theoretical role as "natural contemplation" (θεωρία φυσική)—enjoys a noticeably more positive estimation with Maximus than does "the law" in its strict sense. This has its roots and reasons in the predominantly cosmological, rather than historical, view of the way to salvation that generally characterizes Greek patristic theology, except for Irenaeus; such a view implies that it is precisely the positive, historical aspect of the Old Covenant that appears to be most fully superseded by the appearance of the Logos in flesh. No Greek Father, even Irenaeus, would be at home with the thought that the history of the Church in its phenomenal aspect could

---

[76] Ibid.; CCG 22, 267, 270–82; PG 90, 748AB.
[77] *Ambigua*; PG 91, 1149D.

ever act as an essential source of insight into the economy of salvation as a whole. The elements of symbolic appearance that remain in the New Covenant are due, in their view, to the twofold nature of man as both sensory and intelligent and stand within a constant process of dynamic transition from sense to intelligence. Liturgical symbols are less the permanent place of the realization of salvation than its starting point, which must constantly be left behind. The New Covenant *is* "spirit"; its visible, hierarchical order, the enduring presence of the positive law of the Old Covenant, is only the "springboard" for the New, from which it leaps into our view; it is the means by which the old age dies away, in whose constant disappearance the new age appears to us. We have already met this process of transition, however, as the proper place of *theoria physikē*, the contemplation of nature.

This position is confirmed by a reminiscence of Evagrius Ponticus' theory of steps, in which every spiritual ascent was seen as achieved in the three stages of *praktikē* (πρακτική, the "cleansing" of the soul by the active development of virtue), *theoria physikē* (θεωρία φυσική, the "enlightenment" of the soul by looking through nature toward its divine foundation), and *theologikē* (θεολογική, the "unification" of the soul with God in prayer and ecstasy). What could be nearer Maximus' intentions than to connect this pattern of individual asceticism with his own schema of the "three laws" of salvation history? The consequence of such an assimilation was that the positive law, which corresponds to *praxis*, is pushed still more clearly into a subordinate and preparatory position. And in that the middle step of "enlightenment" is expressly identified as a simple transition from the Old Covenant to the New, from old to new age, the general sense of "movement from" and "movement toward" is still further emphasized.

A third element, in addition to these two, is the idealistic approach to the problem of knowledge itself, as it had been prepared by the Alexandrian tradition and confirmed by Gregory of Nyssa and Evagrius. The two of them, along with Pseudo-Macarius, go almost so far as to deny, more or less radically, the reality of matter in itself and to conceive of it either as the point where universal intelligible ideas and qualities intersect (Gregory) or as a phenomenal intensification of intellectual reality that is connected with our sinful condition (Pseudo-Macarius and Evagrius). Corresponding to the ontic structure of matter, then, as relative nonbeing (μὴ ὄν) in relation to the mind, the basic process of knowing must be seen as an abstraction of ideas from appearances, as lying in the direction of "seeing through" sensible reality without the corresponding counterweight of "seeing in" that reality that one finds in the Thomist "return to appearances" (*conversio ad phantasma*). Here, too, the emphasis points away from particular things to the ideal, and the "contemplation of nature" implies a move in precisely that direction.

In Maximus, these three themes [that is, a cosmological approach to salvation, a scheme of "steps", and a downplaying of the importance of matter] are held in check by the equally strong laws of tension, which lay across this scheme of ascent from matter to spirit a system of balance between them and an affirmation of their equal validity. So even in this context one should not forget that the polarity of positive law and natural law has been expressly designated as an ineradicable tension, in which neither pole "has any advantage over the other or is at any disadvantage with regard to the other".[78]

d. The Contemplation of Nature

The contemplation of nature finds its starting point in man's complete immersion in the natural world that surrounds him. He is nourished by that world in two ways: bodily by what it produces, intellectually by the seeds of truth that the Creator has planted in all things.[79] These seeds have a twofold character:

> God, the author of all visible nature, did not will it to move simply according to the laws of sense, but he scattered among all the species that comprise nature both intellectual meanings and the basic rules of moral behavior; his purpose was that he might not only be praised loudly as Creator by dumb creatures, when the intelligible structure of the world points to him and announces his presence, but also that man might easily find the way of instruction that leads to him, being led upward by the laws and moral instructions that are hidden in visible things.[80]

This "way of instruction", marked out by the "traces of the divine majesty", which leads onward the one who walks it "without leading him into error", is thus just as much a theoretical consideration of

---

[78] Ibid.; PG 91, 1128CD.
[79] *Quaestiones ad Thalassium* 51; CCG 7, 395, 31ff.; PG 90, 477A; *In Eccl. Hier.* 1; PG 4, 120BC (partly by John of Scythopolis).
[80] *Quaestiones ad Thalassium* 51; CCG 7, 395, 7–17; PG 90, 476C.

the meanings, laws, and structural principles contained in [the world's] individual beings as it is the practical imitation of their own unchanging, unmistaken observation of these laws. This "insight into creatures is an immortal food that nourishes the mind";[81] it is thus one of the forms that the creative Word takes on, to become "daily bread" for us, who are "nourished by virtue and insight".[82]

To take something as nourishment is to "use" it, even to "use it up", and so destroy it in its own particular existence. Man is an intellectual predator, who feeds on sensible reality by "digesting" it into something intelligible. It is not an accident that the senses he received are less acute than those of the animals;[83] this lack is richly compensated in him by an intellectual set of senses, through which and into which he is able to transform the external forms of nature and so to "create an intellectual world".[84] Maximus even undertakes to work out a kind of correspondence between the five senses and the spiritual faculties of the soul by conceiving of the former as "exemplary images" of the latter. So the organ and sensible root of the (theoretical) intellect is the eye, the organ of the (practical) reason the perceiving ear, the organ of the emotive soul the sense of smell, that of the passionate soul the sense of taste, and that of the vital principle the sense of touch. Through this correspondence the soul is able "to gather together the dizzying variety of meanings in things by its own power, when it uses its senses appropriately, and to assimilate every sensible thing into itself".[85] So the senses form "the intellectual vehicle of the powers of the soul"[86] yet must themselves continue to be held together and unified through imitation of the laws of action evident in nature—that is, through the moral virtues; in the process, the internal intellectual content of the virtues comes to light as they are realized and becomes in turn nourishment for the soul. So the soul, completely developed—and, so to speak, "satiated"—on both the theoretical and practical levels, reaches its likeness to God. Reaching from the roots of matter and physicality up to the highest unity of the mind, a continuity is developed that

---

[81] Ibid., 39; CCG 7, 259, 11–13; PG 90, 392B.
[82] *Exposition of the Lord's Prayer*; CCG 23, 58, 539–60, 571; PG 90, 896C–897B.
[83] *In Coel. Hier.* 15; PG 4, 105CD (attribution uncertain).
[84] *Ambigua*; PG 91, 1248BC.
[85] Ibid.; cf. on this subject my *Glory of the Lord*, vol. 1.
[86] *Ambigua*; PG 91, 1249C.

has the effect of a growing nourishment of the intellectual through the sensible and a transformation of the sensible into the world of the mind. In fact, this transformation and elevation of the corporeal into the intellectual is precisely its glorification and immortalization, which comes to full realization in the "resurrection of the body". The Asiatic, idealistic style of thought is itself transformed here into the Christian ideal of supernatural transformation.[87]

The soul does not contaminate itself, then, by its turn toward the world of sense. "It is not food that is evil, but our gluttony; not procreation, but fornication; not money, but avarice; not glory, but our thirst for glory. Thus there is nothing evil in things but the misuse [we make of them], which grows out of the disorder of the mind in making use of nature."[88] The right use of things is taught to us in a picturesque way in Peter's crucially important vision at Joppa [Acts 10:9–16]. "Arise," the voice says to him three times, "kill and eat", and a cloth descends from heaven, full of both clean and unclean animals.

> Why is he told to stand up? Why, except to arise from his sensual habits and inclinations, from his over-earthly way of conceiving created things and from his belief that the law made him righteous? In order that he might become capable of being freed from sensible forms and seeing the meanings of sensible things with a mind free from sensible fantasy and that he might gain insight into the symbolism of the intelligible world and learn from it that nothing created by God is unclean.

This "symbolism," however, is once again the mutual indwelling of sense and intellect:

> For if a person can see the visible world radiating its meaning, from the perspective of the intellectual world, or can see the outlines of intellectual things shining out symbolically from the realm of appearances—as the cloth appeared from heaven—he will not consider anything visible as unclean, because he cannot see any irreconcilable contradiction there with the ideas of things.

But why the threefold invitation [to kill and eat]?

> Because one must stand up and kill sensible creation, not just once, but twice and three times, and then consume it intellectually, if one wishes

---

[87] Ibid.; PG 91, 1249D–1252A.
[88] *Centuries on Love* 3, 4; PG 90, 1017CD.

to obey God fully in all things. If one lifts himself up from passionate, lustful patterns of behavior toward the world of appearances, he has killed the movement of sensible things and consumed them within himself through the rule of practical virtue. But if one raises oneself up from deceitful opinions on things, he has also killed the forms of things that appear and has eaten the things they contain that do not appear, in that he has carried out an intellectual contemplation of nature. And if one then raises himself up from the error of worshipping many gods, he has killed the very being of things and has swallowed within himself the power to know God (θεολογία), in that he has incorporated into himself through faith the source of all creation.[89]

If this idealism is to be understood in a Christian sense, it has to be part of the christological idealism of the "elevation" of a sensible human nature into the nature of God, an act through which all mankind, even the whole cosmos, is potentially drawn into that same transformation. It is therefore subject to the same law that determined this divine idealism: "If God plays free with the laws of nature, he does it in such a way that he makes use of nature, in the natural realm, in a supernatural way."[90] Maximus wants his own idealism to be understood as man's religious act, purely and simply, through which he collaborates in achieving his own share in the redemption of all creation.

By giving to the Lord the intellectual meanings of things, we offer him gifts: . . . not as if he needed them, but in order to honor him, as if we were making good our debts, as far as we can, from his own creatures. A person receives gifts, on the other hand, by earnestly pursuing divine philosophy, since by his very nature he needs the ethical laws (woven into things) for his own virtue and their meanings for his own wisdom.

So we only give back to God his own gifts, in a constant interchange of giving and receiving.

The intellectual person [Gnostiker] offers God the intellectual content of things that are given to him as gifts by creation; the practical person [Praktiker] receives gifts, in that he imitates the laws of nature in his behavior, and so reveals in himself, through his way of living, the

[89] Quaestiones ad Thalassium 27; CCG 7, 193, 48–195, 83; PG 90, 353B–356A.
[90] Ambigua; PG 91, 1280C.

whole glorious reality of the divine wisdom that is invisibly implanted in things.[91]

This is, at the same time, the fulfilled meaning of the old harvest festival: bringing to God the firstfruits of creation.[92]

This interpretation of the meaning of the laws of nature, and of our own activity of studying and imitating them, necessarily leads to a kind of universal approach to salvation history, which overflows in every direction the boundaries of God's historical revelation in the people of Israel. Israel is only the "chosen people" in a restricted sense: it is "Israel my firstborn", but not my "only-begotten".[93] Even before Israel was elected, all people were already called in Abraham.[94] More boldly still, echoing a thought of Origen, the scholia on Pseudo-Dionysius say:

> It is not as if God has chosen Israel alone; but Israel alone made the choice to follow God. . . . For God does not love Israel alone, as the Apostle has often shown: Is God not also the God of the pagans? Certainly also of the pagans, for there is only one God! (Rom 3:29). But Israel was the first [people] to walk according to God; and when it later fell away, it also was rejected. Human beings are free; when they choose, they can have God in their midst.[95]

In all peoples, there is something like a shadowy knowledge of Christ, expressed in an innate hope for salvation.

> Every holy person who lived before the coming of Christ and who practiced any kind of virtue, even if he did not fathom the whole mystery of the order of salvation, still had hope by a kind of natural drive, even if only in a partial way (ἐκ μέρους), and expected that the one who had created nature would also save and heal what was corrupted in it.[96]

Perhaps Maximus even considered that a certain spontaneous understanding of the Trinity was possible from a "contemplation of nature",

---

[91] *Quaestiones ad Thalassium* 51; CCG 7, 397, 63–399, 71; PG 90, 480A; CCG 7, 403, 138–44, PG 90, 481C.

[92] Ibid., 65; CCG 22, 281–83; PG 90, 757A.

[93] Ibid., 23; CCG 7, 149, 8–20; PG 90, 325AB.

[94] Ibid., 65; CCG 22, 263, 210ff.; PG 90, 745A.

[95] *In Coel. Hier.* 9; PG 4, 84D–85A (attribution uncertain).

[96] *Quaestiones et Dubia* 16; CCG 10, 48, 3–7; PG 90, 797B–800A. Cf. Gregory Nazianzen, *Orat.* 15; PG 35, 912A–913A.

whose triple potentiality of being, intelligibility, and living movement contains a trace of the threefold existence of God and "proclaims to those who can hear in an internal way, by a triple hymn of praise, the source of its own existence". God's threefold being is, after all, that "invisible reality of God" of which Paul speaks, "which has been recognized intellectually in the world since its very beginning (cf. Rom 1:20)".[97]

e. The Scriptural Law

The great interest Maximus devoted to the contemplation of nature was, however, not to be given at the expense of the law of the Scripture. If one wants to see the positive meaning of that other pole in its true importance, one must not, as we have already said, place the emphasis on contemplating the positive, historical revelation of the Old Testament, let alone simply its juridical and ritual aspects. Maximus is too much an Alexandrian not to sense the transitory and shadowy aspect of this order as its most striking characteristic. But he is also enough of an Alexandrian to value, at the highest level, that positive element that passed undiminished from the Old Covenant over into the New: the Holy Scripture itself. Precisely here he repeats some of Origen's most characteristic ideas, by simplifying them, expressing them in brief and lucid phrases, and building them into his system.

The contemplation of nature is neither the only means nor the preferred means to redeeming knowledge (*gnōsis*). As far as human resources are concerned, it, too, is simply the water that Christ changed into the wine of truly spiritual vision.[98] It represents the sensible, perceivable voice of God in the world, just as things are God's visible garments and form. And just as the world hides God in a revealing way and reveals God in a hidden way, the Scripture is a disguised and confused voice like the rolling of thunder,

> which says nothing clearly; it is a kind of voice of the elements. For every word of God that is written down for man is, as long as this age lasts, the precursor of another word, which uses it as an instrument to proclaim itself to the mind in an unwritten, intellectual way, and which,

---

[97] *Quaestiones ad Thalassium* 13; CCG 7, 101–3; PG 90, 296BC; cf. what we said above in chap. 2, sec. 3.

[98] Ibid., 40; CCG 7, 267; PG 90, 396AB; CCG 7, 271, 96ff.; PG 90, 400A.

in the age to come, will be revealed in a more perfect form. As it is proclaimed, it bears truth within itself, but does not show it in an unveiled, naked way.[99]

So the Scripture can be compared to a holy olive, which must be put into an olive press to produce the holy oil of the Spirit;[100] it is at once indispensable and temporary, just as the candle, which burns itself up, is the necessary support for the flame.[101]

This idea of a progressive self-consumption of the letter is Maximus' most significant attitude toward Scripture, at least as far as the meaning of the Old Testament is concerned. There was a time in which the historic law was necessary for humanity. This stage has been left behind; the fig tree is now withered, at least for those who still cling to the letter.[102] "It was not the season for figs", the Evangelist explains (Mk 11:13): even if the tree of the law still makes a glorious show in the dense, leafy growth of its customs and ceremonies, no more fruit is to grow under these leaves, now that the truth has appeared.

All that remains alive from the Old Law is its spiritual meaning; this, after all, is eternal and can never wither.

> The word of Holy Scripture may well be limited and circumscribed as far as the letter is concerned and may come to an end with the times whose history it tells; yet as far as the spirit and the meaning found within it are concerned, it remains forever unlimited, uncircumscribed. . . . For if the one who speaks [in it] is truly God, and God is in his essence uncircumscribable, the word that is spoken by him must also necessarily be beyond circumscription.[103]

This supratemporal character, however, is not some vague moral teaching, a content abstracted from its context, but a spiritual history constantly coming to fulfillment in human hearts, an event that is constantly coming to pass: "What is written is always being realized in a spiritual way."[104] Spiritually, and only spiritually, the letter still gives

---

[99] *Ambigua*; PG 91, 1252CD.
[100] *Quaestiones ad Thalassium* 63; CCG 22, 161, 269ff.; PG 90, 676D.
[101] Ibid.: CCG 22, 163, 279ff.; PG 90, 676D–677A.
[102] Ibid., 20; CCG 7, 121–23; PG 90, 308D–309B.
[103] Ibid., 50; CCG 7, 379, 9–19; PG 90, 465B.
[104] Ibid., 52; CCG 7, 425, 172; PG 90, 497A.

life today.[105] External sacrifices are alive today only within a larger sacrifice that includes the whole world: in the sacrifice of Christ.[106]

Nevertheless, even the Gospel, despite its role as the "enlivening spirit" of the old body,[107] has a "body" of its own. And even if this "body" is dynamically consuming itself by being transformed into "spirit" ("the more the letter consumes itself, the fuller the spirit becomes"),[108] still this "spirit" is itself only the symbolic representation of a truth that is yet to come. If the Old Covenant is a "shadow", the New Covenant is an "image".[109] The division of Scripture into body and spirit is a line that crosses directly through both Testaments.[110]

Perhaps it was only the unhistorical character of the Greek mind that here prevented Maximus from going on to divide history itself into three periods, related to each other as shadow, image, and truth —into a Kingdom of the Father, a Kingdom of the Son, and a Kingdom of the Spirit.[111] It remained for the Latin Middle Ages, and for Joachim of Fiore, another follower of the Alexandrians, to follow this line to its end. For Maximus as for Origen, the third Kingdom remains transcendent, eschatological. Yet surely this third Kingdom is already completely present now, if only in a way that is still veiled; often, in fact, it seems almost to be simply a matter of the perfection of every individual: the degree to which he brings eschatological, transhistorical reality to fulfillment through his own dying to the world.[112]

Maximus' final attitude toward the heart of Scripture is expressed in a parable. The whole world, he explains, is a game designed by God. Just as one keeps children busy with flowers and brightly colored clothes, and later, when they grow older, teaches them more serious games like the study of literature, so God works our education first through the

---

[105] Ibid. 50; CCG 7, 381; PG 90, 468Aff.; ibid., 18; CCG 7, 117; PG 90, 305D.
[106] Ibid., 36; CCG 7, 243, 30–245, 47; PG 90, 381B.
[107] *Mystagogia* 6; PG 91, 684AD; *Quaestiones ad Thalassium* 63; CCG 22, 171; PG 90, 681AB.
[108] *Mystagogia* 6; PG 91, 684C.
[109] *Ambigua*; PG 91, 1253D; *Centuries on Knowledge* 1, 90; PG 90, 1120C.
[110] *Centuries on Knowledge* 1, 91; PG 90, 1120D–1121A; *Mystagogia* 6; PG 91, 684B.
[111] A hint that he was thinking in this direction, inspired by Gregory Nazianzen, can be found in *Ambigua*; PG 91, 1261A.
[112] See my anthology of Origen, *Geist und Feuer*, 2d ed. (Salzburg, 1953), 453–59; English translation: *Spirit and Fire* (Washington, 1984), 320–25; see also Maximus, *Centuries on Knowledge*, passim.

play of nature as a whole and, when we grow older, through the play of Scripture.[113] So Pseudo-Dionysius and John [of Scythopolis], too, discovered in the truth of Scripture many similarities to the forms of poetic truth:

> The Scripture (as the latter remarks) makes use of certain poetic fictions in order to educate the human mind, which is not yet capable of grasping higher teaching. Heavenly similes are in fact like the fantastic images of the poets—take, for example, those whom the Greeks admire, such as Homer, Hesiod, and the rest—or like certain sculptural images. God's love for us seems to recognize, in its wisdom, that our mind is not ready for lofty insights, so he has prepared for it a way to the heights that suits its nature.[114]

This is the reason, according to Maximus, for the multiple senses of symbolism in Scripture, which is not at all free from ambiguity;[115] this, too, is the reason for those contradictions [in Scripture] which can only be reconciled through a spiritual exegesis.[116] And it is the reason for the pleasure we feel in tasting the delicious meaning hidden under its bitter skin.[117]

But what is play, from God's point of view, is serious from our own. It is, after all, the truth that we find beneath the images: the very Word of God. "The whole content of the dispensation of the law and the prophets leads us back" to this personal Word of God "as to its origin and its goal".[118] It leads to the Word, who stands "above image and truth, . . . above being and appearance, above the present world and the world to come", because he stands above all polarities, even including the polarity of "lies and truth".[119] As we move toward this highest of all goals, the word of Scripture is our hope and our pledge: a hope and a pledge for us who are called, not simply to resemble Christ, but through grace to become Christ himself.[120] In relation to this end

---

[113] *Ambigua*; PG 91, 1413CD.

[114] *In Coel. Hier.* 2; PG 4, 36CD.

[115] *Quaestiones ad Thalassium* 64, CCG 22, 187, 11ff.; PG 90, 693BC

[116] Ibid. 52; CCG 7, 417, 38–45; PG 90, 492B; ibid., 54; CCG 7, 461, 322–463, 335; PG 90, 521A; ibid., 65; CCG 22, 275, 402ff.; PG 90, 753A; *Ambigua*; PG 91, 1244B, 1252D.

[117] *Quaestiones ad Thalassium* 40; CCG 7, 271; PG 90, 397Cff.

[118] *Ambigua*; PG 91, 1164A.

[119] Ibid.; PG 91, 1296C.

[120] Ibid.; PG 91, 1253D.

and this beginning, all laws come to an end: the shadows as well as the images.[121]

f. The Synthesis of Christ

After this discussion of the poles "natural law" and "Scriptural law", all that remains is a look back at the synthesis of them both in the law of Christ. Christ is the place where both lines cross and where they cease to exist separately. His law of death and resurrection touches both nature and the Church.[122] "In Christ, neither circumcision nor uncircumcision is of any avail" (Gal 5:6). "Whoever follows Christ in truth, by practicing virtue, rises above both the written and the natural law."[123] "See, we have left everything and have followed you" (Mk 10:28). Whoever realizes this saying, "inherits the Lord, in place of the law and nature, as the one and only light of truth". Yet precisely in their abolition, as the vision of Tabor shows once again, the lasting meaning of both the law and nature *are revealed* in the purer light of the dawning divinity.

> For just as when the visible sun rises, all physical things begin to shine with it in its pure light, so when God, who is the spiritual sun of justice, rises before the mind, he wills . . . that all the true meaning of material and intelligible things appear along with him. This is proved, I think, by the fact that at the Transfiguration of the Lord on the mountain, when his face began to shine, his garments, too, appeared radiant: this suggests the reconciliation with God of our knowledge of all that is below and around him.[124]

But if the lasting relevance of nature and Scripture is thus confirmed by the fact of their descent from God, so for the soul that is to ascend, the possibility of a synthesis in grace must still be prepared beforehand by a dissolution of even their limited contradictions. "In reality, the termination of the laws of nature has made possible the concrete fulfillment of the world that exists above. For if these laws had not been terminated, the world above would have remained only partially ful-

---

[121] *Quaestiones ad Thalassium* 38; CCG 7, 256, 27–257, 52; PG 90, 389C–392A; *In Eccl. Hier.* 3; PG 4, 137D.
[122] *Quaestiones ad Thalassium* 64; CCG 22, 231, 700ff.; PG 90, 721D.
[123] *Ambigua*; PG 91, 1152C, 1153C.
[124] Ibid.; PG 91, 1156AB.

filled."[125] Only by our sacrifice of the world, by our intellectual "consumption" of it, does the soul rise above "the meaning of the natural and scriptural law" and "entrust itself to a movement beyond them (ἔκστασις), to a kind of abandonment of its whole life and being in order to enter the company of the unique Word of God",[126] "beyond both nature and law".[127] This sacrifice brings to fulfillment the mutual identification of the poles: on the one side, the transformation of nature by the Spirit, in which "the Spirit finally triumphs over nature";[128] on the other, the arrival of the full gospel, "in which all the intelligible meaning of providence and of individual beings are drawn together in the power of a single embrace, made one by a plan that precedes their existence"[129] Pagan polytheism and Jewish monotheism are reconciled here. The former is a self-contradictory multiplicity, without a bond of unity; the latter is unity without inner richness. Maximus considers both to be similarly imperfect, similarly in need of completion. Here, however, they interpenetrate each other to form the idea of a God who is three and one: the Jewish conception of unity, which is, of itself, "narrow and imperfect and almost without substance" and which "runs the danger of atheism", now complemented by the lively, intellectually engaging multiplicity of Hellenistic religion.[130]

In its state of perfection, the creature becomes what Philo and Gregory of Nyssa had already considered to be its vocation: the "borderline" (μεθόριον) between God and its own natural being, between formless being and the created forms.[131] It is "suspended halfway between heaven and earth",[132] and so comes to participate in him who promised, when he was lifted up, to "draw all things to himself" (Jn 12:32). With Christ, it brings to fulfillment that wonderful symbolic act, which represented the interpenetration of the divine and the human walking on water: resting its weight on the fluid matter of the world, it still does not sink into it.[133] It attains that highest degree of

---

[125] Ibid.; PG 91, 1273D–1276A.

[126] *Mystagogia* 24; PG 91, 717A.

[127] *Exposition of the Lord's Prayer*; CCG 23, 55, 485–86; PG 90, 893B.

[128] Ibid.; CCG 23, 47, 354f.; PG 90, 888D.

[129] *Mystagogia* 23; PG 91, 700B.

[130] *Exposition of the Lord's Prayer*; CCG 23, 51, 414–57, 518; PG 90, 892A–896A.

[131] *Ambigua*; PG 91, 1216C.

[132] *Quaestiones ad Thalassium* 55; CCG 7, 507, 425f.; PG 90, 553B.

[133] *Ambigua*; PG 91, 1049CD.

serenity, above and beyond all the laws of nature and Scripture, which "loves all people without placing its hope on any one of them"[134]— that joyful, calm indifference[135] which is the man's attitude of response to the fact that the world is really an insubstantial plaything of God.[136]

Maximus understands nature, Scripture, and man himself as essentially a threefold process of self-comparison: each is a movement that sets off from its basis in matter and reaches fulfillment in what is beyond itself, yet [in each case it is the very movement that] brings it to its own selfhood. This movement gives all three of them, as well, their unity with each other: the purification of the soul, the vision of the heart of nature, and the spiritual interpretation of Scripture together bring "the new world" to perfection, the "cosmos that is from above". "If anyone desires a life and sense experience pleasing to God, he should put great emphasis on the more noble part of these three 'persons': I mean the world, the Scripture, and ourselves."[137]

4. The Synthesis of Three Acts of Worship

The synthesis of the three "laws" was predominantly an intellectual and spiritual synthesis. Even if, in the realm of the [scriptural] law, the presupposition for its intellectual understanding was its application (as *praktikē*)—even if, in the realm of nature, the moral imitation of its lived regularities (τρόποι) stands alongside the contemplation of its deeper meaning—still the tone lay unmistakably on knowledge as an act of "seeing through" the realm of sense to the realm of intellect. The intelligible principle (*logos*) of nature and the intelligible principle (*logos*) of the [scriptural] law revealed themselves to the perfected mind as forms of the one Logos, who is the Truth.

But this Logos is also the Life. Therefore he did not found a society of wise intellectuals but the living organism of a Church. If an intellectual attitude [of reverence] appeared in the time before the Church, as the one "reasonable worship" of God by creatures, so now there arises alongside it a second form of service that is of equal value: the

---

[134] *Liber asceticus*: PG 90, 953C.
[135] "The gentle person remains without passion" (ὁ πρᾶος ἀπαθὴς διαμένει): *Exposition of the Lord's Prayer*; CCG 23, 46, 321; PG 90, 888A.
[136] *Ambigua*; PG 91, 1412AB.
[137] *Mystagogia* 7; PG 91, 685D.

service of the Church in the sacramental realm. The synthesis of the laws becomes, in this way, a simple thesis in itself.

It is clear that Maximus is making a very explicit effort, in this new synthesis, to reconcile his two great teachers, Evagrius and Pseudo-Dionysius. The former had retained only a few traces of the sacramental, hierarchical Church, as a result of promoting a kind of spiritualization through pure knowledge (*gnosis*) that consumed everything external; the latter had presented the sacramental order of the cosmos as something irreplaceable during our life on earth. For Maximus, both kinds of cult take their place alongside each other, implying a mutual interpenetration and transcendence in the direction of a cult that is truly comprehensive. For even the intellectual activity that seeks God through the symbolism of nature and Scripture has a kind of sacramental structure, while the sacrament, on the other hand, needs intellectual understanding if it is to be performed correctly. This understanding, however, is not something that empties the ritual act of its integrity; its intelligibility is possible only within the performance itself, not alongside it, since it "binds us to God through what has been performed, in a condition and a form determined by the [sacramental] thing itself" (πραγματικῇ ἕξει καὶ τυπώσει).[138]

a. Ecclesial and Sacramental Worship

The sacramental worship of the Church and its whole visible, hierarchical structure are treated thematically by Maximus in his scholia to Pseudo-Dionysius and in his *Mystagogia*.[139] This latter work is presented as a supplement to Pseudo-Dionysius' *Hierarchies* and should therefore not be considered apart from them:

> Since the holy Dionysius the Areopagite, who truly directed us to God, also explained, in his work on the *Ecclesiastical Hierarchy*, the symbols performed during the sublime consecratory act of the holy liturgy, in a way that corresponded to his towering mind, we must make it clear that our own discourse will not return to the same subjects or take the same route as his. It would be overly daring, arrogant, almost insane for someone who can hardly grasp or understand his work to attempt to take

---

[138] *In Epist. Dionysii* 9; PG 4, 564C.

[139] The scholia to Pseudo-Dionysius, when dealing with this subject, adhere closely to the texts being commented on and offer little that is characteristic or original.

up again what he has touched on and to offer as one's own discovery the mysteries revealed to him divinely, through the Holy Spirit alone.[140]

Thus it is not correct to present the *Mystagogia*, as is so often done, as a narrow imitation of Pseudo-Dionysius' work; Maximus is going his own way, even in the work's basic conception. Even so, this conscious decision to avoid everything handled by Pseudo-Dionysius may explain the curious fact that precisely the heart of the Church's liturgy, the eucharistic consecration, is passed over in his work without explanation.

Nevertheless, the whole work, as he repeatedly and expressly insists, deals with the holy liturgy in its entire ecclesial and sacramental reality. The liturgy is the midpoint, around which everything revolves, from which—as the single bright point into which one cannot look—everything is explained, whether left or right, up or down (as in Raphael's *Disputa*). Only because the liturgy is everywhere presupposed as the act that makes real the universal presence of the hypostatic Christ—at the midpoint between God and creation, heaven and earth, new age and old, Church and world—can Maximus simplify Pseudo-Dionysius' triadic conception of the world's structure into a dyadic one. The [idea of a] triadic structure comes from late Neoplatonism and retains a taste of emanationism, at least insofar as the middle member of each triad is nothing but the connecting link of the first with the third; if the bishop is the "enlightener", for example, and the people (including the monks) the "enlightened", the presbyters stand between them as both enlightened (looking upward) and enlightening (looking downward). This translation of Neoplatonic sensibility into ecclesial terms lends [Dionysius' picture of] the Church a somewhat fluid and dynamic character but equally allows the role of Christ to slip into the background, located outside and above the triadic scheme.

In contrast, Maximus chooses a wholly different point of departure. He had spent his youth in early seventh-century Byzantium, gazing at the great basilicas and at a liturgy that was already sharply stylized in a hieratic direction. The visible structure, of which Pseudo-Dionysius takes no account at all, stands powerfully before Maximus' imagination; within it, he sees the crucial articulation between clergy and peo-

---

[140] *Mystagogia*, prooemium; PG 91, 660D–661B. Jacoby rightly emphasizes the independence of the *Mystagogia* with relation to Pseudo-Dionysius: "Die praktische Theologie in der alten Kirche", *Theologische Studien und Kritiken* 63 (1890): 472.

ple, the space where the liturgy is performed and the space where the faithful attend it. This emphasis on duality was not without its dangers, and Maximus remains aware of them: he begins from it, only in order to move beyond it. The route by which he made that move, as might be expected, was christological: the unconfused unity of two in one in the visible, hierarchical Church is an application of the Chalcedonian understanding of Christ. With the same move, Maximus has leaped over Pseudo-Dionysius and regained the old Alexandrian world of Origen, with its great symbolic pairings of earth and heaven, body and mind, Old Covenant and New, an old and a new world. The whole system, then, is a Chalcedonian Origenism: this is the uniqueness of Maximus' achievement and something wholly new.

In the *Mystagogia*, the sacramental side of worship is expressed almost exclusively through its symbolic aspect. It is no coincidence that along with the sacramental-gnostic dimension, the great symbol-systems of the world and the Scripture appear here again and that the parallelism and mutual correspondence between the duality of intellect and sense play the major role in all four of them—in the Church, the world, Scripture, and man. E. Steitz seems to be right in speaking of a rediscovery here of Origen's "first principles", and in explaining Maximus' doctrine of the Eucharist as an extension of the earlier Alexandrian conception of symbolism—even though he was less interested in the "heavenly" and "ecclesiastical hierarchies".

> Maximus' *Mystagogia* [Steitz concludes] is in this context the most fragrant flower in the whole Alexandrian garden; the basic views of Alexandrian theology reappear here again, but in such a concentrated and organized form that one may say: What the earlier representatives of this school had only hinted at, in individual, deeply significant aphorisms, here has become a system, whose structural artistry reminds us of the fine architectonic schemes of scholasticism.[141]

One might be concerned that the doctrine of the Church presented in the *Mystagogia* might also end in the same crisis of spiritualization as that of the Alexandrian master; various themes, taken by themselves, could point in just that direction.[142] But one should not overlook the

---

[141] E. Steitz, "Die Abendmahlslehre der griechischen Kirche in ihrer geschichtlichen Entwicklung", *Jahrbücher für deutsche Theologie* 11 (1866): 238.

[142] Cf. A. Lieske, "Die Theologie der Logosmystik bei Origenes", *Münsterer Beiträge zur Theologie* 22 (1938): 74–99.

degree to which both Origen and Maximus are and wish to be "men of the Church": so much so that both became martyrs for the sake of the Church, and especially that Maximus staked his life on the unity of the Church in the highest degree of her historical reality—in her unity of dogma and life, of pope and emperor, of West and East. If the *Mystagogia* sketches out the internal, mystical side of his view of the Church, this is because the Church has, in his eyes, no simply "external" aspect. Even while he is fighting for his formula of Christ's two wills in a tough but seemingly petty series of skirmishes, he always is conscious of being in the Church's inmost heart: the Catholic Church stands and falls with the undiminished humanity of Christ, and with the Church stands and falls every kind of mystical and intellectual interiority.

That is the reason why the symbolism of the *Mystagogia* begins with a building: with a visible church made of stone—something that would have been unthinkable for Origen; and that is why Maximus insists, in a very simple way, on real participation in the liturgy within this building. The "gnostic soul", too, is urgently encouraged to stick to the liturgical order in order to realize his own perfection, by projecting his own subjectivity onto the "objective" pole of cultic worship. Maximus never ceases to

> urge every single Christian to visit the holy church of God often and never to miss the holy liturgy performed in it, both because of the holy angels who are in attendance and always take notice of those who come, bringing them to God's attention and interceding for them, and because of the grace of the Holy Spirit, which is always present in an invisible way but is most especially so during the time of the holy liturgy. This grace enfolds all those who attend, creates them anew, and truly leads each of them, according to his own capacities, to a more divine way of living; it brings each one closer to what the sacred mysteries signify, even when the individual does not experience this consciously.[143]

Here, too, a genuine polarity remains in force, by which the cult of the sacraments and that of theological knowledge only come to their fullness through each other.

In this way, Maximus sums up in a thoroughly orthodox manner another current within patristic spirituality, which had flowed in a heterodox form alongside the main stream—a current that had etched

---

[143] *Mystagogia* 24; PG 91, 701D–704A.

the first semblance of division on the internal face of the Church by distinguishing, in graduated steps, a Church of "fleshly" and imperfect members from a Church of "spiritual" and perfect ones. The Gnostics first developed this distinction by misusing Pauline terminology, as a way of relating the external, official teaching of the Church with their own esoteric, secret teaching intended for the "elect"; Tertullian, the enemy of the Gnostics, made the distinction his own and so constructed the theological basis for Montanist Pentecostalism. True, the Gnostic way of subdividing the Church also found its echoes in Clement [of Alexandria] and Origen. They distinguished within the Church a body of intellectually unformed "simple" folk (ἀπλούστεροι), who are content with believing dogmas, hearing sermons, and receiving the sacraments, from a body of "gnostics" (γνωστικοί), who are genuinely striving to realize their faith fully, to ascend in both theoretical and practical ways to an understanding of faith; yet [Origen and Clement] never conceived this distinction as implying that the Church is twofold or that there is one Church for half-Christians and another for full Christians.

Such a double Church, however, did continue to exist in heretical circles, or in circles close to heresy. One example is the Messalians, whose radical attitudes can be seen glinting behind the more moderate Pseudo-Macarian homilies, where an open break with the hierarchical Church that celebrates the liturgy and administers the sacraments is avoided, but where true worship is still transferred within, to the heart of the person who is genuinely spiritual. The visible Church [in these homilies] is at once something indispensable and something that must be outgrown.[144] Orthodoxy and heterodoxy could come very close to each other on this point. For the Messalians, for example, the fact that sacramental grace works without our knowledge means that a seed of life is planted in the soul, which demands not only to grow but to be experienced.[145] Diadochus of Photike, too, took over this notion almost unchanged,[146] and it appears again in Maximus with the qualification that even a reception of the sacraments or a participation in the holy liturgy that is not felt inwardly can yet be meaningful and necessary, as characteristic of those who are "still children (νήπιοι) with

---

[144] See Hermann Dörries, *Symeon von Mesopotamien*, Texte und Untersuchungen, vol. 55, no. 1 (1941), 214f., 235f., 263f., 369f.

[145] Ibid., 236.

[146] *Centuries*, chap. 77, ed. E. des Places, Sources chrétiennes, vol. 9 (1955), 135.

respect to Christ and are not yet able to gaze into the depths of what is happening."[147]

What holds for Macarius holds all the more for that sinister work whose editor, Kmosko, characterized it as clearly Messalian: the *Liber Graduum*.[148] This strange book makes a sharp distinction between "the righteous" (Christians in the world) and "the perfect" (monks, who have left all things) and develops an ecclesiological dualism that reminds one of Tertullian and may even depend on him—a dualism of a wholly different kind from that of Pseudo-Dionysius. Here the point is not to argue for a symbolic representation of the heavenly hierarchy of the angels in the Church's hierarchy on earth, but to propose a symbolic relationship between an earthly Church of the "body," which is really a kind of parable, and a true, heavenly Church of the "heart" and the "spirit"; the first is only an "educational" prelude to the second.[149] When we have achieved a complete self-emptying,

> then the heavenly Church and the spiritual altar will appear to us; there, in spirit, we will offer our hearts' confession in prayer and in the sacrifice

---

[147] *Mystagogia* 24; PG 91, 704A.

[148] *Patrologia Syriaca* 1, 3 (Paris, 1926). Without being able to offer an adequate proof, I should like at least to raise the question whether or not we have in this work—which so vividly differs from the Macarian corpus in its almost demonically sectarian spirit and in which the main teaching of the Messalians, the call to ceaseless prayer, is less obvious—a Montanist document. The Montanists were not only a powerful sect in Phrygia, with their main center in Pepuza, up to the time of Epiphanius; they were also spread through Cappadocia, Galatia, and especially Cilicia, which bordered on Syria, and they even had members in Constantinople. At the end of the fourth century, they had an organized church with its own hierarchy and liturgy and with special initiation rituals (see G. Bardy, "Montanisme", DTC 10, 2, col. 2368). Bloody persecutions under Justinian, in which some of the members of the sect were burned in their own churches—something that is also reported in the reign of Leo III (the Isaurian), in 729—prove the enormous vitality of the sect and suggest a lively ideology. With its harsh dualism between Christians who are simply "righteous" (and who in fact still belong to the Old Testament, because of their married life in the world and their possessions—however generously they give alms) and the "perfect", who alone come to the vision of God, the *Liber Graduum* seems, like Tertullian, fanaticized to an extreme. [On the *Liber Graduum*, see Arthur Vööbus, *History of Asceticism in the Syrian Orient*, vol. 1, CSCO, vol. 184 (Louvain, 1958), 178–84, 190–207; Antoine Guillaumont, "Situation et signification du *Liber Graduum* dans la spiritualité syriaque", *Orientalia Christiana Analecta* 197 (1974): 311–22; Diana Juhl, *Die askese im Liber Graduum und bei Afrahat: eine vergleichende Studie zur frühsyrischen Frömmigkeit* (Wiesbaden, 1996). On Montanism, see Christine Trevett, *Montanism: Gender, Authority and the New Prophecy* (Cambridge, 1996), esp. 198–232 (on later Montanism); William Tabbernee, *Montanist Inscriptions and Testimonia*, North American Patristic Society Patristic Monograph Series, no. 16 (Macon, Ga., 1997).]

[149] *Sermo* 12: *Patrologia Syriaca* 1, 3, 290.

of our bodies, just as we believe that there is a genuine priesthood that presides also at the visible altar. For everything in this present Church is directed toward that hidden Church by way of parable.

The earthly Church is the holy mother, who raises her children to live in the heavenly Jerusalem; whoever grows up in the direction of this latter community makes his body into a temple and his heart (as an intermediate step) into an altar and ultimately enters the Church of Jesus herself, which is above.[150]

Heretical ecclesiology, whether of Gnostic, Montanist, or Messalian shading, was the first to divide the Church from within; otherwise —as commentaries on the Song of Songs, from Hippolytus to Gregory of Nyssa and Nilus, suggest—she had only one face: that of the pure, beloved Bride. But such division need not be interpreted only in a heretical way; it is true, after all, that in the New Covenant all ceremony, everything that smacks of the "letter", remains precisely an occasion and a starting point for a spiritual union with Christ, understood in faith, just as it is a temporary and temporal foreshadowing of the eternal blessings to come.

The interpretation [Maximus offers] in the *Mystagogia* moves in both of these directions: the mystical and the eschatological. With the mystical or "gnostic" interpretation, the monastic theology of Evagrius is transplanted into ecclesiology; it can be taken over almost entirely, and yet it is relativized by its new context. This tradition now takes over the function of realizing, in an existential way, the mysteries of Christ that are celebrated objectively, ecclesially, in the liturgy; in that sense, it joins with the intentions of Pseudo-Dionysius in his *Ecclesiastical Hierarchy*. But by then developing the eschatological dimension —the relation of the Church on earth with the Church of the resurrection—Maximus moves beyond both Evagrius and Dionysius: in place of a Church of the spirit that is simply disembodied, we find the Church of those risen from the dead; in place of the angelic hierarchies, which are not themselves part of the Church and which form, along with the Church on earth, only a timeless cross-section of the order of salvation, we find the Church in her own process of growth from earth to heaven. Even so, this dimension is not the same as the heretical

---

[150] Ibid. 291–94. Can Epiphanius' remark (*Panarion* 12, 1, 14: Oehler I/2, 37) be correct, that the Montanists go on pilgrimage to Pepuza because they expect that the heavenly Jerusalem will descend to earth there?

Church made of body, heart, and spirit, since her articulation does not arise through the distinction of different categories of believers but through the Church's sharing in Christ's passage from life on earth, through death, to resurrection. The difference also becomes clear in the fact that the *Liber Graduum,* in a separatist, "Jansenist" spirit, only holds the door into the heavenly Jerusalem open for a few elect, while Maximus presents the Church, and the sign that she imprints on the world, in the largest and most open terms possible. The Church lies in the midst of the natural and supernatural cosmos like a source of light that sets all things revolving around itself; in that she represents everything symbolically, she also is an effective guarantee of the transformation of the whole universe. The liturgy is, for Maximus, more than a mere symbol; it is, in modern terms, an *opus operatum,* an effective transformation of the world into transfigured, divinized existence. For that reason, in Maximus' view—again unlike that of both Evagrius and Pseudo-Dionysius—the liturgy is ultimately always "cosmic liturgy": a way of drawing the entire world into the hypostatic union, because both world and liturgy share a christological foundation. This is something new and original and must be regarded as Maximus' own achievement.

Let us consider some texts. "The human hierarchy is symbolic and formed from sensible elements; for we do not come into contact with divine things except through a veil."[151] "The divine hierarchy must always be interpreted symbolically, and the holy gifts are representations of things that are above, which are real."[152] In fact, the whole event of the cultic drama is a presentation of eschatological reality and immediately reveals through itself what is yet to come. In this sense, it is "performed by God himself and then entrusted to man: it works at the formation of gods."[153] So the Church, as a visible community, is already "the image and likeness of God", who holds the whole world, in its variety, together, who draws it up to himself, melts it into unity, and still leaves to each being its own being and its own place. The Church is an image of God,

> because she achieves among the faithful the same unity that God achieves, even when those who are united in faith are very different in characteris-

---

[151] *In Eccl. Hier.* 1; PG 4, 121B.
[152] Ibid. 3: PG 4, 149C.
[153] Ibid. 1; PG 4, 116A.

tics and separated by land and custom—the same unity that God achieves among the essences of things, without confusing them, in that he . . . moderates and brings into harmony what is different among them, by drawing them toward himself as their cause and goal and making them one.[154]

So the eucharistic action recalls the whole providential history of God's salvation: "the entrance rite of the holy liturgy" recalls the first coming of the Savior; the ascent of the bishop to the altar and to his throne recalls his Ascension; the entry of the people, the gathering of the pagans in the Church, or of sinners in grace; the "holy readings", the indication of his will that God makes to each individual concerning his own life; the "holy songs", the desire for God that inflames pure souls; the "greeting of peace", the transition from the bitter soldiering of asceticism to the peaceful "agriculture" of the contemplative life; the reading of the holy Gospel, the descent of the bishop from the throne, the dismissal of the catechumens and penitents, and the closing of the Church doors, all recall the events of the last judgment: the coming of the Lord, the division of the saved from the damned, the passing away of the sensible world; then the "entry of the holy mysteries" [or procession with the gifts] recalls the revelation in the next life of God's ways of salvation; the "holy kiss", the union of all souls in God, which is even now under way; the Creed, the great hymn of thanks sung by all the saved; the Sanctus, the elevation of the blessed into the choirs of angels, who "in the identity of still eternal movement around God . . . acclaim and bless the threefold face of the single God with threefold blessings"; the Lord's Prayer, our adoption in Christ as children of God; the closing hymn, "One is holy, one is Lord", the final and supreme immersion of the creature in the abyss of the unsearchable simplicity of God.[155]

The visible hierarchy, too, is wholly representational, wholly an instrument for realizing the new age. "God has established the priesthood on earth in order to represent himself. There he is visible in a bodily way, and his mysteries do not cease to appear in visible form for those who know how to see."[156] The bishop, as head of the Mystical Body which is the community, stands for God himself. His office, above all

---

[154] Mystagogia 1; PG 91, 664–68.
[155] Ibid., chaps. 1–21.
[156] Epistles 21; PG 91, 604D.

else, is to bring all the members together in unity "and to bind them
in the spirit with the indissoluble bonds of love".[157] Even as late as
the seventh century, Maximus strongly emphasizes several times the
representative character of the priestly office: the name "priest" (sa-
cerdos, hiereus, ἱερεύς) is borrowed from the Old Covenant and now is
only an image for the true, but more modest, term presbyter: "elder"
or "presider".[158] Only Christ is a priest of the New Covenant in the
true sense of the word. The [ecclesial] priest may only "consecrate",
and in the process "be consecrated", by participation.[159] His task is to
unify the Body of Christ, by purifying the faithful like a consuming
fire.[160] But he only unifies the Body through the Eucharist, which is
the mystery of perfect communion and the prelude to that union in
God "which allows no further emptiness that cannot be filled by his
presence".[161]

The sacraments—of which Maximus treats only baptism and the
Eucharist thematically—stand completely within the dynamic of the
movement from sign to reality. The Eucharist is essentially "symbol,
not reality", "an image of true things".[162] This is meant, of course, in
the context of an Alexandrian realism of signs,[163] not in the Calvinist
way in which some have tried to interpret it.[164] Maximus' symbolic
realism acts as the bridge between Origen and the eucharistic doctrine
of Scotus Erigena.[165] In place of the transubstantiation of the bread into
the Body of Christ, the central emphasis is on the transubstantiation
of the communicant into Christ and into his "Spirit".[166] The tone is

---

[157] Epistles 28; PG 91, 621A.

[158] In Ecc. Hier. 5; PG 4, 164C; In Ep. Dionys. 8; ibid. PG 4, 545D.

[159] Epistles 31: PG 91, 625A.

[160] Ibid.; PG 91, 624B.

[161] Mystagogia 21; PG 91, 697A. The texts on baptism and the Eucharist are listed in P.
Sherwood in his translation The Ascetic Life: The Four Centuries on Charity, Ancient Christian
Writers, 21 (Westminster, Md.: Newman Press, 1955), introduction, nn. 325 and 336.

[162] In Ecc. Hier. 3; PG 4, 137A; 145B; Quaestiones et Dubia 41; CCG 10, 11, 5-6; PG 90,
820A (σύμβολα τῆς θείας οὐσίας . . . ἀπεικονίσματα).

[163] Cf. my Parole et mystère chez Origène, 18f.

[164] E.g., Steitz, "Abendmahlslehre", conclusion.

[165] See Erigena, Super coel. hier.; PL 122, 140; Comm. in Joh., frag.; PL 122, 311B.

[166] Mystagogia 24; PG 91, 704A ("transforming, re-equipping and truly re-creating [the re-
cipient] into something more divine": μεταποιοῦσαν καὶ μετασκευάζουσαν καὶ ἀληθῶς
μεταπλάττουσαν εἰς τὸ θειότερον); ibid., 21; PG 91, 697A ("transforming [the recipient]
into itself": μεταποιοῦσαν πρὸς ἑαυτήν).

completely focused on the effect of the Eucharist; that seems to provide its essential definition.

Maximus regards baptism in a similarly dynamic way, seeing it completely as the ontic principle and point of departure for a new life.
In this sense, it takes away original sin (προγονικὴ ἁμαρτία), but not
concupiscence,[167] which is only modified or consumed by the development of this new principle into a conscious way of life. Because
the life given us by God is an intelligent, self-conscious one, such a
development belongs to the essence of the grace of baptism itself. But
every acquired life is, as a phenomenon of the "spirit", both "life" and
"consciousness"; so the principle, too, must be twofold: as sacrament,
the seed of supernatural life, and, as faith, the seed of supernatural vision. Both of these—life and vision—develop from a state of pure
potentiality to such a state of supreme realization.

> The way we are born from God is twofold: the first way gives those who
> are born the grace of sonship, in a complete, if still potential, mode of
> presence; the second gives this grace in perfect, fully realized presence,
> in which all the freedom of those born is transformed, by their act of
> choice, into actual personal being and so is changed into participation
> in the God who gives them birth. The first way involves a possession
> of grace as only a potential presence and depends on faith; the second
> adds to faith the grace that is fully realized in a way corresponding to
> understanding, the grace that brings about in the knower a most divine
> similarity with the one known.

The water of baptism is of no use to us, then, if we do not give it
room, in our freedom, to lead to our conscious moral perfection, so
that "through our daily life the sacramental water might purify our conscience and our consciousness". For only through freedom of choice is
the freedom within us brought to that perfection before God in which
we can no longer commit sin. "For the Spirit does not give birth to
a free will that struggles against him but only transforms those who
desire it with the gift of divinization."[168]

At this point, the "sacramental" and the "gnostic" patterns mesh
with each other. The free moral act, which leads to wisdom and vision by purifying the spirit, rests on the "seed" of divine life sown
beneath it; it is, in fact, only the opportunity that offers itself for this

---

[167] *Liber asceticus*; PG 90, 956A.
[168] *Quaestiones ad Thalassium* 6; CCG 7, 69, 8–71, 51; PG 90, 280B–281B.

grace to develop, in the inner region of the mind (ἑαυτοὺς ὅλους κατὰ τὴν γνώμην ἐμπαρέχειν). Moving upward, it is changed progressively into the act of God himself, who lifts us out of our own freedom into his. (For "when an eye has once seen the sun, it can no longer confuse it with the moon or with other stars": so when we have once glimpsed God, he takes the freedom to do evil away from us). On the other hand, this development of grace into vision can come about fully only by passing through the realm of our freedom of choice. The sacramental reality must become "gnostic", so that the gnostic reality itself can be elevated into a second, eternal rebirth from the womb of God.

b. The Worship of Mind and Spirit

By what we have just said, it is clear that theological worship has found its place within the more comprehensive realm of the sacramental. The whole reality of individual "gnosis" envisaged by Evagrian theology has found its meaning, at least partially realized, within the world of Pseudo-Dionysian liturgy. Yet insofar as sacramental and cultic worship is understood expressly as a way toward the complete liberation of the soul and a means for its complete sacrifice of itself to God, this identification becomes again a polarizing subordination. "The altar of sacrifice is a symbol of God, to whom all of us are sacrificed in spirit", just as "the whole structure of godly deeds and insights rests on faith, which is its foundation."[169]

---

[169] Ibid., 26; CCG 7, 243, 19–24; PG 90, 381A; cf. ibid., 65; CCG 22, 289, 568ff.; PG 90, 760C. An odd comment on a text of Pseudo-Dionysius shows that John of Scythopolis was already contemplating such a shift of emphasis. In his ninth letter, Pseudo-Dionysius mentions two forms of tradition in the Church: the one "makes holy by symbol and by initiation into the mysteries" (συμβολικὴ καὶ τελεστική) and is also called "mysterious and mystical"; the other is "public and on the intellectual plane", is "philosophical and demonstrative" (ἀποδεικτική). The point of Pseudo-Dionysius is unambiguous: the sacramental and symbolic order of the Church represents that "holy veil" through which the believer is "initiated" into the pure truth. For if the "simple and superessential and super-fundamental truth behind the images" was, of itself, "obvious and demonstrative to the human mind" (Epistles 9; PG 3, 1105C–1108A), neither Christ nor the prophets would have made use of holy symbols. But for those who are initiated into these symbols, access is possible to the secret tradition behind openly revealed truth, which is reached through images. The first, symbolic order corresponds to the "sensible part of our being" (τὸ παθητικόν), the second to the intellectual (τὸ ἀπαθὲς τῆς ψυχῆς).

John could not or would not understand the text in this way. For him, it was obvious that "philosophy" and "demonstration" only constitute the anticipatory stage for a "mystical

If the Church is a "world",[170] the world is also a cosmic Church, whose "nave" is sensible creation and whose "choir" is the world of intelligible realities.[171]

> So the soul flees toward the intellectual contemplation of nature, as to the inside of a Church and to a place of peaceful sanctuary; . . . it enters it with the Logos, and under his guidance, . . . for he is our true high priest. And there it learns to recognize the essential meanings of things as if through the readings from Holy Scripture.[172]

In this way, Maximus goes through the whole liturgy and applies its various phases to the inner liturgy of the soul. Man here becomes the true priest of the world, who "offers nature to God on his heart as if on an altar" and penetrates into the inmost parts of his spirit, the "holy of holies", until he reaches the depths of the divine silence.[173] Everything that we said earlier about the value of the contemplation of nature could be repeated here and seen as part of the overarching meaning of worship.

Maximus is even bold enough to interpret knowledge itself as ministry: the same knowledge that according to Paul "puffs up" and that for him seemed to lead, as no other human activity does, to arrogance and to the self-congratulation of the mind. It is not an accident, then, that among all the "capital sins" described by Evagrius Ponticus, it is vainglory (κενοδοξία) that receives Maximus' closest attention. That

---

theology of initiation". So he reverses the order of Pseudo-Dionysius: "The second part of the theological tradition is obvious and understandable to all and does not speak through symbols; he also calls it philosophical and demonstrative; it leads to the ethical, natural, and practical aspects of creation." Only in this part [of theology] can one give "proofs". "The symbolic order, on the other hand, cannot convince the reader, but has a certain hidden, intrinsically efficacious divine power, which communicates itself to those souls who are to be initiated or to enter into contemplation through mystical and symbolic images." With this reversal of the original idea, the higher level of theology is identified as the real realm of worship, and so that parallelism between sacramental and "gnostic" cult is emphasized which Maximus will develop in the *Mystagogia*.

It is, incidentally, very informative to notice how Maximus himself comments on the same text of Pseudo-Dionysius. For him, the "symbolic order becomes a way of pointing to the "legal worship" of the Old Covenant, whereas the "philosophical order" points to "the contemplation of creatures and of God's ways of salvation." Thus he turns his attention back toward the polarity and synthesis of the two laws (PG 4, 561D–564B).

[170] *Mystagogia* 2; PG 91, 668Cff.
[171] Ibid., 2; PG 91, 669AB.
[172] Ibid., 23; PG 91, 697D–700A.
[173] Ibid., 4; PG 91, 672C.

vice is closely connected with envy and covetousness, with the vices
of the hard and dessicated heart, whose opposite in virtue is the humility that gives itself away without a care. And it is not an accident that
precisely this mare's nest is attacked and cleared out at the start of the
Centuries on Knowledge: it is only to the person who serves in humility
that the "gnostic" depths of being are accessible.[174] The patient farmer
who tills his field with no expectations finds the hidden treasure; the
old Platonic notion of the "moment of truth", the sudden (ἐξαίφνης,
ἄφνω) "inspiration" of the divine within the mind, is mentioned, significantly, in just this context.[175] True wisdom is acquired only in service, because it is itself a service given to the salvation of the world
and, so, a "divine service."

c. The Worship of Love

The two kinds of worship—worship in the Church and worship in
the world—are united, without being transformed into each other,
in a total service that is the goal of both sacrament and wisdom: the
worship that is realized in love. Over and above Evagrius, and in close
dependence on Pseudo-Dionysius, Maximus retains a sense for the importance of distance in love, for holy fear, and for a distinction between creature and Creator that shows itself in service. Love, for him,
is "mingling", "the result of fear and longing, consisting of reverent
hesitation and attraction".[176] The law of created existence, that a creature becomes what it is only through its "distinctiveness" from everything else (τὴν διαφορὰν ὡς συστατικὴν τῶν ὄντων καὶ ἀφοριστικήν);[177]
that therefore all things are ultimately similar in this respect: that each
is unlike the others; and that this most general similarity is grounded
in the fact that every creature is defined, as such, by the common notion of nonbeing, which distinguishes the world's being from God and
holds it apart from him[178]—this law is ultimately also the foundation
of the highest form of creaturely relationship to God. The unity of
fear and longing corresponds to the human situation: we must, after
all, take care "that fear does not change into loathing by losing its hold

[174] *Centuries on Knowledge* I, 15–29; PG 90, 1088D–1093C.
[175] Ibid., I, 17–18; PG 90, 1089BC.
[176] *Exposition of the Lord's Prayer*, CCG 23, 27, 9ff.; PG 90, 873A.
[177] *Opuscula*; PG 91, 249C.
[178] *Ambigua*; PG 91, 1312B.

on longing, but also that longing does not change into contempt, if it no longer has a moderate fear as its companion, and that instead love reveal itself as our inner law and take the form of tender inclination".[179] This law is not simply "the combination of longing for the Kingdom of God and fear of the Gehenna of everlasting fire".[180] For

> chaste fear will never be taken away and will even remain for all eternity without any recollection of failures. Its root, after all, is essentially in God himself, so to speak, and in his relationship to creation, through which he manifests all his natural claim on our attitude of humility before that majesty that is his domination over every rule and power. If someone does not fear God as judge, but does possess a humble reverence toward him because of the overpowering excellence of his limitless power, he truly is lacking in nothing; he has become perfect in love, because he loves God with the humility and reverence that are appropriate. This is the sort of person who has the fear that will last, the fear that continues for all eternity.[181]

If sacramental worship is naturally suited to train us in this ultimate "distancing" of love, true wisdom—whose beginning is the fear of the Lord (Ps 111:10)—is equally well suited to do so. "For all intellectual knowledge (*gnosis*) leads the heart to repentance, because it provides us with a living consciousness of the greatness of God's gifts to us."[182] So holy insight elevates the soul to the rank of the angels, who perform in heaven that everlasting "liturgy of the mind" that is their sole occupation.[183] "Whoever offers God his service of worship, in a mystical way, without disordered desires or anger but solely in his capacity of reason, fulfills God's will on earth just as the orders of angels do in heaven. He has become a perfect fellow worshipper with the angels."[184]

Perfect prayer is identical with this service of perfect worship. For if that prayer is truly supplication (δέησις), such supplication becomes "powerful in every way" if it is expressed, not simply through words, but "with substance" (ὑπόστασις δεήσεως), through the fulfillment of God's commandments. Prayer becomes real only in action, which

---

[179] *Exposition of the Lord's Prayer*; CCG 23, 27, 12–15; PG 90, 873A.

[180] *Opuscula* 8; PG 91, 441D.

[181] *Quaestiones ad Thalassium* 10; CCG 7, 85, 57–87, 67; PG 90, 289BC. On the twofold character of fear, see *Centuries on Love* 1, 81–82; PG 90, 977CD.

[182] *Exposition of Ps. 59*; CCG 23, 10, 128–31; PG 90, 861C.

[183] *Exposition of the Lord's Prayer*; CCG 23, 58, 534–36; PG 90, 896B.

[184] Ibid.: CCG 23, 57, 521–25; PG 90, 896AB.

means in service.[185] But service, as we have already seen, is essentially
service to the world, the act of offering the world to God that brings
it redemption. And in this service, the one who serves encounters the
fullness of grace and is made divine. So the goal of prayer is all of
this at once: "knowledge of God (*theologia*), sonship in grace, equality to the angels in dignity, sharing in eternal life, and the restoration
of nature—which now is drawn back toward its own pure state."[186]
But that divinizing participation only comes about in the process of
nature's own coming to fulfillment—in other words, in the law of fear
and of "distancing". The basic acts of prayer (which simply imitate the
fundamental structures of the world's existence and its relationship to
God) continue to be acts of *religio*, whose form is a deifying love that
comes to fulfillment by surpassing its very self but that never comes
to an end.

> The first act of the mind is an act of wonder, when it becomes aware of
> the sheer unmeasurability of God, like an uncrossable sea one has been
> yearning to gaze on. After this, however, it wonders at how God is able
> to bring existent things into being from nonbeing. But just as there is
> no end to his greatness, so you will find no end to his wisdom. For who
> would not be shaken with terror at contemplating that boundless sea of
> goodness, which exceeds all our capacity for wonder? And how could
> one help but be moved, when he begins to reflect on how the reasonable,
> thinking mind has come to be and from what source it comes, along
> with the four elements that form the body, if there was no matter that
> preceded their creation? What can this power be that is at work here,
> giving existence to these things?[187]

Terror like this never fades away; fear like this cannot be quenched.
What shakes here is the very foundation of our being. All love for the
supreme majesty remains service and worship and a complete dependence and self-abandonment expressed in obedience. "Ceaseless prayer
consists in lifting up the mind to God in great reverence and longing,
in depending on him with constant hope, and in trusting him in everything—in all we do and in every experience that comes our way."[188]

---

[185] *Quaestiones ad Thalassium* 57; CCG 22, 23, 11; PG 90, 589D.
[186] *Exposition of the Lord's Prayer*; CCG 23, 31, 81–83; PG 90, 876C.
[187] *Centuries on Love* 4, 1–2; PG 90, 1084BC.
[188] *Liber asceticus*; PG 90, 932A.

5. The Synthesis of the Three Acts

a. Action and Contemplation

The fact that the last syntheses we have discussed end in the worship of love leads us back once again to the intelligent subject, for whom the multiple system of the objective world is revealed in orderly steps. The first synthesis contextualized this subject in the abstract framework of his "faculties", the second immersed him in the great external waves of revelation, the third showed him halfway between objective rite and subjective reflection. The final synthesis is something the subject must bring to completion in his own complete self-realization as subject, as that has already begun to take place through his process of immersion in the objective and ritual realms. Or put another way: the external act has not yet been made the object of reflection; the earlier syntheses are dominated by a one-sided abstract intellectualism that must still "turn into its opposite" to become itself.

Our next task, then, is to show how knowledge, on one side, and action, on the other, constitute the two final polar realizations of the subject, which must interpenetrate "without confusion" (ἀσυγχύτως) in the totality of the subject himself. This totality must, once again, bear the name of love, or one of those other names that move from various extremes toward the middle: calm freedom from passions or drives (ἀπάθεια), gentleness (πραότης), wisdom (σοφία). But the totality must this time be considered as the final form of the subject as such, its full realization.

The problematic side of this synthesis comes from the fact that it is overloaded by the intellectualist heritage of the school of Evagrius. For Evagrius, love was essentially only the more positive name for inner calm, both were the result of the taming of the passions by practical asceticism (*praktikē*), and both were thus oriented, as ways and means, toward the higher goal of knowledge (*gnōsis*). Therefore love comes wholly from the soul's emotional faculty and is its perfection; as the most perfect blossom of the human capacity of desire, it serves —along with inner calm—to prepare the way for the final perfection of the properly intellectual part of the soul, the faculty of reason. There are several places, especially in the *Centuries on Love*, where Maximus himself joins in this traditional way of placing the accent: describing love as a fruit of the sensible, emotional part of the soul[189] and ascribing to it a preparatory function in the practical order.[190] Nevertheless, it is significant that such statements appear mainly in that anthology, while the main works resonate to a different tone altogether. Even if *gnōsis* appears, over and over again, under the weight of tradition, as the dominant pole, there is nevertheless a constant connection of this knowledge with everyday activity (*praxis*); under pressure from Maximus' own conception of the synthesis, the pure domination [of knowledge] yields to a genuinely polar parity.

The concept that brings the two poles together, then—their synthesis—is no longer one-sidedly named *gnōsis*, even a *gnōsis* purified by the practical; rather it is called "wisdom" (*sophia*), as in Origen, since it is the common product of an interpenetration of knowledge and action.

> The proof of the intellectual element is the vital; the radiance of the vital, however, is the intellectual. Praxis is the reality of theory, theory is the mysterious inner side of praxis. To put it briefly: virtue is the form in which knowledge appears to us, but knowledge is the center that holds virtue together. Through them both, virtue and knowledge, one single wisdom comes into being.[191]

This balance between poles is the distinctively Maximian form of the doctrine of human perfection. His image for action and knowledge is provided by the two apostles, Peter and John, hurrying to the grave of the Lord: they rush there together, the one constantly overtaking the other; both are mutually indispensable, and "neither one has an advantage or disadvantage with respect to the other."[192] "Through virtue and knowledge, we come into God's light."[193] "God's gifts are acquired through virtue and knowledge"; virtue sees God "in a mirror", knowledge "darkly".[194] "Through virtue and knowledge, the valley of the flesh" is filled in and "the mountain of pride" is leveled.[195]

Both are simply different modes in which the one Logos manifests his presence in us.[196] Thus both are designed to interpenetrate each

---

[189] *Centuries on Love* 4, 44; PG 90, 1057B; cf. ibid., 4, 61; 1061BC.
[190] Ibid., 4, 86; PG 90, 1069AB.
[191] *Quaestiones ad Thalassium* 63; CCG 22, 171, 390–97; PG 90, 681A.
[192] *Ambigua*; PG 91, 1381AB.
[193] *Quaestiones ad Thalassium* 8; CCG 7, 77, 11f.; PG 90, 285A.
[194] Ibid., 46; CCG 7, 309, 19–28; PG 90, 420D.
[195] Ibid., 47; CCG 7, 319, 119ff.; PG 90, 425C.
[196] Ibid.; CCG 7, 325, 206ff.; PG 90, 429BC.

other. What we encounter here is a new version of Maximus' underlying principle: being is essentially dynamic realization, logos [intelligible structure] made present in act and act struggling toward logos, nature become hypostatic and hypostasis unfolding itself through nature. "The personal face (πρόσωπον) of the *logos* [the intelligible structure] is life, but the natural basis (φύσις) of life is *logos*."[197] Certainly, theology is possible without praxis, but it is the theology of the demons![198] It is like faith without love—the faith that rules in hell.[199] In other words, there is no real knowledge without praxis: "If one seeks for the Lord in contemplation without praxis, one does not find him."[200] Knowledge remains cold and stiff if love does not inflame it.[201] Only such love can protect knowledge from envy and self-importance.[202]

On the other hand, knowledge illuminates action; and because action is only to be realized as a step toward the knowledge of God, it may never become an end in itself. "If someone practices virtue for the sake of the truth, he will not be struck by the arrows of empty vanity; but if someone seeks the truth for the sake of virtue, he already has arrogance and self-importance within him."[203] " 'Seek first the Kingdom of God and his righteousness' calls us first of all to recognize the truth and so to practice a way of life that fits the truth."[204] Simple action, without the enlightening effect of insight, is not even adequate for prayer.[205]

This is not to say that action is simply a means of reaching knowledge. Our actions must certainly make insight possible, purifying, preserving, and confirming our knowledge; knowledge must give a person the power over himself that allows him to resist the temptations of nature and the demons, when they try to cloud his pure mind. But precisely this purity demands that one's view of the world, one's ability to contemplate created things, be constantly renewed.[206] Praxis is what protects the eye that contemplates the world. And in fact the redeemed emergence of the contemplative mind into the world does not come

---

[197] *Opuscula*; PG 91, 9A–12A.

[198] Δαιμόνων θεολογία . . . δίχα πράξεως γνῶσις: *Epistles* 20; PG 91, 601C.

[199] *Centuries on Love* 1, 39; PG 90, 968C.

[200] *Quaestiones ad Thalassium* 48; CCG 7, 339, 151ff.; PG 90, 440A.

[201] *Centuries on Love* 1, 31; PG 90, 968A; cf. *Centuries on Knowledge* 1, 78; PG 90, 1112C.

[202] *Centuries on Love* 4, 61; PG 90, 1061B.

[203] *Quaestiones ad Thalassium* 30; CCG 7, 219, 20–23; PG 90, 369A.

[204] Ibid. 34; CCG 7, 235, 14–17; PG 90, 376D.

[205] *Centuries on Love* 2, 5; PG 90, 985A.

[206] *Quaestiones ad Thalassium* 49; CCG 7, 369, 308–14; PG 90, 460A.

about simply through looking and hearing but in redeemed action, in compassion (συμπαθῶς) toward one's fellowman, which is no longer bound up in the ties of passion (ἐμπαθῶς).[207] Maximus himself—the challenger, the comforter, the confessor—is the best example of his own teaching.

Action and knowledge, then, penetrate each other inseparably and push each other toward a constantly fuller degree of integration. Action, in the end, is only the "revelation" (φανέρωσις) of knowledge,[208] just as knowledge is the bright interior of action. But are not *actives and contemplatives* in the Church, seculars and monks, still in contrast with each other? Surely, their ideals are not the same; yet both are simply predominant emphases within a single overarching ideal, and to that degree—at least in a certain sense—both are of equal value. This way of conceiving the twofold Christian ideal moves in a very different direction from the whole of monastic theology from Evagrius to John Climacus; it is one of the great surprises in all of Maximus' work.

> There are two supreme states, two conditions of pure prayer. One is appropriate for the active person, the other for the contemplative. The soul acquires the first by beginning with the fear of God and holy hope, the second by beginning with the desire for God and the highest possible purification. The characteristic sign of the first kind of prayer is the gathering-in of the mind from all worldly thoughts and the offering up of prayer without confusion or distraction, as if the mind were in the presence of God himself (as it truly is). The characteristic of the second kind is the ecstatic captivation of the mind, within the buoyant activity of prayer, by the infinite divine light, so that the mind is no longer aware either of itself or of any other being, but only of the one who is bringing about this enlightenment within itself through love. And when the mind afterward also concerns itself with ideas about God, it receives clear and precise images from this experience.[209]

The two kinds of prayer, proper to the active and the contemplative person, are really contrasted here as ultimates (ἀκρόταται), each in its own line of development and both as final realizations of possible approaches to "pure prayer". Into the midst of the Alexandrian overestimation of pure ecstatic vision, Gregory of Nyssa's idea that all vision

---

[207] *Mystagogia* 24; PG 91, 716A.
[208] Ibid., 5; PG 91, 677B.
[209] *Centuries on Love* 2, 6; PG 90, 985AB.

remains wrapped in the night of faith and is simply a dark "sense of presence",[210] has here made its entry; so has the mysticism of Pseudo-Dionysius, for whom all ecstatic vision is nonvision. In Maximus, this [combined] approach—which is, at first sight, still purely "contemplative"—is developed to include "active" people as well: they are assigned the activity of "not seeing, but feeling the presence", while the contemplatives are associated more with the side of seeing.

Two further texts must be cited here, which suggest a kind of balance between *the lay and the monastic world*. They emphasize, first of all (with Evagrius), that the monk's task is not fulfilled simply by the external renunciation of things but that the decisive inner renunciation presents a much more difficult challenge.[211] More important, monks and seculars are tempted in the same way, even if the style of the temptations are different.

> The characteristic arrogance of monks is to be overly proud of their virtue and of what goes with it; the sign of a monk's vainglory is that he boasts of his own achievements, holds those of others as nothing, and ascribes everything to himself and not to God. The characteristic mark of a secular person's arrogance and vainglory, on the other hand, is to imagine that he has resources of good looks, riches, power, and intelligence and to boast about them.[212]

Each state in life has its own perfection, and it is precisely the things that constitute perfection for the one that form imperfections and dangers for the other.[213]

First of all, however, Maximus again constantly emphasizes the goodness of created things. "It is not food that is evil, but gluttony; not procreation, but lust; not money, but greed; not reputation, but the desire for reputation. If this is so, then there is nothing evil about things but their misuse, which comes from the carelessness of the mind in controlling its nature."[214] For this reason, the evangelical counsels are not a matter of fleeing from an evil world but of making a "voluntary sacrifice" in love.[215]

---

[210] *Homilies on the Song of Songs* 11; GNO 6, 324, 9ff.; PG 44, 1001B.

[211] *Centuries on Love* 4, 50; PG 90, 1060AB.

[212] Ibid., 3, 84; PG 90, 1041D–1044A.

[213] Ibid., 3, 85; PG 90, 1044AB.

[214] Ibid., 3, 4; PG 90, 1017CD; cf. a similar passage, ibid., 4, 66.

[215] Ibid., 4, 67; PG 90, 1064C.

The balance between *knowledge and action*, gnosis and virtue, has, in
Maximus' view, deep roots in the whole structure of human existence;
in its very foundations, human nature shows signs of a duality that is
constantly striving to resolve itself in successively higher degrees of
synthesis. The *Mystagogia* gives us a detailed description of this series
of syntheses. There Maximus lets a wise old man—obviously a literary
fiction—speak to us about the powers of the soul.

> The soul, he said, has two faculties: one for contemplation, as it is called,
> and one for action. He called the contemplative faculty mind (νοῦς),
> and the active faculty forethought (practical reason: λόγος); these are
> the two basic powers of the soul. And further, he attributed to mind
> wisdom, and to forethought prudence, as the two basic modes of oper-
> ation. Or, to put it more fully: the rational faculty of the soul includes
> mind, wisdom, contemplation (θεωρία), knowledge (γνῶσις), unforget-
> table insight, and, at the end of it all, the Truth; the planning faculty, on
> the other hand, includes forethought, prudence, action (πρᾶξις), virtue,
> faith, and, at the end of it all, the Good. The Truth and the Good,
> however, he said, reveal God; the Truth reveals him when the divine
> seems to be discovered by the interpreting mind in being (οὐσία) itself,
> for Truth is simple, single, unified, identical with itself, free from parts
> or change or fragility, something that cannot be hidden or put away; but
> the Good reveals God when he is discovered by the interpreting mind
> from events, for the Good is benevolent and cares for all the things it
> produces, protecting them, for according to the etymologists the word
> "good" [ἀγαθόν] comes from "being very much" [ἄγαν], "being solidly
> based", "moving forward well", and it gives to all things existence, se-
> curity, and movement.
>
> He next said that the five pairs (συζυγίαι) of beings that we have no-
> ticed in the soul must all be understood to point to the one pair that
> reveals God. The five pairs I am talking about are mind and forethought,
> wisdom and prudence, vision and action, knowledge and virtue, and
> unforgettable insight and faith. The pair that reveals God, however, is
> the Truth and the Good; and when the soul is being moved forward, it
> is united to the God of all things by imitating the unchangeableness of
> his being and the benevolence of his actions, through its being firmly
> grounded in the beautiful and through the steady attitude of its free
> will. . . .
>
> So he then said that the mind is moved by wisdom and comes through it
> to contemplation, through contemplation to knowledge, through knowl-
> edge to unforgettable insight, and through unforgettable insight to Truth;
> there the mind finds the defining goal of its movement, because there

its being (οὐσία), its potentiality (δύναμις), its habitual practice (ἕξις), and its activity (ἐνέργεια) are all comprehensively specified.

For the potentiality of the mind for action, he suggested, is wisdom, and the mind is itself wisdom; contemplation, however, is its habitual practice and knowledge is its activity. The unforgettable insight of wisdom, contemplation, and knowledge (or of the soul's potentiality, practice, and activity) is the endless movement that circles constantly and deliberately around the intelligible reality beyond all insight, whose limits are that one thing that cannot be concealed, Truth itself. And this is truly a cause of amazement, how what is unforgettable can still be circumscribed. Is it not circumscribed simply because it is limited by the Truth which is God? For God is Truth, and the mind moves around him without stopping or forgetting and is unable ever to cease from this movement, because it finds no end at which there is not still room and an opening for movement. The terrifying greatness of God's infinite being cannot be measured in spatial terms; it is utterly without parts and without distances, and no scheme, however cleverly planned, to discover what it really is in its essence can ever penetrate to its heart. But something that has no dimensions, no graspable parts, is also impenetrable to every other being.

Similarly, however, forethought is moved by prudence and so comes to moral action; through action it comes to virtue, through virtue then to faith—to that truly unshakeable, unassailable inner certainty about the things of God, which forethought first had in a potential way through prudence and which afterward proved itself to be a reality when its works were revealed by virtue. For "faith without works is dead" (Jas 2:17), as Scripture says; but what is dead and without effectiveness can hardly be considered a morally good thing. Through faith in the Good, however, forethought finds its limit and comes to rest from its natural action; here its potentiality, its objective reality, and its activity are comprehensively defined.

Then he called prudence the potentiality of forethought, and forethought, in his view, was potential prudence; practiced prudence was moral behavior, and realized prudence, finally, was virtue. Faith, however, he called the internalized, unshakeable confirmation of prudence, action, and virtue (or of potentiality, practice, and realization); and the final limit of faith is the Good, where all forethought ceases its movement and comes to rest. For God is the Good; every conceivable potentiality finds its limits in him. . . . If then the soul . . . comes to have a practically oriented mind, prudent wisdom, actively relevant contemplation, virtuous knowledge, and as a result of them all acquires that unforgettable insight that is indestructible and certain in its faith, and if it offers all these things to God—as effects with their causes, as realizations wisely developed from their own potential—it receives in return the gift of divinization that brings about simple unity.

For forethought is the realization and revelation of mind and is related to mind as effect to cause; so prudence is the realization of wisdom, action of contemplation, virtue of knowledge, and faith of unforgettable insight. And from them all, the interior attitude of the soul toward the Truth and the Good, toward God, is born. And this the old man called divine science, certain knowledge, love, and peace.[216]

This great passage gives full expression to the synthesis of the three acts [of the soul]: the five *syzygies* or syntheses lead upward to the two great transcendental qualities of Divine Being and of all being: truth and goodness. And as the highest possible attitude of man, every way by which the active Christian in the world opens himself toward the presence of God unites him with the ecstatic vision of the contemplative or monastic Christian.[217]

This acknowledgment of *faith* as the highest achievement of the whole "practical" side of the conscious mind is all the more remarkable in that Evagrius always took it as simply the starting point of the way to knowledge.[218] Here, however, faith is seen as the highest act of self-abandonment, the point at which the movement of the mind passes over into the "bright darkness" of the Pseudo-Dionysian God. Faith is not at all an imperfect kind of knowledge here, as it is in Ori-

---

[216] *Mystagogia* 5; PG 91, 673C–680B.

[217] Among the works of Evagrius, there is an exact summary of this passage: an appendix to his "Short Refutation", which is only available in Latin (PG 40, 1275–78). If this text really is by Evagrius himself, and was used by Maximus as a model—although we certainly tend to suppose, because of its content, that it is rather a later addition, summarizing the fifth chapter of the *Mystagogia*—then Evagrius himself must at some point have anticipated the exact structure of Maximus' synthesis, in contrast to his usual line of thought. The text is as follows: "Every soul should attempt to unite and synthesize these things through the grace of the Spirit and through its own labor: practical reason (*sermo*, λόγος) with theoretical (*mens*, νοῦς), action (*actio*, πρᾶξις) with contemplation (*contemplatio*, θεωρία), virtue (*virtus*, ἀρετή) with knowledge (*doctrina*, γνῶσις), and faith (*fides*, πίστις) with unforgettable insight (*cognitio ab omni oblivione libera*, ἄληστος γνῶσις). And it should unite these things so that none of them is less or greater than the other, so that every excess and every deficiency is avoided, and so that the soul itself, to put it briefly, increases its unity tenfold in the truth. For then it will itself be united with God, who is both true and good and who is certainly unity" (PG 40, 1278A).

[218] See M. Viller, "Aux sources de la spiritualité de s. Maxime: Les Oeuvres d'Évagre le Pontique", *Revue de l'ascétique et de la mystique* 11 (1930): 166f.

gen; it is the fullest flowering of the practical faculties. Gregory of Nyssa understood faith in this way,[219] and Philo and the Neoplatonists had also placed faith above knowledge and had described it as the surest and most unitive kind of knowledge;[220] Pseudo-Dionysius followed them.[221] Maximus, too, describes faith here as "the unmediated (ἄμεσος) unity of the mind with God".[222] He writes, more comprehensively:

> Our knowledge of things in the world discovers its own grounds for certainty (λόγοι πρὸς ἀπόδειξιν) in their natural contexts, in which they remain limited by their natures. But God is only an object of faith, known through the meanings of things themselves as one who exists; he is known by bestowing on the faithful the ability to confess and believe in his existence in a way that is more unshakeable than all proofs. Faith, after all, is true knowledge (γνῶσις) resting on principles that cannot be demonstrated, because it is itself the demonstration (ὑπόστασις: see Heb 11:1) of things that lie beyond all theoretical and practical knowledge.[223]

For just this reason, however, faith is itself boundless knowledge, and we can understand how the wise man in the *Mystagogia* can unite both of them in the supreme synthesis of "the most credible of all knowledge" (γνῶσις πιστοτάτη).[224]

b. Love as Unity

It is significant that Maximus' great explanation of the five syntheses does not speak of *love* (ἀγάπη). For love does not find a place as a "member" of any pair: it is rather their highest unity. Other texts show that Maximus understood it simply as *the* synthetic power. Active wisdom spreads outward in widening circles over all that is and embraces it all. But this universal possession is essentially characterized by the fact

---

[219] *Homilies on the Song of Songs*, passim; *Life of Gregory the Wonder-Worker*, PG 46, 901AB; *Contra Eunomium* 12; PG 45, 945Dff. [See also Gregory Nazianzen, *Orat.* 29, 21: Faith is the completion of what counts among us as reason.]

[220] See, e.g., Proclus, *Theol. Plat.* 1, 25.

[221] *De Div. Nom.* 2, 9; PG 3, 648B; ibid., 7, 4; PG 3, 872C.

[222] *Quaestiones ad Thalassium* 34; CCG 7, 237, 33; PG 90, 377B. For John of Scythopolis, it is "the most firm and unshakeable way to possess what we know": *In De Div. Nom.* 7, 4; PG 4, 353CD.

[223] *Centuries on Knowledge* 1, 9; PG 90, 1085CD; cf. ibid., 2, 36; PG 90, 1141C.

[224] *Mystagogia* 5; PG 91, 680B.

that it "gives ungrudgingly" (ἀφθόνως).[225] The wise person necessarily becomes a flowing source of good, while possessiveness is always a sign of disorder, betraying vanity. He loves all people; in fact, since he has himself become universalized, he loves them with the same love as God does.[226] He is the revelation in the world of God's hidden love.[227] Love for God and love for the world are not two different loves but two aspects of the one, indivisible love.[228] Through this love, the total synthesis of mankind comes to realization in a single identity,[229] in which each individual exchanges his own being with the rest, and all with God.[230] Unified in the love of Christ, who is love and therefore unity, the members of his body are also one with each other, so much so that they come to know each other's hearts and thoughts,[231] that they find it impossible to be truly absent from each other,[232] because they have permeated each other's being in love.[233] There is hardly a letter of Maximus that does not begin or end with such thoughts: he is always calling to mind the love that binds him with the addressee in a unity that bridges all distance and is the continuing foundation on which they can exchange their thoughts.[234] This deep consciousness of mutual presence (παρόντων ἀληθῶς ἐπαισθάνεσθαι) has nothing to do with a mere memory or imagination of the absent friend (μὴ ψιλῶς τὴν μνήμην φαντάζεσθαι ὑμᾶς).[235] It is "the law of love, which God has planted in the hearts of all people"[236] and which has nothing to do with sensible feelings or desires. This last element, strong as it may be at times, is always in danger of turning into surfeit and boredom; those who love in a divine way, on the other hand—who bear within

---

[225] *Centuries on Knowledge* I, 29: PG 90, 1093BC; ibid., I, 85; PG 90, 1120A.

[226] *Centuries on Love* I, 61; PG 90, 973A; ibid., I, 25; PG 90, 965B; ibid., I, 17; PG 90, 964D.

[227] *Epistles* 3; PG 91, 409B: "God, who hides himself, is revealed through the just" (κρυπτόμενος ὁ Θεὸς διὰ τῶν ἀξίων ἐκφαίνεται).

[228] *Epistles* 2; PG 91, 401D: οὐκ ἄλλην καὶ ἄλλην . . . , ἀλλὰ μίαν καὶ τὴν αὐτὴν ὅλην.

[229] Ibid.; PG 91, 404B: τοὺς πάντας κατὰ μίαν ταυτότητος δύναμιν περικλείων.

[230] Ibid.; PG 91, 401B.

[231] Ibid., 25; PG 91, 614AB.

[232] Ibid., 43; PG 91, 637BC.

[233] Ibid. 38; PG 91, 620B.

[234] Ibid. 7; PG 91, 433B, 440C–441A, 445B, 509BC, 608BC. Cf. *Quaestiones ad Thalassium*, prologue; CCG 7, 41, 405–17; PG 90, 261AB; *Exposition of the Lord's Prayer*; CCG 23, 27, 4–16; PG 90, 873A; etc.

[235] *Epistles* 8; PG 91, 441A.

[236] Ibid., 24; PG 91, 608C.

themselves the God who is love—are lifted above a fate of this kind. The "tenderness" that melts their hearts is a "capacity to love given to them" by God.[237] The highest synthesis of the soul, the "wisdom" that has penetrated to God's Truth and Goodness, translates itself into this necessity to love. "If someone loves God, he cannot avoid loving all people."[238]

In Maximus' view, love grows so far beyond all the parts and faculties of man that in the end it takes one over completely. Just as it "makes its own anything and everything that is related to it by nature",[239] so ultimately it is also no longer the product of the emotional faculty alone—as it is in Evagrius—but in a "deeper and more genuine" way (μᾶλλον δὲ κυριώτερον εἰπεῖν) the emotions communicate to the whole consciousness the vigor and inner tension (τόνος) of love.[240] But if our emotional and vulnerable side intensifies and, as it were, nourishes the mind itself, then "passionlessness" (apatheia) must also, in the end, have a positive sense for Maximus.

Inner peace and indifference, as we have already seen several times, are not meant to eliminate sensible things or the sensible faculties, but to make them serviceable for the mind, even to sublimate them into mind. Even if it is important at first to learn how to look at things from a sufficient distance so that they will no longer ensnare and over-power us—to retain only the "bare objective idea" (ψιλὸν νόημα) of the "thing" (πρᾶγμα),[241] through a "separation from our passions", and to penetrate through the wild fantasies of sensible illusion and persuasion to a sober view of the world as it is—still this clear, thin air of calm, through which the winds of the earth no longer blow, is not yet divine knowledge. Evagrius may have believed this for a time; for that reason, he ran the danger of confusing such knowledge with a Buddhist ability to "see through" all finite reality and of confusing Christian love with a detached gentleness.[242]

Maximus rejects this kind of rarification; the weight of our vulner-

---

[237] Ibid. 27; PG 91, 617B-D.

[238] Centuries on Love 1, 13; PG 90, 964B.

[239] Exposition of the Lord's Prayer, CCG 23, 27, 3ff.; PG 90, 873A.

[240] Ibid.; CCG 23, 58, 542–45; PG 90, 896C. Cf. Diadochus, Centuries 62 (ed. Des Places, 122), and chap. 5, sec. 5 above, "The Dialectics of Passion".

[241] Centuries on Love 3, 41–44; PG 90, 1029AB.

[242] See my article, "Metaphysik und Mystik des Evagrius Ponticus", Zeitschrift für Aszese und Mystik 14 (1939): 31–47.

ability is not simply a "spirit of heaviness"[243] but also the healthy and necessary gravity of earthly existence. A knowledge of God without *pathos* does not yet lead the mind to its full distance from earthly things but is like a mere mental image of a sensible object.[244]

> Whoever has eliminated his evil passions and has freed his thoughts from material attachments (literally, "has made them insubstantial": ψιλοὺς ἐργασάμενος) has not yet succeeded, by that process, in also ordering his vulnerability (*pathos*) toward the divine. Rather, it can happen that such a person is often touched inwardly neither by human nor by divine reality.[245]

Precisely in people such as this the danger is at its strongest that they will become prey once again to the passions that only seemed to die away "and will wallow like pigs in the drives of the flesh" or reap from their ecstasies a mere "fruitless and pretentious knowledge". Therefore our vulnerabilities must be transformed in a positive way. If someone's mind is always directed to God, his desires have already grown beyond themselves (ὑπερηύξησεν) into a longing for God, his affectivity is completely transformed into love of God; the earthly part of him is translated into something divine and more closely connected and tied with God.[246] So love itself becomes a "divine passion", "the blessed passion of divine love".[247] "All longing and desire is directed toward God."[248] "The perfect soul is one whose whole emotional capability is perfectly oriented toward God."[249] If this soul regards the world "indifferently" from now on, it is not out of contempt for earthly things, but because God is endlessly more beautiful than any of them.[250] From this height, the differences of this world seem so inconsequential that they no longer make a difference, and the soul tends to prefer what

---

[243] Following the thinking of Evagrius, Maximus, in the *Centuries on Love* (3, 56), also occasionally refers to the mind as "light" in weight, as having "the form of light" (3, 97), even as a source of light that the person in a state of ecstasy is allowed to see (4, 79–80; cf. *Centuries on Knowledge* 2, 8). But these reminiscences should not distract us from the fact that Maximus' basic views are quite different.

[244] *Centuries on Love* 3, 66; PG 90, 1036D.

[245] Ibid.; 3, 68; PG 90, 1037B.

[246] Ibid.; 2, 48; PG 90, 1000C.

[247] Ibid., 3, 67; PG 90, 1037A.

[248] Ibid., 3, 72; PG 90, 1040B.

[249] Ibid., 3, 98; PG 90, 1048A.

[250] Ibid., 1, 4–6; PG 90, 961BC; 1, 8; PG 90, 961D.

is apparently less valuable as something more useful, for God's sake. "Knowledge is, of its own nature, good; so is health. But for many, the opposite is more beneficial. . . . The same is true of riches and of pleasure."[251] God created everything "very good", even the things of this world that seem to contradict each other. But when they are weighed on the scales of eternity against the infinitely greater worth of God, a certain distance from them is needed to express the highest degree of righteousness and objectivity. "Use" (χρῆσις), not addictive enjoyment—*uti, non frui*—is for Maximus, as for Augustine, the law of perfection.[252] In his great synthesis of the virtues, Maximus ends by constructing the supreme polarity: prudence and righteousness unite as wisdom; strength and moderation become a calm joy (πραότης), "which is called by many freedom from vulnerability (*apatheia*). Both together, wisdom and calm joy, comprise love."[253]

6. Now and Eternity

The syntheses of the spirit were the realization of the synthesis of Christ in his members. For that reason, they started out from the tendencies and capabilities of the individual subject (each one himself a synthesis of sense and reason), and they returned full circle as the living reality of the same subject (as a synthesis of activity and knowledge). In this way, the subject as such reaches his true fulfillment; but his fulfillment as both a part of the world and a member of the Mystical Body has not yet been thematically developed. Still lacking [in this theological picture] is the realization of the final synthesis in its totality, as Christ, the world's Redeemer, prefigured it: the unification of the world with God. Only with this final synthesis does Maximus put the crowning piece onto his whole achievement; everything in his thought is directed here. With this step, he fulfills the passionate longing of the whole patristic tradition, especially that of Alexandria, for divinization. At the same time, his glowing eschatological vision makes him the great teacher of the Celtic speculator Erigena and, through him, by a long chain of descent, the intellectual ancestor of the German idealists. Here, if anywhere, Maximus reveals what he meant by "godly vulnerability". The

---

[251] Ibid., 2, 77; PG 90, 1009A.
[252] Ibid., 2, 76; PG 90, 1009A; 2, 82; PG 90, 1009C; etc.
[253] *Ambigua*; PG 91, 1249AB.

great final problem still before us, then, is the problem of Maximus'
mysticism.

a. The Centuries on Knowledge

At the crossroads between the world and God, where the restless,
questing movement of creation senses something beyond itself and,
becoming indescribably still, lets itself sink into the rest of eternity
—where eternity descends from above into time, to become a presence constantly annulling time from within—we find the most starkly
challenging work of the theologian-mystic Maximus: his *Centuries on
Knowledge*. Until now, we have used it relatively little; in this final chapter, however, we must examine its meaning within the context of his
whole achievement.

These "Two Hundred Chapters on God and the Order of Salvation"
(or "and the Fulfillment of Creation", which is also a way of translating
oikonomia) are, as we said in the introduction, a synthesis of Alexandrian
mystical theology. Word-for-word quotations from Origen, woven into
the texts like leitmotifs, are developed with thoughts borrowed from
Evagrius and Pseudo-Dionysius, and the whole is placed within the
framework of Maximus' own early mysticism. While the *Centuries on
Love* often transpose the mystical theology of Maximus into an Evagrian mode, and the Scholia transform it to resonate with the song of
Pseudo-Dionysius, here the basic themes of Origen himself are what
clothe Maximus' conception of the world, although surely also in a
form harmonized with Pseudo-Dionysian thought. The first ten chapters are, in fact, tuned to Pseudo-Dionysius' key, and one must agree
with Sherwood when he says that Maximus seems to have wanted to
set forth there the point of view from which one must see and eval-
uate all that is to follow.[254] With intoxicating yet transparent passion,
he describes the return of the world to God, the purification of the
soul from "sensibility", its ascent into ever-more-intellectual realms
and conditions, and the metamorphoses of the Logos into ever-more-
subtle forms of existence; through all of this, the initiates are led upward gradually, step by step, while the gradual dawning of the light of
Tabor, the presence [of God] to intellectual creation, and finally the

---

[254] Polycarp Sherwood, *An Annotated Date-List of the Works of Maximus Confessor*, Studia
Anselmiana, 30 (Rome, 1952), 35.

cessation of all the movement of the ages, God's Sabbath rest, are held up for our praise.

In this work, Maximus reveals himself as Origen's most profound interpreter. Yet he is not simply, not primarily that; to present him in such a guise would be as unjust as to speak of Delacroix' copies of Rubens or Reger's Mozart Variations as their masterpieces. Origenism, portrayed here in such a pure and beguiling way, is only one of the sources and roots of Maximus' conception of the world. In any case, this sketchbook of two hundred little studies allows us to cast a long and revealing look into the deep background of his soul.

One thing, as we have said, must be noticed from the start: the encounter that he immediately arranges between Origen's Logos-centered mysticism, whose central idea is the ascent of the world to God, the Father and source of all, by reason of the successive transforming incarnations of the world's Redeemer, with the transcendent idea of God that characterizes post-Nicene and Pseudo-Dionysian theology. It is the fusion that is already made clear in the title of the work, between *theologia*, the term for reflection on God as he is, and *oikonomia*, the term for God as he is immersed in the world and is returning to himself, step by step, within it. It is the abstract problem of the many and the one, of being "home to" oneself and being "outside" oneself, that is here given a new form. So it is clear that a strong Neoplatonic, spiritualizing, idealist breeze is blowing through Maximus' world; in many places one feels very near to Proclus, Erigena, Cusanus, and Schelling. Correspondingly, the Logos appears in the world here only by way of being "outside" himself, in a guise that is deceptive, but meant for the world's instruction; he is "Logos in essence, flesh in external appearance" (2, 60).[255] The human Christ appears hardly at all. On the other hand, there is also little space left here for the trinitarian God. For in the Origenist perspective, which is preserved here with extreme consistency, the Logos is "the second God", even a unitive concept for the world as a whole, while the highest God is the Father alone; in the perspective of Pseudo-Dionysius, however, the Trinity is again wrapped in the veils of the groundless abyss that separates the absolutely transcendent "essence" of God from the world.

If, then, the two cardinal points of Christian faith [the Incarnation

---

[255] In what follows, the book and chapter numbers will be given in the text and refer to the text of the two *Centuries on Knowledge* in PG 90, 1084–1176.

and the Trinity] thus disappear almost completely here behind the Gnostic idealism that alone dominates, the point of contact between God and the world, at which Maximus aims, becomes the same as the classic starting point of later Romantic and Russian "Sophia" mysticism, both of which can rightfully claim the *Centuries on Knowledge* as their model. In what follows, we will give at least a brief sketch of its basic themes.

God is simply above time and the ages, above the movement of the world, above beginning, middle, and end, and therefore God is inconceivable, only to be approached through faith (1, 1–10): here the Pseudo-Dionysian pedal point sounds from the start! Everything in the world is polarized: as subject and object (1, 82; 2, 2), mind and sense (2, 5), thought and being (2, 3), nature and grace (1, 49); but God is above all duality. For that very reason, God is the midpoint of all things, like the center of a circle (2, 4). The purpose of the *oikonomia*, which the Logos brings to fulfillment, is to lead the polarized, temporal creature across the abyss into God. The Logos, who is himself God, is in his involvement in the world the world's central mystery (1, 66), the one Word, the one Idea in which all the different words and ideas of the world find their complementarity, as in a single totality (*plērōma*; 2, 2–21). Multiplicity is "a falling-away", "a judgment"; return to unity is "providence" and "the plan of salvation" (*oikonomia*), "judgment and providence" (κρίσις καὶ πρόνοια), in the language of Evagrius.[256] In order to gather the world of multiplicity together again, the Logos transforms himself into the whole manifold variety of things: for those who are able to break through the shell of the manifold world of the senses by contemplation and ascetical training, the Logos is always visible and graspable, in an ever purer form, as the authentic meaning and heart of things. He is the spiritual manna that takes on every flavor, according to the ability of the individual to taste

---

[256] Ibid., 1, 33; 2, 16. Maximus uses this terminology in a number of other places: *Quaestiones ad Thalassium*; CCG 7, 207, 89; PG 90, 364AB; CCG 7, 241, 34; PG 90, 380A; CCG 7, 431, 26f.; PG 90, 501C; CCG 7, 457, 238f.; PG 90, 517D; CCG 22, 173, 416ff.; PG 90, 681CD; CCG 22, 239, 831; PG 90, 728C; CCG 22, 281, 485; PG 90, 756D; *Quaestiones et Dubia*; CCG 10, 56, 5–6; PG 90, 825A; *Exposition of Psalm 59*; CCG 23, 10, 123; PG 90, 861C; *Centuries on Love* 1, 78; 1, 99; 4, 16–18; 2, 46; 2, 99; *Ambigua*; PG 91, 1032A; 1121A; 1133–36; 1145A; 1168BC; 1188D; 1205D; 1281D; 1297A; 1305A; 1400A; 1401B. But Maximus is always concerned, as we have already seen, to exclude the purely Origenist sense of these terms.

him: milk to the weak, vegetables to the ill, solid food to the perfect (1, 100). He is "water, mind, spirit, and fire" (2, 63); he is "straw" for the bestial, "bread" for the rational (2, 66); he is dew, water, spring, and river (2, 67); way (2, 68); door (2, 69); light, life, resurrection, and truth (2, 70). So he is the mustard seed, which grows from being a single thing to being the tree of the world (2, 10). He is also the living content of all the commandments (2, 11; 2, 95); those who keep them he nourishes, as their "essential bread" (2, 56; 1, 33). In each particular thing he is "veiled", "densified" (παχυνόμενος); if he is then recognized and understood in them, he casts away the shell and becomes "light", both as radiance and as delicacy (2, 37–38; 2, 61). The challenge, then, is not to isolate him rigidly in the world but to let him "rise", in order to rise with him (2, 45, 47, 73, 94). "Ascent" is the key word, constantly underlined, in this Logos-mysticism (2, 8, 18–19, 23, 77, and so on); its goal is to "catch up with" Christ, to move closer to him (2, 25). For the risen Christ raises all things and draws them to himself (2, 32). Even the sequence from the Old Covenant to the New and from the New Covenant to the "eternal Gospel" is a clear movement away from "flesh" and toward "spirit" (1, 88–96); Holy Scripture itself is a quasi-incarnation, whose purpose is to lead us from the letter to the spirit (1, 91), from the veil to open vision (2, 60). The high light of Tabor, the radiant garments, the divine voice from heaven are symbols for spiritualization (2, 13–15). The three great "days" of salvation history—the death of Good Friday, the burial of Holy Saturday and the Resurrection of Easter Sunday (1, 59–63)—are the "economic" representation of the three "mystic days" of the world: the "sixth day" is the completion and the death of every finite nature; the "seventh day" is the burial of all finitude and temporality; and the "eighth day" is their resurrection in God (1, 51–57). It [the eighth day] is, at the same time, the day of our mystical circumcision from all worldly existence (1, 40–41) and the day of the world's great harvest, when the intelligible meanings (λόγοι) will be gathered into the unity of whole Logos (1, 32, 42–45); so it is the day of our entry into his "bridal chamber" (1, 16).

In this way, the Logos will bring his own totality (*plērōma*) to fulfillment in the world (2, 87); simplicity will rise up from composite reality (2, 74); the "presence" of the Logos, his parousia, comes to its fullness to the degree that he brings all things to fulfillment. The parousia, then, is not a sudden eschatological appearance of some-

thing new, but the gradual process by which eternity, which is always
present in the world, becomes evident, a step-by-step actualization of
an always-potential immanence (δυνάμει ἐνεργείᾳ: 2, 92). It is the gradual dominance of presence over absence (2, 57), of intelligible over
bodily presence (2, 29), of presence through knowledge over presence
merely through virtue (1, 98; 2, 58). This mystical parousia is realized
in those who have reached perfection, but it is hidden in its early stages
(1, 97). It is identified with being "dead to the world", with freedom
from vulnerability (apatheia: 1, 97). It is made possible by the fact that
the glorified Christ no longer has any relationship with the world of
spatial limitation but is present literally everywhere. The goal of the
perfected person is to ascend through all the heavens in the same way
that Christ has risen (2, 18).

All of this is Origenism, of the strictest and most consistent sort.[257]
But while Origen has said most of what he has to say in developing
the above ideas—since for him the delivery of the world, appropriated
and fulfilled in this way, by the Logos to the Father, does not imply
any further major problems of interpretation—Maximus sees here the
beginning of the other side of the problem of mysticism: How is the
fulfillment of the created world in the Logos related to the transcendental incorporation of the cosmos into a God who is absolutely "beyond" the world? The Centuries give no unambiguous answer to this
question but circle around the problem constantly. The chapters with
the strongest Origenist coloring (especially in the second century) naturally lead us to expect that with the parousia of the Logos—who is,
after all, God—the immediate presence of the Father and the Holy
Spirit will also be realized; our mystical ascent in Christ automatically
leads us to the Father (2, 45, 47, 61, and especially 2, 71).

But even Origen's doctrine of the "aeons" itself introduced a new
line of thought: however many types and levels of aeonic systems there
may be, at some point the soul must have crossed over them all and
have reached what is "above the aeons", the actual "Kingdom of God",
where there are no longer shifts and movements but only the stillness
of eternity (2, 86). Origen himself struggled with this critical passage
from the created realm of movement, of the ever-provisional, to what

---

[257] See my anthology of passages from Origen, Geist und Feuer, English translation, Spirit
and Fire, especially the chapters "God-Fire" (German: 452f.; English: 320–50), "The Eternal
Christ" (German: 189f.; English: 133–48), "Food" (German: 364f.; English: 258–67).

is simply eternal; in many places in the *Centuries*, one feels this same mistrust toward the changeability of created nature, the same need to leave behind all the ups and downs of the aeons, the shipwrecks of the world, and to reach at last the terra firma of eternity, the "still point", the state of being "firmly rooted" (ἀκινησία, πῆξις, στάσις, ἵδρυσις, μονή, ἀτρεψία, βεβαιότης) in God himself (1, 39, 45, 81, 84, 86; 2, 13, and so on). So he develops a mystical theology of the eternal Sabbath, in which the creature rests completely from his own movement, and God alone, with whom action and rest are one, accomplishes his eternal work (1, 36–39; 2, 64–65). Maximus decides the question of whether there is eternal progress or a final condition of rest in the direction of Origen rather than of Gregory of Nyssa, by choosing the second alternative (2, 88).

Yet despite the strongly Origenist note, this longing for immovability must have totally different roots in Maximus from those it had in Origen. For Origen, all "movement" was connected with an original "descent" that began in sin; a return to "stability" therefore implied the return of the being to itself, to its best condition (κατάστασις). For Maximus, movement is something basically natural, in Aristotle's sense; complete lack of movement, therefore, can only mean for him a supernatural transcending of the whole created order. Therefore his picture of the Sabbath rest, even in the *Centuries*—despite its Origenist coloring—has a much stronger relationship with the mysticism of Pseudo-Dionysius, with its emphasis on God's transcendence. Maximus simply emphasizes, in contrast to Pseudo-Dionysius' Neoplatonist stress on participation, the "Aristotelian" distance between the God of creation and a self-contained world—a point where one can feel the influence of Gregory of Nyssa—and regards self-determination and natural movement as essential to created being.

This implies, however, that in Maximus' view the passage into God's Sabbath necessarily takes the route of a complete "death" of the creature. For the passage is pure grace (1, 68), completely beyond the creature's own beginning, middle, and end (1, 69). So it does not follow Evagrius' model, where the mind passes over (ἐκδημία) by becoming completely absorbed in its own deepest being. Rather, it comes about through a radical abandonment of itself (ἐκβὰς ἑαυτοῦ; 1, 81). Thus the mind must leave all duality behind itself, even though that is ingrained in its ultimate constitution as a creature (1, 82; 2, 2–3). Only here does God truly become "darkness" (1, 84–85); only here does it make sense to speak of a complete "blindness" of the one who has left the world behind (2, 9). The idea of a "mystical death" thus receives much more emphasis here than in Origenism. For it concerns both mind and body to the same degree, involving the whole of one's nature (1, 67). Even the *Centuries on Love* had spoken of such a death of the mind (2, 62). But in this process, nature only dies to its own mortality, for "everything is dead that lives [only] by participating in life" (2, 36).

What comes to fulfillment in this death of human nature—a death that Maximus sees completely in the light of the cosmic law of the death and Resurrection of Christ (1, 59–63, 65; 2, 27)—is nothing less than the adoption of the internal "activity" of the creature by the divine reality itself. The heart that is completely "pure" knows no further movement of its own but keeps itself in a state of utter simplicity, like a mirror or a writing tablet turned toward God, who writes his own words on it (2, 80–82).

> [It] becomes God itself, by participating in the grace that makes it like God; it brings all its own activities, intellectual and sensible, to rest, just as it brings to rest the natural movements of the body, which is divinized along with it in proper proportion to its own participation in the process of divinization. The result is that God alone, in the end, is visible in both soul and body, and their own particular characteristics are swept up in the overwhelming measure of glory (2, 88).

Our potentiality is realized, in fact, by being developed in the direction of God's actuality (2, 83) and thus takes on its new reality in his endless activity (1, 35). Thus [our final state] is a Sabbath in the sense that God rests from his activity in the action of his creatures, in order to accomplish his own action in creatures from now on (1, 47). Thus one comes to the state of his being present without any mediating distance (ἀμέσως; 1, 46; 2, 25), of the self-revelation of God in and through the perfected creature (2, 79), of the parousia [of Christ] in the soul (1, 46, 93; 2, 98) in its complete nakedness (γυμνὸς νοῦς: 1, 83; 2, 73, 60), of a "face-to-face" relationship (2, 87) in the mutual glorying of God and the soul in each other (2, 72).

The seam between the two groups of problems—the perfection of the world in the Logos as its total idea and the "ecstatic" moving of the world beyond itself in the transcendent God—is occasionally visible in a sharply defined, thematic way. This happens, for instance, when Maximus is attempting to reconcile Paul's conception of a "knowledge in part" [1 Cor 13:12] with the Johannine knowledge of "the glory of the only-begotten of the Father" [Jn 1:14]. The first of these refers to *theologia*, to [our understanding of] God's being, which can never be understood completely; the second refers to the *oikonomia*, to the complete, cosmically realized idea of the Logos' becoming part of the world. Or it happens when Maximus tries to explain the difference between "the Kingdom of heaven" and "the Kingdom of God". The first is the supreme degree of possession of God's world of ideas; the second is the possession of God himself. The first is "the end of all things", the second stands "beyond the end", even though both of them are distinguished only theoretically (κατ᾽ ἐπίνοιαν), not in reality (κατ᾽ ὑπόστασιν: 2, 90).

With this "theoretical distinction", the towering synthesis of the *Centuries on Knowledge* comes to an end: Maximus has built the Alexandrian conception of reality, in an act of supreme stylistic simplification, into the Pseudo-Dionysian system of transcendence, all the while adding his own colors to that system and bringing it into new light, through the notions of a "Sabbath rest" and of a reality beyond the aeons. Whether one should speak of syncretism in referring to this work[258] is a matter of personal taste; its unity, even in its basic conception, seems to assert itself clearly enough.

b. Movement and Rest

Above all, one must not regard the *Centuries on Knowledge* as expressing the only, or even the decisive, form of Maximus' eschatology. They are a brilliant adaptation or variation of his main theme in Origenist terms, but they do not embody the theme itself. This theme may sound similar [when one hears it]; yet it has a purer sound, and in it, above all, the excessive emphasis on detachment from the sensible recedes in importance. And there is another thematic concept, taken from Pseudo-Dionysius, which also leaves its mark on Maximus' eschatology, taking its place beside the ideal of rest (as the cessation of the movement [κίνησις] that for Origen is sinful, for Maximus natural): the ideal of peace (εἰρήνη).

This peace, however, lies beyond movement and rest, because it satisfies and puts to rest all kinds of opposition. It is "ever-moving rest and

---

[258] See I. Hausherr, "Ignorance infinie", *Orientalia Christiana periodica* 2 (1936): 351–62.

steadfast movement at the same time".[259] Thus this coming home to peace also fulfills the positive implications of creaturely longing, even though such longing is experienced sometimes in contradictory terms within the world. Far from turning itself to surfeit (κόρος) and excess, as the [divisive] love of limited and limiting things (περιοριζόμενον καὶ στάσεως αἴτιον) tends to do, godly love is rather the constant expansion and broadening of longing (ἐπιτείνειν μᾶλλον τὴν ὄρεξιν).[260] In this sense of a complete openness, and of the derigidifying effect of love, one can indeed speak of an eternal forward movement of the creature into God.[261] But this forward movement has nothing to do with temporality and "aeonic" duration; it is simply another way of saying that even in laying hold of God, we never wholly grasp him. He remains always "the inconceivable conception".[262]

It belongs ultimately to Maximus' nature, however, to emphasize the gracious immanence of the Absolute One in the creature even more than this transcendence. Here "parousia" ["presence"] becomes, in a way, the concluding concept of his whole train of thought. "This presence leaves nothing empty, nothing unfulfilled."[263] "There will be nothing left to the realm of appearances and nothing that can be put on a par with God; for all things, intellectual and sensible, will be grasped by him through his ineffable self-revelation and presence."[264] Creatures will be like bodily organs to him,[265] for just as the soul dwells in every member of its body and gives it being and movement, so God will dwell in every part of the world.[266] "Through it all, God in his completeness will grow like a soul."[267] The world then is

> the image and appearance of the light that never appears, a perfectly exact mirror, completely transparent, untouched, immaculate, catching in itself

---

[259] *Quaestiones ad Thalassium* 65; CCG 22, 195, 137ff.; PG 90, 700A; *Mystagogia* 5; PG 91, 677A; *Mystagogia* 19; PG 91, 696BC.

[260] *Ambigua*; PG 91, 1089BC.

[261] "We never have enough of being made participants in God" (οὐ λήγομεν θεουργούμενοι): *Quaestiones ad Thalassium* 22; CCG 7, 141, 79f; PG 90, 320D; "the state of transformation toward divinization never ceases" (ὡς μὴ παυομένης ποτὲ τῆς . . . κατὰ τὴν πρὸς θέωσιν μεταποίησιν . . . διαθέσεως): ibid.; CCG 7, 143, 114ff.; PG 90, 321C.

[262] *Ambigua*; PG 91, 1076D.

[263] *Mystagogia* 21; PG 91, 697A.

[264] *Ambigua*; PG 91, 1077A.

[265] Ibid.; PG 91, 1088B; cf. *Quaestiones ad Thalassium* 54; CCG 7, 447, 73; PG 90, 512B.

[266] *Ambigua*; PG 91, 1099AB.

[267] Ibid.; PG 91, 1088B.

—if one may dare to say it—the full radiance of the primordial beauty, made like God yet no less itself, radiating—insofar as it is capable—the goodness of the silence hidden in the abyss.[268]

The unity [of God and the creature] will go as far as the point of "indivisible identity"[269] and will stop just short of the irreducible difference of natures.[270] It is a "sameness due to assimilation",[271] an identity in the "realization" of two natures, like the bridge reaching out from two shores and meeting over the abyss. It is the final synthesis built on the synthetic person of Christ, the last of the "towers" he has constructed.[272]

Now the world is totally transfigured into God; its totality rests within the inner realm of God's totality,[273] its unity encounters the primordial unity.[274] The radiance of God's glory streams over it, as the splendor of the sun overpowers the light of the stars.[275] Beings that exist as parts entrust themselves to the dominance of the whole.[276] Every will that wills for itself is now annulled, since the creature no longer desires to belong to itself.[277] There is only one activity (μία ἐνέργεια) left now, the activity of God—and that is precisely the highest level of freedom.[278] The image of the burning bush will then be completely realized: "That ineffable, overwhelming fire, which burns away, hidden in the essence of things as in the bush",[279] will then burst out: not to consume the world,[280] for it needs no fuel to burn. It will be a flame of love at the heart of things, and that flame is God himself.

This presence of God is peace. The philosophy and theology of synthesis are ultimately a vision of the presence of eternal calm and peace, simultaneously existing in and above all opposition within the world,

---

[268] *Mystagogia* 23; PG 91, 701C.

[269] Ibid., 13; PG 91, 692D.

[270] *Quaestiones ad Thalassium* 22; CCG 7, 139, 36ff.; PG 90, 320A.

[271] Ibid., 59; CCG 22, 53, 136ff.; PG 90, 609A.

[272] Ibid., 48; CCG 7, 335, 80f.; PG 90, 436B.

[273] *Ambigua*; PG 91, 1088A.

[274] Ibid.; PG 91, 1200B.

[275] Ibid.; PG 91, 1077A; *Mystagogia* 1; PG 91, 665AB.

[276] *Mystagogia* 1; PG 91, 665B.

[277] Ibid., 23; PG 91, 701B.

[278] *Ambigua*; PG 91, 1076BC; note the refinement here of the easily misunderstood expression in *Opuscula*; PG 91, 33AB.

[279] *Ambigua*; PG 91, 1148C.

[280] *In Coel. Hier.* 13; PG 4, 97A; cf. ibid., 15; PG 4, 105B.

opposition that will vanish, in the end, like mist in the blue sky of eternity. All discord and conflict in things are simply a superficial phenomenon.[281] The "natural, innate war of substances",[282] a war that is naturally given with the contrasting essences of things[283] and that leaves its mark even on the moral life,[284] can never burst the bonds of this eternal peace.[285] God's goodness exceeds all bounds and is not bound naturally to any partial reality. This transcendental goodness is the first and final quality of God. For Origen, that quality was "unclouded truth", for Gregory of Nyssa—the poet of the eternal pilgrimage—a "hopeless beauty" that the soul endlessly seeks. But Maximus, who was gripped more than either of them by the deep goodness and blessedness of nature, had to find that ultimate mark [of God] in goodness. Goodness is God's most perfect name;[286] everything that is shares essentially in it, and it forms the substantial core of every being.[287] "Goodness, noblest of all words!"[288]

c. Restoration

Nevertheless, one question remains open. In this ecstatic final picture of the reentry of the world into God, how can an eternal hell exist? Should not this final contradiction, too, be resolved within God's peace? Maximus often uses the word *apokatastasis*—a word that had denoted the forbidden theory of the abolition of hell since the time of Origenism—but he gives it a much broader and vaguer meaning.[289] Yet one knows that even in his own lifetime Maximus was accused

---

[281] "Appearance, by which the constant war of perceptible things with each other has come into being" (τὴν ἐμφάνειαν, καθ᾽ ἣν ὁ διηνεκὴς τῶν αἰσθητῶν πρὸς ἄλληλα συνέστηκε πόλεμος): *Mystagogia* 23; PG 91, 697CD.

[282] As John of Scythopolis, alluding to ancient Greek tradition, says, there is "a natural war . . . that is part of the family heritage of things" (φυσικὸν πόλεμον . . . ἐμφύλιον): *In De Div. Nom.* 11; PG 4, 392CD.

[283] *Centuries on Love* 3, 27–28; PG 90, 1025AB.

[284] *Quaestiones ad Thalassium* 51; CCG 7, 403, 166ff.; PG 90, 484A.

[285] *In De Div. Nom.* 11; PG 4, 397B.

[286] Ibid., 5; PG 4, 312B.

[287] Ibid., 4; PG 4, 280D. (Attribution uncertain.)

[288] Ibid., 13; PG 4, 280D. (Attribution uncertain.)

[289] *Opuscula*; PG 91, 72B; *Exposition of the Lord's Prayer*; CCG 23, 31, 83; PG 90, 876C; and especially *Quaestiones et Dubia* 13; CCG 10, 17, 1–18, 21; PG 90, 796A–C. This was noticed long ago: see the letter of Maximus Margounios to David Moeschel of 1599 (PG 91, 656A).

of "following the teachings of Origen and being of one opinion with him on all subjects".[290] It has been made sufficiently clear [here] that this was false, at least on the subject of the preexistence of souls and also on the theory that the created multiplicity of things, especially in the world of sense, came into being through a fall from the original "henad". But is this true of the "restoration of all things"? The works of Maximus must be allowed to give us their own answer.

Maximus speaks of hell in many places.[291] The most famous passage is the great exhortation in the *Liber asceticus*, which employs a strict and sober eloquence to wring from the heart contrition and a sense of sin.[292] On the other hand, we can find a number of passages that use the language of Gregory of Nyssa to speak, in general terms, of God's universal will for human salvation and of the redemption of the whole of human nature because of its indivisible ontological unity.[293] Maximus speaks of the unity of the Mystical Body as if no member should ever be missing from it.[294] The incarnation of God is realized in everyone,[295] the whole species will be saved from death,[296] "the works of sin will disappear into nothingness",[297] all will share in the resurrection,[298] the whole world, in the Son, will be "subject" to the Father [1 Cor 15:28].[299] The sheep that was lost and found again is

---

[290] *Acta*; PG 90, 93A; cf. ibid.; PG 90, 120AB.

[291] *Quaestiones ad Thalassium* 11; CCG 7, 91, 33–38; PG 90, 293B; *Liber asceticus*; PG 90, 941–48; *Ambigua*: PG 91, 1237B; 1252B; 1373B; 1376B; 1392D; *Epistles* 24; PG 91, 612C; *Mystagogia* 14; PG 91, 693B.

[292] *Liber asceticus*; PG 90, 941–48.

[293] *Epistles* 17; PG 91, 580C; *Ambigua*; PG 91, 1044B; 1044D; 1280A (first line); 1280C; 1314AB; *Quaestiones ad Thalassium* 2; CCG 7, 51; PG 90, 272; *Quaestiones ad Thalassium* 21; CCG 7, 127f.; PG 90, 312F; *Quaestiones ad Thalassium* 23; CCG 7, 153; PG 90, 328B; *Quaestiones ad Thalassium* 63; CCG 22, 145–47; PG 90, 663C; *Quaestiones ad Thalassium* 64; CCG 22, 195–97; PG 90, 700AB; *Exposition of Psalm 59*; CCG 23, 3; PG 90, 857A; *Centuries on Love* I, 25; 56–57; 61; 70; 86; 2, 34; 44; 46; 3, 2; 29. In the *Centuries on Knowledge*, because of the work's basically Origenistic orientation, Maximus never speaks of hell but often speaks of a "universal homecoming" (διόλου κατάντησις) (1, 47: PG 90, 1100B) or of a complete subjection (2, 27, PG 90, 1137B).

[294] *Ambigua*; PG 91, 1088B, 1092C.

[295] Ibid.; PG 91, 1084D.

[296] *Exposition of Psalm 59*; CCG 23, 3, 14f.; PG 90, 857A.

[297] *Quaestiones et Dubia* 73; CCG 10, 111, 19f.; PG 90, 848A.

[298] *Exposition of the Lord's Prayer*; CCG 23, 36, 172ff.; PG 90, 880C.

[299] *Ambigua*; PG 91, 1312AB.

the one, complete human nature.[300] The whole world will be brought home by the Logos,[301] for he saves everyone,[302] the whole race,[303] just as his ineffable mystery embraces all ages and every place.[304]

On the basis of this second series of texts, E. Michaud[305] concluded, somewhat hastily, that Maximus taught *apokatastasis*. Apart from the fact that Michaud uses as proof several texts that are not genuine and forces the meaning of others, these general pronouncements [on the universality of salvation] are hardly decisive and cannot neutralize the others that assert the opposite, restricting salvation to the "elect". The dispute can be resolved only by a third series of texts, which Michaud missed.

Origen saw the event of the restoration of all things mysteriously expressed in the double identity of the tree of Paradise, as the tree of life and the tree of the knowledge of good and evil. According to Origen, this corresponds to the double symbolism of the tree of the Cross, as well, on which both good (Christ) and evil (the devil, according to Colossians 2:14–15) were crucified.[306] Gregory of Nyssa followed and abundantly embellished this interpretation of the trees of Paradise.[307] When Thalassius asks him about the meaning of these trees, Maximus first gives a purely moral interpretation. Then he continues: "Thus the passage on the tree is to be understood according to the spiritual interpretation appropriate for the general public. The hidden, better meaning, however, must be reserved for those who have a deeper understanding of mysteries. We must 'honor it by silence'."[308] Thalassius also asks for an interpretation of the Pauline text, "He has despoiled the principalities and powers" (Col 2:15). Maximus again first gives a generally understandable interpretation, then continues: "We could have given another, more secret and more sublime interpretation of this text. But since one should not spread the more hidden divine teachings

---

[300] *In Coel. Hier.* 14; PG 4, 104A; *Epistles* 29; PG 91, 621C.

[301] *Ambigua*; PG 91, 1165D.

[302] *Quaestiones ad Thalassium* 47; CCG 7, 325, 225ff.; PG 90, 429C.

[303] *Opuscula*; PG 91, 93C.

[304] Ibid.; PG 91, 92D.

[305] E. Michaud, "St. Maxime le Confesseur et l'apocatastase", *Revue internationale de théologie* 10 (1902): 257–72.

[306] *Homilies on Joshua* 8, 6: ed. Baehrens (GCS), 7:338–42.

[307] *Homilies on the Song of Songs* 12; GNO 6, 348, 9–350, 9; PG 44, 1020B–1021A.

[308] *Quaestiones ad Thalassium*, prologue; CCG 7, 37, 350–53; PG 90, 260A.

publicly in books, as you realize, let what we have said here suffice."[309] In a later question, he again comes back to the two trees and repeats the same reservation:

> The teachers of the Church, who were in a position to say many things about this passage thanks to the grace that had been given to them, considered it wiser nonetheless to "honor it by silence"; for the intelligence of the majority of people did not seem to them prepared to grasp the depth of these words.[310]

Hints of such an approach can be found fairly often in Maximus' works.[311] And we find a similar attitude expressed later in the work of the last of the great Alexandrians, Anastasius of Sinai.[312]

These texts are clear enough: Maximus is not in favor of proclaiming a universal restoration in the straightforward way in which Gregory of Nyssa and even Origen himself did it, despite their assurances to the contrary. The history of Origenism was proof of the bad effects of such a lack of prudence. The esotericism practiced by Origen was only a halfway measure; true esotericism means "to honor [a doctrine] by silence".[313] Beginners and the imperfect should not simply be guided by kindness and by glimpses of the depths of [God's] mercy; they need fear as well.[314] And who is so perfect that he is no longer in danger of falling away?[315]

---

[309] Ibid., 21; CCG 7, 133, 108–12; PG 90, 316D.

[310] Ibid., 43; CCG 7, 293, 6–10; PG 90, 412A.

[311] *Ambigua*; PG 91, 1277 (four interpretations of the "fullness" [*pleroma*] of Christ); ibid.; PG 91, 1356BC; ibid.; PG 91, 1384C ("according to the most obvious meaning" κατὰ τὸν πρόχειρον νοῦν).

[312] *On the Hexaemeron* 8; PG 89, 971Cff.: "For what Holy Scripture passes over in silence should not be examined closely. . . . Thus when the Holy Spirit is silent about the name and the nature of those two trees, it is obvious that it is neither necessary nor useful for the Church to examine closely and divulge what has been hidden by God." In the same passage, Anastasius mentions the "unhappy Origen". Cf. ibid., 10; PG 89, 1013B.

[313] [This phrase, used by Maximus in the passages von Balthasar mentions, appears several times in the works of the Cappadocian Fathers: see Gregory Nazianzen, *Orat.* 28, 20; Basil of Caesaraea, *On the Holy Spirit* 18, 44, 30, 78. For a discussion of von Balthasar's suggestions on *apokatastasis* in Maximus, see Brian E. Daley, "Apokatastasis and 'Honorable Silence' in the Eschatology of Maximus the Confessor", in Felix Heinzer and Christoph Schönborn, eds., *Maximus Confessor* (Fribourg, 1982), 309–39, and von Balthasar's reply: *Dare We Hope "That All Men Be Saved?"* (San Francisco, 1988), 245–48.]

[314] *Centuries on Knowledge* 2, 99: PG 90, 1172D.

[315] *Centuries on Love* 4, 34; PG 90, 1060C.

We should not, then, be more curious than Scripture allows us to be. With Paul, we may say that grace is far more powerful than sin, that all die in Adam, but that all will also be raised to life in Christ, who will lay a perfected creation at the Father's feet [Rom 5:12–21; 1 Cor 15:21–22, 28]. But we must also stand with Christ himself, and with his gospel, at the edge of eternal destruction and gaze down into it. To want to overcome this final antinomy through a premature "synthesis" is not appropriate for theology in this present age. The serious possibility of being lost must never be watered down, if the seriousness of Christian life is not to be transformed into a mere game.

> And the brother asked, Why, Father, do I not have a contrite heart? And the old man replied, Because we do not have the fear of God before our eyes. Because we have become a pit full of all kinds of evil and so despise the dreadful judgments of God as a mere fiction.[316]

We must hear the threats of God "not simply because of the evil we have committed, but equally because of the good we have neglected and because we do not love our neighbor enough".[317] Only in fear may we raise hopeful eyes, with Paul, toward that full complement of the Kingdom of Heaven, which will one day include us all in its number.

> Thus the world above will reach its fullness; the members will be united with their head, each according to his merit. Through the constructive skill of the Holy Spirit, every part will have the place it deserves in a harmonious way according to the degree of its progress in virtue. So each of us will bring to completion that Body that itself brings all things to completion in each of us, filling everything and itself brought to fullness by all things.[318]

---

[316] *Liber asceticus*; PG 90, 932C.

[317] Ibid.; PG 90, 936AB.

[318] *Ambigua*; PG 91, 1280D–1281A. God alone knows the final goal of his providence: *Ambigua*; PG 91, 1169A.

THE PROBLEM OF THE SCHOLIA
TO PSEUDO-DIONYSIUS[1]

Maximus entered the history of theology not only as the victor in the dispute over the doctrine of two wills [in Christ] but also as the man who assured a lasting home in the Church for the writings of Pseudo-Dionysius, thanks to his orthodox interpretation of them. Whether Pseudo-Dionysius in fact needed such justification, whether he really was the half-Neoplatonic, half-Monophysite mystic that one likes to make him today, and was not rather one of the most powerful Christian thinkers of all time (as Hugo Ball—in my opinion rightly—has characterized him),[2] need not be decided here. It is certain that he aroused a divided response very early: alongside enthusiasm, scepticism, and

---

[1] [This study of the scholia to Pseudo-Dionysius first appeared as an article, "Das Scholien-werk des Johannes von Scythopolis", in *Scholastik* 15 (1940): 16–38; it was reprinted, with a postscript, in the 1961 edition of *Kosmische Liturgie*. Over the past two decades, Beate Regina Suchla has published three important studies of the scholia on the *Corpus Areopagiticum* attributed to John of Scythopolis and Maximus the Confessor, continuing the research begun by von Balthasar in this article. These three articles, all of which have appeared in the *Nachrichten von der Akademie der Wissenschaften in Göttingen, Philologisch-historische Klasse*, are as follows: B. R. Suchla, "Die sogenannten Maximus-Scholien des Corpus Areopagiticum" (Göttingen, 1980); "Die Überlieferung des Prologs des Johannes von Skythopolis zum griechischen Corpus Dionysiacum: Ein weiterer Beitrag zur Überlieferungsgeschichte des Corpus Dionysiacum" (Göttingen, 1984); and "Verteidigung eines platonischen Denkmodells einer christlichen Welt: Die philosophie—und theologiegeschichtliche Bedeutung des Scholienwerks des Johannes von Skythopolis zu den areopagitischen Traktaten" (Göttingen, 1995).]

[2] *Byzantinisches Christentum*, 2d ed. (1931), 63–249. Although a dilettante, Ball is fearlessly clear, in his long essay on Pseudo-Dionysius, in saying that even verbal borrowings from Proclus and Neoplatonism do not present any problem for the author's Catholic orthodoxy. Ball rightly complains of the narrow historicism of modern research, which no longer has an intellectual ear for the whole tone of a work. One might only add that even the Monophysitism of Pseudo-Dionysius, which one often assumes to be an evident fact, is not at all proven. [On Dionysius' orthodoxy, see now Alexander Golitzin, *Et Introibo ad Altare Dei: The Mystagogy of Dionysius Areopagita* (Thessalonike, 1994).]

cool diffidence, even suspicions of being an Apollinarian forgery.[3] It is also certain that Maximus belonged to those who grasped the value, the originality, and the fruitfulness of the *Areopagitica* and that through his spirited championing of their genuineness, as well as his work of interpretation, he became one of the heralds of what was to be their triumphal march down through the Latin Middle Ages. What is doubtful is only whether it was *his* scholia that achieved the decisive step of "baptizing" Pseudo-Dionysius. This present study will attempt to show that this had already been achieved a century before Maximus, about thirty years after the appearance of the Pseudo-Dionysian writings, by a theologian who has received little notice until now but who is the real author of the most extensive and materially significant parts of the scholia that have circulated under Maximus' name.

In what follows, we can only spread out the materials for a theological and philosophical examination of these unusually rich scholia; we cannot undertake such an examination here. Yet it would be an extremely welcome study, not only because it would allow us a glimpse of the thought of a highly cultivated, broadly interested theologian and humanist, but also because it would shed new light on the history of Christian Neoplatonism. From their contrast with the notions contained in these scholia, Maximus' own ideas and his interpretation of Pseudo-Dionysius' view of the world would certainly stand out more clearly.

The demonstration that the core of the extant scholia (in volume 4 of Migne's *Patrologia Graeca*) are the work of someone other than Maximus amounts to something new only in the radicality with which we here carry it out. It is based on surmises, even certainties, that have long been in circulation. Even the prefaces to the older printed editions point out that the scholia, in their present form, are a mixture of commentaries by various authors. It has been known, too, that along with Maximus' scholia, the comments of a sixth-century scholar, the "scholastic" [lawyer] John of Scythopolis, appear prominently in the tradition and, in fact, occupy an important place there.[4] Other com-

---

[3] On the history of the reception of Pseudo-Dionysius, see J. Stiglmayr, *Das Aufkommen der pseudo-dionysischen Schriften* (Feldkirch, 1895).

[4] Commenting on the first printed edition of the scholia, that of Morelli of 1562, Archbishop Ussher says: "John of Scythopolis, along with Maximus, wrote scholia on Dionysius the Areopagite. In fact, in the books of Dionysius . . . *the scholia of John and of Maximus are combined*: these are distinguished not only in the older editions, in circulation at the time of

ments are ascribed to Germanus of Constantinople.[5] One scholion also appears, in confusing circumstances, in the works of Anastasius of Sinai.[6] In addition to this variety of authors, we must also keep in

---

Cyparissiotes (the fourteenth century; this is in fact untrue—see below, n. 11) but also in the two manuscripts used by Morelli. In one of them, the scholia of John of Scythopolis are written in the margin without a name; in the other, after the whole text of Dionysius, scholia appear under the name of Maximus—shorter than the former because separated from the longer scholia of John, with which Morelli joins them (see J. A. Fabricius and G. C. Harles, *Bibliotheca graeca* 5, 1 [Hamburg, 1796]; cf. PG 3, 64CD).

[5] In later manuscripts, many scholia have a Greek numeral in their margin, about which a Venetian manuscript remarks: "Note that the scholia that are marked with a number come from Germanus the Patriarch, but those without a number are by Maximus the Monk" (De Rubeis: PG 3, 71A). Angelo Mai found the same note in a Vatican manuscript, with the addition: "Forgive me, my brother, for bringing both authors together in this book under a single number." Mai therefore repeats Morelli's doubt "whether the distinction of Maximus' scholia from those of 'Germanus' on the Areopagite is justified" (*Spicilegium Romanum* 7 [Rome, 1842], 74; PG 98, 87–88).

[6] This is scholion 1 on the fifth chapter of the *Celestial Hierarchy* (PG 4, 60): Τί δήποτε, μιᾶς οὐσίας εἶναι πάντας ἁγίους τοὺς ἀγγέλους λεγούσης τῆς ἐκκλησίας (al.: Γραφῆς), ὁ θεῖος Διονύσιος πολλὰς ὀνομάζει δυνάμεις; Ὁ γοῦν μέγας Διονύσιος ὁ Ἀλεξανδρείας ἐπίσκοπος, ὁ ἀπὸ ῥητόρων, ἐν τοῖς σχόλ οἰς, οἷς πεποίηκεν εἰς τὸν μακάριον Διονύσιον τὸν αὐτοῦ συνώνυμον, οὕτω λέγει, ὅτι ἀγέννητον εἴωθε καλεῖν ἡ ἔξω σοφία πᾶσαν ἀόρατον φύσιν, ὁμοίως καὶ οὐσίας τὰς ὑποστάσεις· κἀκ τούτου φησίν, ὅτι κατὰ τοὺς ἔξω εἴρηται τῷ ἁγίῳ Διονυσίῳ αἱ τοιαῦται φωναὶ καταχρηστικῶς· "Why, then, if the Church (variant: the Scripture) says that all the holy angels are of a single essence, does holy Dionysius call them many powers? Now the great Dionysius, bishop of Alexandria and rhetor, in the scholia that he wrote on blessed Dionysius, his namesake, says that pagan scholarship tends to call every kind of invisible nature 'unbegotten', just as it calls concrete individuals (ὑποστάσεις) 'essences' (οὐσίας); therefore he says that such words are used metaphorically by holy Dionysius, following the custom of the pagans." In Anastasius' *Hodegos* (ed. K.-H. Uthemann, CCG 8, 298f.; PG 98, 289CD), this passage is introduced with the words, Πάλιν τε μίαν οὐσίαν λεγούσης τῆς Ἐκκλησίας εἶναι πάντας τοὺς ἁγίους ἀγγέλους: "Again, since the Church says that all the holy angels are a single essence . . . ," and forms a single unit with the body of the comment. The passage is missing, in fact, in a tenth-century manuscript. Hilper (*Dionysius der Areopagite*, 120) believes that the passage, which is also missing in the oldest manuscripts of Pseudo-Dionysius, according to Lequien (see *Dissertationes Damascenae* 2: PG 94, 278 n.), was added after 1200, based on a note in Nicetas Chroniates' *Thesaurus Orthodoxiae*. Stiglmayr (*Aufkommen*, 71) considers this a likely explanation. Nonetheless, there seems to be an easier solution.

Where does the name of Dionysius of Alexandria come from? At the beginning of the sixth century, George of Scythopolis, one of the first defenders of the genuineness of the Pseudo-Dionysian corpus, circulated a [putative] letter from the Patriarch Dionysius of Alexandria to Pope Sixtus II, as evidence for the authenticity of the works (text in Pitra, *Analecta Sacra* 4, 414); in this letter, Dionysius is supposed to have defended the genuineness of the *Areopagitica* as early as the year 268. This forgery existed, then, from the early years of the corpus' existence, so that one should not be so surprised to find Anastasius using scholia attributed

mind the impression we get on reading the scholia: that a later reader of the whole complex added glosses of his own, in the form of short summaries appended to the end of many sections.[7]

to the bishop of Alexandria. One may surely ask: Did such scholia ever exist? Joannes Cyparissiotes cites "scholia of Maximus and Dionysius of Alexandria" in his *Decades of Symbolic Theology*. But the passages ascribed to Dionysius are the same ones that Ussher (quoted by Fabricius and Lequien in PG 4, 1034A) knew under the name of the first great commentator, John of Scythopolis (compare also Anastasius, εἴωθε καλεῖν ἡ ἔξω σοφία πᾶσαν ἀόρατον φύσιν: "Pagan philosophy usually calls every invisible nature", etc., with the formula in Pseudo-Maximus, οὓς εἴωθεν ὀνομάζειν κατά τινας τῆς ἔξω φιλοσοφίας: "Whom they usually call, according to some representatives of pagan philosophy" [PG 4, 188C]). One might wonder, then, whether the scholion in Anastasius does not also belong to those of John. In fact, we find among the pieces ascribed to Maximus one passage (PG 4, 372D–375A) that we must give back to John (see below) and which contains a discussion of the use of the word ἀγέννητον: Εἰπὼν ἀγέννητον τὸν Θεόν, τὰς παλιμφήμους ἑρμενείας τοῦ ὀνόματος ἀποκαθαίρει. . . . Ἤδει οὖν εἶναι δόγμα τινῶν αὐτῶν λεγόντων τὰ νοητὰ πάντα καὶ ἀθάνατα, καὶ νοερὰ γεννητὰ πάντα καὶ ἀγέννητα . . . Φησὶν οὖν ὁ μέγας Διονύσιος, ὅπως ποτ᾽ ἄν λέγοιτο τὸ ἀγέννητον, εἴτε ὡς ἔφην, εἴτε ὡς οἱ Ἕλληνες, μὴ ἐπὶ τοῦ Θεοῦ τοῦτο δέξῃ, τὰ μὲν ἄλλα αἰτιατῶς λέγεται ἀγέννητα, ὁ Θεὸς δὲ ἀναιτίως: "In saying God is unbegotten (ἀγέννητον), he purges away the contradictory meanings of the word. . . . For he knew that it was the opinion of some (that is, the philosophers of the Ionian school in Ephesus at the time of Pseudo-Dionysius) that all intelligible realities (νοητά) are also immortal and that all intelligent beings are either begotten or unbegotten. . . . Now the great Dionysius says that however one uses the word 'unbegotten', whether as I have said or as the Greeks use it, he would not accept it as applying to God; other things are said to be 'unbegotten' owing to some cause, but God is 'unbegotten' without any cause." In addition, one must remember Anastasius' practice of inexact citation; he often complains of not having any books in his desert cell! So it is not unlikely that Anastasius is referring to the commentary of John. At the end of the seventh or the beginning of the eighth century, then, this would have been circulating as a work of Dionysius of Alexandria. Who was the forger? Is it the same person who circulated the so-called letter of Dionysius? And would this not be George of Scythopolis himself, who also incorporated the preface of John in his own preface to the *Areopagitica*?

What we possess of this George is preserved by Phocas bar Sergis, who published the Syriac translation of the Areopagite corpus prepared by Sergius of Reshaina (d. 536), including his translation of the two prefaces of John and George, along with John's scholia. In his preface (see below), John had tried to prove the genuineness of the Pseudo-Dionysian writings; in his own preface, George expands on this proof through the purported letter of Dionysius of Alexandria to Xystus (see Rubens Duval, *La Littérature syriaque* [Paris, 1907]; O. Bardenhewer, *Geschichte der altkirchlichen Literatur*, vol. 4 [Freiburg, 1924], 296f.).

[7] There are also scholia of this type to the other genuine works of Maximus. Wilhelm Soppa (see below, n. 10) proved their inauthenticity. In the commentaries on Pseudo-Dionysius they are usually introduced with "signifies" (σημαίωσαι). A few examples will suffice: In PG 4, 93BC, the text reads, Δοκεῖ πως ἐνταῦθα λέγειν ὅτι κατ᾽ ἀξίαν αἱ ἀγγελικαὶ διακοσμήσεις δημιουργικῶς ἐτάχθησαν "He seems to be saying here that the angelic orders were arranged by the Creator according to their dignity." At the end of the paragraph, the reader finds the

Confronted with this multiplicity of authors, we may at first doubt the usefulness of such a compilation. Yet there is light in our confusion. The secondary scholiast is so unimportant that for large sections he is not noticeable at all. The problem raised by Anastasius can probably be solved satisfactorily (see n. 10). The share of Germanus, too, can easily be shown to be a red herring;[8] The real task remaining, then,

---

sentence (probably originally in the margin): Σημαίωσαι δὲ· πῶς κατ᾿ ἀξίαν αἱ ἀγγελικαὶ διακοσμήσεις δημιουργικῶς παρήχθησαν: "Signifies: how the angelic orders were set up by the Creator according to their arrangement [but probably, 'according to their dignity', κατ᾿ ἀξίαν]." In PG 4, 104D–105A the text comments on the idea of fire as a symbol of God. The reader finds: Σημαίωσαι δέ, διὰ τί Κύριος ὁ Θεὸς πῦρ ἐθεωρήθν πολλάκις καὶ κατὰ τί ἡ ὁμοίωσις τοῦ πυρὸς πρὸς τὸν Θεόν "Signifies: why the Lord God is often imagined as fire, and in what the comparison of God with fire consists." Cf. also PG 4, 136C and 136D; 188BC and 188C; 212B and 212C; 280C–281B and 281C; 340D and 341D; 344D; 344D–345A and 345A; 348D–349A and 349A; 349BC and 349C; 404D–405A and [διὰ τί] 405A; 412AC and 412D; 537D–540B and 540BC; 561D–564B and 564D; etc. More often, however, "signifies" (σημαίωσαι) is part of the commentary itself: e.g., PG 4, 329D–332A. For the content, the distinction of these primary and secondary scholia is hardly ever important.

[8] Nowhere else is there the slightest trace of a commentary authored by Germanus. In any case, the Greek numbers reproduced by Migne are mostly wrong. Passages marked in this way are often in very close relationship to others, without numbers, or else they betray by their contents the hand of John. A few examples: 32AB deals with purely grammatical questions on the language of Pseudo-Dionysius: Attic versus Ionic declensions. But such considerations are clearly a concern of John. One scholion, for instance, begins: Νόας καλοῦσι καὶ οἵ παρ᾿ Ἕλλησι φιλόσοφοι τὰς νοερὰς, ἤτοι ἀγγελικάς δυνάμεις, ἐπειδὴ τὸ πᾶν νοῦς ἐστιν ἕκαστος αὐτῶν, καὶ τὴν οὐσίαν ἅπασαν νοῦν ζῶντα εἰς τὸ εἶδος τὸ ἑαυτῶν οὐσιωμένων ἔχει· νόες καλοῦνται πρὸς τὸ εὐφωνότερον τῆς κλίσεως γενομένης: "By 'minds' (νόες), the Greek philosophers mean intellectual or angelic powers, since each of them is completely mind, and possesses the whole essence that is living mind as the form that gives it being. They are called νόες [i.e., rather than the more predictable form νόαι] to make the declension more euphonious." This should be compared with the unnumbered scholion at 188BC ἀλλὰ καὶ περὶ τῶν ἀγγέλων, οὓς εἴωθεν ὀνομάζειν κατά τινας τῶν τῆς ἔξω φιλοσοφίας νόας· οἵτινες τῶν ἄνω ταγμάτων νόες εἴρηνται, ὡς τὸ πᾶν νοῦν οὐσιωμένως ὄντες: "but also concerning angels, whom he is accustomed to call 'minds' (νόες), following the usage of some of the pagan philosophers; these members of the higher orders are called 'minds', because they are completely mind in their essence". On the other hand, the author—who deals with philological questions—loves to cite Homer and the ancient poets. He is therefore probably the source of 36CD. In 301CD, we find a strictly "scholastic" definition of ὅρος (definition, limit). This can only come from the same author who pours the concepts of Pseudo-Dionysius into this form of definition in a series of unnumbered passages: 200C (τελικὸν αἴτιον); cf. 332D, and especially 260B (ὅροι εἰσίν . . .).
The long passage 296B–297A is very closely connected with a whole group of unnumbered scholia. The expression at 297A, "in things contrary to nature" (ἐν οἷς δὲ παρὰ φύσιν), recurs at 289BC, a passage that is itself connected with another group, of which nothing can

is to unravel the scholia composed by Maximus from those by *John of Scythopolis*.

Now the confusion, despite Archbishop Ussher's assurances to the contrary, seems not to be rooted in the printed editions but to exist even in the manuscripts.[9] There is one sure proof of this: the Pseudo-Maximian compilation of "Five Hundred Chapters", which Soppa and Disdier[10] showed to be a work of the eleventh century, probably of Antonius Melissa, already contains some fragments that can be shown with certainty to come from John.[11] Likewise, the ten "Theological Decades" of John Cyparissiotes (fourteenth century) include, under Maximus' name,[12] a large number of scholia that should be ascribed

---

be ascribed to Germanus. But then one must also remove from his authorship the scholion 301D–304A, where there is a similar expression (ἀσθενείᾳ δὲ . . .); and this, in turn, is connected with 309CD. In the scholion we are considering (296Bf.), there is a theory that φύσις (nature) and λόγος (intelligible structure) are identical. This is echoed, in turn, at 353 AB, an unnumbered passage. The examples could be multiplied in this same direction. It seems that there never was a commentary of Germanus, as De Rubeis himself already surmised (PG 3, 71).

[9] This is unquestionably true of the manuscripts that we were able to consult: Parisinus 440 (twelfth century) and 438. In the first of these, the great prologue, which is undoubtedly the work of John, is itself ascribed to Maximus, along with many of the scholia. The variants here with respect to the edited text are constant and often considerable.

[10] W. Soppa, *Die Diversa Capita unter den Schriften des hl. Maximus Confessor in deutscher Bearbeitung und quellenkritischer Beleuchtung* (diss., Dresden, 1922); M. T. Disdier, "Une Oeuvre douteuse de St.-Maxime: les 5 centuries théologiques", *Echos d'Orient* 30 (1931): 160, 178.

[11] Excerpts from Pseudo-Dionysius himself comprise Capita 5, 66; 5, 68; 5, 82; 5, 83; 5, 86; 5, 90; 5, 91. Scholia are excerpted in 5, 63; 5, 64; 5, 65 (which is a summary of the one that follows); 5, 67; 5, 69; perhaps one sentence in 5, 83; 5, 87; 5, 88; 5, 89. From these, the Syriac translation establishes as certainly by John 5, 64 (= PG 4, 120C); 5, 65 (= 204BC + 205C); and the first half of 5, 69 (= 344A; the second half, from ἕνωσιν on, has every chance of being by Maximus). Uncertain is 5, 67 (= 225BC). The last three mentioned, 5, 87–89, are not included in the Syriac and could be by Maximus. In any case, the expansion had already taken place.

[12] We give here a list of quotations from Maximus in Cyparissiotes, taken from the scholia on Pseudo-Dionysius, which shows clearly that both works—Maximus' commentary and John's—were already integrated when Cyparissiotes used them. The first number here refers to the *Theological Decades* (PG 152, 737–992), the second to the scholia (PG 4). "Sc" stands for the scholia that are identified in Phocas' Syriac translation (cf. n. 14 below) as the work of John of Scythopolis. "[Sc]" denotes scholia that seem to belong to John on internal grounds, even though they are not included in Phocas' collection. "M" denotes scholia that could belong to Maximus.

782A = M 376D–377A; 788B = Sc 52D–53A; 789B = M 221C; 790C = Sc 229D–232A; 790D = Sc 381D; 793A = Sc 205A; 793B = M 225BC; 809A = M (?) 252A;

to John of Scythopolis, while the *Century* on hesychastic prayer by [Nicephorus] Callistus [Xanthopoulos] (fourteenth century)[13] presents a long quotation from Pseudo-Maximus that unquestionably also belongs to John. The ascription to Maximus of works by John thus seems to have taken place very early.

Nevertheless, there remains one very valuable means of distinguishing [their work]: the Syriac translation of the prologue and scholia of John by Phocas, preserved in a manuscript dated to 804.[14] Admittedly, this manuscript contains only a *selection* of the scholia of John, as is evident from a mere glance at the Greek edition; but it contains the most valuable and elaborate comments on *The Divine Names* and the complete introduction as well. But John, in this introduction, develops a precise program for the content and goal of his commentary; in the scholia themselves, he sticks to it conscientiously and also connects his comments to each other by frequent cross-references ("as we said above in the fifth chapter"; "as we will explain later in our commentary on the *Divine Names*"). So it is not difficult to form a tentative but fairly exact picture of his work, which must suffice until the appearance of a

---

809C = M 413B; 810A = M 413C; 817B = M 317CD; 822B = Sc 380B; 822A = M 401AB; 885B = Sc 221B; 893A = [Sc] 388C; 906AB = [Sc] 348BC; 919BC = Sc 372CD; 919C = Sc 375B; 950D–951A = Sc 329A; 951B = Sc 353AB; 964A–965A = Sc 65BC; 981A = [Sc] 332C; 981AB–Sc 352A; 982BC = Sc 320BC; 988B = M (?) 429B.

[13] A. M. Amman, *Die Gottesschau im palamitischen Hesychasmus: Ein Handbuch der spätbyzantinischen Mystik* (1938), 117.—It is worth mentioning that Scotus Erigena only knew the *Ambigua* and the *Quaestiones ad Thalassium* from the works of Maximus. The latter he called "scholia": something that Dräseke missed, who thought he should identify the "scholia" mentioned in *Div. Nat.* 4, 26, and many other places as scholia to Pseudo-Dionysius ("Zu Maximus Confessor", *Zeitschrift für wissenschaftliche Theologie* 47 [1904]: 20f., 204f.). Thus we can find no help for our present question in Erigena.

[14] MS Add. 12151 of the British Library (see Wright's description in his catalogue of the Syriac manuscripts of the British Museum, 494); and see the end of n. 12 above.—I owe heartfelt thanks to Prof. Hengstenberg of Munich and to Fr. W. de Vries, S.J., for their kind and unselfish help in translating this manuscript, which at times was more a laborious work of deciphering.—Robert Grosseteste, bishop of Lincoln, is supposed to have translated these scholia of John into Latin (according to Ussher, PG 3, 64D–65A). But Ezio Franceschini, "Grosseteste's Translation of the ΠΡΟΛΟΓΟΣ and ΣΧΟΛΙΑ of Maximus to the Writings of the Pseudo-Dionysius Areopagita", *Journal of Theological Studies* 34 (1933): 355–363, showed that Grosseteste found the scholia of Maximus and John already mixed together in his source and that he did not even know the author of the whole collection of scholia (356–57). So this statement of Ussher, too, remains "without verification" (Franceschini, "Grosseteste's Translation", n. 2).

critical edition. Here external and internal evidence cooperate to form an organic whole.[15]

The work of John of Scythopolis reveals a personality of significant dimensions; he is a great scholar and no mediocre philosopher. In his elegant style, limpid in comparison with Maximus, he develops his thoughts with a kind of humanistic ease and a relaxed air. In the process, he enlists the doctrines and conceptual definitions of the academy to cast light on the dark passages of his mystical text; he cites poets and historians, philosophers and theologians of pagan and Christian antiquity; he corrects what may seem unorthodox with unobtrusive skill, employs for it the expressions canonized by tradition, sometimes weaves in his own favorite ideas, and everywhere arouses the impression of comprehensive, effortless, even playful learning.

The *Prologue* (PG 4, 16–21C) develops the purpose of the work in a masterful way. John wants to present the genuineness of the Pseudo-Dionysian writings by proving their age and their complete orthodoxy. Starting with the address of Paul on the Areopagus, in which he used Hellenistic philosophy as an instrument of the proclamation of Christ, John insists that the pagans must be converted by their own intellectual means (21A). The mention of the Areopagus is the occasion for an excursus, in which John gives free rein to his knowledge (includ-

---

[15] Lequien and De Rubeis themselves pointed out several such internal criteria (PG 3, 66–68): (1) The scholia of Maximus "are shorter" (according to Ussher). This is strikingly true, if we use the Syriac manuscript as evidence. One must understand this, of course, in a relative sense, since John assures us in his introduction (PG 4, 21C) that he, too, is interested in brevity. (2) John speaks of "the Origenist myths that even now are in circulation" (καὶ νῦν δὲ οἱ ἀπὸ τῶν Ὠριγένους προσερχόμενοι μῦθοι: PG 4, 176C), something that can only be true for John's own time, the Palestine of c. 530. (3) Twice there is mention of "Nestorians and Basilians" (PG 4, 72A; 181C). The latter can only be the followers of Basil of Cilicia, who had attacked John of Scythopolis and had written an important book against him (cf. Photius, *Bibliotheca* cod. 95). Basil had attacked the orthodox under the pretext of fighting the Nestorians. He was, then, presumably a Monophysite. He answered John with a diatribe in sixteen books (Bardenhewer, *Geschichte der altkirchlichen Literatur* 5:116). By Maximus' time, Basil had long since been forgotten. (4) The scholia are often interrupted by the words "alternatively" (ἄλλως) or "on the same point" (εἰς τὸ αὐτό); this clearly shows two different commentators at work. This criterion is theoretically excellent but of little use in practice. For it only rarely gives us a way of distinguishing the authors (e.g., 228C; 428C; 429A; 536BC). Often, the explanations are very different, even opposed (e.g., 264BC and 264CD, 336D and 337A). Often, too, one commentator can give two different explanations (e.g., 429A–432C: εἶτα καὶ ἄλλως; 240D: δύνῃ δὲ καὶ ἄλλως νοῆσαι). These four criteria occasionally offer some help in distinguishing the commentators; but they are far from sufficient for carrying it through completely.

ing a quotation from Philochorus' *Attides*, another from Androtion, and a historical observation on the legal situation of the Athenians and Lacedaemonians under Roman rule) and where at the same time he can hint at the high rank of the newly converted Dionysius (16B). If one adds to this the testimony of Polycarp in his letter to the Athenians, cited in the works of Dionysius of Corinth, one has staked out the intellectual position of the great convert: "initiated by the powers of Saint Paul into all the dogmas of salvation, taught and further formed by the mighty Hierotheos". And Dionysius himself writes to Timothy, Paul's disciple who was at that time bishop of Ephesus. Ephesus was, in fact, the stronghold of Ionian philosophy, and Timothy, pressed by a number of subtle philosophical attacks, had to ask the wise Dionysius for advice on how to answer (20D). Dionysius answered him in the most natural way possible, by citing his contemporaries "without affectation"—something that clearly supports his credibility.

In fact, Dionysius undertakes to translate this whole profane, esoteric philosophy into Christian terms (17D). In this adaptation, one can admire his "straightforwardness" just as much as "his great learning" and his "unbroken fidelity to the Church's tradition".

> What a pity that so few people are capable of this achievement and that these few are then measured by the great majority according to the measure of their own laziness and ignorance! Yes—and worse still, these ignorant people are always the ones who stand ready with censures and who explode in anger over things they do not understand, rather than letting themselves be instructed by those who can teach them something! Such are the people, too, who today are so rash as to stamp the divine Dionysius as a heretic (even though) they themselves have no notion of what heretics really teach.

Was it not rather Dionysius who refuted all heretics in advance? Then John proceeds to develop his whole plan:

> What will they say, in fact, in response to all his explanation of the Trinity, which alone is worthy of adoration? What will they say about the unique Jesus Christ, one of the Holy Trinity, the only-begotten of God and the Word, who willed to become fully flesh? Did he [Dionysius] not develop the doctrine of the rational soul and the earthly body [of Christ] like ours and all the rest of the teachings of the accepted doctors? Who could rightly criticize what he says about intelligible beings (νοητά: the higher angels) and intellectual beings (νοερά: the lower angels) and sensible beings, about our final resurrection with our human body

and our soul, about the judgment that then will be passed on righteous and unrighteous? For, to put it briefly, that is where our salvation is moving; so we should not tarry here, since the explanations in our scholia will explain everything at an appropriate time (20AB).

There follows a deft explanation of why Origen and Eusebius know nothing of the Dionysian corpus and, finally, an appeal to common sense, which must recognize that the obvious holiness of the author cannot be simulated by any forger.

This brief but well-constructed introduction reveals a clear, and certainly not a narrow, mind, which feels at home in the milieu of pagan humanism but which clearly represents the dogmatic tradition and does not lust after the dark secrets of mystery cults. John is too experienced a scholar to be fanatical on any issue; later he will become a vigilant bishop, who made no bargains with heresy. The literary, even encyclopedic element is also strongly represented in the introduction. John speaks of Ionian philosophy, of Epicurus, of the Stoa; he knows of the quarrel between Ares and Poseidon, the charge of the latter that Ares had killed his son Halirrhotion—whence the Areopagus received its name; he knows the *Apostolic Constitutions*, Polycarp, Dionysius of Alexandria, Clement of Rome, Pantaenus, the literary habits of Origen and Eusebius; he claims to know that the books of the Areopagite are kept in the library of holy books in Rome.

From all of this, we can infer three groups of internal criteria for the scholia that belong to John—criteria that are completely supported by the Syriac selection:

1. An interest in proving that the author lived in the apostolic age, in attesting his good faith, and also his efforts to translate the profane philosophy of the Greeks into Christian and orthodox terms.

2. An interest in defending the author against the suspicion of heresy (or against the charge of being an Apollinarian forgery). The main points of the doctrine to be defended are set out in the introduction.

3. An interest in Greek antiquities, in Greek history, poetry, and philology.

These internal criteria, supplemented by the external criteria of the Syriac tradition, are sufficient to allow us to establish with assurance John's most important scholia. In what follows, we offer a list [of these passages] arranged according to subject matter. An asterisk after a number means that the passage is attributed to John in the Syriac translation.

I

One constantly finds in the scholia the effort to show "how Dionysius *adapts* the false teachings of the pagans and heretics to Christian truth". One should compare with this statement: 32AB*, 32D*, 33D–36B*, 77BD*, 157A*, 272AD*, 281D–284C*, 288BC*, 300CD, 312A*, 329D, 332C, 337BC*, 368D–369A*, 388C–389C* (the Syriac breaks off at παρελεύσεται [389B]), 392BD*, 397BC*. Cf. also 180AB*, 248AB* (καλῶς).

Equally clear is his effort to prove the genuineness of the writings through their *antiquity*: 29B–32A*, 32A* (πατέρας, and so on), 125CD, 136B, 136C, 136D, 137A (cf. 148B), 145A, 165A, 165BC, 177A, 184A, 196D, 249C, 360C–361A*, 393A*, 420AB. A passage thoroughly in tune with the prologue is 373 AC*. The possibility that Dionysius may have already used the [Chalcedonian] word "unconfused" (ἀσυγχύτως) is explained in 196D, 197A*. The impossibility of an Apollinarian forgery: 176CD*, 85C.[16]

II

The second group of scholia, which concern the *orthodoxy* of the Pseudo-Dionysian teaching, can be divided into four sections, corresponding to the prologue.

1. Trinity

192C (? because of the citation of Gregory [of Nyssa] in 221AB*), 209D–212A*, 220AB (?), 221AB*, 216A* (κατὰ ἀφαίρεσιν), 216A* (κατὰ κοινοῦ), 221D–224A*, 229D–232A (because the "phantasiasts" are often mentioned in the Syriac scholia).

2. Christology

We know that John was an enthusiastic defender of Chalcedon. A fragment of his writing against Severus is preserved in the *Doctrina Patrum*

---

[16] John considered the question of Apollinarian forgeries in other places, as Leontius of Jerusalem expressly attests (PG 86, 1865C). See Loofs, *Leontius von Byzanz* (Leipzig, 1888), 269–72.

de Incarnatione Verbi,[17] where he argues for two activities or energies in Christ, "undivided and unchanged" (ἀμερίστως τε καὶ ἀναλλοιώτως). The argument first discusses his divine activity (ἐνέργεια), then the rationality of the soul of Christ (in contrast with Apollinarianism), which must possess its own ability to reason (διανοεῖσθαι). This is in accord with the anti-Apollinarian thrust of the prologue to the scholia. One should compare with this the following scholia: 56C* (σημείωσαι), 57BD*, 60AB* (a quotation of "Basil the Cappadocian", clearly to distinguish him from John's opponent, Basil of Cilicia), 72AB* ("Basilians"!), 149D–152A ("against the Apollinarians"), 157A*B, 181D–184A*, 196CD, 196D (ἔμεινε), 197CD, 216B*, 221D–224A*, 229C*, 533A (ἀνθρώπου). Especially important is 536A*, where John already distinguishes three levels of activity in Christ, long before Sophronius and Maximus: the purely divine, the purely human, and a mixed mode. 149A gives a list of all the heresies that Dionysius opposes.

One may add here a group of scholia that provide similar lists of heretics or otherwise well-known people. John loves to show his learning in this way: 57CD* (Nestorians and Akephaloi [a sixth-century pejorative term for anti-Chalcedonians]), 57A–C* (from σημείωσαι to κατὰ Νεστοριανῶν is a single scholion in the Syriac), 60AB* (Arians), 133D* (*Apostolic Constitutions*), 192C (Arius, Eunomius), 173D–176A* (Bias of Priene, Plato, Simon Magus, Menander, Valentinus, Marcion, Manes, "the recently resurgent myths of Origen" [see n. 15 above]), 169D–172A (Lampetians, Messalians, Adelphians, Marcionites), 557B (Messalians), 397BC* (Valentinians, Manichaeans), 272D–273 B* (Manichaeans), 285AB (Manichaeans), 285B* (Manichaeans), 209D–212A* (Arians, Eunomians, Nestorians, Akephaloi), 176BC* (Simon Magus, Origen, Methodius of Olympus, Olympius of Adrianople, Antipater of Bostra), 337C–340A* (Simon Magus, Irenaeus, Origen, Hippolytus, Epiphanius), 312A* (Simon Magus), 52CD ("Titus [of Bostra] in his book against the Manichaeans"), 340D*, 341D (Chrysostom), 545C (Simon, Irenaeus, Hippolytus, the Origenists). 176CD* (Papias of Hierapolis, Apollinarius, Irenaeus), 48C–49A* (Timothy, Papias, Clement of Alexandria [*Paedagogos*]; what he says about Dionysius and Timothy corresponds exactly to the pro-

---

[17] Edited by F. Diekamp (Münster, 1907), 85–86. [It seems more accurate to say, on the evidence available, that John was a "Neochalcedonian" or proponent of the strongly unitive interpretation of the Chalcedonian formula that gradually won acceptance in the middle decades of the sixth century.]

logue), 536BC (Nestorius, Arius, Apollinarius; this also belongs to group I), 573BD* (Polycarp, Irenaeus, Clement of Alexandria [*Quis dives salvetur?*]; also part of group I), 576B (ὡς ἔφημεν: "as we have said" refers to the passage just mentioned), 536D–537A (Polycarp of Smyrna, Irenaeus [cf. prologue, 17C!]), 377AB* (Aristotle [*De generatione animalium*], Irenaeus), 225D–228A* (Nestorians, Clement of Alexandria [*Hypotyposes*]), 421AC* (Clement of Alexandria [*Hypotyposes*], Ariston of Pella [*Disputatio Papisci et Jasonis*]), 372C–373A (up to ἐπί Θεοῦ is not in the Syriac; Justus, mention of Scylla and the Chimaera), 393A* (Justus: cf. group I),[18] 241D* (the *Shepherd* of Hermas), 244A* (the *Shepherd* also), 528A* (two writings of Philo; the identification of the Caius, to whom Dionysius writes), 241A (Philo, *De cherubim*), 113D and 185A (Justin "the Philosopher"), 65CD* (Ammonius of Adrianople, *De resurrectione*: an anti-Origenist work), 561C (?: Theodore of Mopsuestia).

Although Maximus, too, is an admirer of the Cappadocians, the majority of the citations from them here are also the work of John. Basil is usually designated by the epithet "divine" (θεῖος), to distinguish him from the Cilician. See: 40B* (Basil), 68AB* (Basil), 108BC* (Basil, with a reference to his theory of a vegetative πνεῦμα: *In Hexaemeron* 8–9), 309BC* (Basil, *In Hexaemeron*: theory of light in the first three days of creation), 388C–389C* (reference to the same theory), 129B* (Basil, "Know thyself"), 44BC* (Basil: "Know thyself"), 413A* ("Basil and the divine Gregories").

The designation of the two Gregories presents an unusual problem. One passage extant in Syriac names the author of the *Contra Eunomium*,

---

[18] A questionable passage, in my opinion, is 377D–380A, since Maximus also likes to cite Clement of Alexandria. (He calls him the "philosophers' philosopher": PG 91, 317C; cf. ibid., 264B, 276C, 1085A; also Stählin's edition of Clement, GCS 3:219–20). The Syriac securely assigns to John a quotation from Clement of Rome: 329AD*. John has to solve two subtle chronological questions in connection with De Div. Nom. 4, 12 (264B–265A): Dionysius cites Ignatius, "My love is crucified." First John argues that Ignatius died before Domitian, yet [the apostle] John, on Patmos in the reign of Domitian, received a letter from Dionysius. But how can Ignatius have written this sentence in his letter to the Romans, and mention the bishop of Ephesus, Onesimus, in his letter to that community (*Eph.* 1, 3; 2, 1; 6, 2), if Onesimus was the successor of Timothy, to whom Dionysius—in *his* letter—has already cited the phrase of Ignatius? Truly a thorny problem! John solves it elegantly, by explaining the passage—which makes sense without the quotation from Ignatius—as an interpolation; alternatively, the phrase might be a favorite saying of Ignatius. In any case, Dionysius does not cite [Ignatius'] letter to the Romans expressly but speaks very generally of a saying of Ignatius!

Gregory of Nyssa, "Gregory the Theologian" (221AB*). This same title is used in connection with the theory of aeons, which also occupied Gregory of Nyssa (338B), and in 40C, where the apophatic theology ascribed to "Gregory the Theologian" also better fits Gregory of Nyssa. On the other hand, Gregory Nazianzen is also called "the Theologian" [in the scholia] (as he generally is by Maximus), and precisely when two passages are being cited that Maximus comments on in the *Ambigua* (557D: καὶ ὅτι ἡ Μόνας, εἰς Τριάδα προελθοῦσα, μέχρις αὐτῆς ἵσταται: "and that the Monad, having proceeded toward Trinity, comes to rest there", referring to the fifth theological oration and the second oration on peace). The same is true of a reference to the phrase, κιρναμένων ὥσπερ τῶν φύσεων: "mixing up the natures", in 533C, although the Syriac only begins two lines later (πῶς δέ: "but how . . . ?"); also in 264AB, where one hears the style of the Maximus of the *Ambigua* and where the Gregorian theme of Μονάδος κινηθείσης ("the monad in motion") is echoed; also probably in the sentence (404B), "So say the two Gregories, the Theologian and the Nyssen." For the same reason, 149B points to Maximus' side, too. So far, so good; but one text seems to cross the lines of demarcation: in 429B we read, Οὕτω καὶ Σέξτος ὁ ἐκκλησιστικὸς φιλόσοφος εἶπε καὶ ὁ θεόλογος Γρηγόριος ἐν τῷ τρίτῳ τῶν Θεολογικῶν αὐτοῦ: "Thus said Sextus, the ecclesiastical philosopher, and also Gregory the Theologian in the third of his theological orations." That Maximus would have cited the so-called "Sentences of Sextus" (see Bardenhewer, 2:643) is somewhat unlikely; but why does John [if he is the author of the scholia] here change the title from Gregory of Nyssa to Gregory Nazianzen?

In the light of this catalogue, the incredible learning of John "the Scholastic" cannot be disputed. But let us return, after this tour of names and quotations, to the development of his doctrine.

3. Spirit and Body

The prologue (20B) promised to discuss intelligible (νοητά), intelligent (νοερά) and perceptible (αἰσθητά) realities. The scholia that realize this promise are the heart of the commentary and its most original sections. John here develops the Pseudo-Dionysian texts in all directions: he changes the theory of emanations into a Christian theory of ideas, which is among the clearest approaches to the problem by Christian thought up to that time; he includes notions from Aristotelian philosophy, from Stoic physics, and seems to be able to brighten and disperse the dark clouds of the Pseudo-Dionysian vision with a sure hand.

a. *The theory of "intelligible" and "intelligent" reality* plays a large role, corresponding to the announcement in the prologue.
109BC* (enlightenment of the lower angels [νοεϱά] by the higher [νοητά]). From the reference here to the commentary on *The Divine Names* we learn that John composed that work *before* the commentary on *The Celestial Hierarchy*. 120BC* (νοητόν as the spiritual food of the νοεϱόν); 153BC* ("We have often explained in the book on *The Divine Names* what νοητόν and νοεϱόν are"; philological explanation of the word θεωϱοί); 240B–241A* (νοητόν as food of the νοεϱόν; but the νοητά, too, are "subsistent intelligences", exalted above material change; ideas are related to existent things as potency to act); 257AB* (νοητόν as food; the soul as the lowest level of spiritual being); 269AB (νοητόν as food; the angels as beings of love [ἐϱῶτες] and as intuitive minds, while souls think discursively); 309BC* (angels as νοητά; souls as νοεϱά; food); 344C–345A* (νοητά, nourished by God, are themselves the food of νοεϱά; the soul as the lowest, discursive level of mind).

b. *The Theory of the Spirit of Life*. One group of scholia insistently develops a theory that is as foreign to Maximus as it is to Pseudo-Dionysius: the theory of the vital soul as a kind of natural fire, as the Stoics and Aristotelians understood it.[19] The hierarchy of structural forms in man, according to this theory, ascends from body to mind in the following way: body (σῶμα)—sense faculties (αἴσθησις)—spirit (πνεῦμα)—soul (ψυχή)—mind (νοῦς). The soul, in order to think, must "descend" into the multiplicity of sensible things; it does this by means of spirit, which is the container and memory of sense impressions and is, as such, the connecting link with the multiple world, with separation (μεϱισμός) and distention (σκεδασμός): 108BC* (Basil as witness for the theory of pneuma [πνεῦμα], the heart as the center of the vital system and natural warmth), 193D–196A* (main text on the turn of the soul toward

---

[19] See Hans Meyer, *Geschichte der Lehre von den Keimkräften von der Stoa bis zum Ausgang der Patristik* (Bonn, 1914), 18.

the spirit and thus toward the senses), 201AC* (equation of the bodily [σωματικόν] and the spiritual [πνευματικόν],[20] as that which retains
sense perceptions; distinction of three kinds of imagination; difference
between thought, which resides in the mind and is active, and imagination, which has its home in the body and the spirit and receives
passive impressions [τυπώσεις]), 205B–208A* (detailed passage on the
intelligible [νοητόν] and the intelligent [νοερόν], mentioning the "living spirit" [ζωτικὸν πνεῦμα, 205D]), 292B (τί ἐστι φαντασία ἐν πρώτῳ
κεφαλαίῳ εἴπομεν: "we said in our first chapter what imagination is":
reference to 201AC*), 320B–321A* (main text on John's theory of
ideas; at the end, the presence of the vital soul through all fibers of the
body, to make sense perception possible; new explanation of imagination), 336B–D* (on the vegetative pneuma as fire[21]), 372BC* ("soul
and pneuma" in Hebrews 4:12 is taken to refer to the spiritual soul and
the bodily pneuma; the latter is also called by the Greek philosophers a
"potency" [δύναμις; cf. above 201AC*] and a "second soul" [δευτέρα
ψυχή; cf. 196A*, "second knowledge" δευτέρα νόησις], and it extends
through all the arteries and bones and limbs), 393D–396A* (reference
back to 193D–196A*; important discussion of the return of the mind
to itself ["reflection"] from the self-alienation of discursive thinking).

c. *Theory of the "Descent" of Thought.* The circle of discursive thought,
as "a descent below yourself" into multiplicity and a return through
this multiplicity to unity, is developed by John at great length. In doing
this, he worked out the positive meaning of material multiplicity and
of the mind's "turn to appearances" (*conversio ad phantasma*) along lines
Maximus never took and, in some ways, more clearly than Maximus;
as a result, he avoids the danger, very real in Maximus, of a one-sided
spiritualism. John lives completely in the Aristotelian and Stoic academic tradition and is internally a stranger to the ascetical-mystical tradition of monasticism.

---

[20] The text is found (see above, n. 13) under Maximus' name in the *Century* of [Nicephorus]
Callistus [Xanthopoulos], ed. Amman (1938), 117. Since in Maximus the term "spiritual"
(πνευματικόν) never occurs in this Stoic, cosmological sense, but always in a theological or
mystical sense, Amman translated it as "intellectuality", which of course is not intelligible.

[21] One should notice that this scholion takes the passage from Pseudo-Dionysius in question exclusively as referring to the vital soul (περὶ γὰρ τῆς τῶν νοητῶν ζωῆς ἢ τῆς καθ᾽ ἡμᾶς
οὐ νοεῖ ταῦτα: "for he does not understand this as referring to the life of intelligible beings
or to our own life"), while the following scholion, which may be by Maximus, understands
it quite differently, as referring to the human soul (337A).

73A–74A* (long commentary on the circular movement of the mind: its movement outward into multiplicity and its return into itself; λέγεται οὖν ὁ νοῦς ἐν ἑαυτῷ εἶναι καὶ πρὸς ἑαυτὸν σπεδεύιν: "The mind is said to exist in itself and to be in motion toward itself" [73C]; therefore it is rest and movement at the same time, a "dance" around God), 241A–C* (movement of the mind outward and back), 257BC* (multiplication of the mind through descent into thoughts; it comes to itself "from other things" [ἐξ ἀλλοτρίων]), 264A*, 288D–289C* (theories on the intellectual activity of daemons, on their potency [δύναμις] and activity [ἐνέργεῖα]; δύναμις τοῦ νοῦ τὸ εἰς νοήσεις κατιέναι: "the potentiality of the mind is to descend into thoughts" [289C]), 344A* (in the Syriac up to "instead of what is thought" [ἀντὶ τοῦ τῶν νοουμένων]; superb summary of the theory of descent; the end of the Greek chapter, missing from the Syriac [from ἕνωσιν δέ φησι: "he says that unity . . ." on] shows, on the other hand, strong traces of Maximus' terminology and thought).

Since the soul, as we have seen already, is the lowest form of a thinking being and thinks in a discursive (διεξοδική, λογική) mode, the division of mind can also take a threefold form: νοητά (the intelligible; the highest angels), νοερά (the intelligent; lower angels), and λογικά (reasoning; souls). So 384BC. A variant is the division into νοερόν (as "inner", intelligent man) and λογικόν (as "outer", sensitive man). So 249AB*.

In three texts we have already cited (201AB*, 288D–289C*, 372BC*), we find the interesting parallel of mind and act (ἐνέργεια), on the one side, with sensibility and potentiality (δύναμις), on the other. John develops this theory in such a way that he conceives the essence of pure mind as an identity of being and action; its δύναμις (potentiality) is identical with its ἐνέργεια (activity), its accidents with its substance. So 65BC*, 97AC (the virtues of the angel are not accidents), 120C* (ἔσωθεν, οὐ θύραθεν αἱ ἐλλάμψεις: "the illumination is within, not outside"), 157CD (the "essential states" [οὐσιώδεις ἕξεις] of angels; reference back to 65BC*), 240AB* (no distinction between substance and accident in angels; their light comes from within), 288D–289C* (essence [οὐσία] = activity [ἐνέργεια], whereas potentiality [δύναμις] is a distancing of the mind from itself), 292A (reference back to the preceding text).

All these passages form a strict unity. Most appear in the Syriac tradition; the few that do not are shown to belong to John through

references to other texts or through agreement with the theories and
terminology of John.

d. *The Physical World.* The prologue promised, along with a theory
of intelligible (νοητά) and intelligent (νοερά) beings, a theory of perceptible things (αἰσθητά). Many different theories about matter and its
physical qualities are connected with this doctrine in the scholia. The
author obviously takes a good deal of trouble to focus his extensive
knowledge in this area on the author with whom he is dealing.

44D–45B*, 132C* (multiplicity [πολλάκις]; description of material
change [ἀλλοίωσις]), 148D (τί ἐστιν: substance, or "what it is": reference back to 381BD*), 244D–245B* (movement of the heavens),
256C–257A* (on rest and movement, on the preservation or destruction of the underlying subject [ὑποκείμενον] in the latter case), 257CD*
(on three kinds of material movement, which the commentator puts
parallel with the three intellectual movements in the text of Pseudo-
Dionysius; Aristotelian physics; the rod of Moses used as an example
of change [τροπή], since it is changed into a snake), 257D–260A (on
change [ἀλλοίωσις] and decay [φθορά], similar to 381BD*), 381AD*
(on change [ἀλλοίωσις] and decay [φθορά] and all forms of intellectual
and material movement; again the example of Moses' rod), 333CD (on
the three kinds of movement, with reference back), 384B* (on mixture
[κρᾶσις]), 393C* (two kinds of mixture [κρᾶσις]: that which also destroys the subject and that which leaves it intact), 392AD* (how God
prevents the decay [φθορά] of sensible things), 397AB (reference back
to 381BD* [ἐκ παραλλήλου: "from the parallel", etc.]; that the ancients
called sensible reality nonbeing and intellectual reality being), 417CD*
(intelligible reality [νοητά] as "being in the true sense" [κυρίως ὄντα];
to this corresponds the explanation of the essence of matter as "inequality" [ἀνισότης] or "nonidentity" [ἑτερότης]: 77BD*, 368BD*; in
other places, however, John also includes sensible things among "beings" [ὄντα]: 52D–53A*, 100AB [referring back to the preceding]).

e. *The Theory of Ideas.* The transformation of the Pseudo-Dionysian
system by John reaches its climax in the theory of ideas. We have already mentioned the main text, 320B–321A*. Like those we are about
to list, it shows a consistent effort to exclude anything that suggests
a model of emanation. The ideas, which John, in contrast to both
Pseudo-Dionysius and Maximus, *calls* "ideas" (εἴδη, ἰδέαι), are first of

all simply God's "thoughts" (νοήσεις). God does not know them, how-ever, as objects, but within himself, just as he also "knows the things that are, in that he is himself being" and thus also "the original idea of the world". On the other hand, John also has his own conception of the immanence of ideas in things, and even of what Pseudo-Dionysius sees as the basic principles of being ("being-in-itself", "life-in-itself", and so on). John calls these the "immaterial materials" (ὕλαι ἄϋλοι) of beings, in which beings participate. The ideal meanings (λόγοι) of things are also their natures (φύσεις).

These passages include: 200BC*, 260C* (ιδέα as "coming into being along with nature" [ἐνεστὼς τῇ φύσει] and as final cause), 297C–300B* (presentation of the Neoplatonic theory of matter; the "matter" [ὕλη] of the mind), 316D–317C (ideas as "immaterial material" [ὕλη ἄϋλος]), 324A–D* (ideas as "the eternal thoughts of God"), 325AB*, 329A–D* (reference back to the foregoing text; ideas as "eternal creation of the eternal God"), 329D–332A (ideas in Plato and their transposition in Dionysius), 332AB* (on the "primordial ideas" [ιδέαι ἀρχικαί]), 332C (ideas as "thoughts" [νοήσεις] of God), 340AB* (the idea as the mind's "matter" [ὕλη]; exclusion of pantheism; on the basis of this text, we can also ascribe to John 248BC [with a reference to 340AB*] and 328D–329 A [with the same reference]), 345BD* (ideas as "thoughts" [νοήσεις], the simplicity of the angels; reference back to 320B–321A*), 348B–349B (three larger scholia that belong together and that are prob-ably by John; the last of them seems to refer back to 320BD*; cf. 109AB), 349BC* (the same notion; God does not come to know things by experience [πεῖρα] and the process of learning [μάθησις]), 349C–352B* (we come to know God through ideas in things, which are his thoughts), 352BC* (the same notion; the soul, too, is the likeness of an ιδέα), 353AB* (the Logos contains all ideas within itself; these are God's thoughts and, at the same time, the "natural principles" [λόγοι τῆς φύσεως] of things), 353BC* (the Logos is thus simple "knowledge of beings" [γνῶσις τῶν ὄντων]), 377CD (idea as "immaterial under-lying matter, which is life" [ὑποκειμένη ὕλη ἄϋλος ζωὴ οὖσα]; in their identity, things come to resemble each other), 384CD* (ideas as God's eternal thoughts), 429C–432C (the same notion; in the second half of the scholion, the ascription [to John] is uncertain, because of the des-ignations "in other words" [ἄλλως] and "on the same point" [εἰς τὸ αὐτό]), 569CD.

As a by-product of [this identification of scholia dealing with] the theory of ideas, we can identify a group of scholia, some of them already mentioned, that deal more fully with the hierarchical arrangement of being. Here we repeatedly find the expressions "in descending order" (καθ' ὑπόβασιν) and "[union that is not] in arithmetical sequence" ([ἔνωσις οὐ] σωρηδόν), as a kind of leitmotif: 209AB*, 241AC*, 256AC*, 297C–300B*, 300CD*, 312A*, 312C–313A*, 316D–317C*, 329AD*, 357BD*, 384AB*.

f. *The Theory of "Aeons"*. A consistent theme in John's scholia is the treatment of the concept of "age" (αἰών) as the "time" of the mind: its definition, its etymology (from "always being": ἀεὶ ὤν), finally its difference from the "eternal" (αἰώνιον). Some of these scholia we have already met elsewhere, but we will put them together here again systematically:

313B–316B* (main text on the "age" [αἰών]), 208BC*, 229AB*, 373AC*, 385C–388B* (with reference back to 316*), 388C–389C*, 324AD*, 336A (with reference back to 316*). Part of this complex, too, are the reflections on eternity and number: 385AB*, 385BC*.

4. Resurrection and Eschatology

The fourth group of dogmatic scholia deal, as the prologue programmatically suggests, with the resurrection of the body (20B). John obviously is aiming at Origenism (cf. 176A*), and we will therefore add to this group a series of scholia that deal [in other ways] with Origenist issues. This group contains:

69A (the Redeemer sits with his body at the right hand of God), 71AB* (same subject), 173C (same subject), 176B (same subject), 197C* (condition of the blessed), 197CD ("the divinized body" [τὸ θεῖον σῶμα]), 345BD* (complementing Dionysius' thought by referring to the bodily resurrection).

John directly approaches the struggle against Origenism, even naming names, in the following passages: 176BC* (distinguishes in Origen himself two opinions about the glorified body), 172C–173B* (attacks the Origenist myth of the fall with a citation from the *Peri Archōn* and two from Evagrius' *Centuries*), 173B* (against *apokatastasis*), 76D–77A* (a new quotation from "the unholy Evagrius" [ἀνόσιος Εὐάγριος] on the Trinity, but obviously not in a way that suggests he rejects it), 65CD* (anti-Origenism), 337C–340A* (John acknowledges that Origen taught the resurrection of the body; Origen is quoted alongside Irenaeus, Hippolytus, and Epiphanius—something a passionate anti-Origenist would never have done! John is a historian and knows how to let justice take its objective course), 545C (against spiritualism, including that of the Origenists), 549B (quotation from Origen's commentary on Lamentations. Maximus, who takes over Origen's ideas anonymously, would not have dared to quote him in such an open way.)

This whole group of passages reveals John to us as decisively opposed to Origenist spiritualism, but as generous enough, on the other hand, to allow Origen and Evagrius their just due, when it is appropriate, and to quote them just as readily as he does other authors who have not been condemned.

This raises a serious question. One large group of scholia—not part of the Syriac tradition, as far as we could ascertain[22]—asks the question, not asked by Pseudo-Dionysius, *why* the essential ranks of the angels were created different, why their natures and their ability to receive the divine light are unequal. The commentator feels that this question is raised by the Origenists and looks for a moderate solution. He explicitly underscores the freedom (αὐτεξούσιον) of all created spirits and asks, in constantly new contexts, whether this could not stand in some kind of causal relationship with the differences between natures. In the end, he comes to the conclusion that God foresaw the strength of each spirit's love and so gave each, at creation, the natural perfection that is appropriate to this strength. This solution is similar to Origen's but is distinguished from Origen's in that the scholiast places the basis for the difference of these beings, not in the degrees of their negative fall away from God, but in the intensity of their positive turning toward him. For the author of the scholia is determined not to admit any kind of culpability among the (higher) angels; even the "cleansing" Dionysius mentions is not to be understood in Origenistic fashion, as a cleansing from sin. From what we have already seen, we know that there is no difference in the angels between essence and activity; from the first moment, the spirits are firmly grounded in the good by grace, despite their freedom. The scholiast concludes his treatment with a question mark: "But if someone else understands this better, I am ready to learn" (93BC).

---

[22] The manuscript is, at this point, confused and full of lacunae; in addition, the microfilm was hardly legible.

Everything points to the conclusion that John is the author of this group of texts. For much as Maximus may have assimilated Origenist ideas, on this one point he is completely inflexible: the differences between beings and their ranking belongs, in his view, to the positive value and meaning of the world. The length of some of the scholia, too, points to John. Phocas may have had good reasons not to include the most outspoken texts of this group in his selection. One of the main texts (97AC) undoubtedly contains ideas of John: the nondistinction of essence (οὐσία) and accident (συμβεβηκός) in a pure spirit (while Maximus says the opposite; see PG 90, 1125CD; PG 91, 1400C), spirits as forms (εἴδη). Here is the complete list of scholia that deal with this question:

61AC, 65CD* ("self-determining" beings [αὐτεξούσιοι]), 68C, 68D* (with a double reference to earlier texts, as is frequently the case with John), 84CD, 84D–85A, 85AB, 85B, 85CD, 85D–88A, 88A–C*, 88C–89A, 89A, 89B, 89B–D (reference to the following text), 92BC, 93BC (final solution of the question), 96D–97A (reference to 85AB), 97AC, 101BC, 128D–129A, 156A (a critique [κριτικόν]; cf. on this 84CD, 85AB), 249D* (beginning τῷ γὰρ), 249D–252A* (to ἄλλως; the same quotation of Scripture, Matthew 5:45, as in 88C–89A), 305D–308B*, 308B* (καλῶς), 360AB*, 364AB*, 377CD.

<h1 style="text-align:center">III</h1>

The third group of scholia is comprised of texts that display an express interest in Greek antiquity, in poetry, history, grammar, and philosophical systems. These texts are very numerous; the commentary is teeming with allusions and references that must come from a widely educated humanist, even from a polymath. We give here only the most important examples:

a. *Poetry and Philology.* 32AB* (on the Attic declension), 52B ("an Ionic form" [Ἰωνικῶς]; also on Attic), 188BC*, 148A (on Attic forms, with a reference to 188BC*, from which it is clear that John composed the commentary on the *Ecclesial Hierarchy* after that on the *Celestial Hierarchy*), 36CD* ("Homer, Hesiod, and others"), 69AC (on Attic forms; quotations from Homer, Plato, Euripedes), 152BC (on Attic and Lacedaemonian forms; quotation from Plato), 185AB* (on lost writings of Dionysius), 420B (on accents; quotation from Homer), 421D–424C (on the literary use of ἄγαλμα; quotations from Euripedes, Homer, the *Lithika* of the poet Dionysius, with reference to 216D–220A*), 553A (philological material; a quotation of Homer), 572D (philological material; a quotation from Homer).

Alongside these passages, there are numerous little philological explanations of words, of which we may mention a few: 49B, 53C, 53D, 65B, 68D–69A, 72D, 209BC, 212D (variants in the manuscripts), 236A.

b. *History and Literature.* 249C* (κατὰ τὸν; mention of Old Comedy), 368D–369A* (description of herms in classical sculpture), 553D–556A (on Athenian marriage customs and liturgies), 556AB (on the feasts of the *Hilariai*; quotation from Demophilus, *On the Sacrifices and Feasts of the Ancients*), 532BC* (quotation from Africanus' *Chronographies*), 560B–561A (mention of "the historian Phylarchus"), 569A (διαβαίνειν: a philological comment; quotation from Diogenianus), 541C–544B (chronological calculations; quotations from Africanus, Eusebius, Phlegon. These calculations correspond to John's taste, as is confirmed by 573BD*; so 540D–541B should also be ascribed to him). Phocas, who obviously was interested only in theology for his selection, did not include most of these longer pieces.

c. *Scholastic Philosophy.* John's philosophical education, as we have already said, was comprehensive—dazzling rather than deep. He has all the academic definitions present in his mind, and cannot hear the word "condition" (ἕξις) without being reminded of its explanation, "a lasting quality" (ποιότης ἔμμονος). He also has an excellent knowledge of the different [philosophical] systems. For example, he quotes the Stoic phrase, "At once God and all things" [ἅμα Θεὸς ἅμα πάντα] (388D*; 569DC; both texts have already been mentioned several times), and knows the Neoplatonic theories on matter (77BD*, 297C–300D*, both of which have also been mentioned). He uses Neoplatonic terminology, which Pseudo-Dionysius avoids for good reason (for example, the Proclian "flower" or "summit of the soul" [ἄνθος τοῦ νοῦ], 185B). But he also knows exactly where every pagan philosopher needs correction. Thanks to this sensitivity, he became the great "Christianizer" of Pseudo-Dionysius. With a bold touch, he transforms his "emanations" into "God's thoughts" and interprets vague expressions such as "a pouring forth of light" (φωτοχυσία), "outflow" (ἀπορροή), "bring out" (παράγειν), "be gifted" (δωρεῖσθαι), "a support" (ὑποστάτης)— all of which Pseudo-Dionysius uses to describe God's creative action —into the clear terms of "make" (ποιεῖν) and "maker" (ποιητής; for example, 261A*, 313D*). He knows the whole academic organization of philosophy, in all its subsidiary branches (568C*[23]) and includes it in his commentary, even though it makes only a modest contribution toward explaining the text. Similarly, John knows the academic organization of theology (561D–564B*) and includes it in his commentary, even though it positively reverses Pseudo-Dionysius' train of thought. Here is a list of scholastic definitions: 33C, 65C*, 73A, 205A, 208A*, 244BC (with reference back to the preceding text), 260C* (definition of cause; three definitions of final cause), 213CD* (three definitions of scientific knowledge [ἐπιστήμη]), 260B and 301CD* (definition of a definition), 361D–364A (six definitions of justice), 332D (reference to 260C), 537B, 425D–428C* (definition of the affirmative and the hypothetical modes of argument), 424BC (definition of affirmation [θέσις] and negation [ἀφαίρεσις], referring back to 216D–220A*), 565A–C* (from ὅρα δὲ: scholastic theory of mind).

These are all the scholia that one may identify with John on the basis of the prologue and the criteria it provides. Beyond these, the Syriac manuscript provides us with a number of other scholia, which we list here. Since they deal with the widest imaginable variety of subjects, we can only bring them into a provisional order.

1. On Hierarchy, Liturgy, etc.

29A*, 29AB*, 33B* (on φαινόμενα), 37A* (ἀπότομον), 48C* (κατὰ), 49A*, 49BC*, 49D–52B*, 52B* (ἐνταῦθα), 56A*, 64B* (ἱεροτελεστήν), 81C–84A*, 117CD*, 121C–124A*, 125B* (σημείωσαι), 128AC*, 133AD*, 177B* (οὐδέν), 197B*, 236B* (ὅτι).

2. On God, His Transcendence and His Relation to the World

32BC*, 40C*, 40D–41A*, 41AB*, 45C–48A*, 76C*, 185C*, 189AB*, 193CD*, 201CD*, 204D–205A*, 213AC*, 252CD*, 252D–253A*,

---

[23] We have treated this text in *Zeitschrift der katholischen Theologie* 63 (1939): 95–96, in connection with the *Hiera* of Evagrius.

253C–256A*, 260AB*, 308D*, 332D–333A*, 369BD*, 369D–372A*, 373D–376B*, 376CD* (up to ἄπειρον), 380D–381A*, 381A*, 396CD*, 404CD*, 404D–405A*, 408BC*, 425C*, 572A*.

3. On Participation in God, Matter, Evil

261A*, 268B–269A*, 269CD*, 272D*, 273CD*, 276AC*, 276D–277A*, 277A*, 277BD*, 277D–280A*, 280A*, 281CD*, 284D–285A*, 285C–288A*, 288AB*, 292C*, 293BC*, 293C (ἔφημεν)–296A*, 296B* (ὅτι οὔτε), 296B–297A*, 297B* (ὥσπερ), 301A*, 301B* (καὶ), 301D–304B*, 304BC*, 305AB*, 305C*, 308B* (σημείωσαι), 308C* (ὅρα), 380BC*, 397D–400A*, 401BD*, 405AC*, 405CD*, 529BC*.

4. On Angels

37B* (ποσῶς), 37B* (θεοειδεῖς), 37C* (αὗται), 37C* (ζῶα), 37D–40A*, 48BC*, 61D–64A*, 64CD*, 64D–65A*, 65AB*, 65D–68A*, 68B* (both scholia), 68D* (σημείωσαι), 69C* (σημείωσαι), 72CD*, 84A* (πῶς), 84B* (ὅτι), 92AB* (and with it 160B), 201D–204B*, 417A* (οὐ γὰρ).

5. On the Trinity, God the Logos, the World of Ideas and the Incarnation or Self-Emptying (Kenosis) of the Logos

132C* (on τοῦτο), 132D*, 133A*, 176D* (on ἑτέρους), 177CD*, 196B* (on σημείωσαι), 212B*, 212D* (on σημείωσαι), 213C* (on θεοπρεπῆ), 220CD* (and with it 220AB), 224D–225B*, 228AC*, 228C–229A*, 232B–233A*, 340D*, 340D–341C*, 344BC*, 353C–356B*, 356C–357A*, 361AC* (to τὸν Υἱόν; the conclusion, dealing with the "natural will" (θέλημα φυσικόν) of Christ, presupposes Monothelitism and is missing in the Syriac), 372D (from εἰπών)–373A*, 532A*.

6. On the Mystical Knowledge of God

This group is the most important, because it contains several elaborate treatments of Pseudo-Dionysian mysticism that largely anticipate Maximus' interpretation. Like Maximus, John also attempts to bring the new views of Pseudo-Dionysius on negative knowledge and divine "unknowing" into harmony with the traditional principles of Alexandrian (Origen and Evagrius) and Cappadocian (the two Gregories) mysticism. Apart from attempts to describe ecstatic "unknowing" more in psychological terms (like the important text 216D–220A*, to which John likes to refer in later parts of the work), he introduces into Pseudo-Dionysius the Philonic-Evagrian notion of the transcendence of all discursive movement and of the divine unity as the firm foundation of all knowledge, without allowing his explanations to become an extrinsic, inorganic synthesis. In general, John sticks here, too, to an already traditional body of knowledge, but he does not abandon his own sure instincts and his gift for wise distinctions.

a. *On the Knowledge of God through Symbols and Images*: 32C* (σημείω-σαι ὅτι δίχα), 33A* (σημείωσαι δὲ τίνα λέγει), 69CD*, 200A* (on ὅτι ἐκ), 265A (σημείωσαι). On the "distant echo" (ἀπήχημα): 48B*; the imitation of the angels: 204BC*.

b. *On the Unknowability of God and Mystical Ecstasy*: 113CD*, 185B*, 188B*, 188D*, 189BC*, 189CD*, 189D–192A*, 193AB*, 201C*, 216C*, 216D–220A*, 224CD*, 233CD*, 244C*, 352CD*, 416C–417A*, 528BC*.

This completes our outline of the important work of John, the Scholastic of Scythopolis—at least in its main features. It will be possible to make a fully valid division of his scholia from those of Maximus only when the whole manuscript material is collected. Inner criteria for judging content and style can probably not reveal more than what we have been able to establish in these pages, since John and Maximus are to some degree dominated by the same tendencies—to reconcile Dionysius with Alexandrian theology, to emphasize Chalcedonian Christology, and so on—and since many scholia are so colorless that they render any clear decision of this sort impossible. One thing is clear from what we have presented here: if our division of the material is correct —and that means, above all, if the Syriac selection from John's work is reliable (and there is no reason to doubt that it is)—then by far the most important part of the scholia is to be identified as the work of John. Maximus' contribution is limited to brief, usually unimportant scholia, the marginal notes of an attentive reader, which are in no sense intended to be a work of their own.

That a commentary of such importance, which attempts to defend the authenticity of the *corpus Areopagiticum* with all the arts of humanistic disputation, could have appeared so shortly after the appearance of the corpus itself—in any case before the Three Chapters controversy and probably before 520—and in its own native region, must, in any event, give us grounds for reflection. Was John really convinced of this authenticity—he who otherwise appears so sceptical in philosophical and historical questions? Does one not have the sense—at least in the introduction—of something almost unnoticeable, something that cannot be put into words, but that sounds like a gentle, overriding irony? Can John have belonged to the author's accomplices, even have been an initiate in his circle of friends? It would be worth the trouble to look more closely at this circle, and especially at that extraordinary personage who provided the Syriac translation of the Pseudo-Dionysian writings, Sergius of Reshaina. Perhaps one would find, in this very circle, their real author.

Postscript, 1961

What I have said here has met with no contradiction over the past twenty years. Charles Moeller (in A. Grillmeier and H. Bacht, eds., *Das Konzil von Chalkedon*, vol. 1 [Würzburg, 1951], 642, 675) added a few complementary details, for which I am grateful; more than anything else, he acknowledged the enormous importance of John the Scholastic. Jean-Michel Hornus, who at first suggested an untenable identification of Pseudo-Dionysius with John of Scythopolis ("Les Recherches récentes sur le Ps.-Denis", *Revue d'histoire et de philosophie religieuses* 35 [1955]: 350ff.), has now given up that approach, "after we began a personal study of the scholia. But we are still of the opinion that with John we are not far from the solution (to the problem of authorship)". ("Recherches dionysiennes de 1955 à 1960", *Rev. hist. phil. rel.* 41 [1961]: 37). I myself have never considered identifying Pseudo-Dionysius with John (as Elorduy has suggested I have done), nor have I even intended to insinuate it indirectly (as Hornus thinks, "Recherches dionysiennes", 40, n 89). Naturally, Pseudo-Dionysius can also not simply be equated with Sergius of Reshaina. Yet I would still like to assume, with Père Hausherr ("Note sur l'auteur du Corpus Dionysiacum", *Orientalia Christiana Periodica* 22 [1956]: 384–85), that the unknown author—who will probably always remain unknown—must be looked for in the circle of these people.

Meanwhile, the rest of what is known about John of Scythopolis[24] has been integrated with the new texts [we discussed]; until now, however, no new edition has appeared. Very recently, J.-M. Hornus has announced plans for such an edition, along with an edition of the Syriac translation of Pseudo-Dionysius and of John of Scythopolis.

Polycarp Sherwood, O.S.B., has dealt with the problem of the scholia in a number of places: "Sergius of Reshaina and the Syriac Versions of the Pseudo-Denis", *Sacris Erudiri* 5 (1952): 181;[25] *The Earlier Ambigua of St. Maximus the Confessor and His Refutation of Origenism* (Rome, 1955), 117–20; article, "Denys", in *Dictionnaire de spiritualité* (1954), 295a. He concludes that even the limited commentary that I would like to associate with Maximus cannot be ascribed to him with certainty. The reason is the fact I have already emphasized, that the Syriac translation only offers us a selection of John's scholia and so is no guarantee that the rest of the Greek sections are not also by John. That was clear to me also; I simply wanted to argue that what is attested in Syriac cannot be by Maximus (and this axiom seems to me, in the meantime, beyond dispute). And on the basis of the Syriac, one can, as I have shown, reclaim a good deal more of the Greek for John. To ascribe a text to Maximus, on the other hand, one would need further criteria, which I propose here once again:

1. A very strong internal relationship between a scholion and a genuine work of Maximus. An example of this is PG 4, 265CD, with *Ambigua* 1260CD; also PG 4, 317D (on κατὰ πρώτην προσβολήν), also

---

[24] See Loofs, *Leontius*, 269–72, corrected by F. Diekamp, *Origenistischen Streitigkeiten* (1899), 127f.; M. Richard, "Leonce de Jérusalem et Léonce de Byzance", *Mélanges de science religieuse* 1 (1944): 44, n. 35 (also in M. Richard, *Opera minora*, vol. 2 [Louvain, 1977], no. 59); O. Bardenhewer, *Patrologie*, 5:16; H. G. Beck, *Kirche und theologische Literatur im Byzantinischen Reich* 376–77; and above all C. Moeller, "Le Chalcédonisme et le néo-chalcédonisme en Orient de 451 à la fin du VIᵉ siècle", in A. Grillmeier and H. Bacht, *Das Konzil von Chalkedon: Geschichte und Gegenwart* (Würzburg: Echter, 1951), 1:675f., and J. M. Hornus, "Recherches dionysiennes" 37–38.

In B. Altaner, *Patrologie*, 5th ed. (Freiburg, 1958) 473, one unfortunately finds the misleading sentence: "Maximus Confessor integrated most of this work (John of Scythopolis' commentary) into his scholia on the *Areopagitica*." Even less true is the following sentence (ibid., 484): "In his exegesis of Pseudo-Dionysius, he (Maximus) is almost completely dependent on John of Scythopolis."

[25] See also the corrections to this article in Hornus, "Recherches dionysiennes", 36, n. 72 and addenda.

with *Ambigua* 1260. Further, 314A (from ἕνωσιν on) is only imaginable as coming from the mouth of Maximus.

2. Two opposed ways of speaking, as with the titles given to the Cappadocian Gregories.

For the moment, that is admittedly not much. But my purpose was not to save a work for Maximus but to claim one for John. What remains, after we have removed the scholia that belong to John, *can* partly belong to Maximus; but it is certainly not a work of great weight and character.[26] Even if that remainder must someday be taken away from Maximus, the loss would not be substantial. In this present book, I have made only decorative use of the scholia, but I have not built any arguments on them.

---

[26] Photius does not know the scholia. One could ask oneself, in any case, whether there were not also others, besides Scotus Erigena, who understood by Maximus' scholia on Pseudo-Dionysius the *Ambigua* and whether this was not the reason for attributing to him the scholia of John.

BIBLIOGRAPHY

I. Editions and Translations of Maximus' Genuine Works:

1. *Ambigua* [explanations of difficult passages in Gregory Nazianzen and Pseudo-Dionysius]. Edited by F. Oehler. Halle, 1857. In J.-P. Migne, *Patrologia Graeca* [PG] 91, 1032–1417.

———. In Latin translation of Scotus Erigena: edited by E. Jeauneau. In *Corpus Christianorum, Series Graeca* [CCG] 18. 1988.

Translation: J.-C. Larchet, E. Ponsoye, and D. Staniloae. *Saint Maxime le Confesseur, Ambigua*. Suresnes, 1994. [French translation; notes by Dumitru Staniloae.]

2. *Two Centuries on Knowledge* ("Gnostic Centuries"). Edited by F. Combéfis. Paris, 1675. PG 90, 1084–1176.

Translations: H. U. von Balthasar. *Gnostische Centurien*. Freiburg, 1941. Reprinted in *Kosmische Liturgie: Das Weltbild Maximus' des Bekenners*. 2d ed. Einsiedeln, 1961. [German paraphrase, with interspersed commentary; rearranged systematically.]

———. A. Ceresa-Gastaldo. *Il Dio-Uomo. Ducento Pensieri sulla conoscenza di Dio e sull'incarnazione di Cristo*. Milan, 1980. [Italian; brief introduction and notes.]

———. G. C. Berthold. *Maximus Confessor*. New York, 1985. [English; with commentary.]

———. J. Touraille. *Philocalie des Pères Neptiques*. 6:81–245. Abbaye de Bellefontaine, 1985. [French translation, as part of translation of classical Greek collection of ascetical writings; the "two hundred chapters" are followed, in this collection, by a further three hundred excerpted from the *Quaestiones ad Thalassium*.]

For a full, critically annotated biography of all editions and translations of Maximus, and all secondary works dealing with him, up to 1986, as well as a useful, brief summary of his doctrines, see Maria Luisa Gatti, *Massimo il Confessore. Saggio di bibliografica generale ragionata e contribute per una riconstruzione scientifica del suo pensiero metafisico e religioso* (Milan, 1987).

3. *Four Centuries on Love* ("Centuries on Charity"). Edited by F. Combéfis. PG 90, 960–1080.

———. A. Ceresa-Gastaldo. *Capitoli sulla carità.* Verba Seniorum, n.s., 3. Rome, 1963. [Critical edition with introduction, Italian translation, and notes.]

Translations: J. Pégon. *Centuries sur la charité.* Sources chrétiennes, vol. 9. Paris, 1943. [French, with brief introduction and comments. No Greek text, unlike later volumes of Sources chrétiennes.]

———. P. Sherwood. *The Ascetic Life. The Four Centuries on Charity.* Ancient Christian Writers, no. 21. 136–208. Westminster, Md., and London, 1955. [English; with introduction and commentary.]

———. H. U. von Balthasar. *Kosmische Liturgie: Das Weltbild Maximus' des Bekenners.* 2d ed. 408–81. Einsiedeln, 1961. [German, with brief introduction and comments.]

———. G. C. Berthold. *Maximus Confessor: Selected Writings.* Classics of Western Spirituality. New York: Paulist Press, 1985. [English, with commentary.]

———. J. Touraille. *Philocalie des Pères Neptiques.* 19–80. Abbaye de Bellefontaine, 1985. [French.]

4. *Computus Ecclesiasticus.* Edited by D. Petau. 1630. PG 19, 1217–80. [Introduction to method of calculating liturgical feasts, with summary of biblical and secular chronology. Composed between October 640 and February 641.]

5. *Disputation with Pyrrhus.* Edited by F. Combéfis. PG 91, 288–353.

Translations: A. Ceresa-Gastaldo. *Umanità e divinità di Cristo.* Rome, 1979.

———. J. P. Farrell. *The Disputation with Pyrrhus of Our Father among the Saints Maximus the Confessor.* South Canaan, Pa., 1990. [English, with notes.]

6. *Epistles* (45). Edited by F. Combéfis. PG 91, 364–649.

———. Epistle to Abbot Thalassius. Edited by J. D. Mansi. *In Sacrorum Conciliorum Nova et Amplissima Collectio*, 10:677–78. Paris, 1901. Cf. Latin translation in PL 129, 583–86.

———. Epistle to Anastasius. Edited by F. Combéfis. PG 90, 132–33. [With *Acta* of events leading to Maximus' death.]

———. Second Epistle to Thomas (not included in Combéfis ed.). Edited by P. Canart. "La Deuxième Lettre à Thomas de S. Maxime le Confesseur". *Byzantion* 34 (1964): 415–45.

7. *Exposition of the Lord's Prayer*. Edited by F. Combéfis. PG 90, 872–909.

———. Critical edition by P. Van Deun. CCG 23 (1991).

Translations: A. Ceresa-Gastaldo. *Umanità e divinità di Cristo*. Rome, 1979.

———. G. C. Berthold. *Maximus Confessor: Selected Writings*. Classics of Western Spirituality. New York: Paulist Press, 1985. [English, with commentary.]

———. J. Touraille. *Philocalie des Pères Neptiques*. 247–67. Abbaye de Bellefontaine, 1985. [French.]

8. *Exposition of Psalm 59*. Edited by Combéfis. PG 91, 856–72.

———. Critical edition by P. Van Deun. CCG 23 (1991).

Translation: R. Cantarella. *S. Massimo Confessore: La mistagogia ed altri scritti*. 4–25. Florence, 1931. [Italian.]

9. *Liber Asceticus*. Edited by F. Combéfis. PG 90, 912–56.

Translations: R. Cantarella. 30–99. Florence, 1931. [Italian.]

———. M. Dal Pra. *Breviari Mistici* 19. Milan, 1944. [Italian.]

———. P. Sherwood. *The Ascetic Life. The Four Centuries on Charity*. Ancient Christian Writers, no. 21, 103–35. Westminster, Md., and London, 1955. [English, with introduction and commentary.]

——. P. Deseille. *L'Evangile au désert: Des premiers moines à saint Bernard.* 161–91. Paris, 1965. [French.]

——. A. Ceresa-Gastaldo. *Umanità e divinità di Cristo.* Rome, 1979.

10. *Mystagogia.* Edited by F. Combéfis. PG 91, 657–717.

——. C. G. Sotiropoulos. Athens, 1978. [Critical edition, with introduction and translation into modern Greek.]

——. Ξαράλμπος Γ. Σωτιρόπουλος, Ἡ Μυσταγωγία τοῦ Ἁγίου Μαξίμου τοῦ Ὁμολογητοῦ (Athens, 1978) [privately published thesis].

Translations: M. Lot-Borodine. "Mystagogie de Saint Maxime". *Irénikon* 13 (1936): 466–72, 595–97, 717–20; 14 (1937): 66–69, 182–85, 282–84, 444–48; 15 (1938): 71–74, 185–86, 276–78, 390–91, 488–92. [French.]

——. H. U. von Balthasar. *Kosmische Liturgie: Das Weltbild Maximus' des Bekenners.* 2d ed. 363–407. Einsiedeln, 1961. [German.]

——. G. C. Berthold. *Maximus Confessor: Selected Writings.* Classics of Western Spirituality. New York: Paulist Press, 1985. [English, with commentary.]

——. J. Stead. *The Church, the Liturgy and the Soul of Man: The "Mystagogia" of St. Maximus the Confessor.* Still River, Mass.: 1982). [English, with introduction.]

11. *Opuscula Theologica et Polemica.* Edited by F. Combéfis. PG 91, 9–285.

Translation: Opusc. 3, 6, 7, 15, 16, and 24 (all dealing with the agony of Jesus): A. Ceresa-Gastaldo. *Massimo il Confessore: Meditazioni sull'agonia di Gesù.* Rome, 1985. [Italian.]

12. *Quaestiones ad Thalassium.* Edited by F. Combéfis. PG 90, 244–785;

——. Critical edition by C. Laga and C. Steel. CCG 7 (1980) [Qq. 1–55]; CCG 22 (1990) [Qq. 56–65]. Includes edition by E. Jeauneau of the Latin translation by Scotus Erigena.

Translation: J.-C. Larchet and E. Ponsoye. *S. Maxime le Confesseur: Questions à Thalassios.* Suresnes, 1992. [French.]

13. *Quaestiones ad Theopemptum.* Edited by F. Combéfis. PG 90, 1393–1400.

Translation: R. Cantarella. *La mistagogia, edaltri scritti.* 104–17. Florence, 1931. [Italian.]

14. *Quaestiones et Dubia.* Edited by F. Combéfis. PG 90, 785–856.

———. Critical edition by J. H. Declerck. CCG 10 (1982).

II. Editions and Translations of Doubtful Works of Maximus

1. *In De Coelesti Hierarchia:* scholia on Pseudo-Dionysius, *The Celestial Hierarchy.* Edited by Corderius (1889). PG 4. (See appendix, above.)

2. *In De Divinis Nominibus:* scholia on Pseudo-Dionysius, *The Divine Names.* Edited by Corderius. PG 4. (See appendix, above.)

3. *In Ecclesiaticam Hierarchiam:* scholia on Pseudo-Dionysius, *The Ecclesial Hierarchy.* Edited by Corderius. PG 4. (See appendix, above.)

4. *In Epistulas Dionysii:* scholia on the Epistles of Pseudo-Dionysius. Edited by Corderius, PG 4. (See appendix, above.)

5. *In Mysticum Theologiam:* scholia on Pseudo-Dionysius, *Mystical Theology.* Edited by Corderius. PG 4. (See appendix, above.)

6. *Life of the Virgin* (extant only in Georgian translation, which draws, at least to some extent, on later sources). Edited and translated [French] by M.-J. van Esbroeck. *Corpus Scriptorum Christianorum Orientalium* 478 [text] and 479 [historical introduction and translation]. Louvain, 1986.

7. *Moscow Centuries on Knowledge* [probably not authentic]. Edited (along with thirty-one other fragments attributed to Maximus) by S. L. Epifanovich. *Materialy k izučeniju žizni i tvorenij prep. Maksima Ispovědnika* [Materials to Help the Study of the Life and Works of Maximus Confessor] 33–56. Kiev, 1917.

III. Anthologies of Translated Passages from Maximus' Works

1. E. von Ivánka. *Maximos der Bekenner: All-eins in Christus*. Einsiedeln, 1961. [German; with brief introduction and notes.]

2. A. Louth. *Maximus the Confessor*. London and New York, 1996. [English translation of Epistle 2; Ambigua 1, 5, 10, 41, and 71; Opuscula 3 and 7. With extensive introduction and notes.]

3. M.-H. Congourdeau and F.-M. Léthel. *Maxime le Confesseur: L'Agonie du Christ*. Paris, 1996. [French translation of passages dealing with Jesus' agony in the Garden.]

IV. Sources for Maximus' Life

1. Michael Exaboulites the Studite? *Life*. Edited by F. Combéfis. PG 90, 68–109.

2. Briefer accounts of his life and martyrdom. Edited by S. L. Epifanovich. *Materialy k izučeniju žizni i tvorenij prep. Maksima Ispovědnika* [Materials to Help the Study of the Life and Works of Maximus Confessor] Kiev, 1917. 1–25; see also R. Devreesse, "La Lettre d'Anastase l'Apocrisiaire sur la mort de S. Maxime le Confesseur et de ses compagnons d'exil. Texte grec inédit". *Analecta Bollandiana* 73 (1955): 5–16.

Translation (of Epifanovich's text): C. Birchall, *The Life of Our Holy Father Maximus the Confessor*. Boston, 1982. [English, with introduction.]

3. *Acta* and documents of trial. Edited by F. Combéfis. PG 90, 109–221.

Translation: G. Berthold. *Maximus Confessor: Selected Writings*. Classics of Western Spirituality. 17–31. New York: Paulist Press, 1985.

4. *Syriac Life* [hostile, from Monothelite source]. S. P. Brock. "An Early Syriac Life of Maximus the Confessor". *Analecta Bollandiana* 85 (1967): 285–316.

V. Modern Works on Maximus

P. Argárate. "El hombre como microcosmos en el pensamiento de San Máximo el Confesor". *Recherches de théologie ancienne et médiévale* 63 (1996): 177–98.

———. "La unidad dinamica del Cósmos en San Máximo el Confesor". *Teologia* 33 (1996): 35–51.

E. Bellini. "Maxime interprète de Pseudo-Denys l'Areopagite. Analyse de l'Ambiguum ad Thomam 5". In *Maximus Confessor*, edited by F. Heinzer and C. Schönborn (hereafter referred to as Heinzer-Schönborn). 37–49. Fribourg, 1982.

G. C. Berthold. "Maximus the Confessor and the *Filioque*". *Studia Patristica* (Kalamazoo, Mich.) 18 (1985): 113–17.

———. "History and Exegesis in Origen and Maximus". *Origeniana Quarta* (Innsbruck), 1987, 390–404.

———. "The Cappadocian Roots of Maximus the Confessor". In Heinzer-Schönborn, 51–59.

———. "Levels of Scriptural Meaning in Maximus the Confessor". *Studia Patristica* 27 (1993): 129–44.

P. M. Blowers. *Exegesis and Spiritual Pedagogy in Maximus the Confessor: An Investigation of the "Quaestiones ad Thalassium"*. Notre Dame, 1991.

———. "The Logology of Maximus the Confessor". In *Origeniana Quinta*, edited by R. J. Daly. 570–76. Louvain, 1992.

———. "Maximus the Confessor, Gregory of Nyssa, and the Concept of 'Perpetual Progress'". *Vigiliae Christianae* 46 (1992): 151–71.

———. "The Anagogical Imagination: Maximus the Confessor and the Legacy of Origenian Hermeneutics". In *Origeniana Sexta*, edited by G. Dorival and A. LeBoulluec. 639–54. Louvain, 1995.

R. Bornert. *Les Commentaires byzantins de la divine liturgie du VIIe au XVe siècle*. Paris, 1960. [On *Mystagogia*: 83–124.]

R. B. Bracke. *Ad Sancti Maximi vitam: Studie van de biographische documenten en de levensberijvingen betreffende Maximus Confessor (ca. 580–662).* Diss., Louvain, 1980.

―――. "Some Aspects of the Manuscript Tradition of the Ambigua of Maximus the Confessor". In Heinzer-Schönborn, 97–109.

I. I. Bria. "La Conaissance de Dieu selon S. Maximu le Confesseur". *Studii teologice* 9 (1957) 310–325 [Romanian].

P. Canart. "La Deuxième Lettre à Thomas de S. Maxime le Confesseur," *Byzantion* 34 (1964): 415–45.

E. Caudel. "La gracia increada del *Liber Ambiguorum* de S. Maximo". *Orientalia Christiana Periodica* 27 (1961): 131–49.

A. Ceresa-Gastaldo. *Il codice Vaticano Palatino gr. 49 (fine IX sec.) continente i 'Capitoli sulla carità' di S. Massimo Confessore.* Varese-Milan, 1955.

―――. "Appunti dalla biografia di S. Massimo Confessore". *La scuola cattolica* 84 (1956): 145–51.

―――. "Die Überlieferung der *Kephalaia peri agapēs* von Maximos Confessor auf Grund einiger alter Athoshandschriften". *Orientalia Christiana Periodica* 23 (1957): 145–58.

―――. "Dimensione umana e prospettiva escatologica in Massimo Confesore". *Renovatio* 12 (1977): 324–29.

―――. "Tradition et innovation linguistique chez Maxime le Confesseur". In Heinzer-Schönborn, 123–37.

―――. "Il motivo del sangue in Massimo Confessore". In *Sangue e antropologia nella letteratura cristiana: Atti della settimana*, edited by F. Vattioni. 1421–31. Rome, 1983.

P. Christou. "Maximos Confessor on the Infinity of Man". In Heinzer-Schönborn, 261–71.

P. K. Chrysou. "L'Homme sans commencement et sans fin". *Klēronomia* 12 (1980): 251–81. [Based on Maximus; Greek.]

M.-H. Congourdeau. "L'Animation de l'embryon humain chez Maxime le Confesseur". *Nouvelle revue théologique* 111 (1989): 693–709.

V. Croce. *Tradizione e ricerca: Il metodo teologico di S. Massimo Confessore.* Studia Patristica Mediolanensia, 2. Milan, 1974.

V. Croce and B. Valente. "Provvidenza e pedagogia divina nella storia". In Heinzer-Schönborn, 247–59.

B. E. Daley. "Apokatastasis and 'Honorable Silence' in the Eschatology of Maximus the Confessor". In Heinzer-Schönborn, 309–39.

I.-H. Dalmais. "S. Maxime le Confesseur, Docteur de la Charité", *La Vie spirituelle* (1948): 296–306. [Includes a translation of Epistle 2.]

———. "La Théorie des 'logoi' des créatures chez S. Maxime le Confesseur". *Revue des sciences philosophiques et théologiques* 36 (1952): 244–49.

———. "L'Oeuvre spirituelle de S. Maxime le Confesseur: Notes sur son développement et sa signification". *La Vie spirituelle*, suppl. 21 (1952): 216–26.

———. "Un Traité de théologie contemplative: Le Commentaire du Pater de S. Maxime le Confesseur". *Revue de l'ascèse et de la mystique* 29 (1953): 123–59.

———. "La Doctrine ascétique de S. Maxime le Confesseur d'après le 'Liber asceticus'". *Irénikon* 26 (1953): 17–39.

———. "L'Anthropologie spirituelle de saint Maxime le Confesseur". *Recherches et débats du centre catholique des intellectuels français* 36 (1961): 202–11.

———. "Saint Maxime le Confesseur et la crise de l'Origénisme monastique". In *Théologie de la vie monastique.* 411–21. Paris, 1961.

———. "La Place de la *Mystagogie* de S. Maxime le Confesseur dans la théologie liturgique byzantine". *Studia Patristica* 5 (Berlin, 1962): 277–83.

———. "La Fonction unificatrice du Verbe Incarné d'après les oeuvres spirituelles de S. Maxime le Confesseur". *Sciences ecclésiastiques* 14 (1962): 445–59.

———. "L'Héritage évagrien dans la synthèse de S. Maxime le Confesseur". *Studia Patristica* 8 (Berlin, 1966): 356–62.

————. "Le Vocabulaire des activités intellectuelles, volontaires et spirituelles dans l'anthropologie de S. Maxime le Confesseur". In *Melanges offerts à M. D. Chenu.* 189–202. Paris, 1967.

————. "Mystère liturgique et divinisation dans la *Mystagogie* de S. Maxime le Confesseur". In *Epektasis*, Festschrift J. Daniélou, edited by C. Kannengiesser and J. Fontaine. 55–62. Paris, 1972.

————. "Théologie de l'Eglise et mystère liturgique dans la *Mystagogie* de S. Maxime le Confesseur". *Studia Patristica* 13 (Berlin, 1975): 145–53.

————. "Maxime le Confesseur". *Dictionnaire de Spiritualité* 10 (1980): 836–47.

————. "La Manifestation du Logos dans l'homme et dans l'Eglise: Typologie anthropologique et typologie ecclésiale d'après Qu. Thal. 60 et la Mystagogie". In Heinzer-Schönborn, 13–25.

————. "La Vie de Saint Maxime le Confesseur reconsidérée?" *Studia Patristica* 17 (Oxford, 1982): 26–30.

J. H. Declerck. "La Tradition des Quaestiones et dubia de S. Maxime le Confesseur". In Heinzer-Schönborn, 85–96.

E. Dekkers. "Maxime le Confesseur dans la tradition latine". In *After Chalcedon: Studies in Theology and Church History Offered to Professor Albert van Roey for His Seventieth Birthday*, edited by C. Laga, J. Munitiz, and L. van Rompay. 83–97. Orientalia Lovaniensia Analecta, 18. Louvain, 1985.

E. des Places. "Maxime le Confesseur et Diadoque de Photicé". In Heinzer-Schönborn, 29–35.

R. Devreesse. "La Vie de S. Maxime le Confesseur et ses récensions". *Analecta Bollandiana* 46 (1928): 5–49.

M. Th. Disdier. "Les Fondements dogmatiques de la spiritualité de S. Maxime le Confesseur". *Echos de l'Orient* 29 (1930): 296–313.

————. "Une Oeuvre douteuse de saint Maxime le Confesseur: Les cinq Centuries théologiques". *Echos d'Orient* 30 (1931): 160–78.

———. "Elie l'Ecdicos et les *Hetera kephalaia* attribués à saint Maxime le Confesseur et à Jean de Carpathos". *Echos d'Orient* 31 (1932): 17–43.

M. Doucet. "Vues récentes sur les 'Métamorphoses' de la pensée de Saint Maxime le Confesseur". *Sciences et Esprit* 31 (1979): 269–302. [On the conception of Maximus' theological "evolution" presented in the books of J.-M. Garrigues and A. Riou.]

———. "Est-ce qu le monothélisme a fait autant d'illustres victimes? Réflexions sur un ouvrage de F. M. Léthel". *Science et Esprit* 35 (1983): 53–83. [Critical of Léthel's *Théologie de l'agonie du Christ* (1979).]

———. "La Volonté humaine du Christ, spécialement en son agonie. Maxime le Confesseur, interprète de l'Ecriture". *Science et esprit* 37 (1985): 123–59.

G. D. Dragas. "The Church in St. Maximus' *Mystagogy*". *Theologia* [Athens] 56 (1985): 385–403.

V. L. Dupont. "Le Dynamisme de l'action liturgique: Une Étude de la *Mystagogie* de S. Maxime le Confesseur". *Revue des sciences religieuses* 65 (1991): 363–88.

M. L. Gatti. *Massimo il Confessore: Saggio di bibliografia generale raggionata e contributi per una ricostruzione scientifica del suo pensiero metafisico e religioso.* Milan, 1987.

J.-M. Garrigues. "L'Energie divine et la grâce chez Maxime le Confesseur". *Istina* 19 (1974): 272–96.

———. "La Personne composée du Christ d'après saint Maxime le Confesseur". *Revue Thomiste* 74 (1974): 181–204.

———. *Maxime le Confesseur: La Charité, avenir divin de l'homme.* Théologie historique, 38. Paris, 1976.

———. "Le Sens de la primauté romaine chez S. Maxime le Confesseur". *Istina* 21 (1976): 6–24.

———. "Le Martyre de saint Maxime le Confesseur". *Revue Thomiste* 26 (1976): 410–52.

———. "Le Dessein d'adoption du Créateur dans son rapport au Fils d'après S. Maxime le Confesseur". In Heinzer-Schönborn, 173–92.

R. A. Gauthier. "S. Maxime le Confesseur et la psychologie de l'acte humain". *Recherches de théologie ancienne et médiévale* 21 (1954): 51–100.

D. J. Genakopoulos. "Some Aspects of the Influence of the Byzantine Maximos the Confessor on the Theology of East and West". *Church History* 38 (1969): 150–63.

E. Gilson. "Maxime, Erigène, S. Bernard". In *Aus der Geisteswelt des Mittelalters*, Festschrift Martin Grabmann, edited by A. Lang, J. Lechner, and M. Schmaus. 188–95. Beiträge zur Geschichte der Philosophie und Theologie des Mittelalters, supplementband 3/1. Münster, 1935.

V. Grumel. "L'Union hypostatique et la comparaison de l'âme et du corps chez Léonce de Byzance et S. Maxime le Confesseur". *Echos d'Orient* 25 (1926): 393–406.

———. "Notes d'histoire et de chronologie sur la vie de S. Maxime le Confesseur," *Echos d'Orient* 26 (1927): 24–32.

———. "Recherches sur l'histoire du Monothélisme, I–III". *Echos d'Orient* 27 (1928): 6–16, 257–77; 29 (1930): 16–28.

———. "Maxime le Confesseur". *Dictionnaire de théologie Catholique*, vol. 10, 1 (1928): 448–59.

S. Gysens. "Les Traductions latines du *Liber Asceticus* (CPG 7692) de S. Maxime le Confesseur". *Augustiniana* 46 (1996): 311–88.

J. F. Haldon. "Ideology and the Byzantine State in the Seventh Century: The 'Trial' of Maximus Confessor". In *From Late Antiquity to Early Byzantium: Proceedings of the Byzantinological Symposium*, edited by V. Vavrínek. 87–91. Prague, 1985.

I. Hausherr. "Les Grands Courants de la spiritualité orientale". *Orientalia christiana periodica* 1 (1935): 126–28.

———. "Ignorance infinie". *Orientalia christiana periodica* 2 (1935): 351–62.

————. *Philautie: De la tendresse pour soi à la charité selon S. Maxime le Confesseur*. Rome, 1952.

J. Heintjes. "Een onbekende leeraar van ascese en mystiek: S. Maximus Confessor". *Studia catholica* 11 (1935): 175–200.

F. Heinzer. *Gottes Sohn als Mensch: Die Struktur des Menschseins Christi bei Maximus Confessor*. Paradosis, 26. Fribourg, 1980.

————. "Anmerkungen zum Willensbegriff Maximus' Confessors". *Freiburger Zeitschrift für Philosophie und Theologie* 28 (1981): 372–92.

————. "L'Explication trinitaire de l'Economie chez Maxime le Confesseur". In Heinzer-Schönborn, 159–72.

F. Heinzer and C. Schönborn, eds. *Maximus Confessor. Actes du Symposium sur Maxime le Confesseur, 1980*. Paradosis, 27. Fribourg, 1982. [Individual articles are listed here with references to Heinzer-Schönborn.]

E. Jeauneau. "Jean l'Erigène et les Ambigua ad Iohannem de Maxime le Confesseur". In Heinzer-Schönborn, 343–64.

V. Karayiannis. *Maxime le Confesseur: Essence et enérgies de Dieu*. Théologie historique, 93. Paris, 1993.

I. Kirchmeyer. "Un Commentaire de Maxime le Confesseur sur le Cantique?" *Studia Patristica* 8 (Berlin, 1966): 406–13.

W. Lackner. *Studien zur philosophischen Schultradition und zu den Nemesioszitaten bei Maximos dem Bekenner*. Diss., Graz, 1962.

————. "Quellen und Datierung der Maximosvita". *Analecta Bollandiana* 85 (1967): 285–316.

————. "Der Amtstitel Maximos des Bekenners". *Jahrbuch der österreichischen Byzantinistik* 20 (1971): 63–65.

C. Laga. "Maximi Confessoris *Ad Thalassium Quaestio 64*. Essai de lecture". In *After Chalcedon: Studies in Theology and Church History Offered to Professor Albert van Roey for His Seventieth Birthday*, 203–15. Edited by C. Laga, J. Munitiz, and L. van Rompay. Orientalia Lovaniensia Analecta, 18. Louvain, 1985.

————. "Maximus as a Stylist in Quaestiones ad Thalassium". In Heinzer-Schönborn, 139–46.

————. "Judaism and Jews in Maximus Confessor's Works: Theoretical Controversy and Practical Attitude". *Byzantinoslavica* 51 (1990): 177–88.

J.-C. Larchet. "Le Baptême selon S. Maxime le Confesseur". *Revue des sciences religieuses* 65 (1991): 51–70.

————. *La Divinisation de l'homme selon Maxime le Confesseur*. Paris, 1996.

M.-J. Le Guillou. "Quelques réflexions sur Constantinople III et la sotériologie de Maxime". In Heinzer-Schönborn, 235–37.

F.-M. Léthel. *Théologie de l'agonie du Christ: La Liberté humaine du Fils de Dieu et son importance sotériologique mises en lumière par Saint Maxime le Confesseur*. Théologie historique 52. Paris, 1979.

————. "La Prière de Jésus à Gethsémani dans la controverse monothélite". In Heinzer-Schönborn, 207–14.

J. Loosen. *Logos und Pneuma im begnadeten Menschen bei Maximus Confessor*. Münster, 1941.

A. Louth. "St. Denys the Areopagite and St. Maximus the Confessor: A Question of Influence". *Studia Patristica* 27 (1993): 166–74.

J. D. Madden. "The Authenticity of Early Definitions of Will (*thelēsis*)". In Heinzer-Schönborn, 61–79.

N. Madden. "The Commentary on the Pater Noster: An Example of the Structural Methodology of Maximus the Confessor". In Heinzer-Schönborn, 147–55.

————. "Composite Hypostasis in Maximus Confessor". *Studia Patristica* 27 (1993): 175–97.

G. Mahieu. *Travaux préparatoires à une édition critique des oeuvres de S. Maxime le Confesseur*. Licentiate thesis, Louvain, 1957.

J. L. Marion. "Les Deux Volontés du Christ selon saint Maxime le Confesseur". *Résurrection* 41 (1973): 18–66.

S. G. Mercati. "Maxximo Margunio è l'autore degli inni anacreontici attribuiti a San Massimo Confessore". In *Mélanges Bidez*. 619–25. Brussels, 1934.

P. Miquel. "*Peira*. Contribution à l'étude du vocabulaire de l'expérience religieuse dans l'oeuvre de Maxime le Confesseur". *Studia Patristica* 7 (1966): 355–61.

I. D. Moldovan. "La Théologie de la résurrection dans l'oeuvre de S. Maxime le Confesseur". *Studii teologice* 20 (1968): 512–27. [Romanian.]

L. Negri. "Elementi cristologici ed antropologici nel pensiero di S. Massimo il Confessore: Nota critica sulla bibliografia sull'argomento". *La scola cattolica* 101 (1973): 331–61.

A. Nichols. *Byzantine Gospel: Maximus the Confessor in Modern Scholarship*. Edinburgh, 1993. [A survey of modern theological work on Maximus, which curiously omits any discussion of Balthasar's *Kosmische Liturgie*.]

T. Nikolaou. "Zur Identität der *makarios gerōn* in der Mystagogia von Maximos dem Bekenner". *Orientalia christiana periodica* 49 (1983): 407–18.

J. Pelikan. " 'Council or Fathers or Scripture?' The Concept of Authority in the Theology of Maximus Confessor". In *The Heritage of the Early Church*, Festschrift for G. V. Florovsky. Edited by D. Neiman and M. Schatkin. 277–88. Orientalia Christiana Analecta, 195. Rome, 1973.

———. "The Place of Maximus Confessor in the History of Christian Thought". In Heinzer-Schönborn, 387–402.

P. Piret. *Le Christ et la Trinité selon Maxime le Confesseur*. Théologie historique, 69 Paris, 1983.

———. "Christologie et théologie trinitaire chez Maxime le Confesseur, d'après sa formule des nature 'desquelles, en lesquelles et lesquelles est le Christ' ". In Heinzer-Schönborn, 215–22.

P. C. Plass. "Transcendent Time in Maximus the Confessor". *The Thomist* 44 (1980): 259–77.

———. " 'Moving Rest' in Maximus the Confessor". *Classica et medievalia* [Copenhagen] 35 (1984): 177–90.

J. J. Prado. *Voluntad y naturaleza: La antropología filosófica de Máximo el Confesor*. Rio Cuarto, Argentina, 1974.

L

A. Radosavljevic. "Le Problème du 'présupposé' ou du 'non-présupposé' de l'Incarnation de Dieu le Verbe". In Heinzer-Schönborn, 193–206.

R. Riedinger. "Die 'Quaestiones et Dubia' des Maximos Homologetes". *Byzantinisch-neugriechische Jahrbücher* 19 (1965): 260–75.

———. "Die Lateransynode von 649 und Maximos der Bekenner". In Heinzer-Schönborn, 111–21.

A. Riou, *Le Monde et l'église selon S. Maxime le Confesseur*. Théologie historique, 22. Paris, 1973.

———. "Index scripturaire des oeuvres de S. Maxime le Confesseur". In Heinzer-Schönborn, 405–21.

K. Savvidis, *Die Lehre von der Vergöttlichung des Menschen bei Maximus dem Bekenner und ihre Rezeption bei Gregor Palamas*. S. Ottilien, 1997.

C. Schönborn [= von Schönborn]. "La Primauté romaine vue de l'Orient pendant la quérelle du monoénergisme et du monothélisme". *Istina* 20 (1975): 476–90.

———. "Plaisir et douleur dans l'analyse de s. Maxime, d'après les Quaestiones ad Thalassium". In Heinzer-Schönborn, 273–84.

———. and F. Heinzer. *Maximus Confessor*: see Heinzer above.

A. Schoors. "Biblical Onomastics in Maximus Confessor's *Quaestiones ad Thalassium*". In *Philohistor*, Festschrift Carllaga, edited by A. Schoors and P. Van Deun. 257–72. Orientalia Lovaniensia Analecta, 60. Louvain, 1994.

A. Schoors, and P. Van Deun, eds. *Philohistor*. Festschrift Carl Laga. Orientalia Lovaniensia Analecta, 60. Louvain 1994.

R. Schwager. "Das Mysterium der übernatürlichen Natur-Lehre: Zur Erlösungslehre des Maximus Confessor". *Zeitschrift für katholische Theologie* 105 (1983): 32–57.

G. Sfameni Gasparro. "Aspetti di 'doppia creazione' nell' antropologia di Massimo il Confessore". *Studia Patristica* 18 (1985): 127–34.

I. P. Sheldon-Williams. "The Greek Christian Platonist Tradition from the Cappadocians to Maximus and Eriugena". In *The Cambridge*

History of Later Greek and Early Medieval Philosophy, edited by A. H. Armstrong. 421–533. Cambridge, 1967.

P. Sherwood. "Notes on Maximus the Confessor". *American Benedictine Review* 1 (1950): 347–56.

———. *An Annotated Date-List of the Works of Maximus the Confessor*. Rome, 1952.

———. *The Earlier Ambigua of St. Maximus the Confessor and his Refutation of Origenism*. Rome, 1955.

———. "Exposition and Use of Scripture in St. Maximus as Manifested in the *Quaestiones ad Thalassium*". *Orientalia christiana periodica* 24 (1958): 202–207.

———. "Maximus and Origenism, *Archē kai telos*". *Bericht zum XI. internationalen Byzantinisten-Kongress*. Munich, 1958.

———. "A Survey of Recent Work on St. Maximus the Confessor". *Traditio* 20 (1964): 428–37.

C. G. Sotiropoulos. "η έννοια τῶν πειρασμῶν εις την πνευματικην ζωην κατα τον αγιον Μάξιμον τον Ομολογήτην και Συμεων τον Νέον Θεόλογον". Θεολογία 64 (1993): 683–706.

A. Squire. "The Idea of the Soul as Virgin and Mother in Maximus Confessor". *Studia Patristica* 8 (1960): 456–61.

J. Starr. "St. Maximos and the Forced Baptism at Carthage in 632". *Byzantinisch-neugriechische Jahrbücher* 16 (1940): 192–96.

C. Steel. "Un Admirateur de S. Maxime à la cour des Comnènes: Isaac le Sébastocrator". In Heinzer-Schönborn, 365–73.

———. "'Elementatio evangelica'. —propos de Maxime le Confesseur, *Ambigua ad Joannem* 17". In *The Four Gospels*, Festschrift Frans Neirynck, edited by F. Van Segbroeck et al. 3:2419–32. Louvain, 1992.

———. "Le Jeu du verbe.—propos de maxime, *Ambigua ad Joannem* 67". In *Philohistor*, Festschrift Carl Laga, edited by A. Schoors and P. Van Deun. 281–93. Orientalia Lovaniensia Analecta, 60. Louvain, 1994.

E. Stephanou. "La Coexistence initiale du corps et de l'âme d'après S. Grégoire de Nysse et S. Maxime l'Homologète". *Echos d'Orient* 31 (1932): 304–15.

H. Stickelberger. "Freisetzende Einheit: Uber ein christologisches Grundaxiom bei Maximus Confessor und Karl Rahner". In Heinzer-Schönborn, 375–84.

H. Straubinger. *Die Christologie des hl. Maximus Confessor*. Bonn, 1906.

B. Studer. "Zur Soteriologie des Maximus Confessor". In Heinzer-Schönborn, 239–46.

B. R. Suchla. *Die sogenannten Maximus-Scholien des Corpus Dionysiacum Areopagiticum*. Nachrichten der Akademie der Wissenschaften in Göttingen, philologisch-historische Klasse, no. 3. Göttingen, 1980.

S. Tache. "La Theologie du Logos chez S. Maxime le Confesseur". *Studii teologice* 29 (1977): 516–26. [Romanian.]

L. Thunberg. *Microcosm and Mediator: The Theological Anthropology of Maximus the Confessor*. Lund, 1965. 2d ed., Chicago, 1995.

———. *Man and the Cosmos. The Vision of St. Maximus the Confessor.* New York, 1985.

———. "Symbol and Mystery in St. Maximus the Confessor. With Particular Reference to the Doctrine of Eucharistic Presence". In Heinzer-Schönborn, 285–308.

C. N. Tsirpanlis. "Acta S. Maximi". *Theologia* 43 (1972): 106–24.

K.-H. Uthemann. "Das anthropologische Modell der hypostatischen Union bei Maximus Confessor. Zur innerchalkedonischen Transformation eines Paradigmas". In Heinzer-Schönborn, 223–34.

B. Valente. See Croce and Valente [above].

P. Van Deun. "Deux Textes attribués à tort à Maxime le Confesseur". *Scriptorium* 46 (1992): 87.

———. "La Symbolique des nombres dans l'oeuvre de Maxime le Confesseur (580–662)". *Byzantinoslavica* 53 (1992): 237–42.

———. "Les Extraits de Maxime le Confesseur contenus dans les chaînes sur le Nouveau Testament, abstraction faite des évangiles". *Orientalia Lovaniensia Periodica* 23 (1992): 205–17.

————. "Les Extraits de Maxime le Confesseur contenus dans les chaînes sur l'Évangile de Matthieu". In *Philohistor*, Festschrift Carl Laga, edited by A. Schoors and P. Van Deun. 295–328. Orientalia Lovaniensia Analecta, 60. Louvain, 1994.

————. "Les Extraits de Maxime le Confesseur contenus dans les chaînes sur l'Évangile de Marc". *Orientalia Lovaniensia Periodica* 25 (1994): 169–73.

M. Viller. "Aux sources de la spiritualité de S. Maxime: Les Oeuvres d'Evagre le Pontique". *Revue d'ascèse et de mystique* 11 (1930): 156–84, 239–68.

W. Völker. "Der Einfluss des Ps.-Dionysius Areopagita auf Maximus Confessor". In *Universitas*, Festschrift Albert Stohr, edited by L. Lenhart. 1:243–54. Mainz, 1960.

————. "Der Einfluss des Ps.-Dionysius Areopagita auf Maximus Confessor". In *Studien zum Neuen Testament und zur Patristik*. Festschrift Erich Klostermann. Texte und Untersuchungen, vol. 77. 331–50. Berlin, 1961. [Although the title is the same, this is a different article from the preceding item.]

————. "Zur Ontologie des Maximus Confessor". In . . . *und fragten nach Jesus: Beiträge aus Theologie, Kirche und Geschichte*. Festschrift Ernst Barnikol. 57–79. Berlin, 1964.

————. *Maximus Confessor als Meister des geistlichen Lebens*. Wiesbaden, 1965.

E. von Ivánka. "Der philosophische Ertrag der Auseinandersetzung Maximos' des Bekenners mit dem Origenismus". *Jahrbuch der Österreichischen Byzantinischen Gesellschaft* 7 (1958): 23–49.

S. Zañartu. " 'Las naturalezas de las cuales, en las cuales y las cuales en el Cristo'. Máximo el Confesor como culminación de un proceso de inculturación cristológica en torno a los conceptos de φύσις ὑπόστασις". *Teologia* 29 (1992): 21–55.

C.-A. Zirnheld. "Le Double Visage de la passion: Malédiction due au péché et/ou dynamisme de la vie: *Quaestiones ad Thalassium* de S. Maxime le Confesseur XXI, XXII et XLII". In *Philohistor*,

Festschrift Carl Laga, edited by A. Schoors and P. Van Deun. 361–
80. Orientalia Lovaniensia Analecta, 60. Louvain, 1994.

VI. The Background of Maximus' Theology

S. Gersh. *From Iamblichus to Eriugena: An Investigation of the Prehistory and Evolution of the Pseudo-Dionysian Tradition.* Leiden, 1978.

F. X. Murphy, and P. Sherwood. *Constantinople II et Constantinople III.* Histoire des conciles oecuméniques, 3. Paris, 1974.

J. M. Sansterre. *Les Moines grecs et orientaux à Rome aux époques byzantine et carolingienne (milieu du VI⁰ s.–fin du IX⁰ s.).* Mémoires de la Classe des lettres, 2d series, vol. 66, 1 fasc. Brussels: Académie Royale de Belgique, 1983.

C. Schönborn. *L'Icône du Christ: Fondements théologiques élaborés entre le Ier et le IIe Concile de Nicée (325–787).* Paradosis, 24. Fribourg, 1976. English translation: *God's Human Face: The Christ-Icon.* Translated by Lothar Krauth. San Francisco: Ignatius Press, 1994.

GENERAL INDEX

INDEX OF CITATIONS
FROM MAXIMUS' WORKS

Acta

PG 90, 89C	40	PG 91, 1052B	210
PG 90, 93A	355	PG 91, 1053	104, n. 69
PG 90, 93D	43	PG 91, 1053B	215; 258
PG 90, 101B	44	PG 91, 1053C	259; 259, n. 245;
PG 90, 112C	38–39		279
PG 90, 117AB	41–42	PG 91, 1053CD	209; 215
PG 90, 120AB	355	PG 91, 1056A	202; 256; 259
PG 90, 121A	43	PG 91, 1056BC	262
PG 90, 121BC	40, n. 15	PG 91, 1056D	256
PG 90, 128B	42–43	PG 91, 1056D–1057A	214
PG 90, 128C	43	PG 91, 1057A	209; 214; 215
PG 90, 132C	40, n. 13	PG 91, 1057B	146
PG 90, 145C–148A	42	PG 91, 1058C	213
PG 90, 149A–D	53–54	PG 91, 1060B	257, 258
		PG 91, 1068ff.	258
		PG 91, 1069A	127–28
Ambigua
		PG 91, 1069B	128
		PG 91, 1069C	129; 129; 130
PG 91, 1032A	346, n. 256	PG 91, 1072AB	145–46
PG 91, 1036B	104; 217, n. 42;	PG 91, 1072BC	144
	232	PG 91, 1072C	144
PG 91, 1036C	105	PG 91, 1073B	155
PG 91, 1037A	256	PG 91, 1073BD	143
PG 91, 1040C	251	PG 91, 1073C	145
PG 91, 1041C	264	PG 91, 1073CD	153
PG 91, 1044	214	PG 91, 1076BC	353
PG 91, 1044A	193; 269	PG 91, 1076D	352
PG 91, 1044B	355	PG 91, 1077A	87; 88; 352; 353
PG 91, 1044BD	258	PG 91, 1077AB	131
PG 91, 1044D	237, n. 143;	PG 91, 1077B	127, n. 40
	262; 355	PG 91, 1077BC	132
PG 91, 1044D–1045A	215; 239	PG 91, 1077C	126; 156, n. 66
PG 91, 1045AB	277	PG 91, 1077C–1080A	131
PG 91, 1048A	215	PG 91, 1077D	231
PG 91, 1048B	215	PG 91, 1078A	146
PG 91, 1048C	259; 269	PG 91, 1080A	133
PG 91, 1048D–1049A	96–97	PG 91, 1081A	119; 126
PG 91, 1049A	257–58	PG 91, 1081AB	117
PG 91, 1049CD	313	PG 91, 1081B	217, n. 42
PG 91, 1049D	214	PG 91, 1081BC	133
PG 91, 1052A	215	PG 91, 1081C	121; 133

Centuries on Love

Quaestiones ad Theopemptum

Quaestiones et Dubia

Scholia on Pseudo–Dionysius

In Coel. Hier.

In De Div. Nom.